The Spiritual Path

A Conversation Between Professor Ali A. Allawi and Shaykh Fadhlalla Haeri

On His Life, Thought and Work

Publisher: Zahra Publications

ISBN (E-Book): 978-1-919826-99-8

ISBN (Paperback): 978-1-928329-11-4

http://www.zahrapublications.pub

Published in June of 2019

© Haeri Trust and Shaykh Fadhlalla Haeri

All rights reserved. Except for brief quotations in critical articles or reviews, no part of this book may be reproduced in any manner without prior written permission from Zahra Publications.

Copying and redistribution of this book is strictly prohibited.

Table of Contents

About This Book i
About Shaykh Fadhlalla Haeri ii
About Professor Ali A. Allawi iii
Growing up in Karbala 1
Life in England 68
Career in the Oil Industry 83
Time with Chinmaya 102
Sufism 124
America 161
After America 181
It's All About Oneness 192
Other Sages and Realized Beings 231
Reaching Luminosity 257
Spiritual Realm 272
Religion 295
The Sacred 334
Consciousness 350
The Teacher 389
Societies, Nations, and Civilizations 396
Imaginal and Natural Sciences 437
Glossary 461
eBooks By Zahra Publications 473

About This Book

This book is a transcription of extensive interviews between Professor Ali A. Allawi and Shaykh Fadhlalla Haeri, conducted in South Africa during January-February of 2014.

In them, Shaykh Fadhlalla Haeri discusses his life story, the spiritual journey and the path he has been on ever since.

Professor Allawi's questions highlight Shaykh Haeri's life-changing encounters with Sufi Masters and other spiritual teachers and his travels and teaching with Sufi communities.

Drawing out Shaykh Haeri's far-reaching views on the future of religion, Sufi orders and global spirituality, the conversations probe deeply into how one attains enlightenment and what it means to live in the light of the Absolute in a relative world.

Deeply engaging and inspiring for any serious seeker.

These interviews were transcribed by Julia Khadija Lafene and edited by Anjum Jaleel.

In order to publish it as a book, chapter headings, subheadings and footnotes have been added, many gaps within the conversations have been filled, and footnotes and a glossary have been added.

About Shaykh Fadhlalla Haeri

Acknowledged as a master of self-knowledge and a spiritual philosopher, Shaykh Fadhlalla Haeri's role as a teacher grew naturally out of his own quest for self-fulfillment.

He travelled extensively on a spiritual quest which led to his eventual rediscovery of the pure and original Islamic heritage of his birth, and the discovery of the truth that reconciles the past with the present, the East with the West, the worldly with the spiritual – a link between the ancient wisdom teachings and our present time.

A descendant of five generations of well-known and revered spiritual leaders, Shaykh Fadhlalla Haeri has taught students throughout the world for over 30 years. A prolific author of more than thirty books relating to the universal principles of Islam, the Qur'an, and its core purpose of enlightenment, he is a gifted exponent of how the self relates to the soul, humankind's link with the Divine, and how consciousness can be groomed to reflect our higher nature.

The unifying scope of his perspective emphasizes practical, actionable knowledge that leads to self-transformation, and provides a natural bridge between seemingly different Eastern and Western approaches to spirituality, as well as offering a common ground of higher knowledge for various religions, sects and secular outlooks.

About Professor Ali A. Allawi

Prof. Ali Allawi has had a distinguished career in the Iraqi government, serving as Minister of Trade, Minister of Defense and most recently, Minister of Finance in 2006. Dr. Allawi has been a Research Professor at the National University of Singapore, and at Oxford University. In 2009-2010 he was elected Senior Visiting Fellow at Princeton University and at Harvard Kennedy School of Government. Dr. Allawi holds an S.B. in Civil Engineering from MIT and an MBA from Harvard Business School.

New York Times Book Review called his book *The Occupation of Iraq: Winning the War, Losing the Peace*, the most comprehensive historical account of the aftermath of the American invasion.

Also, in October 2009 the Washington Institute for Near East Policy announced that Dr. Allawi's book *The Crisis of Islamic Civilization* was awarded the silver prize of its annual book prize.

In March 2014, his major political biography of *Faisal I of Iraq*, set against the fall of the Ottoman Empire and the formation of the modern state system in the Middle East, was published. In December 2014, the *Economist* placed the book on its list of Best Books for 2014.

In April 2016, Ali Allawi was nominated as the Distinguished Fellow at the Rajaratnam School of International Studies at the Nanyang Technological University, Singapore.

He is presently working on a book commissioned by Yale University Press, entitled *The Chasm*. This will be an economic history of the developing world, tracing the evolution of development paradigms and policies from the end of World War II to the present.

Growing up in Karbala

Spiritual Lineage

AA: Al-Salaam alaikum, Shaykhna. Thank you for agreeing to hold this interview. I hope it will be more like a conversation or dialogue so it will not be structured in any way except along the lines that you choose or along the lines of the conversation itself.

We'll start at the beginning, which is your own childhood and youth. You mentioned it at some length in the book, '*Son of Karbala*', but I felt that there were a number of things that could have been elaborated on, but the length that this may have forced the book to take, it may have been unreal to go beyond the outline you provided in the book. But to me it's clear that in early childhood there are significant elements in the formation of a person's character and predisposition.

Before we get into that, I'd like to ask more about your lineage, for lack of a better word, your *spiritual* lineage, in the sense that again, following in part your own teachings, genetic inheritance is a significant element in the formation of spiritual predisposition, so can I know something more about the Haeris, before they came to Iraq, when they came to Iraq and something about your grandfather, if you can recall that? I'm speaking now of the paternal line.

SFH: I remember very well an inner certainty that my genetic, material or physical lineage, or background had been very blessed. I grew up feeling very confident and content since my earliest childhood – may be the age of two or three. And I didn't really dig a lot into that, except that I know, from relatives and others who dug into it, that the family had come from Shirvan, which is near Dagestan. They were Shirvanis, of Persian, Aryan extraction.

AA: Not Turkish?

SFH: They may have been a mixture – I don't know – my mother was half Turkish – Turkic – and they were landed people, leaders of whatever

– both religious and secular lands, and with the Russian wars, in the early 1800s, there were waves of killings, and they ended up in Northern Mazandaran, where they had family links and friends. They ended up in Babul – Mazandaran now – as of 1840-50. And they had a very strong affinity to the *Ahl al-Bayt* teachings of Islam and a very strong inclination towards *`Irfan* and Sufism without them being part of a *Tariqah*.

AA: Were they all religious teachers and *`ulama*?

SFH: They were both *`ulama* and landowners at the same time; they were merchant princes – land and *`ilm* combined.

AA: There was not a real distinction between being a landowner and an *`alim*?

Great Grandfather Shaykh Zayn al-`Abidin

SFH: Correct. For example, my mother's father was a great tradesman, wholesaler in Iraq, in Baghdad, and ended up in Karbala, and his library was known to be one of the best in terms of the handwritten manuscripts. As far as names, I know, my great grandfather, Shaykh Zayn al-`Abidin, was the greatest *marja`* of his days. His father was known to be a big advocate of combining outer and inner, and his name was '*Karbala Muslim*' – his title.

AA: You were not known then as 'Haeri'?

SFH: No. Haeri came with Shaykh Zayn al-`Abidin (1850/60). He ended up in Najaf as a youngster because there was no other teacher who could teach him in Northern Iran. So the people around said, 'this young man is worthy – at the age of 9 or 10 – of being under the best tutelage.'

AA: So this was around mid 1800s?

SFH: 1850-1860. So he ended up as being the greatest *marja`* in his 50s in Najaf – he was not married. Several people knew a lot more about him than I do – Ansari was his main teacher and he told them, 'I've never had such a being as this man.'

AA: He became then a *mujtahid* in Najaf?

SFH: Absolutely, in Najaf. And the story is that at the age of fifty, he would often go to Imam Ali's shrine and they would lock him up overnight. So that night – this story was told to me by Seyyed Mehdi al-Hakim, and others knew it. I never investigated it, I was so confident in the love of my parents – especially my mother. So I really did not have an unhappy childhood. I grew up quite content inwardly. Those were the happiest times for me. As a youngster, in Karbala, I often found myself sitting in the corner of one of the four houses that were all contiguous. I never needed any attention or toys or anything – I was quite happy singing to myself.

AA: Did you ever need confirmation of your part of the lineage or did you take that for granted?

SFH: I took it for granted. I remember the earliest time my father called me 'Shaykh Fadhlalla', my mother said, 'what is this?', and he said, 'he is a Shaykh'.

AA: 'Shaykh' in an endearing way or as a title?

SFH: I don't know – I really have no idea. I didn't care either.

AA: I suppose moving to Iraq, the Haeri *laqab* was attached to it.

SFH: Only when he moved from Najaf to Karbala?

AA: Karbala.

SFH: It may have been 1880s or 90s – I don't know my dates very well, but before 1890.

AA: Was he involved in the events of the period – the various religious disputes? Especially, this was the time when the *Babis*[1] had become quite a serious threat to the established religious authority in Iran anyway, and had an extension in Iraq, so in this period, when your great grandfather was active, it was also the period of religious and spiritual turmoil.

SFH: My personal reading and interpretation of religious and political turmoil – later on in the British rule – is that this family was aware of it, but they were never embroiled in it.

AA: So they were sort of detached from it.

SFH: Absolutely. For example, I know there were a number of incidents with Shaykh Zayn al-`Abidin when there were disputes, when somebody saw someone else in the public bath doing *ghusl* and part of the back had not been wetted and he would call them to task – there were dozens of such stories. He would say: 'it is not your business – you are not religious police. If a man is doing his *ghusl*, what's that to do with you as an observer?' So he was in a way, I wouldn't say, above the law, but he was considered to be not embroiled in the day-to-day '*mullahdom*' activities.

AA: He had a kind of elevated station, didn't he?

SFH: No doubt about it. I know from all the stories I have been told from Shaykh al-`Abidin, 150 years ago, that these people were considered to have a voice of higher *haqq*, or original *Muhammadi Light*, without them taking a side line, if you like, away from the day-to-day activities. They were aware of the day-to-day activities, but, if you like, it touched them lightly.

AA: Did he teach Shaykhna?

---

[1] An offshoot of Shi`a Islam who emerged in 19th century in Iran, generally considered heretics by both the Shi`a and Sunni Muslims.

SFH: He died in his 90s, still teaching.

AA: So he had a group of students.

SFH: He had more than that. He moved and went to Iran. He complained to Imam Ali [in his supplication], 'I am in my fifties, I am not married, I have lived on bread and water, and enough is enough.' Apparently Imam Ali came to him and reprimanded him: 'What are you talking about? I have never heard you before. You have never asked for anything. But if you want all of this, it's not here. Leave for Karbala.' This story was told to me by Seyyed Mehdi al-Hakim and many others. So in his early fifties he goes by caravan from Najaf to Karbala, then stopped half way at Khan al-Nus – with two or three donkeys carrying his books, and Imam Ali tells him, 'This is my son, Imam Hussain, he will take care of you. Don't stay here, go to Karbala. This is a place of austerity and nothingness.'

Shaykh Zayn al-`Abidin's Move to Karbala

AA: So his movement from Najaf to Karbala was inspired. When did he move?

SFH: In his late fifties.

AA: So he was given clear Instructions.

SFH: Yes, he was given instructions. So he comes to Karbala, and they say, as he is nearing the gate where the cemetery is in the desert, he sees a very distinguished man on a white horse with his servants, who calls him, saying, 'I'm waiting for you. Are you Shaykh Zayn al-`Abidin?' He said 'Yes'. He said, 'Last night I had instructions from Imam Hussain. I am the biggest trader and businessman in Karbala, if not in Iraq, and I have had instructions that I have to wait for you and I have to give you my daughter. You're not married. You're in your mid-fifties – it's late.' Shaykh Zayn al-`Abidin doesn't know, he says, 'I have a *madrasa* here, and I have my students. I'm going to the *hawza*. I'm not going to your house.' So food arrives and after six months he ends up marrying that daughter, whose name was Khurshid. I have her *tasbih* of a thousand beads – it's made of mud of Karbala. Apparently she was a very pious, a very beautiful, mixed Mazandarani, woman, and this fellow was also Mazandarani, but his family ended up being the founders of the Ottoman bank and it was said that if they withdrew their money the bank would collapse. So he was married to a big merchant, as was the custom. So in his mid fifties he gets married and they have four sons and maybe one or two daughters.

AA: No daughters?

SFH: I don't know. Now there is Shahla Haeri you can contact – she is part of the same Haeri clan. Ha-er means, 'next to Imam Hussain'. That's where the name 'Haeri' comes from; there were no ayatollahs at that time. And then in 1890, or something, the Shah of Iran commissions the production of the first printed *risala* in Lucknow. I have one copy from 1890 or something. And it is '*hajar*'[2] – I have it in type – no doubt the thing is already written but this was commissioned to be printed and made available by command of Nasreddin Shah – and his favorite wife was always at his side – you know, coming and going with him to Karbala, in 1890 or something.

AA: Has anything about him been written or researched?

SFH: Yes, yes, there are one or two pages.

AA: Within the literature?

SFH: Yes, yes no doubt about it.

AA: Such as [the compendium] *`Alam al-Najaf* by Ja`afar Khalili?

SFH: That's right – no, I think before that – I have some copies – I will show you.

---

[2] Printing using stones.

AA: When did he die, Shaykhna? Before the turn of the century?

SFH: I really don't know, in 1910 perhaps. He died a very old man. My dates are not right – you need to string it together to make some sense out of it.

AA: Well I suppose if he came in his 40s and 50s in the 1840s, he died in the 90s.

SFH: 90s. And it was written that he died teaching. During the last half hour of his life he was still teaching.

AA: What did he teach, *Fiqh, Usul, `Irfan*?

SFH: I don't know if it was classified as *`Irfan*. It was a complete package, not a separate field. That's how I grew up – without having to classify something as '*`Irfan*' or 'Sufism.' It was the same. There is only one path. You do your best and live it.

AA: So it wasn't as structured formally.

SFH: No, there well may have been structured in the *Hawza* but not in our household. I did not get a whiff of any of these things.

AA: Were there permanent students – I'm sure there must have been.

SFH: There must have been – I don't know.

AA: If he passed away at the beginning of the turn of the century, was the mantle transferred to your father?

Grandfather – Shaykh Muhammad Hussein

SFH: No, it was transferred to my grandfather, Shaykh Muhammad Hussein. He was one of the four sons. One of them was called Shaykh al-`Iraqain because he was very much involved in disputes, and the others were Shaykh Muhammad, Shaykh Ali, and Shaykh Muhammad Hussain.

AA: Your grand uncle, not your uncle.

SFH: I had one uncle – Shaykh Muhammad Hussain, who had two sons; one of them, my father, the eldest, Shaykh Ahmed his name was, and his brother Shaykh Baqi. He went to Iran and became exceptionally prominent. He was the head of the judiciary for many, many years – I forget now, but he had a title meaning, 'the son of the Shaykh.'

AA: *Shaykh Zadeh!*[3]

SFH: The Iranian brother was Shahla Haeri's grandfather and she is an anthropologist in Boston; she also tried to package it together, but there wasn't this separation of *zahir* and *batin* – they were one. You are accountable for all your actions, and you should be watchful of what you are doing and where your *qibla* is.

AA: Do you remember your grandfather yourself?

SFH: Not at all. I never saw him. My grandfather became exceptionally prominent in India because Shaykh Zayn al-`Abidin inspired the people in Lucknow, in 1860s, 70s.

AA: I read in Nakash's book on the "Lucknow legacy" which played a large part in financing the *Hawza*. When the British came, all the people in Najaf were trying to draw proximate to the rulers and a number of documents that dealt with the various, and sometimes groveling, way in which they handled the relationship with the British authorities [came to light]. Then there was a section on the `*ulama* of Karbala which mentioned your grandfather – how they were very distant and formal in their relationship [with the British] – they were not part of the bequest of the Awad[4] legacy. Your grandfather had some degree of financial independence that was probably not available to the normal `*alim*.

---

[3] Son of a Shaykh.
[4] Arabic word for the Indian province of Oudh (currently known as Uttar Pradesh).

SFH: It began with Shaykh al-`Abidin around 1870's, and its influence with the kings of power was immense – especially with Mahmoodabad. Until now in Mahmoodabad, old palace there is a huge *ijaza* that says that this man can do this, he can do that. So he was a great influence on them, and my father, I remember as a kid, did something, which was very unusual, I remember it vaguely – he went to Baghdad to perform a marriage. He'd never ever done these things and I remember vaguely as a child that the story was that this was the son of somebody who mattered a lot to my grandfather and great-grandfather, and he was the Rajah of Mahmoodabad, father of Suleiman. They were getting married and wouldn't do it unless my father performed the marriage. So he went for them. So there was a strong link with that part of India, and also with further on away to the east. And there were also links with North Africa.

AA: Really?

SFH: There were links. I remember once a man from North Africa coming and staying with us, because we had a guest house – and there were always guests. This guest was from North Africa, a practicing alchemist. He was very upset – I remember at 5 or 6 years – screaming away at my father, saying, 'You are not showing me, you are not giving me, you are not telling me anything.' My father was a practicing alchemist, and I didn't understand what was going on – I just remember vaguely the notion of the conversation. This man wanted a recipe and my father was saying to him that: 'you are the recipe – you have to be transformed – YOU are the recipe, you are going to be the elixir.' So there was something like that, and it went on and on for a few hours.

AA: And you were listening?

SFH: I was coming and going and it had an effect on me, in that what this man was looking for in the outer, my father was saying, 'it's all about your inner?', that is what left an impression.

AA: So the term Ayatollah came into common use by then?

SFH: That time was after my grandfather, and they talked about Ayatollah Abu Al-Hassan Qasim, and my father said, 'People need them.' He was not elevating them, he was not being condescending; he was just saying that it's not our business.

AA: Need them for the outer definition of their religion.

SFH: People need them and that's it.

AA: But it wasn't in common use in Karbala?

SFH: Not at all; neither that, nor the name, 'Imam'. 'Imam' was always reserved for Imam Ali. So when I heard Imam Khomeini being called 'Imam', for me it was a new thing, and I accepted it. New thing, new life, new days.

Father – Shaykh Ahmed

AA: So now we come to your late father. How do you recall him? What are your first impressions of him?

SFH: There and not there. I felt there was a great – if you like – umbrella of referencing, because that is what Karbala referred to him also. Most of the `ulema every now and then would come over and so would be the governor. Every Thursday he would come quietly early morning to have 10-15 minutes with him and talk about the day-to-day affairs. My father was the voice of *haqq* not remote or distant from day to day, but he was not embroiled in the day-to-day. The same thing with me. Whenever I had something very serious, I would ask and he would answer me according to my level of understanding. I felt his availability all the time.

AA: Was he a remote figure?

SFH: No. He was always available when needed. I never felt him remote, but I knew he was at another level than I, but would condescend to be at my level and talk to me and ask my help. Every other day he would be doing something, pottering around one of the four or five houses, fixing something; he would always be either planting and pulling plants and palm trees. We had four houses and each had a courtyard with gardens in it.

AA: Did you have orchards in Karbala?

SFH: We had a very big orchard, called *Bagh e Jamal*, within five minutes walk from the shrine.

AA: Was he spending much of his time there?

SFH: No, there were farmers coming and the people who looked after it would be coming and going – every other day there would be two or three donkeys coming with produce to the door so we always had fresh stuff available to us.

AA: You didn't feel any scarcity of food?

SFH: Not at all, no. In my grandfather's time, Indian envelopes arriving ... very tough envelopes... also during my grandfather's time. I remember he died young – he was stabbed..... for those people. He died in his late 60s.

AA: He was murdered?

SFH: He was stabbed coming back from the *salaat* to the house: apparently somebody was waiting for him in the *barani* and stabbed him because that day he had received a big envelope from the British agency with money in it. So he considered him as a British agent and stabbed him.

AA: He died of his wounds?

SFH: After a few months, of infestation. My aunt told me the story; he died of the wounds, and apparently the man who stabbed him ended up nursing him in the last two or three months.

AA: *Subhanallah!*

SFH: He nursed him, saying that, 'I really thought you were an agent and that's why I stabbed you. But now I know you aren't an agent, …'

AA: He then forgave his attacker!

SFH: Totally. This came clearly from my aunt, who was with him until he died.

AA: But it was a lingering wound, and it took a long time for him to die.

SFH: My aunt got married to the Asad Khan's family…

AA: So on your grandmother's side, who was your paternal grandfather? Were they Ayatollahs?

SFH: I don't know.

AA: So you don't have a connection there?

SFH: I really don't know. But I have inherited a few things. It is interesting that as time went by there remained only a few things that I inherited. For example, that printed *risala* from the 1880s or 90s. It was kept somewhere and it ended up with me. I also had the first printed Qur'an *hajjar* used by my grandfather and my father – all these ended up with me as custodian. Not that I wanted them. This Qur'an, for example, was given to my eldest brother – Sadreddin his name was from my father's first family. Sadreddin died 20 or 30 years ago in his 80s, and he inscribed on it: 'There is always a line of light and we have to follow it, and that line of light came to you, so I am sending you this Qur'an. I was only a keeper of it for you.' So I have about a dozen or twenty of these things that came to me. I'm also not that good a keeper – I don't really care for these things, but there are there.

Three C's – *Connectedness, Continuation and Consciousness*

AA: I have heard Shaykhna that you have described the exalted status of your great grandfather – the significant status of your grandfather – their orientation towards inner knowledge and *`Irfan*, their distancing themselves from power and authority and the common set of *`ulama*. Do you think these developed any kind of spiritual legacy that was somehow transferred generationally? Could that legacy be transferable?

SFH: I see the patterns of connectedness throughout life. I see the life force is based on three things: 'three 'Cs', I call them. First force is Connectedness: there is Connectedness, Connectedness, Connectedness, beyond our ability to imagine. That's why we want to connect, that's why we want the Internet and Facebook, etc. – to connect, connect. Everything is already connected. *Al-Jami`* is one. From that immensity of singularity the whole universe and apparent diversity have come about. So I see the most important power is Connectedness. The baby wants to connect with the nipple, the mother and with the father – on and on and on.

The second force is Continuation: Connectedness ends space; Continuation ends up as the illusion of time – the *fitra*, crack, it's an illusion, which Adam had to fall into. You and I also have to fall into it in order for us to get out of that prison and exile.

The third one is Consciousness.

So there are three 'Cs': Connectedness, Continuation – eternal – and Consciousness.

AA: If we visualize it as a kind of virtual spiritual pipeline which connects and continues, consciousness is the flow that goes through them, then would that prevail in terms of its transferability into the world of matter – across generations?

SFH: True, there is that. But I won't give it too much emphasis. I'm sure there is genetic, I'm sure there is culture, I'm sure there is nurture and nature – all of these do play a role, no doubt about it.

AA: No, I'm not trying to fix the contours, I'm not trying to say there is a kind of pipeline architecture that links generations, but it is a fundamental part of a network – the end result is that the flow of consciousness through this virtual pipeline can be a conflicted pipeline or it can be a broad pipeline. If your starting point is infinite and then it becomes in the realm of finitude – it goes to individuals, that connectedness may continue across generations.

SFH: Yes, no doubt about it.

AA: There is a biological element.

SFH: No doubt about it, but also bear in mind, there are many biological or genetic advantages that get blocked later on. So many people have that potential – they have inherited something but they are not worthy of it. It doesn't work for them.

AA: That's the other side of it.

SFH: The other side. I have absolutely no doubt. In my case, I really had no qualms about the fact that I – it wasn't egotistic, it wasn't *nafsi*, it wasn't a *selfie*; it was just that I took it for granted. I grew up quite naturally with that confidence. All is there already. So, I had realized that I needed to participate in this world and needed to have some skills. Fine – I took it quite naturally. If you look at it from a biographical point of view, eight times I was uprooted in my life. Eight countries, eight different times.

AA: But the travel was in your family. The big up-rootedness was when your family moved across continents – moving from Mazandaran to Najaf.

SFH: …and before Mazandaran, from Dagestan.

AA: From Dagestan one *hijra*; from Mazandaran to Najaf, and then from Najaf to Karbala.

SFH: You're right. I remember as a fourteen year old ...

AA: So the aspect of movement in order to achieve a degree of spiritual realization ...

SFH: ...to be an exile in this world. You are happy to take that in your inner world. I remember as a 14/15 year old in Karbala, because the house had no fence or no distance from the shrine. I remember being on the roof – clearly it was Muharram and the black flag was waving on the roof – I could hear the flag, it was next to me – I asked Imam Hussain, because my birthday is the same as his birthday, the third of *Sha'ban*, so whenever they celebrate it I felt quite chuffed. .... without really being esoteric... but I asked Imam Hussain, 'What shall I do? I now have a scholarship; should I go abroad or stay here?' I wanted to do medicine in Iraq – I didn't want to leave Iraq and I could almost hear the voice that said, 'Flow with the wind of your destiny. Go with Selma, wherever she goes. And follow the winds of destiny wherever it turns.' And that came to me later. I knew my destiny wasn't there; I had to move and accept whatever came. And then when my name was announced as one of the earliest winners of the scholarships – and I was number two in Iraq – I was chuffed. I said, 'That's it, flow with the flow.'

Spiritual Pipeline Across Generations

AA: I want to go back to the earlier question – to go back to the idea of the movement across generations, the spiritual pipeline. If you think of yourself as the end of a parenthesis, you can alter the bracket, at your parents or your grandparents – you can open it at the ultimate point – with Adam and so on. So the whole thing with these brackets is to enclose something so that you can understand it within the limits of the mind. What I'm trying to ask is, if you take yourself as a spiritual teacher, and you close the bracket in the sense that that aspect will be closed with you; if you open the bracket with your great grandfather, you can see patterns, within this limited frame for this infinite pipeline where the three 'Cs' as you mentioned flow. You can see the movement but there are certain repetitions and characteristics. They may not be inherited equally; the characteristics of movement – call it *hijrah*, the characteristic of having an inclination. Now I don't know how many descendants there are of your great grandfather, maybe several hundred …

SFH: More.

AA: Thousands? You stand out from amongst them as the inheritor of that spiritual legacy. If I were to structure the question, I'd put it this way: Is there any, firstly, validity, and secondly, any purpose, in talking about this genetic predisposition?

SFH: There is. But I look at the other side of it to understand it. In other words, I am not the only inheritor, I am not the exclusive spiritual inheritor, I am not the selected inheritor, and I am not the exclusive being. What happened to me, fortunately, at a very young age is to realize my attention; my focus has to be to be weary of the shadow, not of the light. So I was very fortunate at a very young age to realize that my business is not to claim the light of God or the *ruh* – it is to realize the shield or the handicap of identity, of separation, of my reality, my ego. I was very fortunate at an early young age to discover that it is the removal of the 'I', it is *la ilaha – il-Allah* is already there – it was almost intuitive, that is, don't claim anything – higher, lower, inheritor of light; just watch out for the shadow that covers that light which is universal and in every soul. In other words, if you tell me now that there are another five hundred, if you like, *arwah* from Karbala, Muslim or whatever, who have that, I say, of course, but you personally, everyone personally, every individual has to know it. Everybody is enlightened, but to know that enlightenment or the potential enlightenment or illumination, or the *nur* of Allah in your heart, your *ruh*, is covered by your illusion that you are separate – that's all. So I accept the idea of the special people, selected people, exclusive people, but I think that is the cover up of everybody and it is inclusive. All human beings have that potential.

AA: It has to be earned by every generation.

SFH: Absolutely – by realizing the shadow that covers it. Not by wanting the light.

AA: No, but the outcome, the end result is that there are people who are more pre-disposed to that.

SFH: Correct.

AA: And there are others who are less able to receive that light.

SFH: Because they have simply looked at the shadow by their insight – when the shadow disappears the *nur* of Allah prevails – this is Reality.

AA: But the acknowledgement of the Reality in terms of action, in terms of personal characteristics, in terms of spiritual composition, requires a person to actually switch on that light, or to say that there's always been light there. It's like you must have a pre-disposition to say that the emperor has no clothes.

SFH: True, and that pre-disposition needs to be encouraged, to be nourished.

AA: Every person in this world has that pre-disposition, but the degree to which it's opened is partly a function of spiritual inheritance.

SFH: Could very well be. Again, nature and nurture. I remember myself as a three or four years old, crying because they didn't wait for me to pray with them. So later on I eventually came to realize that the Muhammadi package has it all. The *wudhu* is to disconnect, for a little while, this continuing connectedness with your worldliness, with your *nafs*, with your body, your mind, your senses, your desires, and the connection will come naturally when you go into your prostration. For me a few things that Muhammad's[5] teaching – such as *'Assalatu mi'raj*

---

[5] In the Muslim tradition, Peace be Upon Him, is invoked whenever the Prophet Muhammad's (PBUH) name is mentioned. When his blessed name appears in this book, PBUH is implied.

al-mu'min'[6] – *mi`raj* is taking off to another zone of consciousness. I live that zone; I don't talk about it.

AA: But Shaykhna, I find a reluctance on your part to accept the elite functions of this knowledge, but its intrinsic limitation to a few. You said before that it's a question of *dhawq*; I think it's a question of *dhawq* as well as pre-disposition.

SFH: I accept all that, but I don't see it. I accept what you say make sense to the mind, but I'm not the mind, I'm the heart.

AA: If you look at most of the people.

SFH: I accept that ... in the Qur'an – most of them do not have an intellect, most of them do not see... of course... *Wama yu'minu aktharuhum billahi illa wahum mushrikoon*[7] ... I accept that, but I don't see it as such – I see it as the potential in everyone. The first thing I see in anyone is a *ruh* – really, it's the truth. So I can accept it.

AA: For yourself, it becomes transparent, but I mean those, the vast majority of people, even those who are on this path, are not yet at that level where they can only see.

SFH: Sure.

AA: So if you don't mind, I'll pull you back to the level that – in the sense that if you look at nearly all the great beings of the world, and all the great traditions, there's some peculiar characteristics about their make-up. They seem to have this in-born ability. It's very unlikely that, for instance, you'll find an accountant who suddenly becomes an accepted shaykh. There's something in their inner make-up.

SFH: Connection, connection, continuation – *Baba Jaan* – it is continuous... so watch out! *Bismillah* is there. Where are you putting

---

[6] *Salaat* is the *mi`raj* (ascension to Heavens) of a believer.
[7] "Most of them will only believe in God while also joining others with Him." (Qur'an 12:106)

your foot? Why are you doing this? Why are you talking to this fellow? Why? Because one thing will lead to another. Suddenly you find yourself in another valley. Somewhere else – you don't know where it is. Complete alienation, of course.

Family Life

AA: Shaykhna – about your family life, your father. Your father had two families – is that correct?

SFH: He had married one of the relatives from Mazandaran and he had five sons and two daughters. His wife died from cholera or something, and he remained without a family for five, six, seven years. And then he married my mother.

AA: His first wife died and then he remarried?

SFH: That's right.

AA: Was there any connection in your youth between the families of his first wife and his second wife, because there must be a generational gap between you and your step (half) brothers and sisters.

SFH: It was a very good, a very healthy connection. My mother was rejected for the first two or three years…

AA: By whom?

SFH: By the rest of the family.

AA: Were they living in the same enclosure?

SFH: Connected houses that were next door to each other. Karbala…

AA: A kind of *Haush*…

SFH: Three or four houses – for example, my aunt and her sister – two sisters – there were three aunts…living in a house next door.

AA: Married or not?

SFH: The aunt that told me about Shaykh Muhammad Hussain's fascination in a way was, as I said, was married to the Asad Khan family – that's why there's a …

AA: …Shams ul-Mulook's family…

SFH: She was married to Mulook's father's brother – he was the head of that family – Majid Khan was his name ...

AA: Kabulis – they were from Afghanistan?

SFH: Majid Khan – they came from Isfahan.

AA: Originally they came from Kabul.

SFH: They originally may have been connected. There was a direct link to the Agha Khan, he used to come every now and then to Karbala; he had connection with my father. So there were three aunts living next-door – the houses were connected outside and from the roof – you know fairly sizeable houses. So my mother was not accepted because she was an Arab, a Seyyed from Assad, Bani Assad. But within two years she learned Persian, and she started writing poetry, so she was fully accepted, and they really honored her.

AA: Did you have any connection with your half brothers and sisters?

SFH: Very much so. One of them was...

AA: Was there an age gap?

SFH: Of course – a big age gap – one of whom was living in England – he looked after me as I went as a scholarship student.

AA: But when you were young, I mean, when you were seven, eight years old.

SFH: They would come and go and visit. Yes – there wasn't much interaction.

AA: I mean there wasn't a formal distance between you and them?

SFH: Not at all. I never observed this. I felt favored.

AA: I'm speaking about your relations with your aunts …

SFH: As I said, I felt favored by all of them.

AA: Really?

SFH: Absolutely. The eldest half-brother, Sadri – I took liberties with him, he allowed me to do anything, cuddle him, kiss him, jump on him – and the second one, the third one and the fourth – they all loved me – I was totally favored. One of them came to America, visited us, and stayed with us for a while. And he said he came to America to see whether he could live with his son, who was quite a successful IT top man in California, but he said, 'I can't stay here, there's no life here,' so he went back to Iraq. No, I never ever felt rejected by anyone.

AA: Would you say your household was culturally Persian, Arabized, Muslim or Karbalayi.

SFH: No – Persian culture to begin with, but Arabized in the Seyyedi/Muhammadi sense – Karbalayi and beyond. For example, during Muharram our house would be closed, we wouldn't go out for days, like being in a closed enclosure. I remember myself as a kid, the first language was Persian, but the Qur'an was in Arabic and I loved the Qur'an. I remember myself as a very, very young three year old, going up and down on different roofs reciting the Qur'an aloud. I enjoyed the sound of it. Persian was the first language, Arabic went with it, Qur'anic

Arabic especially, and I grew up Persian, Arab, Iraqi, Karbalayi, without much of a difference – a seamless connectedness.

AA: So it all seemed to be part of multiple cultures.

Son of Karbala

SFH: Yes, I grew up really as a son of Karbala[8]. I mean I really felt I am the son of this town. Wherever I went I was respected, people knew who I was.

AA: But what did you feel as, within the fold of Islam – Iraq, the Arab world, southern Iraq.

SFH: Not so much – I never felt that barrier – I felt connected with Imam Hussein, with Ali, Muhammad and the universe. I really didn't see myself as an Iraqi.

AA: There was no sense of national affiliation?

SFH: No. None at all, none whatsoever.

AA: You dealt with authority, right? I mean with officials as something that has to be done?

SFH: I really felt I perched on this land for a while – it is my temporary abode, and wherever I am, it doesn't matter since it is a temporary abode. I never felt emotional, or, if you like, strong affinity to land or people – I felt they were fine, they were all good people, or bad people – it doesn't matter.

AA: Were there *muhallas* in Karbala?

SFH: Of course.

---

[8] See Shaykh Fadhlalla Haeri's autobiography, "*Son of Karbala*".

AA: Which *muhalla* were you in?

SFH: This was *Baab al-Qibla – Zainabiyya*.

AA: So you were in the elite of the elite *muhalla*.

SFH: No, I didn't feel that elevated. I regarded all the poor as equals and I'd be very happy to sit with any one of them and enjoy them.

AA: But in Karbala was your geographical, sacred space.

SFH: That is right. You know I got into a lot of trouble in the oil company – I was among the first batch of Iraqis returning and I was covenanted staff, and there were nine different levels before being a staff. And I would love these people – I would go to town, I would sit with them in Kirkuk, with my employees. I'd sit with them and enjoy them – go to their houses. Occasionally, I was not reprimanded by the British top brass, but I would be questioned, and they'd say something like, 'Look you know you are a higher level…' … but I enjoyed them … I really enjoyed them. It was one of my five degrees below me employee who would be a very good shoemaker, maybe make my shoes. I'd go to his little shoe shop in Kirkuk and I'd sit with him and I enjoyed that.

AA: What I know is that most of the rest of Southern Iraq disliked Karbalayis, because they saw them as introverted, arrogant and very, very elitist, and they always favored their own, and they were not prepared to accept others, and not just people from Najaf and Kadhimain with whom I have a connection through my mother. And there was long-standing feuding in the relationship with Karbala. Did you feel a sense of superiority and elitism?

SFH: None at all.

AA: …that you were special people?

SFH: Not at all. I felt there was something about me individually as special and I felt everybody else was special too, potentially special. I really never had the sense of separation or elitist or whatsoever. Not at all. Not once. In fact the only time I was reprimanded was when I was going to school, swinging my new satchel bag with my books in it, and I hit somebody. He held my hand and said, 'Who are you? Ccome, come you can't do that.' So he took me back home and said, 'He was not behaving himself properly in the street.' That was the only time I felt reprimanded. I never felt special – I felt confident, without knowing that I was confident, without a reflection of confidence or elitism. So I knew I am chosen, but the same as everybody else.

AA: You came from a very secure family, and had a very protected life.

SFH: Totally. Totally, totally, totally! In every way.

AA: Did your father make a special effort to fend off the problems from the outside world?

SFH: I don't think he made any effort. I don't think so – not overtly. I don't think he made any effort because his presence was strong, as was my mother's and her friends'. No, I felt accepted by all. The men – I would go to the *burani*, I would sit with them, talk with them, say a few things. I never felt in any way having to be put in a place, or something. The same thing with the women. For example, I favored a few of my mother's friends – beautiful women – I'd go and jump on their laps and they'd accept it.

AA: Well, you were only 4 or 5… "Shame on you!" [smiling]

SFH: five, six until seven…

AA: So they made you stop around 7, 8.

SFH: Around 6, 7 – I remember going to the women's bath one day. This time when they admonished me, they were right, so I didn't go there again. …It was never hurtful. I never felt that I'd been deprived or I'd not been accepted. I never ever felt that.

AA: Did you have a special nurse or maid?

SFH: I had, of course. There was this Meshti – I wrote about her in '*Son of Karbala*'. Now, she was the wife of someone very well to do from northern Mazandaran, next to the Russian border. He had land, he had a lot of wealth, he had orchards and he had also fishing, and I think he was caught between two of the boats that he owned and died. Within two or three months her son died, so she was very bereft. They told her, 'go to Karbala, there is a sanctuary.' So she arrived in Karbala. I was the same age as her son who died, so she adopted me, she took care of me. And I would tease her, I took her for granted, used to pull her hair, kick her, whatever.

AA: Have you found any difference between those who are nursed by their mother and by a wet nurse?

SFH: I have come to know that you need both – you need a mother, you need others, you need an extended family. You need public school, whatever. Later on I realized I grew up in an extended family environment.

AA: But you were not wet-nursed?

SFH: I don't think so.

AA: I mean – this was a common practice amongst the elite of the Arabs.

SFH: I wanted my mother exclusive to me. I even prayed that everybody else should die except her. She'd just be exclusive to me.

AA: So what happened with the person who had a wet nurse?

SFH: I don't know. I think it's good – it's good to have more than one mother.

AA: As I said, it was a common practice.

SFH: The earliest memory in my life is – I was probably over two – when my mother tried to wean me unsuccessfully. I remember coming with a wet cloth to wipe her nipple because she put something on it – aloe which was bitter – to wipe that and suckle her.

AA: But you are the youngest?

SFH: yes....

AA: The word 'Fadhl' seems to run in the family.

SFH: yes, yes – my mother, her name was Fadhila.

AA: But you're named by your father...

SFH: I think he liked that. There were four of them with the name 'Fadhl' – I was the third.

AA: I think there was – they probably ran out of permutations with the name 'Fadhl'.

SFH: Whatever. No, also I think she didn't want any more children after me. I would tease my younger sister that, 'you were not expected' ...

AA: So your mother came from the Bani Assad tribe?

SFH: Correct.

AA: From the Karbala area?

SFH: Baghdad and Karbala. Her father came to Karbala as a wholesaler – he was a very big wholesaler, but based in Baghdad.

AA: There's a common saying in Iraq that two-thirds of the person follows their maternal uncle – Did you have good relations with your maternal uncles?

SFH: I did. I had good relations with two that I knew – there were three of them – one of them was the first merchant in Baghdad to open a department store – the first ever in Iraq. His name was Mahmoud Assadi. And he was famous by having ready-made clothes brought to Baghdad.

AA: Before Orosdi Beck?[9]

SFH: Before Orosdi Beck he was the first merchant – an exceptionally successful young man. Brilliant. And he settled in Baghdad a famous person, and died in his thirties from an exploded appendicitis.

AA: Fatal…

SFH: Very fatal, he died. And the two others – one of them was a very cultured man of literature – Mashkur al-Assadi. He was very close to King Faisal and was very much in his entourage. A writer and author, he had at the time a very extensive library of culture and literature. He had his degrees from Cairo and elsewhere. He was also a withdrawn man, a man of literature. He was very much into his books. And the other one was a very successful *sarrab*, called Mohammad Hussain Sarrab. I remember as a kid we would brag and say, 'do you think I am like Muhammad Hussain Sarrab?' He made a lot of money through *"kacha"* – through the Second World War, through contraband. I remember very well he favored me. His car was called Karbala No. 1 – he had an American car. So some other people said, 'No you can't have it. You must give it to this other person.' So he became no 2.

AA: He gave it to the governor?

SFH: Or someone, and I remember once in that car coming from Karbala to Baghdad – because he favored me, he liked me – Muhammad Hussein, his name was. In the middle of the way between Karbala and Baghdad which was not asphalted, the car developed some trouble, so they called for another car, and I remember very distinctly sitting in the

---

[9] A department store.

back; so they had to lift the thing and there were bundles of gold inside the car trunk.

AA: Really? Gold bars or ingots?

SFH: No I think they were *majidis* or something. Because there were about ten or twelve of them – heavy. So I was sitting there and wondering why was this in the car – that's why they were worried.

AA: You thought that all cars were stacked with gold!

SFH: Mohammad Hussein Sarrab and the driver were very concerned. So when I learned about the gold in the car, I knew why.

AA: You don't remember the make of the car?

SFH: I think it was Buick.

AA: Was this before World War II?

SFH: No – I don't know. I must have been 8 years old. So, yes, it was during the war.

AA: Do you remember anything of the war?

SFH: I only remember the end of it. Somebody was calling in Karbala, 'the war is coming to an end,' I said, 'what is the war?'

AA: You mean the war was going on and you didn't know?

SFH: I didn't know.

AA: How old were you?

SFH: I was born in 1937, so I was 8. Then somebody said, 'But don't you remember brown sugar? That was because of the war.' There was also white sugar in the house…

AA: This is quite an interesting observation. 8 is not very young. I remember, for example, at that age, the Suez crisis – I was in fact younger than that. But it means that you are not pre-disposed to be interested in public events.

SFH: But it also didn't affect me – didn't affect the household, didn't affect anybody.

AA: Were there any rations or shortages?

SFH: None at all; none at all. I remember British people coming to the house to see my father, especially British ladies. I had the first experience with the West, where two British lady explorers coming to the house, with police and so on accompanying them, because I suppose that was the only household they could come to without *hijab*.

AA: Really?

SFH: Yes.

AA: Your father allowed them in.

SFH: Of course. And they gave me two books. One of them was pictures of Hyde Park, with women pushing prams about London. I can't remember the other one – they were nice books with colored pictures.

AA: Did they make you want to visit these places or were you just curious?

SFH: Not really. I was indifferent. It didn't touch me. I was so content that it didn't make a difference. But I remember them asking my father – he was very hospitable to them – you know whenever there were odd things like this, the governor of Baghdad would send them to us.

AA: Because you were the only household –

SFH: The only household that was not questionable – people did not consider it as a wrong thing, because, as I said, he was regarded as a non-controversial and respectable man.

AA: Above the fray...

SFH: In a sense. Absolutely.

AA: What do you remember of the town?

SFH: I remember the two shrines of Imam Hussein and Abbas connected with the bazaar.

AA: Did you have daily contact with the shopkeepers?

SFH: Well, whenever I was with my father, they would all jump from the shops to kiss his hand and he would pass very quietly ...

AA: Was it a pious town?

SFH: It was a very pious town.

AA: A town that lived off the pilgrims...

SFH: Also trade. They were workers, shoemakers, dressmakers of every nationality, every Kabuli[10] face was there.

AA: Even agriculture?

SFH: I remember the town itself was a bit of a microcosm. It was beautiful; I loved it.

AA: Did you go to the river a lot?

SFH: Yes, I did. I had one of the earliest bicycles in town, and I would go along the river.

---

[10] From Kabul (Afghanistan).

AA: Swim?

SFH: Not really, I wasn't sure about that. But one day, I remember my friends trying to cross the river on a little steel bridge and one of them fell in, so we had quite fun pulling him out and the bicycle. No, I enjoyed myself going around the river and going to our orchard, and picking up fruits. There were all kinds of fruits under the palm trees.

AA: Was it a very verdant area?

SFH: Very verdant. Beautiful. I really had a good childhood; good friends; many, many friends. The son of a tailor, Sahab Mahsin, he was one of the top people, number one in Iraq for his scholarship. He went to *Dar al-Hikma – Kuliyat al-Malik Faysal*. So I had many friends like that.

AA: Who were your best friends? Did you have any best friends?

SFH: Yes, I had two or three very best friends – Sahab Mahsin was one of them, and there were a few others.

AA: Jamil Sami ...

SFH: Jamil Sami was a relative – a grandson – great grandson of the fellow who was waiting for Shaykh Mohammad Hussein in the door of Karbala.

AA: So it was a self-contained, contented atmosphere.

SFH: Fantastic! It was beautiful. As I said it was really like a microcosm. I could go anywhere in Karbala. I never had any money – until I left Iraq, I only had a coin in my pocket once – somebody gave it to me.

AA: Didn't you want to buy something? *Lablabi* or something?

SFH: Whatever I wanted people would give me. Also, I wouldn't buy these things because I wasn't sure about their health. But things like pencils, books, magazines I would buy. There were about a dozen shops in Karbala where I would just go and take what I wanted, and they would always write it to my father's account.

AA: All on credit?

SFH: Yes, on credit. My father had a batman named, Baba Mahmud. My father died when I was in England. When I came back after his death, Baba Mahmud said to me, "Your father knew exactly when he was going to die. Two days before his death he asked me to go and settle accounts. So I never had so much money in my hand or in my pocket. And I went and they all were surprised – 'why are we settling accounts?' He said he should settle all the accounts." So when he died, he told the undertaker where he wanted to be buried. Ours was the only mausoleum closest to where Imam Hussain is buried. Even the Agha Khan lost theirs. Ours was the only one left. So it was a big thing that he told the undertaker where he wanted to be buried – way out, the furthest from the public cemetery in the desert. So there was a dispute. And according to my brother, the king sent his representative to read the *Fatiha* and he said whatever he [my father] wished you had to perform. And he got the undertaker who said he had wished to be buried there. And apparently the place where he was buried became very popular. So a year or so later when I came back from England, I didn't want anybody to accompany me; because Baba Mahmoud said, 'I'll take you.' I said, 'No I want to go alone.' I couldn't find it – it was in the middle of a huge new cemetery. So the next day I had to go with Baba Mahmoud. And apparently next to where he was buried, there was some water coming out and they called it the 'Spring of Ahmed.'

AA: Did you travel at all or did your father travel?

SFH: To Baghdad.

AA: Did you have a car?

SFH: No. A few cars were sent to Baghdad and a few other places – between Karbala and Baghdad, Saddat al-Hindiyya[11].

AA: But you didn't go to Beirut or Lebanon for holidays?

SFH: No.

AA: There was no notion of...

SFH: No, not in our case. In Saddat al-Hindiyya we stayed for a month. The government gave us a house as an official resident, and people who were responsible for it took care of us, and a few other places like that.

AA: And you didn't see any need of leaving the town.

SFH: I never did. I didn't want to – I wanted to stay. I never considered travelling was going to do much, except for the notion that Imam Hussain gave me – 'you have to go' – that notion was re-confirmed later on by some other *awliya*, like Sufi Barkat Ali. When I went to his place later on in life, it felt the same as Karbala. I said to Sufi Barkat Ali, 'I want to stay here'. He was on a fast of not speaking for thirty years.... and then he spoke a few times. He said, 'No place here for you.' I said, 'Why?' He said, 'You have to go north, south, east, west; you have no place here. I am here, I am you', he said. 'You go – you are my eyes, my ears, my mouth.'

AA: Pakistan does that to you the first time you see it. You think you are back in Iraq very quickly.

SFH: Except for Outch...

AA: that Illusion...

SFH: Except for Outch ... all Iraq – Outch Sharif. You go there, now you feel at home. And the cemetery, it is one of the most blessed places on earth. There's nobody around, a few stray cats and dogs. I wandered all around Outch Sharif many times.

---

[11] The Indian Barrage, a dam near Karbala.

AA: Trying to find a replacement for Karbala?

SFH: No, no. Smelling ... I said, 'These people are more alive than those living.' And I restored a few of the old cemeteries – ancient cemeteries, 800, 900 years old. Beautiful tiles. It's the only place livable...

AA: What was your food like in your youth?

SFH: Mixed. I think Iraqi, fresh, a lot of rice, a lot of *maragh* every day there was some rice. Normal Iraqi food.

Alchemy and Metaphysics

AA: Shaykhna, going back to our conversation, there's one thing I want to ask you – your father was known as an alchemist, and a physician who was engaged in transmutation of substances and so on – how did you understand this work?

SFH: I was very curious, because I would often go with him to his lab. It was stinky. There would be five or six different little primuses and heaters boiling things, and there would be quite a number of organic substances, burning, boiling, and there was a furnace – I'm sure the temperature was very, very high – a few 100 degrees. Every two weeks or so, the furnace would be stoked with special coal that would be brought from India. I've been to that lab maybe 50 times – once every week. He would go every day, in the morning, for about half an hour, and then in the afternoon, for, may be, twenty minutes to half an hour, to put things off and on. A lot of things were being distilled. I knew this was his hobby, I knew this was something he had a passion for and from his speaking I also knew it was not about a final product. It was the process and the process was to do very much with himself. I knew then that this was something to do with inner development – I knew that. He mentioned it many times, because people would ask him – visitors or amateur alchemists would ask him.

    He also had 3 or 4 books that were very handy. One of them I still have – it's a very rare book, maybe 5 or 600 years old. The paper – I think it's parchment or something. I have it; I can show it to you. Maybe I'll collect all these for you next time you are here – you can see them. It is a most incredible book. Every now and then I go to it. Again, it came to me in a most unusual way – it was rescued as one of the most precious things in his library. And it says, for example, 'and the sulfur of it will surface, and on the surface it will glow.' I read it, and it wouldn't make sense to me. So, after a day or two, I'd give up. And then it would say, 'when it glows, you know it is in the right balanced situation. Then, when you know that, you have to leave it until it again calls you back, and then you know you have to go back to it and do the same process again to it.' And on and on and on. A lot of symbolic stuff, a lot of physical stuff, and it would say things like, 'but do that; hold it until it burns so bright that you can almost not see it.' And on and on and on.

AA: Was the lab off limits to the family?

SFH: No, not at all.

AA: Anybody could walk in?

SFH: You had to go onto one of the roofs. We had seven roofs connected, of the different houses. This was tucked away on the back of his own quarters. He had his own quarters. He had his bedroom, his library, a small courtyard, and this lab – you go to the roof and the back of the courtyard. You couldn't get to it from the house. So it was not off limits and the entry to it was the *turshi* house, where they made all the pickles – a reasonable size room. You go to the *turshi* house and then you descend into this cave. A big cave, which was the lab, not really below ground because you were going into it from the roof level.

AA: Windows?

SFH: I think so. There were actually *shubbak* ...and light, it was there for a long time.

AA: You took it as part of the house environment...

SFH: Yes, absolutely …

AA: He didn't make a secret of it?

SFH: Not at all. There were a few occasions when someone would say, 'Well, you know, if we had more money, we could do more of this ... buy more clothes – ' (he would say?), 'Are you short of clothes? Don't you have everything you need? The biggest thing is waste, waste, so what do you want?' And then, two of the last years of his life, his rings, which were often like *aqiq* or *shadhar*, or something, became gold-like. And I remember my mother said that he had done it. And then he stopped, stopped going to his lab. A year or so before he passed away. So I asked him, I remember, before I left for England, I said, 'Are you content?' He said, 'Yes! I've done what I wanted and that's it.' And I didn't ask whether silver had become gold, or whatever... I knew I was interested only about the being.

AA: How it affected him?

SFH: How it affected him. He said it's done, all done.

AA: What is your understanding of alchemy?

SFH: My understanding is the connection of physics and metaphysics, and I have felt that a few times in my own life.

AA: And its manifestation is metaphysics in the unseen?

SFH: Yes. Although I can't describe a channel, a tunnel, if I have not been through it, the tunnel I've been through is that I've had occasions in my complete stages of abandonment when I've felt as though I've been given a glimpse of the ultimate power of the universe. And I'd ask myself, 'Can I make any changes in it? Isn't it perfection beyond perfection?' And I knew I couldn't do it. Occasionally in my youth I felt if I were given power, or if I were the king of a land, or if I were the ultimate authority of a land, like my great grandfather, I thought that would be wonderful – I could do a lot of things, I could bring a lot of goodness, I could change the world, I could make a mark on the world. But I have had utter inner total experience of that. *farji'i albasara hal taramin futoor*[12]. You cannot make changes if you are given power, because then that becomes translated later on. If somebody comes to me now with a trillion dollars, I honestly do not think I can touch it. I'd say to them, 'please don't come near me. It's a problem. It's trouble. Getting it is a problem, keeping it, spending it; everything is a problem – I don't want it; please do not, I've had my troubles, you go for your troubles.' So I've come to the same conclusion in a different way.

AA: An extraordinary thing. But how can you teach others this kind of spiritual alchemy – it's only open to very, very few people who can see this dividing line or non-dividing line between physics and metaphysics.

SFH: You know in those few occasions in my life, when I've had night vigil, or two or three days of complete seclusion, I could feel that the empowerment is so immense that I've been frightened. I knew that if I touched a thing, the whole thing would change as I had wished or imagined or willed. So, in other words, I got close to that immense voltage of the power of Allah, of the '*kun*' or whatever it is ... billions of degrees of Celsius, before singularity exploded into universality. I could almost be the *qaba qawsayni aw adna*[13] – so it's not done – what are these fancies of wanting this and wanting that?

AA: Can you visualize it as the slowing down or freezing of the atoms and electrons, giving you the authority to rearrange them – was it something like that?

SFH: I almost felt everything was possible. The exchange of energy and matter, the seamlessness of it all. I remembered the *Shahadah*, it shows that everything is totally connected. It's the illusion of separation that makes one feels that one is the doer, that one can play at alchemy, this or that, or one can change things. I know that now. I have no illusion – it's not a question. Question doesn't arise; I can't even get near the question.

---

[12] "Look again! Can you see any flaw?" (Qur'an 67:3)
[13] "two bow-lengths away or even closer" (Qur'an 53:9)

AA: And once you know you don't need to go through the process of rearranging the atoms...

SFH: It's not knowledge any more – it is *Yaqeen*, not knowledge, not a quest.

AA: You don't need physical manifestations.

SFH: Nothing – physical, literal, nothing.

AA: Is it just a metaphorical process?

SFH: The only thing that I can say is that I have compassion for the rest of humanity, who have the same potential, the same purpose, being born as human beings, and they don't do it. It used to be sorrow, it used to be anger. Not any more. It's compassion now.

AA: Pity?

SFH: Not even that. The same compassion. And I will respond to those who are …

AA: Very Buddhist.

SFH: Fine, whatever you name it – I don't know names…

AA: The centrality of compassion in relation to humanity.

SFH: I don't know who is Buddhist. If he knows himself then he is wrong.

Schooling in Karbala

AA: This is a universal principle. It's interesting to see… in terms of categories… Shaykhna, coming back to your life in Karbala, what was your first school? Primary school?

SFH: Primary school... A nice [government] school near by, called *Madrassa Sibt-al-Hukumiyya*... excellent teachers – they were amongst my heroes. Especially Muhammad Jawad, one of the teachers – wonderful man.

AA: What did he teach you?

SFH: Arabic, *Hisaab*, a bit of this and a bit of that, and curriculum Arabic – Qur'an was a subsidiary subject. I enjoyed the Qur'an – Arabic, *qira'* – a bit of history, a bit of geography, rudiments of science.

AA: Who was the headmaster?

SFH: I can't remember, but I liked the teachers. There were three most likeable teachers that I had until six. I enjoyed Mathematics or *Hisaab* very much. I did very well in all of them.

AA: Grammar? Language...

SFH: Language, Grammar. I did very well in the *Baccalaureate*.

AA: Were they rigorous teachers?

SFH: Good teaching, good quality teaching.

AA: The teachers were interested?

SFH: Very interested. I was also considered the favored pupil, so I had to behave myself.

AA: Because you were the son of one of the most respected men in Karbala?

SFH: I think so, but I also remember the teachers coming to the *burani* with my father, and one of them was called Awad. So it was very good schooling, very enjoyable schooling. And then once, which was a little bit further, I went on a bicycle to the *madrasa*...

AA: You were not accompanied by anyone?

SFH: In my first *madrasa*, yes, by Baba Mahmoud, most of the time, specially the first two or three years.

AA: Wait for you?

SFH: No, they would come back for me. I remember also, the second or the first year, I fell into the toilet – it was a bad accident – it was a very old-fashioned hole in the ground, and I slipped in it, and I was very, very upset.

AA: So you had to go home and do ablution?

SFH: No, I wanted to disappear, to be whisked off, so someone took me home very quickly. I didn't want to be seen by anybody. I wanted to be elegant and nice and clean. So that was a bad accident. And I was scared…

AA: Were you pushed?

SFH: No, I slipped in it. I think only my leg got dirty.

AA: Scarring experience?

SFH: No. I remember that quite clearly now.

AA: Were you walking?

SFH: I went on my bicycle, I enjoyed it.

AA: …bicycle? Hercules or Raleigh?

SFH: It was one of the early bicycles in town – Hercules. I remember my brother bringing it for me.

AA: A bell on it?

SFH: A bell – I think one or two, and a lock. I enjoyed riding on it. One or two of my friends also managed to get bicycles, so we would often go for a little bit of an out of town excursion.

AA: Did you form a group or a gang or something?

SFH: Not really, but we were a few close friends from *Karbalayyi* families, with me at school. One or two of them were a year ahead, and one or two were with me in the same year – The Awad Family and ...

AA: Kamal Khan?

SFH: Kamal Khan was older than I. His youngest brother Talib Khan whom you know was with me in the same class, in the primary and the intermediate. He wasn't doing very well, and every now and then the teacher expected me to help him more.

AA: So he became a businessman.

SFH: Yes – and then I ended up in England with him also – we went to the same town in England.

AA: Were you friends or just acquaintances?

SFH: We were his relatives and we really enjoyed each other's company.

AA: And you shared things in common.

SFH: A lot of things. In England, the first year, we were together in the same school, preparing for the GCE and we worked during the summer in a petrol station, both of us.

AA: Did they pay you?

SFH: Of course.

AA: How much?

SFH: Enough for two months for us to buy a little scooter each – a Vespa or Lambretta... can't remember. I always had a very good time with Talib. And he always had a good link. Soon after that I went to university, he went to some other schooling, and then he returned to Iraq. I took the challenge of the academic world and the profession far more seriously than he did.

Early Religious Life

AA: What about the role of outer religion in your daily lives? Were you strictly governed by the prayer times and so on?

SFH: The first year very much so. The second year I had a lot of difficulty with ablution and time for *salaat*.

AA: In Karbala?

SFH: No, In England...

AA: No, I'm talking about Karbala.

SFH: In Karbala there was a norm and I wanted to be part of it.

AA: When did you first start?

SFH: I remember at a very, very young age wanting to join the *salaat* with the others.

AA: Was it always done in *Jama`*?

SFH: No, in the house whoever was available at the time, the ladies and the men, they would be praying in one room...

AA: So no one actually taught you, you just followed the others?

SFH: Absolutely. No one gave me any strict formal or out of the norm instructions and training.

AA: It's something that you do.

SFH: I imbibed it and I asked and they answered.

AA: What about the various commemorations and anniversaries of Karbala and the *Shi`as*?

SFH: I was aware of it all, but it was never part of our household, and we were never in any way pushed or encouraged to join anything, or discouraged.

AA: Did you have *qurayyas* in your house?

SFH: Yes, *qurayyas* – there would be lady *qurayyas*.

AA: Who used to recite?

SFH: Mullah Zakiyyah in Karbala – women – I can't remember if there were any men.

AA: Did you see any of the leading clerical lights – the `ulama*?

SFH: They would come to my father and the more senior they were, the more it would be one to one: otherwise there'd be two or three where he sat in the *burani*. The first two would sit next to him; it would accommodate about 30/40 people who were present in a nice pavilion in a courtyard with a big, big mulberry tree close by – people knew their position. So anybody would go and take a seat according to their perception of their own position.

AA: There was a natural hierarchy?

SFH: Natural hierarchy, absolutely.

AA: And did you sort of imbibe that natural hierarchy?

SFH: Totally. I remember once in England with *Bahr al-Ulum* We were sitting quietly in a very intimate atmosphere in the center. And there was a lot of noise downstairs. People were screaming and so on. So after five minutes we realized there were three people from Najaf scrambling to get to a man. The fellow at the door was saying, 'It's somebody, keep quiet'. But they came barging in in a most vulgar state, sat there, complaining and swearing at a distance. And after 15 minutes they left. He turned to me and said, 'Who are these people? Look, in Iraq, forty or fifty years ago there'd be a natural filter – it has gone, so your culture has gone. This is your future.'

AA: What a future! So in Muharram, you went along with the activities?

SFH: We hardly left the house; especially near *Ashura*, we never went out of the house. Because the streets would be full of filth. People would be camping, sleeping, and defecating everywhere.

AA: But you didn't go to any public events?

SFH: No ... I don't remember – Occasionally I went to the *tashbih*, on the last day.

AA: But you didn't act in it?

SFH: No, no. I just looked from a distance, and the lion cubs... also I remember one year, the fellow who acted Shimmar[14]; he nearly was killed by the crowd.

AA: He must have been a good actor.

SFH: No, but – I mean they caught him – also, I remember every year in the `Azza of Twairij[15] as it is called, thousands of people would be running down – quite a few people would be trampled on.

AA: Did it leave any profound effect on you? Did it engrave itself on you?

---

[14] The killer of Imam Hussein.
[15] The lamentation of Twairij – part of the Ashura ritual in Iraq.

SFH: Other than an event, not really. I knew people needed to commemorate something. I knew people loved this anniversary repetition. Later on I came to understand that this is how we touched to that of continuity, of ongoing-ness.

AA: You were not touched emotionally by the story of Imam Hussain?

SFH: No, but I do remember, until now, whenever I am in a bit of inner resonance with Imam Hussain, I weep. But not the `Azza of Twairij, none of these things.

AA: So why do you say '*Ya Hussain!*' when you drink water? I have noticed that....... It must have had a powerful impact; but it wasn't something around which you built your inner life.

SFH: No. As I grew up, specially the last twenty 30 years, I started to feel the presence of these beings.

AA: But it's unrelated, you think, to your youth.

SFH: I can't say unrelated. Everything is related. *Wa anna ila rabbika almuntaha*[16].... I can't say unrelated, no way.

AA: But when somebody comes and says, 'We're commemorating some saint in, say, Florence,' you would not feel that attachment.

SFH: Nor if they tell me they're commemorating Imam Hussain – I say 'Good luck to you!' I feel I'm not separate from his presence. As I have just told you, in Karbala, they called me to participate ... they said, 'Why aren't you here? You are a son of Karbala', I said, 'You know, the *nur* of Karbala is in my heart. You need the stones of Karbala. You need that, I need the *nur* of Karbala; Allah gives us all according to our wishes. *Bismillah!*'

---

[16] "that the final goal is your Lord." (Qur'an 53:42)

AA: But Shaykhna, you relate to the symbol of Karbala. You don't say the same thing about, say, St. Francis of Assisi.

SFH: No, I don't.

AA: Because you are not a Christian.

SFH: I have to accept my physical, biological, cultural lineage. I don't deny that. That's why Chinmaya returned me to my religious origins. He said, 'You don't need Sanskrit, you don't need your habit. Now that you have touched the truth, you go back and find that all of it is the same. Go!'

AA: The filter is your youth, your childhood and adolescence.

SFH: I think it is more of a diet, more of a familiarity rather than a filter.

AA: Equivalent to eating certain dishes?

Allah's Nur and Culture

SFH: Sure. With a diet, you get used to it, you want familiarity, the same thing that you know. Because ultimately what you know is your own soul. You know Allah, you know Allah's *nur*. So everything else you want starts from the gross, the outer, until you find that what you are looking for is looking for you – it is your own *ruh*, which gives you life.

AA: But the tools, as it were, are to some extent, cultural.

SFH: Sure.

AA: And culture is to some extent connected to your earliest exposure.

SFH: Sure, but once you have the house and are living in the house, you don't commemorate the tools. Finished. It doesn't matter. All the way your path, path, path. Once you're in the city, it doesn't matter. I once asked one of the great ones, 'Why don't I hear a lot about *Tariqah*,

Tariqah, Tariqah?' He said, 'You are in the city, don't ask about the road.' So I accept the tools, I accept the need of it. I also accept that you have to give up that – like Ibn `Arabi's nearly 300 pages of the virtues of *zuhd*, and the virtue of leaving *zuhd*.

AA: But he still wrote in Arabic, which imposes on him certain limitations.

SFH: Fine. You have to get out of that imposition, get back to the root of it. Water has to come out from somewhere, but once it comes out, you say, it's a well, in so and so location …

AA: No, I'm not trying to say, Shaykna, that one is a prisoner of these things, that you're predisposed in this direction because you're bound to act in a certain way because you're exposed to these sights and sounds – there are still significant.

SFH: I don't deny that.

AA: But they also give it a certain twist, familiarity.

SFH: I don't deny where I was born, the culture, the *dīn*, the mother, and the environment – but more than that I acknowledge the Light that transcends it all. And the more I acknowledge that Light, the less important will be all of the tools, background and biographies. The biggest need we have is a biography, but more than that need is to get rid of the identity.

AA: But it's facilitated, if you agree with me, by your own experiences, as your experience is being detached and distanced from an early age, you're no longer culturally specific… it helps.

SFH: Absolutely. It helped then to be attached to it and it helps even more when, without knowing what detachment is, to go past it. It becomes yet another obstacle – 'I have to be detached' – what do you mean, detached? Detached from what? There's nothing detached –

there's only one. No ... 'you suffer from attachment, you suffer' – what attachment? There's only One. It's the illusion of my own mind.

AA: No, it's not attachment as much as a frame with which you pose these questions. They can be posed differently. As you know in science, the way that you frame an experiment, to some extent it generates the desired or the un-desired result, as it were.

SFH: True. And that's why science is so limited.

AA: What about language?

SFH: The language is a bridge, but it can also be a great canyon that divides, like everything else. Every goodness can also be the worse of worst.

The Absolute

AA: We'll talk about that later. The issue of culture and language at an early age I think is extremely significant in the way that you comprehend the world.

SFH: Probably.

AA: You don't agree with that?

SFH: Yes I think so. But as I said earlier, once you touch something that is Absolute, all of these relative issues become so insignificant.

AA: But the path to it must come through these frames.

SFH: Sure.

AA: You don't enter the route to Absolute without these terrestrial weapons in your armory.

SFH: On average yes, but not always.

AA: If somebody tells me, for example, that the best way is to know Serbo-Croat, I'll find it next to impossible. The multiplicity in which this is manifested demands that you work to this principle.

SFH: This is absolutely correct when the intellect is aroused, reasoning, `aql and all of that. But I have also known people who didn't need any of that – they just in their simple simplistic way found the Absolute – as Ibn `Arabi says, 'The *Jannah* is full of simpletons'. But those simpletons cannot help or teach others, cannot help to show the path or the way. A person like you needs both – significant attention to the path, and to all of its idiosyncrasies, and a better understanding of the ultimate destinations, but it's not a necessary condition.

People with Clear Minds and Pure Hearts

AA: When you talk about simpletons – simpleton or simple as in non-compound – it's different. If you are simple it sounds as if you are reduced to a singularity. It's different from being a simpleton, which can mean idiotic.

SFH: No, I don't mean idiotic, I mean somebody whose heart is clear, whose mind is not yet fully challenged or developed. So they are almost mindless. No, they are pure. They have clarity in their minds and purity in their hearts. I have known people who have not had the sophistication of education and all that. In my own language also, education is to do with bringing out what is in – the Latin origin of educate – *educare* (brought-up; trained) –

AA: But a simpleton cannot be a Shaykh.

SFH: True. They will not be able to teach, but their presence is *baraka*. It's why they've killed it.

AA: It's like an AC-DC current – it's just one type of current – it's not both. So they are of little use to people who are seeking.

SFH: No, I can't say little use in an obvious sense. It doesn't mean their presence is not good. In Karbala it was wonderful in our own household, all of the five, six, sometimes fifteen, people – women and men sitting there doing their chores quietly – sifting through the rice – it was goodness. We have reduced everything – unless you can do this or do that, you are incompetent. I think this is denuding humanity of its divinity, which in some cases is coming out of people whom we disregard as being simple, uneducated – I think this is a big, big loss to humanity.

AA: Did you have mendicants or *qalandars*?

SFH: Often – in our house as well as Karbala. I remember one man coming during Muharram ....

AA: Local?

SFH: No, they were foreigners. You could see from the robes, the cap – they were often people with *kashkol*, sometimes without. This one man would stand in front of Bab al-Qibla supposedly, he only ate one almond a day – he would be standing on one leg reciting, and halfway through reciting, he would change to the other leg. I think I must have seen him a few times but I didn't check whether it was 24 hours. There were a number of cases.

AA: What did you think of him? Were you intrigued by it? Or was it just part of the landscape?

SFH: I considered him to be just part of the landscape. I thought of him as just another being, another tuning. I was neither curious nor uncurious, I just accepted it as it was.

AA: You're describing, Shaykhna, a medieval city.

SFH: It is true.

AA: Which had its lepers, beggars, its merchants, ...

SFH: It's true. Three mad people in the city. One of them was a lady – Layla Diwina was her name '*diwina*' means 'mad' – Layla was her name.

AA: And then all of this was then shattered by...

SFH: I left ...

AA: ...by the opening of the officers' club?

SFH: (laughs) I don't know – yes. You know by the time I left for the UK.

Accepting Change/Inner Reliance

AA: When did it begin to lose its medieval-ness?

SFH: I would say I began to notice its loss of medieval-ness when I was about, may be 10, 11, 12, and my father stopped going to his *burani*.

AA: Do you think it was a good thing in those days or a bad thing?

SFH: I knew it was an end of an era. I never judged it as good or bad.

AA: Really? Just something that happened.

SFH: Something that happened. Because, again, my talking to Imam Hussain – 'shall I stay, shall I go [to England]? I don't want any movement, I didn't want any change.' He said, 'No! You have to go! There's nothing else for you.' So I went.

AA: And you were not like, you were, enthralled with change. You loved it – new cars – TV.

SFH: Yes and no – not really.

AA: Did you like TV?

SFH: TV came in England when I went – 1955.

AA: It came to Iraq in 1956.

SFH: You see I wasn't enthralled.

AA: Like air coolers. Did you have air coolers in Iraq?

SFH: They had some, yes, desert coolers. No, I wasn't enthralled. I just took it as – 'fine, it helps and gives ease and comfort.' I took things in my stride. I was never over-enthusiastic about anything. I was always mild, but pleasantly attached…

AA: Attached?

SFH: Not really. I didn't know attachment or detachment.

AA: I'm applying the term retroactively.

SFH: I can't say I was detached or attached. But it never really shocked me to a thrill or excitement.

AA: You're describing supreme comfort, a form of serenity.

SFH: Inner serenity. Even the bicycle, which was a big event – I was excited the moment it was given to me, but that was it. A few minutes later on, that was it. There was nothing more.

AA: Do you remember an episode that jarred you? Did you do an injustice without thinking, and then deeply regret it?

SFH: I think there were a few occasions in our playgroups with my relatives, wanting to have one of their toys or something – it just passed, it was childish.

AA: You were not an acquisitive person?

Growing up in Karbala

SFH: No – I remember I hid a few times nuts and things, which were eaten by rats, and I felt at the same time, I would say to them, 'You deserve it!' I remember once there was a wonderful packet of special Persian nuts that I hid in one of the rooms in the *burani* – there were several rooms empty – there was a little cupboard so I put it in there, and after two or three weeks when I went there it was mostly chewed away, so I felt, 'you see, that's what happens.'

AA: I think it seems that it was inevitable that you would become a Shaykh....(laughing)...... unless you reverse that which is difficult....I think you were earmarked like these people seeking the new Dalai Lama. No inequality...No sibling rivalry, no jealousies, none of these vices that condemn individuals…

SFH: If I have to say one thing again, I repeat, I had immense inner, if you like, trust, or reliance or confidence, without it being too vain or arrogant – I had that.

AA: You were at a middle point.

SFH: Yes, self-contained. I would be very happy being left in the house for long hours – I would find something to do – I would find a book to read, something to do, or a bit of gardening – you know I would occupy myself.

AA: But it's extraordinary, Shaykhna that you were not swept up by the political currents of the time: this was a time of great change in Iraq.

SFH: I had a lot of, again, insight. For example in the oil company, where my friends were the top Ba'athists, what was the first Ba'ath thing that came? Ali Saleh Al-Sa`di, well, you know his wife was a very close friend of mine – one of the closest. Because the wife's brother was part of one of our groups, like (Shaykh) Hosam, his name was Tariq al-Umari. Tariq was one of the closest in our inner circle – we were four or five of us, and his sister, Hana, was very close to me and some of our friends.

AA: Also a big Ba'athist?

SFH: Top Ba'athist – chief of the radio.

AA: Yes, I know her – sister of Tariq al-Umari…

SFH: So when that regime came she came to my house and hid with us for a month – she came to the house and hid – nobody knew where she was. But I felt all of this would pass. And they asked me to do this and that, and be head of this and I said, 'this is all rubbish.'

AA: But Shaykhna, this is later...

SFH: This was later, yes. But this was when I was tested...

AA: I mean the crisis that emerged in Iraq in the 1950s didn't really reach you.

SFH: No – as I say, even the World War I didn't notice.

AA: If you don't notice the world war, what are you going to notice?! May be an earthquake! Even that you probably wouldn't notice. Were there any sectarian feelings in your household?

No Sectarian Feelings

SFH: No. I knew there was one major Sunni family who had a Sunni mosque in Karbala.

AA: But you knew you were Shi`a?

SFH: Of course – and I knew they were Sunnis and they were nice people – his name was Khatib, and his son was with me at school: we played sport. That's about it. I really had no negative feelings towards the Sunnis whatsoever, nor against Christianity. As I said eariler, quite a number of Christians would visit our house. I knew they were different, but I didn't feel any discrimination towards them.

AA: But it was an overwhelmingly Shi`a environment. You didn't conflate being a Muslim with being a Shi`a?

SFH: No – I think from an early stage I knew that there would be distractions and there would be different streams and different levels of light or knowledge and I knew that where I'd come from had been very privileged in that, and I accepted that – I acknowledged that I was in gratitude.

AA: But that's different. A decade later things changed.

SFH: No doubt about it.

AA: It became more intense.

SFH: I was spared all of that, and that's why wherever I went after that, I tried to create a similar ambience, as though it's nothing to do with this world, like here in South Africa – what can you do? And I'd been privileged in the way that wherever I'd gone I managed to have a bit of an ambience like this – I could have been anywhere, and still feel and experience that.

Simple Life in Karbala

AA: Did you own a radio?

SFH: No – my sister wanted a radio – she was older than I – and she had a tiny little radio, a beautiful little Pye – her name was Fadhila – and she would hide it in her room – my father was quite – you know – not happy with it – so she would be very quiet listening to some music and so on. Later on he would ask her to bring it to him for the news. So I think he became well-disposed to it.

AA: What did he listen to – Saut al-Arab?[17]

---

[17] Voice of the Arabs – A radio station.

SFH: I don't know – things like this ... I never...

AA: Were there cinemas in Karbala...?

SFH: No –

AA: That came very late.

SFH: It came much later.

AA: About *Chai Khanas* and so on?

SFH: Full of them.

AA: But you were not allowed to go there?

SFH: I was never deprived – I never took to it...I much preferred at home.

AA: I was just thinking – did you go to the souk?

SFH: Often.

AA: And did you talk to *Bazaaris* and stallholders.

SFH: Often with Baba Mahmoud or with somebody else.

AA: Part of the life of the town, that fellow sells carpets, that fellow sells this or that.

SFH: I had no needs...I had everything in the house. People would gift us. I often had enough clothes. I was also never desirous of acquiring so many things, like clothes or shoes. I often had people gifting me – from Iran, from Baghdad – shoes, clothes, shirts, etc.

AA: Clothes were just provided for you?

SFH: Provided – often my mother would sew – she would alter some of these things for me, I remember a couple of occasions, things that were altered for my brother – I liked the stuff, but I wasn't very happy about my having altered stuff.

AA: Hand-me-downs –

SFH: Hand-me-downs. They were good and she did a super job. Until now, most of my nightshirts were sewn by my mother. Until now.

AA: You were wearing western clothes?

SFH: In Karbala, yes.

AA: You didn't wear traditional clothes?

SFH: No, I wore western clothes.

AA: Did they shave your head?

SFH: No.

AA: Did you go to Friday *ghusl* and so on?

SFH: No.

AA: So you didn't have special rituals?

SFH: By that time my father had stopped everything. There were no more rituals; he was no longer involved in public life.

AA: But the daily articles of use – did you use Laural soap or Pears soap?

SFH: Both – most ......I preferred Laural soap – I continue with them up till now.

AA: And toothpaste, or a *miswaak*.

SFH: I think so – I never had a *miswaak*.

AA: I mean the common articles of the modern world began to seep in.

SFH: That's right –

AA: From clothes to toothpaste –

SFH: Yes... bicycles, blocks of ice and iceboxes.

AA: Air coolers.

SFH: Air coolers – we didn't need it because we had *sirdabs*.

AA: Fans...

SFH: No, we didn't do so much, but I knew it was done nearby... we had *sirdabs* and we had fans.

AA: The only article of modern consumption you didn't have was a car.

SFH: That's right – there was no need for it. You could walk. And whenever it was for trips, people would send their cars, or a few cars were available.

Visiting Baghdad

AA: When was the first time you went to Baghdad, Shaykhna?

SFH: I think maybe with my uncle.

AA: What did you think of it? Did you want to get back?

SFH: It really didn't matter. I tell you what I liked in Baghdad; it was *simsimiyya* that was a big association with Baghdad – nice bars of *simsim* and sugar, or honey. I am still fond of it. Actually, I did like Baghdad, I didn't mind it, but I was never overly fascinated by it.

AA: Was it a day trip, you came back to Karbala the same day?

SFH: No, no, a few days, two or three days – it was a long trip.

AA: You stayed with family?

SFH: Stayed with uncles, families and Jamil Sami, and with others, the Mazandarani families; they were three of them and many elsewhere.

Interactions with Adults

AA: Shaykhna, we come to – you said that your heroes were your teachers.

SFH: In school, yes definitely.

AA: Did you have any other heroes?

SFH: Yes, I had a few visitors to my father. There was one Iranian prince, who would come every year, either the head of the Iranian Hajj delegation, a very princely being.

AA: Qajari prince?

SFH: Qajari prince. There was another one resident in Karbala called Shahzadeh – I also loved him. He would always give me sweets; he lived in a most beautiful house – with a huge garden, a little pavilion. He was a wonderful man. There was another man, who was a Sayyed close to my father, from Peshawar, a Peshawari, also a wonderful man. He would always be there, every day with my father in their *burani*.

AA: You just liked them as individual beings...

SFH: I looked up to them. I found these beings were of substance...

AA: People worthy of being admired.

SFH: I loved them and they never condescended to me, they treated me as one of them.

AA: It's very traditional – a habit that seems to have died out now, to treat children as if they were part of the adults.

SFH: I was treated as one of them.

AA: They wouldn't say, 'go away!' if you were there with them?

SFH: No, never, never.

AA: Did you ever talk to them?

SFH: Often –

AA: In a conversation?

SFH: I often talked to them. Again in a real way – I would ask them, 'What is this?' 'What is that?' 'Why do you do this?' and they would answer me. I would have them really as older friends. I never felt in any way being condescended to or had to put up with anything of that sort.

AA: I remember you related once a story where a person was involved in interest-taking...

SFH: Yes, yes, in the *burani* there were often 3 or 4 of these low level mullahs, and they would do their deals. In this particular case somebody wanted to borrow money and they wanted interest and the mullahs found this solution. They said, 'look, buy from him this cigarette for £10 and you'll get your way.' So I told them that on the day of reckoning God would put him in a barrel and set the barrel on fire and say, 'I didn't throw you, I threw the barrel.' They looked at me quite unhappy. On occasions I would say things like this to others as well as relatives. So that's it.

AA: So how did your father react?

SFH: He didn't know. It didn't reach him. It was not that important.

AA: It was quite a daring thing to do.

SFH: As I said, I was allowed to, without it being funny, without it being clever – it was natural for me. And I was allowed self-expression. Later on, when I saw what goes on in the inner self, that it reflects the *al-Mutakallim*, I really felt that I had been so fortunate, that the Expresser in me had been allowed to express its voice from early on, at that young age.

AA: What did you think of the notion of the deity at that age?

SFH: Didn't really think much. I knew deep down that all of what we were doing was a human attempt and I had to be in it. I felt deeply that I had no option other than accepting whatever came, including the skills I developed, including the work I had to learn for business or engineering or whatever. I took it that this was part of a cycle, and I accepted it in a way, occasionally with a bit of grumbling, occasionally with a bit of reluctance. So deity and the higher I somehow, maybe subconsciously, knew it without questioning it, without knowing it.

AA: Did you relate it to *khawf* – fear?

SFH: Not that much. I visualized paradise, I visualized Hell, but I somehow did not fall into that excessive, if you like, synthesis or analysis. I somehow trusted that all was well.

AA: You were too young, I suppose, but usually, at that age, ten or twelve, you have a sense of the deity, driven either by fear or, I won't say, hope, but some kind of reward at the end.

SFH: I never had that. You know, later on when I discovered the meaning of *khawf* and *raja'*, I really found that perhaps I'd been very fortunate in being between the two.

AA: And you were not told, 'If you don't do this...'

SFH: No.

AA: '…you'll be in the fire.'

SFH: No. Never, never. Nor did I look for more *thawab*. I really, as you said earlier, I was much more in the middle somehow. It was one of those muddling through by *rahma*.

Pre-University/England Scholarship

AA: We come now to the last phases of your pre-university – secondary school. You also went to *thanawiyya* in Karbala?

SFH: Of course.

AA: Which one was it?

SFH: *Thanawiyya Karbala* – it was good, I enjoyed it and –

AA: All your friends moved with you?

SFH: Yes. I did very well. I excelled. Strangely enough in my most favorite topics, which was Mathematics, and science, either I would do 100% or fail. It happened twice.

AA: Why was that?

SFH: I don't know. Either I get it all, or somehow just below par. It happened to me at the *mutawasia* – the third … and then in the *thanawiyya* a month or so before the exams, I began to wake up – I wanted to do well. And of course came first in Karbala, second in Iraq, and strangely enough, I was top in Mathematics. Arabic was 100% – can you imagine somebody getting Arabic 100%?

AA: No, it's impossible!

SFH: Impossible. That's why.

AA: *Baccalaureate* is not an easy exam –

SFH: In the interviews of scholarship they asked me, for example, 'What is this?' So, there were some of these odd things.

AA: I think you were first in Karbala, second in Iraq, all the options were open to you – where to go to university. Did your father expect you to go to England?

SFH: Not at all. He never, ever interfered, never said anything or suggested anything. Whatsoever.

AA: If you had wanted to become a blacksmith, say?

SFH: I don't think he would have objected. But somehow, his presence was for me a good reference, and somehow, automatically, I wanted to do medicine. He wasn't very happy with that because of the strenuous life it would bring upon me. He mentioned to me, for example that one of my elder brothers decided against medicine, because he said, 'My life would be completely taken by being in the service of others.' And then when my name was announced on the radio that I was second and was selected for scholarship, that notion began to tick within me. And then I knew – Sahib Mohsin was already in England, because he was two years ahead of me – so one thing led to another, so I said, 'All right, never mind'. I actually thought I'd apply and then I would refuse it. Pachachi was the examiner –

AA: Nadim?

SFH: Nadim. And he asked me, 'why do you want to do biology?'

AA: He interviewed you?

SFH: He interviewed me and two others for the scholarship; so I applied for organic something.

AA: Who provided the scholarship? The government or the IPC[18]?

SFH: The government.

AA: It wasn't the IPC?

SFH: No, it was the government – I think so. I'm not sure. Nadim was the head of the examining committee. The other one was that fellow who became minister of oil, also went to the Gulf, nice man, from the north.

AA: Abdullah Ismail?

SFH: Abdullah Ismail. He was the secretary, he was sitting there with others; they were all there. They remembered me later on. So he asked me, 'Why do you want to do this?'

AA: So there was no sectarianism?

SFH: Not at all. I never felt sectarianism. He said, 'You have done so well.' Without being arrogant, I said, 'Yes, if you don't accept me, don't. It doesn't matter.' He said, 'No, we want you.' So I went. And it was shock upon shock. Cultural shock was the greatest. You asked me what were the shocks. It was this. The cultural shock. It was a killer.

AA: Did you know the language?

SFH: Some English, because the last two years at the secondary school we were taught English.

AA: Could you converse in English at that time?

SFH: Very poorly.

AA: But you could read a bit.

SFH: I could converse, read a bit, like now!

AA: No, not like now!

---

[18] Iraq Petroleum Company.

SFH: Slightly less.

AA: You are not cluttered by what you have learnt since! It was elemental...

AA: Did you know what you were going to study in England?

SFH: Initially I was interested in organic chemistry – that was the subject.

AA: What did you know about it?

SFH: I liked Chemistry. I had always liked Mathematics and Physics. I wanted Chemistry because it was far more basic, fundamental at the molecular atomic level – I liked that sort of thing. Investigative. I wanted to know what was inside the molecule, inside the cells, inside the organic life. It's part of my – if you like – curiosity about the origin of life. So I thought organic would be better – I didn't know what it was – really had no idea as to what subjects there were. And that is why the Examiners for my scholarship objected. He said, 'Why are you doing this? You are so good at this and that...' So when I got to the GCE first, two years, I applied for London.

Travelling to London

AA: How did you get to London? How did you take leave of your family? Did you leave in a rush?

SFH: No, not in a rush – there was quite a bit of resistance. For example, I was about to leave for the airport – my own nanny just wept; she said, 'I will die'. I said, 'Die', I said, 'You're born to die.' So the poor woman, she quietly left the house and took a taxi to go to the airport to Baghdad, not knowing what time I was leaving – and the taxi took her somewhere else, dropped her somewhere else. The poor woman was two days in the sun, she got sunstroke. She died a week later, literally. I didn't know. She had eczema. We used to send her stuff we found in England, they said it's good for eczema. So after about a year my brother or someone wrote to me, and said, 'please don't send her any more things. She doesn't need it.' I suspected she must have died. So Baba Mahmood would not call for a taxi to take me to Baghdad. He said, 'I can't do that. I don't want you to leave. How can I go and help you leaving.' So it was a bit of a drama over my leaving for England.

AA: It must have been rather traumatic for you to leave.

SFH: A bit traumatic – and in the airport I found two or three other people on the same scholarship.

AA: How did you find out about your scholarship? You were accepted by the committee – they wrote you a letter?

SFH: They wrote me a letter. They said, 'This is your flight. You're booked on KLM. You stay one night in Beirut…'

AA: 1955?

SFH: 1955. 'One night in Beirut, and you'll be on your way to England and there you'll have somebody in the airport, from the embassy to greet you.'

AA: What about financial arrangements?

SFH: I really can't remember whether they gave me some money or not. Can't remember. But they were quite organized. There was a Mr. Pearce from the embassy who was in charge of the scholarship students.

AA: You had to get a passport.

SFH: Yes… Iraqi passport – the usual stuff, not that difficult, took 2/3 weeks. In Karbala it was easy, my brother and others helped me.

AA: There were no visas then.

SFH: No, I don't remember. But anyway, I didn't have any hassles; there were no restrictions. But on the plane to Beirut I was quite surprised to see waitresses – that was the first cultural shock for me.

AA: Stewardesses…

SFH: Stewardesses, sorry, I was surprised. "Isn't this shameful," I thought, "Women watching!" So in Beirut we stayed in a hotel, in downtown on the sea front – Normandie – there were 3 or 4 and a certain Alwan and 3 other students, and the next day we took the flight to London.

Life in England

SFH: There [in London], there was somebody from the embassy. I can't remember where they had booked us – some bed and breakfast place – and then a week or so later, they assigned each one of us to a college to do the GCE. I was assigned to Brookland College in Weybridge, Surrey.

AA: It was quite a pleasant summer.

First Impressions

SFH: Very pleasant. And there I stayed with a family. There were three of us Iraqis in the same house, with a landlady and the smell of bacon and so on was overwhelming. And the next morning we came down in our pajamas, and she said, 'No, No, No, no such thing. This guesthouse cannot allow this. Go back and dress up. Come back properly dressed.'

AA: You were used to walking in pajamas in the street!

SFH: So I learned that. And then what was very embarrassing for me a week or two later, I had a little brass jug for the toilet, which I had hidden behind the door in my bedroom. I suddenly found that on the mantelpiece – as though it was an ornament. It was a brass thing. So I was so embarrassed. They didn't know what it was for. And then, about 2/3 weeks later, I bought a radio to listen to the news to improve my English.

AA: What was your first impression of London. Did you like it? It was summer time.

SFH: It was summertime – it was all right. I was surprised at the gender mix – that really shocked me more than anything else.

AA: But *hijab* was not really that common in Iraq.

SFH: Karbala was full of *hijab* and *abaya – pushiye*, some of them.

AA: Did you go out in the streets bareheaded?

SFH: No-one, except some of the Europeans who came to visit us.

AA: So you were surprised to see mixed couples.

SFH: I was surprised also at the interaction – a woman sitting with a man, talking with a man – it was a very big shock to me.

AA: So what was the outer aspect?

SFH: I think I had seen enough pictures in those tourist travel books that I was given by what looked liked ... type of ladies – Freya Stark – I wasn't that surprised, I wasn't that shocked. Then Sahib Muhsin and a few others were there, and they warned us, they said, 'Look, you know there will be a lot of girls smiling at you and laughing with you – it doesn't mean anything, so be careful, don't be too concerned about it – this is normal here.' So we were soon educated that women were not loose or whatever and don't get any ideas. I found the biggest difficulty was that I was expected to be self-reliant in studies, in the lectures. I couldn't quite catch up.

AA: But I'm sure the college is designed to teach foreigners English.

SFH: No, Brookland College was preparatory but for everyone, it was not for foreigners, not specialized in anything.

AA: Like a sixth form college…

SFH: Something like that, absolutely. It was not specialized. We were in a minority in the class. We had to do exactly as everybody else and they were far ahead. It was very depressing. The first three months, most of us were very depressed.

AA: I had the same experience in my time. I was much younger.

SFH: No, it was very depressing – several of us suffered from that. I remember one of our friends who later went to the ministry of foreign affairs, nice man, Ferhan something; after two or three months he was weeping day and night. We asked him why, he said he had not heard from his family. He said, 'Every day I'm sending them a letter.' In Weybridge it was very nicely organized – all the street corners had 'litter' boxes, he was throwing his letters into the litter box! Day after day – no answer. So there were a number of tragedies like this, which were comic tragedies. So somebody told him, "This is 'litter' box, not letter box." And there were a lot of tragedies; somebody ate bacon, they told him it was 'ham', he thought it was 'hen'. It was ham. So he cried. There were quite a number of incidents. We were not sufficiently guided. We didn't have anybody to tell us much or show us or give us a little book to introduce us to the British culture. There wasn't any of that.

AA: Dropped in the deep end.

SFH: Dropped in the deep end. I too found it quite difficult and depressing but I had a lot of good support from a few friends and also, as it happened in Weybridge, there was somebody I knew very well from Karbala, who was in university at that time. His name was Khalil Iraqi, nice man, close to us, knew my family. He would be visiting me, so I had quite a bit of support. And my brother – one of my brothers from my father's first wife, he was a businessman, quite well off, export-import to the Middle East, nice man, wonderful man. So I would almost end up every weekend, if not every other weekend, in his house, in Wembley. He'd take care of me – food, parcels. So I was quite supported, but I still felt lonely, depressed. I remember a very brief letter – my father used to write to me – it wasn't that long, but I kept it. I got one letter from him five six months after I arrived in London. He said, 'Had I known it would be so hard on you, I would not have allowed you to go but I thought based on what is coming you might as well be exposed to the rest of the world. But I know it's been very hard on you, and on your mother, although she doesn't show it. She never showed it in her letters.'

AA: Later on when you reflected on this time, was there any benefit of being thrown in the deep end?

SFH: No doubt there were, but at the time I would have told you, 'Please take me out of the deep end.' So of course there is always with hindsight –

AA: If someone had offered you a return ticket, would you have taken it?

SFH: I think so, I think so. Although once I had it in my pocket, I would have wondered what I was going to do with it in Iraq. ... whether I would have returned, I am not sure. I wasn't really happy, I wasn't well. Then one of my friends…

AA: What was the food like?

SFH: Terrible, Terrible.

AA: English stodge?

SFH: English stodge; also don't forget, they were still on ration. Everything, including eggs, were rationed. I was used to produce from our farm, so I would go to the grocery shop and you could only buy a quarter of a cucumber. For one shilling or something. Half an onion – that sort of thing. It was horrible. I would have from our farm tons of beautiful oranges and there you had to buy half a one or one.

AA: Did you sort of reflect on how this was a mighty power and it had such a miserable narrow life?

SFH: No I didn't–

AA: I mean this half an onion – things you never saw in Iraq – to see them in what was supposed to be a great power. Did that not make you think?

SFH: No. As you said, I wasn't at all looking at the power maps of the world. I just thought they were technically, materially very advanced, but they were a different people and I didn't think I would belong to them or like to. So I really took it from day one, 'I am here on a trip to gain some skills, some training, a degree, and that's it.' I never thought I would have a great deal of connection, long-term association with it. Nor did I know how temporary it would be or how long. I just accepted this period as being very different, and I had to put up with it and that's it. There was no alternative. What else could I do? So the first year was harsh on me.

AA: Was it a two-year program?

Return to Iraq for a Holiday

SFH: Two years. I returned to Iraq the next year for a holiday. I bought a scooter, so I drove all the way to the tip of Italy – Brindisi – to Venice and from there I took a boat. On my own steam.... and then – I might have had some help from my family.

AA: Did they expect you to return?

SFH: No, no.

AA: So you went across Europe on a scooter, by yourself?

SFH: By myself, staying in youth hostels along the way.

AA: An adventure!

SFH: Yes, I joined the Youth Hostel Association and it took me 8-9 days from London to Venice; from there I took a boat.

AA: You had to take a visa from Italy and a transit visa.

SFH: Yes – all the time.

Life in England

AA: It was quite easy in those days.

SFH: Yes easy, from there I took a boat, it was one of the famous old ship.

AA: There was the Achilles, the Agamemnon, the Esperia.

SFH: The Esperia, I was on; then from there to Beirut. From there I took the Nairn[19] to Baghdad.

AA: It must have taken you weeks…

SFH: I was in Iraq for a month.

AA: Were they all happy?

Final Meeting with Father

SFH: Very happy. I was also very happy and that time I knew I wouldn't see my father any more, because I said goodbye to him. He looked well. I said, '*Inshah Allah*, I'll see you again when I come back maybe in a year or two.'

AA: He was in his seventies?

SFH: No, in his eighties.

AA: But he wasn't ill then?

SFH: Not at all. In his early mid-eighties. So, as I was leaving his courtyard – this was another house that he had – a little courtyard with orange trees and all of that and his own library and bedroom – beautiful setup – and the lab was, as I said, behind – you could get into it from the

---

[19] The Nairn Transport Company was a pioneering motor transport company that operated a trans-desert route from Beirut, Haifa and Damascus to Baghdad, and back again, from 1923. Their route became known as "The Nairn Way". The firm continued, in various guises, until 1959.

roof. So I turned around again just to look at him; he deliberately, I think, tried not to have eye-to-eye contact. So I knew that's it, I won't see him.

AA: A premonition.

SFH: Absolutely. And the rest of the time, especially with his batman, he said he knew exactly which day he'd die when he was leaving, and how he prepared for it.

Back to England

AA: What happened to your scooter? You left it in Venice?

SFH: I went back – I had left it in Venice. Went back to Venice, took the scooter and drove back to England. It stayed with me for a year or so. I had one or two little accidents, turning around a bit too fast on a gravel road, you know they are a bit skiddy – and I enjoyed it very much. Then I sold it later on. Occasionally I gave lifts to one or two people –

AA: The summer of 1956? Before the Suez crisis?

SFH: Correct. So basically I returned, then I applied to different universities – I wanted some place that was a bit less hectic.

AA: Did they indicate where you should go or was it your decision?

SFH: No, they helped me to apply to one or two universities. I thought of St. Andrews but I learned it was much colder and I wanted some place where it was a bit more homely – I was homesick. I was really homesick. And I was fortunate that I had a wonder British old lady as my landlady for a long period of time – her name was Mrs. Cubicle. She was married to a Frenchman, a very fine and interesting Frenchman. She always plied me with fruits and stuff.

AA: In Weybridge?

SFH: In Weybridge. So then I had three or four possibilities. I didn't do very well in my A levels – middle grades.

AA: C-D –

SFH: Something like that – so I knew I won't get-

AA: What subjects?

SFH: Eventually I decided there and then that I would choose basic science: Physics, Mathematics and Chemistry.

AA: For your A levels?

University Life

SFH: A levels. So I got accepted to the University of Wales. North Wales – I preferred that, I felt it was more homely, small university, and not too stressful, not too demanding.

AA: It was a University College then?

SFH: It was University College of North Wales.

AA: Aberystwyth?

SFH: No, Aberystwyth is south. This is Bangor – North Wales. Next to a beautiful island. Anglesey. I lived in Anglesey.

AA: Is it connected to the mainland?

SFH: Yes, yes. There is a bridge – beautiful. There are a couple of islands.

AA: Did you visit the college or prior?

SFH: People told me there were Iraqis there – I heard from the grapevine there were 4 or 5 Iraqis; one of them was doing a PhD, the others were undergraduates.

AA: And were you limited by your grades?

SFH: I was limited to two or three universities; I preferred not to go up north, so it was limited.

AA: Were you offered St Andrews University College and others?

SFH: It was possible – St. Andrews – maybe another one.

AA: They gave you an indication?

SFH: Yes – and being a foreigner we were given a certain amount of leeway – they made allowance for our low grades –

AA: Do you think you had low grades because of lack of familiarity with the system?

SFH: No doubt – I began to catch up towards the end. It wasn't very easy, but I wasn't too unhappy about it either.

AA: You weren't aiming for Cambridge or Imperial College?

SFH: No, I think from early on I excluded the top five or six English Universities, definitely also Oxford. Cambridge was out of my reach.

AA: Did the embassy direct you or did you decide on your own?

SFH: No, they gave us again a short list of what was appropriate and I think most of us Iraqis in that batch received second year scholarship in a big way. Fadhil Khan was just one year ahead of me.

AA: The scholarship started in the 1920s but not in a big way.

SFH: No, not that number – we were 50 that year. There were also from the Development Ministry and a few other places. I think in total there may have been 70, 80, 90 people.

AA: Was Islam al-Khalisi, my cousin, one of them?

SFH: Yes, a year ahead of me – I knew him from Iraq, Karbala. His father, I knew him very well from Karbala. We were close friends. His father was very close to my father. Almost every day he was with my father. Abdul Rasul Al-Khalisi almost every day.

AA: In many ways stubbly upright person.

SFH: They were very close together – I'll never forget them. He would travel with my father in their car going to orchards; they had a lot of photographs together.

AA: You knew Isam from Karbala?

SFH: I knew Isam very well from Karbala. I was very fond of him. Exceptionally good at school – bright – he was a year ahead of me.

AA: So he didn't suggest you go to Sheffield. I thought you were going to go to Sheffield. You were then accepted at Bangor.

SFH: I was accepted at Bangor and I went.

Summer Holidays

AA: You didn't go home for the summer holidays?

SFH: No.

AA: So what did you do in the holidays, did you work?

SFH: That year I worked in Sweden. I applied to the university of Uppsala to work as a research assistant in a farm. They were gaging why this immune hybridized clover was not getting fertilized by the bees. So I was given this task for two months, with a girl who was the granddaughter of Tolstoy, to measure how long the bees stayed on the flower, and we found that quite clearly –

AA: Did you do it by photography?

SFH: No, timing – it doesn't stay long because it cannot get the pollen. So the stem was longer than the bee can pollinate. So the professor congratulated us because of that – they gave us a bonus.

AA: How did you find the job – in the newspaper or –?

SFH: No, in the university board – I applied; so that was my first year.

AA: It was between your A levels and the first year, or the first year?

SFH: No, after the first year.

AA: So it was it was a job that was put on the university bulletin board.

SFH: Exactly, after the first year at university I went to Sweden.

AA: So how was your first year in college?

SFH: All right, jogging along, not too happy.

AA: No Iraqis there?

SFH: There were, maybe 7, 8.

AA: Shaykh Hosam?

SFH: Shaykh Hosam was ahead of me one or two years, I think 2. So Hosam was very close in terms of age, and a few others. They were my friends.

AA: Did they see you as junior?

Life in England

SFH: No, they were my close friends. Tariq was my year – Tariq al-Umari – there were a total of 6/7 Iraqis.

AA: Your friends were all Iraqis?

SFH: No, they were not all Iraqis. There were non-Iraqis as well. For example, there was one nice Englishman and a lovely lady, who was actually his girlfriend.

AA: Did you keep up with them later on?

SFH: Not so much – only three years after I had graduated, and that was it. There was one Iraqi, brilliant, a bookworm, very religious, doing his PhD. There was a Syrian who was doing a PhD. There were a total of maybe 10, 12, middle Easterners, Arabs; an Iranian, very nice boy – he was my friend. Very close friend.

AA: Did Iranians and Iraqis exile, or abroad, became quite friendly?

SFH: Yes, three or four Iranians, I wasn't really very happy. I had no real intimacy, no connection with the culture. And the weather depressed me a lot. I didn't know that I was subject to Seasonal adjustment – SAD[20] – I really didn't know that. I discovered it much later.

AA: That was the cause for depression?

SFH: Also the lack of sun – sea air, and all of that. And I met a few very fine people outside the college. I didn't stay in the hostel. Some did.

AA: Dorms or...?

SFH: I didn't stay in the dorms. It was a very old, beautiful, small boutique university, with may be 2000 students; brilliant residents and a wonderful lecture hall; though a bit stiff and pretentious.

AA: You wore ties?

---

[20] Seasonal Affective Disorder.

Life in England

SFH: Yes, you had to wear a gown, always.

AA: And instruction was good?

SFH: It was excellent. They had high quality professors.

AA: 50s and 60s were the peak.

SFH: Our Professor of Physics was an FRS.[21] The Professor of Chemistry was an FRS. Top people.

AA: Do you remember anybody in particular?

SFH: Yes, I remember the Professor of Physics, Professor Andrew; the Professor of Chemistry was Professor Agnes – Angus.

AA: And you stuck to basic science?

SFH: I stuck to basic science, pure science, and pure Mathematics.

AA: I thought your degree was in Chemical Engineering?

SFH: No. Chemistry, Physics and Mathematics; I did courses in Chemical Engineering in the oil industry. They sent me to America for a while to Esso that time as it was in Houston, Texas; again it was very depressing and lonely.

AA: Much more depressing than in England!

SFH: Very depressing. And I, from nowhere, was there for six months. I was at the IPC for 8 years; more than half of it I was abroad.

AA: So when you were in Bangor, did you feel the need to go to a big city, like Manchester?

SFH: We did occasionally.

---

[21] Fellowship of the Royal Society.

AA: By coach or bus?

Planning to Return to Iraq

SFH: Coach, bus – with the Iraqis, sometimes with cars, one or two of them had cars. We had an enjoyable group. One of us, Ghazi Kufaishy, became a very prominent Ba'athi member; Ghazi Ayoub too became a very prominent Ba'athi member. Saddam killed him because he told Saddam, 'Now that you are so unpopular, step down for a while and then you come back.' The next day he was killed. There were a lot of things like that. But we had a nice group.

AA: But it overlapped with the revolution in Iraq (1958). Did that affect you in any way?

SFH: No, it didn't affect me.

AA: Were there any pro- or anti-revolution people?

SFH: I don't think it affected our group in Bangor so much. Hosam may know more. I wasn't affected, I didn't feel it. There were several of these people already becoming Ba'athists, and there were two or three of them a bit more religious.

AA: Where would you classify yourself?

SFH: Myself – really indifferent. I wasn't in any camp.

AA: Did you stick to religious practices?

SFH: No – by the second year at university I couldn't keep up my *salaat* – I began to drift. The last year, I remember myself beginning to smoke, especially with the studies and things, and by the end of it, I was beginning to feel the lack of the need, a vacancy in my life. It was there, the last year, that I met Zainab, Inge. She was there for a scholarship and we used to meet in the cafe, talk and so on. I was about to return to Iraq and I felt very lonely, so I told her, if I went back, and got a job, would you come, and so on? It was already clear that I'd marry her.

AA: You were young –

SFH: I was very young – 23.

AA: What about Karbala?

SFH: My father had died – I knew everything was over… I was going back to Kirkuk to the oil company.

AA: You already had a job lined up?

SFH: The scholarship must have been the IPC, now that you ask…

AA: Nadim Pachachi (The Examiner) was Minister of Oil.

SFH: He was a Director; he wasn't yet the minister. They were both in the directorate. No, it was an IPC scholarship.

AA: Nadim Pachachi was a Minister with my late father with him in 1956…

SFH: It was IPC and I knew I'd have a job straightaway there. When I returned, there was the question of National Service or the Army. But they found I had flat feet, which is not true actually. That was discovered also, later. The doctor there said I had flat feet, so I was exempt. So I went straight to the oil company. Whilst I was with the oil company, people like Hosam, Sahib were still doing the military service. So we all started together.

Career in the Oil Industry

IPC/Residence/Travelling Abroad

AA: You moved to Kirkuk?

SFH: Kirkuk, from the beginning. They gave me a house –

AA: You'd just come – a 23 year old, recently married. You have a house?

SFH: Absolutely. I had a house, everything, service. The house could have been anywhere in the suburbs of any major city, 3-4 bedrooms, beautiful garden; everything is done for you.

AA: Was there a club?

SFH: A beautiful club – every night cinema, tombola.... and we had a gardener, a servant. If a bulb went off, they'd come every day to inspect, and they'd replace it. Pampered beyond – we had a car, a driver.

AA: All at 23!

SFH: I was put into the production department and there was a very fine head of the department – an Englishman, Joe something – fine man, decent, very fair; he really took me on and took me through training.

AA: How was your language?

SFH: Fine, okay, I was comfortable. I could think in English. He put this fellow who came raw with basically good science into more engineering related position – gas, pressure, this and that. So I was promoted very rapidly from being what they called a Trainee Assistant Engineer to have become, within three or four years, Production Engineer. Within four years, I was in charge of all of the gassing stations in Northern Iraq, a million barrels per day production.

AA: Obviously you must have been very effective.

SFH: I was very effective – I worked hard day and night and was on call 24 hours.

AA: Were you responsible for people?

SFH: Absolutely – 4 or 5 hundred people. Junior engineers, but people who were far more qualified than engineers who were in charge of the stations – people who had been brought up on the stations for 40 years. They knew far more than any engineer. I learnt a lot from them, and by being with them, sitting with them – they were very obliging, so I picked a lot of training from the supervisors who were many, many ranks lower than I.

AA: NCOs.[22]

SFH: Yes, I liked them, loved them, and they loved me – I had the best of everything. So did Hosam. Hosam too was the same as I, in connecting, relating to people.

AA: Were they recruited locally?

SFH: All of them – for years and years and years they'd be recruited – knowledgeable, loyal, constantly training, wonderful people.

AA: A very well self-sufficient operation.

SFH: Exceptionally well-run. We were totally self-sufficient. In the company you did not need a thing whether it's transport – we had a fleet of a few thousand cars and an airline. You could go to Beirut anytime you wanted to – there were several company aircraft – anything you could imagine – maintenance, supplies, supermarkets-

AA: You must have been living the life of the top point one per cent.

---

[22] A military rank.

SFH: Absolutely. I remember once one of the Ministers of the Cabinet of Iraq came for a visit and he told us, 'We as ministers, we envy each one of you. Your salary is more than ours, your way of life is better, your condition is better, your efficiency – you are a super country within an underdeveloped country.' That was clear.

AA: Did these contrasts and contradictions impinge on you?

SFH: It did. I tell you, in many ways. For example, my house was on the perimeter – a huge fence. And I could see these Kurdish shepherds on the other side, living as though it was 3000 years ago. And here I was in the lap of luxury, connected with walkie-talkies – we had our own transport, telecommunication – the contrast was obvious. Then the general in charge of a big military division in Kirkuk befriended us and invited us to the club. We would love to come; we had to be invited. And I learned that my salary was twice his. How was this going to last? Impossible! A 27-year-old engineer in this company, with a salary twice the salary of the divisional commander, a general. I knew this was artificial, it could not last. The IPC could not last, and I began to feel insecure. I began to feel that this was artificial, out of place, out of context, and I shouldn't stay. That is how I began to think of going back to do a masters degree and get out –

AA: As you said, you were constantly agitated.

SFH: Constantly. Every time I was about to leave, they would send me on a course. I had maybe five courses, two to the States and then at the end I was sent on a special Reservoir Engineering course in the States – that is the elite, because Reservoir Engineering is what determines how much you are going to extract, you had to learn how much weight, also maintaining pressure in the field, so I was sent also to that and then 6 months or a year to CFP[23] in Paris, so I lived in Paris for a year, and visiting Hassi Messoud in Algeria from Paris, as a Reservoir Engineer.

AA: A lot of High powered people, it was like a club.

---

[23] Company Francis de Petrol.

SFH: High powered – they were really grooming me.

AA: So they must have identified you with career potentials.

SFH: Identified, fully, fully – fast track, but too fast. And my two daughters, Muna and Dina, would be with me wherever I went, for example, England; I was in London the equivalent of about a year. In England I was given 6 months training with IBM because the company had just installed punch card computers system – 1401. I went to IBM, but I had a beard and they wouldn't accept it so I said I won't come.

AA: Because you didn't like it?

SFH: It was winter, terrible winter, one of the worst winters in England – black smog and so on-

AA: This was when? 1961?

SFH: Must have been.

AA: 1961 – you lost each other in the fog.

SFH: Terrible! Muna had asthma. Anyway, I was quite rebellious, I trusted somehow that everything would be fine. I wasn't rebellious in an angry, horrible way. I said, 'No I'm not going to stay because of winter, because I feel cold, I am wearing a beard, if you don't like it I'll leave.' There wasn't any animosity –

AA: No hostility.

SFH: No hostility. But I wanted to leave. So I spent at least 3 to 4 years abroad. Then one day 8 years later, I was in the bathroom reading the Observer and there was an advertisement for the First MBA Course in England. The University of Birmingham, in conjunction with another university – a 2-year course, but you could combine it in 1 year with a dissertation the second year. I came out of the bathroom and immediately sent them a telegram, saying I am this, and that…

AA: 1965?

SFH: Yes, 65-66.

AA: And all the turbulent events in Iraq had no effect you. What about the Kirkuk riots?

SFH: I don't know whether I was there – I may have been abroad on a course.... Maybe I was in Huston. It never affected me. It was really skimming across…It didn't touch me; didn't affect my life.

AA: There were major killings in Kirkuk – 800 people died.

SFH: I wasn't there; also don't forget the camp was outside Kirkuk, so I arrived there in our own aircraft at our own airport and went to the house.

AA: So if somebody asked you, 'what was going on in Kirkuk?' you'd say, 'Why? Is something going on there?'

Reading

SFH: Also, I was very much into reading.

AA: I was going to ask you – what were you reading?

SFH: I was very much influenced by the existentialist movement – Camus was one of my favorites.

AA: When did that start – University?

SFH: Earlier – I had actually read something of Camus, or maybe Sartre in Iraq – and then I went to the *Wujudi* movement in Iraq at that time.... and then I was very much interested in theatre of the absurd – 'Waiting for Godot' and I would go to the theatre-

AA: Becket?

SFH: Really – Becket was my hero, and the 'angry young man' …

AA: Why is that? Why do you think, Shaykhna ... people of that age with that inclination – it is a kind of nihilism –

SFH: Absolutely – nihilism – because we want to see the alternative...

AA: Rhinoceros…

SFH: The status quo was unacceptable: the establishment for me was anathema.

AA: But it did not push you into the political arena.

SFH: Not at all – or not even in a social direction.

AA: So you were reading the existentialists, the theatre of the absurd, various plays by Becket –

SFH: Absolutely. And also very much the – A.J. Ayres – positivism, the other fellow – Russell.

AA: So it pushed you away from religion?

SFH: It in a way, I tried to replace it. I wasn't irreligious but I was not practicing it properly.

AA: Did you have recourse to the Qur'an in those days?

SFH: I did.

AA: I always loved and enjoyed the Qur'an. Any time the sound of the Qur'an came, I would feel it. I was always touched. I'd feel something missing.

AA: Why do think people immediately react to the Qur'an?

SFH: I think it's the sound, the effect of sound. From the womb. It is *The Sami`*.

AA: If you hear a very sonorous and melodious *Adhan*, it immediately wakes you up, even if you are not religious.

SFH: I know. Zainab took on the *dīn* and religion far more than I did when I married her. She said, 'This is it!' She had a great influence on me. The sound of the Qur'an affected her. I am convinced of *Sami`* and *Basir*, *sami`* and *basir* – also, the first thing a fetus is impacted upon, other than the physiology, is sound.

AA: And this is metaphysical, but the actual response – Shaykhna, what about things like – this was the late fifties, early sixties – you mentioned the existentialists, Bertrand Russell – did you try to read any of the Christian scholars, like Paul Tillich?

SFH: No, none of that–

AA: And the psycho-analysts…?

SFH: No, none. Not at all. I didn't come across it. In fact Bertrand Russell; I read most of the things he wrote – and the thing that impressed me most was an obscure little book called, '*In Praise of Idleness*'. It really affected me – I said, this is amazing from this man. I was always interested in this nothingness in a subconscious way – 'don't do anything' – you know, the power of aimlessness, that sort of thing – I was always interested in this sort of things.

AA: But you didn't go deep into philosophy?

SFH: In a way I always tried to attend lectures that were like that; I wasn't interested in the 'cultural club' of it, I was interested in a personal way – for my own sake – the content – I wanted to know –

AA: But you were obviously not convinced by any of it – you did not frame your life around it.

SFH: No, not at all.

AA: It was still a question of –

SFH: It was drifting into this side, that side, this way, that path.

AA: How did you buy the books – from Mackenzies bookshop or [in Baghdad]?

SFH: The other one, the big shop in Charing Cross road –

AA: Foyles.

SFH: Folyes – no, I didn't go to Mackenzies. Foyles – I had often been in England – no, Foyles was my main bookstore.

AA: Wonderfully disorganized.

SFH: Wonderful – a rabbit warren.

AA: They used to give you a chit every time you bought a book to take to another counter.

SFH: Yes, but I was also fortunate in my book selection – often the book calls me. I've often had that. Something pops up. You see, it always increased my trust that there is something else that is driving me.

AA: But you were not reading literature, novels.

SFH: Not much. Every now and then I would. I tried, but it never attracted me. Creative writing never touched me.

AA: Fiction ...

SFH: I never read fiction; biographies maybe. I wanted to have something that is going to change me.

AA: Did anybody catch you – any prominent figure, intellectual, political? Educational figure? Scholar? Anybody?

SFH: I was fascinated by some of the more highlighted profiles, like even Churchill. So I read quite a few biographies…Gandhi, etc.

AA: Was it an essential element of your life?

SFH: No – my social life was adrift – I had finished my MBA.

MBA at Birmingham

AA: At Sheffield?

SFH: No, at Birmingham. I went to Birmingham – paid all by myself.

AA: You took your family with you?

SFH: I took my family. Zainab was in Kirkuk and didn't know. I went to Baghdad and had an answer to my telegram from Birmingham saying, 'you're accepted, you have to be here on the so and so' – only 2 weeks, 10 days-

AA: It was free?

SFH: No, I paid – It was expensive for me, the payment, the travel, staying there –

AA: The IPC didn't support you?

SFH: No, I resigned. Just that year, the IPC had, for the first time, a general manager who was an Arab, Dr. Helmi Samara, a brilliant being, ex-Cambridge PHD in Mathematics –

AA: Egyptian?

SFH: No, Palestinian, brilliant being, wonderful man, who had come from the lowest rank of Reservoir Engineering, so he knew me well, although there were 5 or 6 levels between the top man in Iraq and myself as an engineer. He kept an eye on me. So when he heard I was resigning he insisted I should go back to Kirkuk and see him. He took me to his lavish room, showed me a chart and said, 'You are supposed to be General Manager in 12 years time.'

AA: All mapped out.

SFH: He said, 'Look, I will need you when you get to that position; you are already slated for that.' I said, 'No, I'm sorry I can't; I've been accepted at this place; I'm going there.' He said, 'You are making a mistake. This is yours. Your country, your land.' Then suddenly something came to me – an amazing thing. I told him, 'Dr. Helmi, you will not be able to keep to this post for more than two years.' He said, 'What do you mean?' I said, 'I guarantee – in two years time you will not be sitting in this chair. This country is going to hell.' He said, 'How do you know this?' I said, 'I don't know. My heart tells me that. I must leave. I'm leaving.'

AA: 1967?

SFH: '68. No, a bit later, after the Ba'athists – this was after my MBA…

AA: The IPC was nationalized by then?

SFH: In 1965 or '66.

AA: So several years before the nationalization.

SFH: Before the nationalization. Again, Hossam can tell you a lot about Helmi – magnificent, wonderful man, married to a Christian, beautiful, wonderful lady. So then I go back to Baghdad, arrange for my travel; he calls me and says, 'Your wife says you can't do that.' So Zainab phones me – she said, 'This is what Helmi's saying. You can't leave.' I said,

'Then you stay, I am leaving!' She'd just furnished her house, beautiful Scandinavian furniture, wood, beautiful. I said, 'Sell everything.'

AA: It can't be just a chance ad in the Observer!

SFH: It was – there is no chance in life.

AA: An ad in the Observer – there must have been a preparatory ...

SFH:.... I just wanted a sign to leave. I was beginning to feel sick – a lot of acidity, I was not well and I knew it was not a normal sickness – it was something much more psychic, psychological – I felt I was in a –

AA: Doomed ship?

SFH: No, it was more. I felt I was in a volcano exploding – honestly, I felt like that. Jittery, jittery, jittery – ask Zainab. So I said, 'If you do not come here in 3 days time, I'm leaving. Pack everything, sell everything.' She had a beautiful new car.

A Trip from France Back to Iraq

What I didn't tell you was an interesting trip I made from France back to Iraq in a car. I got a nice big station wagon, newly bought, with Zainab and the two girls. We drove all the way through North Africa, Egypt, then to Lebanon and then Iraq.

AA: Very few people make that journey. Most go by car across the Balkans –

SFH: I made the whole journey. We had a number of incidents. It was then that I discovered Ahmed al-Alawi. I was in Algeria – the revolution was just over – it was horrible, and I went to Mustaghanam I don't know why. We stayed in a normal concrete hotel – horrible place – on the edge of the town. Something drew me to go to the center of the town. I heard the *dhikr* for the first time. I had no idea about *dhikr* or Sufis. Zainab was interested in all of that in her youth. I wasn't. She was interested in

Sufism – she did a course in the AUB[24] in all of these things with a very fine Professor from Syria, who ended up in America, lovely man, whose name will come to me – but I wasn't. When I heard the sound it drew me like a magnet. I went to the *Zawiya* – people running after the car and so on. I never forget the impact on me that there is somebody buried here who called me. And the song remained in my heart. So then we drove back and I had a problem in Egypt in Cairo. Because – catch 22 – the car didn't have this paper or that paper, you can't get this because you don't have that. And you don't have this because you can't – I had a cousin, Hayder, who is still alive – living still in Cairo, I think he is still alive – I called Hayder – he said, 'Leave it to me, come.' So we went to the main police station – one of these old buildings, two or three floors, people hanging on this and stairs. He asked for the *Rais* – we went upstairs and when we came to Hadhrat Al Rais he said, '[your honor!]'. We opened the door, Hadhrat al-Rais comes out, hugs Hayder as though they were bosom friends, and in three minutes it was all done, he signed everything. So I come out with Hayder, I say, 'You must know him very well.' He said, 'No, I never knew him.'

AA: What a story! How can you tell!

SFH: Absolutely. None of them dares to say, 'I don't know you!' …. so I managed to get back to Iraq with that car.

AA: What happened? You couldn't have crossed Israel, Shaykhna.

SFH: No, by boat from Alexandria to Beirut.

AA: Beirut. You came by sea – what an extraordinary trip! I don't know anybody who has made this trip. Hundreds have made the other.

SFH: No, no, I have made the trip from the desert of Libya. From Tripoli to Benghazi -

AA: What about petrol?

---

[24] American University of Beirut.

SFH: We arranged all that – I stopped in the middle of nowhere on that road, at night. Dogs came around – from nowhere. At the hotel in Benghazi I said to the fellow, 'there is hair on this sheet!' He said, 'Only one night they stayed there.'

AA: Why did you choose this route? Nobody has taken this route.

SFH: I wanted to explore – explore –

AA: You started from Morocco or Algeria?

SFH: No, I started from France. France, to Spain, crossed to Morocco, Algeria, all of it, Tunisia – all of it.

AA: So what are your impressions? ... destitute?

SFH: Not really. I felt familiar. Just like passing by. I wasn't after anything specific-

AA: And the goal was to get to Baghdad?

SFH: Yes, the goal was to get to Baghdad. I said to myself, 'I'm in Europe, I may as well use this occasion once in a while.'

In a Quasi-Secular State

AA: You were still in a quasi-secular state then?

SFH: Absolutely. Praying occasionally. Making mistakes. Going to the mosque and being repelled. Not liking it-

AA: What did you do about Ramadan?

SFH: I think I fasted sometimes, part of it, and sometimes not. I remember taking on to it occasionally.

AA: And was there a culture in the IPC of religiosity?

Career in the Oil Industry

SFH: Hardly. Not really. I think –

AA: I think in Iraq in those days very few people were religious; it was considered reactionary-

SFH: It was. In the meantime I made a lot of other friends – non-Arabs; for example, I had a Jesuit friend in Iraq ... he was one of the senior Jesuits. He did his research on the Assyrians. He would stay with me whenever he came to the IPC. I loved that man. We were so close in the spiritual sense. He had quite a lot of influence on me.

AA: You were not very religious, but not exactly secular?

SFH: No.

AA: – and you were still trying to practice religion.

SFH: All the time – but I didn't know how to maintain, how to contain –

AA: Did you visit Karbala and the shrines?

SFH: Yes, but I never was a shrine visitor. It never touched me. I always felt the light of Imam Ali.

AA: So you were not drawn into the shrine in Karbala or Samarra?

SFH: Not at all, not at all. I hardly visited shrines. Quite a few times I went with Zainab to visit our home, our orchard, my mother and others. But no, I had no nostalgia as such for any places.

Work/Writing Papers at the IPC

AA: You didn't go to Baghdad on a regular basis?

SFH: Not that regularly.

AA: Because the IPC head office was in Baghdad.

SFH: Not regularly. Head office was a nominal head office. The main production was in Kirkuk and the General Manager of the IPC was in Kirkuk.

AA: And Basra Petroleum had its own management?

SFH: Yes, lesser, it was much smaller – it had about 20% the size of Kirkuk-

AA: Did you make any major work as an engineer? Was it dramatic or routine?

SFH: Routine and enjoyable – I wrote a lot of papers on reservoir engineering, and that's why people like Helmi and others knew me and noticed me, and there was a General Manager, top man, called George Dobb or Todd – a most unusual man. He really ruled Iraq, and his assistant was Kaan, a Dutchman. They both were very strongly connected again because of reservoir engineering. They saw the papers I was writing on pressure maintenance and on one well we drilled there was enough production for the whole of Germany – 100,000 barrels per day, without any pressure maintenance. So I did a few of these things and I enjoyed it. I would be working day and night. I'd be out at night in my car with my walkie-talkie and a driver, going to the wells, and to the mountains, into the tulip fields. It was for me an incredible period. I must have written about maybe 15 papers, research papers on topical things, wells, pressure maintenance, and this and that – oil and gas levels.

AA: Published in the IPC magazine –

SFH: Published in the IPC and distributed – no not in the magazine; the magazine of IPC – whose man was in Baghdad, nice man – wrote a few articles on me, including my paintings-

AA: Really? Maybe you should dig up those articles.

SFH: He was a Christian, lovely man.

AA: Do you have these articles – they may be in some archive in London.

SFH: It was strange – at my level, as I said, I had these links with the top guys. George Todd told me, 'if you want to leave, tell me.' So I wrote to him – at that time I think he had become a director of one of the top Scottish banks, in Edinburgh and he said to me, 'go to Dubai and be based there,' then what happened was the I set up a consulting company with Tariq Shafiq [a well-known Iraqi oil expert].

AA: This was after you graduated from Birmingham?

SFH: Yes, after I graduated, Helmi Samara contacted me. He said, 'I'm going to recruit you back as an expatriate from London. So you'll have your passage back, and your salary, your payment, your pension will be exactly as an expatriate's.' So I went to the IPC with only a few pounds in my pocket.

AA: IPC London?

Recruitment Consultant in England

SFH: IPC London, and he gave me beautiful lunch in the boardroom in Oxford Street and he said, 'Don't refuse me again. You refused my staying; now I'm getting you back.' I said to him, 'I don't think you'll last even months – please excuse me, I can't do it. It's wonderful, I'm tempted – the cushiness, the ease – my heart tells me it won't last.' So we parted company. He paid me for my day coming, a few pounds, and then I looked around for jobs in London. Then there was a job offer from a special recruiting firm for specialist in operational research – that was the key word in those days – so because of my mathematical background, model building, reservoir engineering, and I was an OR[25], so the offer was for BP[26]. They were looking for OR people. So as it happened that day the recruiting company, the person who was supposed

---

[25] Operational Research.
[26] British Petroleum.

to interview me wasn't there. So the head of the firm was there. His name was William Key. Brilliant man. A top firm in Park Lane. Ten partners and he was the top man.

AA: A recruitment specialist?

SFH: Recruitment in this specialized areas – computers, or arms, data processing, so Bill Key had finished interviewing me, he said, 'Are you all right for lunch?' I said, 'No,' He said, 'I'll take you for lunch.' He said, 'Look I really am tempted you should join us.'

AA: Join the company?

SFH: As a recruitment consultant.

AA: Which one was that? PA Associates?

SFH: No, it was called William Key and Partners. A small boutique firm with 10 partners. Top people, wonderful people.

AA: Offered you a job –

SFH: Offered me a job there and then.

AA: Forget about the OR.

SFH: Forget the OR. He said, recruit people in these spheres, and open up to oil companies to the east. So I did. I worked for him for a year, and lived in Surrey. Found a rented house.

AA: Zainab and the children?

SFH: Yes, they were with me. We rented a house near Guilford, not too far from there, and I commuted by train.

AA: Was the aim that you wanted to leave Iraq also?

SFH: No, I wanted to change that job. I didn't want to be in oil because it was in the east – in Iraq – I don't like these places.

AA: And the thing was you could sense that the change was fast approaching.

SFH: Absolutely. One thing in my life Ali I can tell you – from childhood, I knew what was not going to work. I didn't know what would work. I knew *La ilaha*...repeatedly, repeatedly, I can give you dozens of incidents when I said, 'they won't work'. That I knew. It would come to me.

AA: It was the end of an era.

SFH: No, but all together my own psyche, I knew this was not workable – this arrangement, this relationship, this money, this job was not working. So then the interesting bit I wanted to share with you is that after William Key –

AA: Were you successful in your job?

SFH: Very successful. My advertisements were all over the place in the Sunday Times, the Observer.... I was quite successful, I made money. Every week we had a review, how we had performed, how much money we made. William Key was brilliant. Every Monday you had a review of what you produced during the past week. So that was very good discipline for me. Then there was another job coming from BP again. It was to do with setting up our type of activities in different BP related companies in the Middle East. So I accepted it.

AA: This was Scicon. They tried to recruit you? Sigi Latif [the GM of Scicon]?

SFH: ...... and others.

AA: This was '71.

SFH: That's right.... so I became a director of the company, and set up the office in Beirut.... and in Tripoli, Libya, and in Tehran and Kuwait. Four offices.

SFH: I remember that, I could have been working with you then!

SFH: Exactly. I got to Beirut. We set up a company with Tariq Shafiq as consultants, oil consultants.

AA: so you left Scicon.

SFH: No, I was still with them. Then we met... I had a few jobs for him, then suddenly one day Helmi Samara arrives from Iraq, emaciated, to our office in Beirut. He had a *tasbih* in his hand, a small one and would throw it up in the air, and say, 'Look, gravity, it comes down.' Nearly deranged. Two months in prison. They beat him up. He escaped. So we recruited him. Helmi, you are a partner, come...' He said, 'I came for you.' It was amazing. And after two years with Scicon something amazing happened.

Time with Chinmaya

SFH: In Beirut I met Chinmaya......

AA: I remember in Beirut, you were in the Gefinor Center. I think I came across you when I visited your company. This was in '73/'74.

SFH: I established that office – it was a partnership called Arab consultant.

AA: But it was a partnership between you and Shafiq....

SFH: 50% with Shafiq. And then I found them [Shafiq and Tariq] not getting on together – a lot of childishness – a lot of ego – 'whose desk is bigger' kind of things. So after a year or two, I said, 'please excuse me, I'm leaving' – and I just walked out...

AA: So what happened – did they buy your share or...?

SFH: I don't know – I think they did – I was not interested…

AA: Then you moved to Sharjah, Shaykhna?

Mediterranean Containers

SFH: No, I'll tell you what happened with that. The Sharjah situation –

AA: The war was still not on…

SFH: Not yet – it was '73/'74.

AA: Where were you living?

SFH: I was living in a beautiful apartment on Majdani building right across from the Pigeon Rock on the Sea. Right across – the best location... and I had a balcony on which I had avocado trees – on the balcony, giving avocados.

AA: Mediterranean ones...

SFH: I had the best of lives.... But what happened was that I was involved in a project in Saudi Arabia for the King Feisal Hospital, and King Feisal wanted this huge monument, several hundred million dollars, and didn't trust anybody, so he put his brother-in-law in charge, a doctor…

AA: Kamal Adhem...?

SFH: No, another man... Kamal Adham was on the board but not so much in the center – he actually – yes! I'm sorry. The doctor was involved in the technical thing; Kamal Adhem was intermediary and they wanted this whole thing on a turnkey basis, in every way. I suddenly found that the managing director was a Canadian bypassing me, involved directly. Within two or three months I found that he was on the take sharing 10% of the gross, which he was partly giving away partly and partly keeping it. I knew that. So without making a fuss I said, 'I want to change my full-time executive thing to a consultant'. By that time I was with Chinmaya and I wanted to follow him, to see how things fit, also. So he said, 'fine; we'll do it, we'll arrange things.' So without cut in salary or anything, I was made a consultant, with no recourse to the number of hours I had to be available. In fact not even half an hour I became available for the following two years...Two years, full salary. It was during that period I began to look at the Gulf. Kaan who was one of the top men of the IPC sought me out in Beirut and he introduced me to Gulftainer. At that time it was a small Lebanese shipping company, which had retained him. It was a big – for that industry big – container ship between Europe and Lebanon. So he said, 'Look, let's take it to the Gulf.'

AA: Was it called Gulftainer then?

SFH: It was called Mediterranean Containers – It was not called Gulf.

AA: So this was when, Shaykhna, 1975?

SFH: 1975-76.

AA: So you were now a full-time consultant ...

SFH: Not full-time; I was paid for the consultancy...

AA: But you had flexible hours – do what you want…

SFH: Of course, entirely my own hours.

AA: Flexible hours – when they wanted something, they'd ask –

SFH: It never happened.

AA: So you were just there on retainer.

SFH: Absolutely, never happened. Not once did they ask me.

AA: They met all the expenses?

SFH: Not expenses, but they paid my salary, and for house rent.

AA: So in 1975 you come back to this former IPC director, who became a director in this Mediterranean company who suggested you look at the Gulf – meanwhile you had not travelled to the Gulf at all?

SFH: I had. I'd been to Abu Dhabi for the oil company as an IPC man in the '60s – Abu Dhabi Oil Company was an IPC... as an oil engineer I had travelled on a very short visit because of reservoirs – and there was nothing there. No place to stay except the IPC compound. Then in '75 the war in Lebanon broke out – I remember Chinmaya warning me, 'why are you here?'

Meeting Chinmaya

AA: So when did you meet Chinmaya, Shaykhna?

Time with Chinmaya

SFH: I met him in 1972.

AA: My sequences are off...so you met Chinmaya on one of your consulting visits?

SFH: No, I was in Beirut, based in Beirut. I was coming back from Kuwait to Beirut when I met him.

AA: You had said you were intrigued by him, and you asked him what was that mark on his forehead –

SFH: It was after setting up the offices in Kuwait.

AA: But you said that you were intrigued by seeing this man on the plane; you asked him about the dot – he said you were asking the wrong question.

SFH: No – he said, 'You are not asking about this.' I was also intrigued at the airport, first. It touched me. I said to myself that this is another being.

AA: Before that, did you ever show any interest in spirituality?

SFH: None.

AA: You had no interest or knowledge of that.

SFH: No.

AA: So you see this fellow in saffron robes in Kuwait airport – was he in first class? Going to Beirut where he had a number of followers with him, and what did he say to you that suddenly drew you to him?

SFH: He didn't say anything – it was his state. I knew this man was in another state than mine, being simply grappling in the *duniya* and trying to make sense of it.

AA: How can you tell, Shaykhna?

SFH: I don't know. I just felt it in my heart and knew that he was above me in terms of inner state.

AA: Was he glowing – did he have a certain radiance?

SFH: Yes, you can say that. He did have something else, another demeanor, about him. He was in this world, not of this world. That's what I can say now.

AA: The fact that he was of the Hindu tradition had no effect on you.

SFH: Absolutely none.

AA: You just wanted to know what this was all about.

SFH: I was intrigued. I said, 'this is a man of Light – I have not seen anybody like this for years.' It reminded me also in a way of some of the other characters in Karbala but not quite the same.

AA: There were a number of not so evidently knowledgeable people in Syria or in Lebanon; you never tried to seek them out or –

SFH: I never sought out anybody.

AA: Okay, so you come on the plane with him to Beirut. What happens after that?

SFH: Then the next day in Beirut I visited him at the house of the Air India manager and I was completely bowled over. I knew that this man was in touch with another zone of life that I was not of. And this is what I wanted. There was a vacancy obviously in my life, and suddenly it was, like filled with passion.

AA: It was like a hole inside you was filled.

SFH: Absolutely! I didn't know the hole until I saw somebody else who had no hole. When I saw that wholesomeness, I realized my own hole.

AA: So before you met Chinmaya how did you manage that hole?

SFH: I was avoiding it; I always tried to be distracted. More promotions, more business, a bit of this, a bit of that – and also, my own livelihood thing was in balance. I had to be careful – I had to weigh what income was coming in – it was just about making a reasonable life. There wasn't a great deal of income coming. Also, my future was not certain – nor was I worried. But I was in and out, doing consulting work, earning a bit of this, a bit of that. I had the Japanese government giving me a nice job for two years as consultant to the government to MIIT[27] on monthly report basis. It wasn't a struggle, but I had to be in the marketplace. So that's what filled the hole – children, schooling. Muna had gone to an English boarding school in Ascot. I kept an apartment in London –

AA: So next day you ring the office manager and –

SFH: And I know this is the man, it's confirmed. This is a special being – and as I said, I decided there and then that I must follow this man.

AA: You told him you wanted to be his follower?

SFH: No. He knew, I knew and he said, 'Sonny, come wherever I am.'

AA: He used to call you 'Sonny'.

SFH: Sonny – child – a child.

AA: Then what?

Work in the Gulf

SFH: He was going to Switzerland because he had a heart attack – he was going to stay for a few weeks in the Bircher Berner clinic, and within a week I had a letter from him – I still have it, a beautiful letter. He said, 'You came into my life with such an abruptness that I could

---

[27] Ministry of Industry and International Trade.

only sit back and reflect upon this amazing encounter.' A beautiful, long letter. Again he called me, 'My Child'. It touched me very deeply that I wanted to be with this man, by hook or by crook. I didn't want to abandon my family or my career, and that is when my consulting came. Soon – within a few months; it coincided. Then, at the same time, I had a few people in England asking if I could help them to establish something or another in the Gulf – Abu Dhabi, Dubai – the first one was turnkey operations for hospitals. So I went to the Gulf, I went to Hamid. [Jafar, his partner, subsequently] told them there was this company and they wanted to do this. They said, 'Sharjah has just built a hospital, badly built, in the shape of an eagle, impossible to manage' – so that was the first serious job. So we ended up having a terrific contract – they did some tendering to supply, to take it on a turnkey basis. To turn this horrible building into a real functioning hospital. Bring in the doctors, nurses, equipment, etc. And that was the first of several such big jobs.

AA: You stayed in Beirut or moved to…?

SFH: Ah, no you are right. In 1976 I moved to England. I used my apartment in England –

AA: Which was where, Shaykhna?

SFH: It was in Queensway [London], on top of the skating rink. I had an apartment there. And also in 1977, I was there more, and then I rented a place in Sharjah, a house. Hamid was beginning to do property deals, so whatever money I had – maybe $50,000 – I gave it to him to do that and he rolled it quite well.

Spending Time with Chinmaya

AA: So throughout this period you were going to see Chinmaya?

SFH: Yes, that was my main preoccupation, to meet him wherever he was.

AA: How did that control ... I mean, did you go to India? Were you part of some kind of retinue or what?...what practices did you go through....what did he instruct you to do?

SFH: I think quite a bit of this is in '*Son of Karbala*'. But the thing I can really share with you is that neither he nor I cared for anything except intimacy – being together. He didn't say it, I didn't say it, but that was it. I'd be with him as long as I could. From early morning till night, as long as I am not exhausted all the time, and he would tolerate me. He never asked me to do anything. I never asked him, 'what about this or that?' The intimacy I began to absorb – because I was like a sponge – absorbing his inner state. There was nothing more effective than that.

AA: It wasn't some late night discussions – and so on?

SFH: Never. No, I listened to him, I accompanied him – that was it – it was companionship. It was total *sadaka*, and he accepted me unconditionally and never ever once tried to impose anything on me – religious or spiritual. I just observed, observed, observed – and I learned very soon that I could be totally silent in my mind. I enjoyed the chanting, the Indian chanting.

AA: Did he teach you meditation techniques?

SFH: Nothing whatsoever.

AA: So you must have been a unique follower in the sense that you weren't pushed into a structure.

SFH: I was, I was – and I remember often I was – not clearly or overtly – an object of envy. Because I had the money – I could travel with him anywhere. Many a time we were the only two travelling by air and staying together. That's how I picked the whole thing from him – the hours of being with him. One day I remember very early morning in a small plane – we were coming from somewhere in central India to the north, it was dawn; the plane landed in a tiny little airport somewhere, nowhere – there were only two of us on the plane – to refuel. We came out onto the tarmac to walk, the sun, the light was just beginning. So I turned to him and said, 'what an amazing day! What an incredibly spiritual, this and that!' He said, 'Sonny, you are talking nonsense. If you are in a good mood, nothing to do with the day; you have just stopped reducing your inner agitation.' It was always like this. This is how I learnt. I was with him – there was a hospital he had in Bangalore – a big hospital. The top ten doctors were beginning to jockey for positions. So he said one day, 'come let's go, they are in trouble'. So we go – the two of us; he sits there in the boardroom, one of them accusing the other. He listens, he said, 'Look all of you are highly qualified, you could get far more salary than you are earning here. I thought you were interested in your own inner evolution also, inner awakening by serving; otherwise you'd be much better elsewhere.' So he said to this fellow, 'you seem to be older than others,' and he told the others, 'why don't you people accept him?' Within two minutes he sorted it all out. And he turned to me and said, 'Let us run away before they discover the whole thing is rubbish.' This is how I learnt. 'So let us leave before they discover the whole thing is rubbish – because once they discover that, they won't be working. Let's get out.'

AA: This is how you were immersed in the truthful paradoxes –

SFH: Yes, and because I was not from the culture, I was not entrenched in anything, I really absorbed it.

AA: Where would you put him in terms of teachers? Top of the list?

SFH: Absolutely.

AA: He was a living guide?

SFH: Absolutely! No doubt about it.

AA: And all of this apparently chance encounter – all part of a Divine Plan?

SFH: *Wa `ala niyyatum turzakoon*[28]. Not once he tried to convert me – in fact I was at one period interested in Sanskrit; he said, 'you don't need it', and after four or five years he began to mention to me every time I came, '*Allahu akbar. Assalaam alaikum.*' I said, 'What is he saying? I am sick of these Muslims.' He said, 'Not the Sufis – the Sufis, the Sufis.'

AA: He knew that there were two Islams – *Islam al-Dhahir* and *Islam al-Batin*?

SFH: Yes. He kept them separate, and then later in America, when I was at the peak of trying to help, turn the whole world, he sent me a warning with Batul. He came to Houston. I sent Batul to see him, and he told her, "warn him that this business of '*ummah*', community, is rubbish. You mustn't waste time on it." It was already too late. I'd already done it, a mess.

AA: If you had to count the days and hours you spent with him, these five years, was it very intensive? 8 years, you were in regular reference with him.

SFH: It was my *Qibla* – At least 3 or 4 times every year, two or three weeks at a time, and many times I took my wife and the children with me.

Chinmaya's Ashram

AA: Did he have an ashram?

SFH: Of course he had a center outside Bombay. After a few months I went to the ashram as a *sanyasi*, stayed there, and I didn't want to do anything other than what the *sanyas* was doing. I was given a simple basic room, quite small with a charpoy which is where I slept, and we were given two meals a day – very thin hot vegetarian soup in the morning – hot in the sense of pepper. I was quite ill actually after two or three weeks.

---

[28] "You will be granted according to your intentions." (A Prophetic Saying)

AA: What did you do?

SFH: Listen to all the talks and the chants –

AA: English or Hindi?

SFH: His talks were mostly in English. Chanting and other things would be in Hindi. I ignored them. I just imbibed the atmosphere.

AA: What was the atmosphere like?

SFH: Exceptionally potent in an inner sense. You had to be inward, inward, inward, thoughtless, mindless. But it took its toll on my body – I became very sick, and after a few weeks, there was a lady, her name was Kamlaji, who saw me suffering. She would accompany Chinmaya on his travels, and had earlier seen me and met me in Beirut. I didn't want to say it, I didn't want to buy anything. I was determined not to be different from the others. So I was sitting one morning a week or two weeks after I was there, ill, and it was a morning talk by Chinmaya, beautiful setup in a park – it was called Poway Park – I suddenly saw an enormous tray of fruits being carried by someone ten meters from me, and I said, 'my God, what a wonderful delight.' Then I saw Kamlaji with it, and I new it was for me, and I saw them taking it to my room. I was desperate for some fruit, something interesting, like bananas – so in my mind I began to distribute some of it to some other students, and to keep the nice ones for me. I didn't know when the discourse would finish so I could get to my room and eat the fruit. After maybe half an hour I go to the room and saw that the monkeys had been there before me and mucked it all up. Every bit of fruit was thrown everywhere. I only managed to rescue very little. So I thought, this serves you right! 'Here you were, scheming and look what happened.'

AA: Abu Hamid al-Ghazzali was doing his *salaat* and his brother Ahmed said, "Under the tree."

SFH: Under the tree – that's it, that's it.

AA: I know you don't like these terms, but that period with Chinmaya, was it an abrupt encounter – abrupt in the sense that you met him suddenly unexpectedly, then over the next 8 years 7 years, you were involved more in the practices than anything else. There were no teachings as such that you could refer to, or was it just an atmospheric thing?

SFH: Yes, it an atmospheric thing, and it was personal. For example, out of the blue one day he said, 'You know you plan for the weekends to go out and so on – for the next two or three weekends, don't plan. Just sit and see what comes to you. You don't be the instigator. Respond to what comes to you.' So he would give me a lot of such instructions.

Chinmaya's Teachings

AA: I'm surprised that he didn't have a kind of structured program, or some kind of spiritual course.

SFH: Oh he did – sorry, there was a full two-year correspondence course. Every week I had to work about two or three hours on it, and that's from where I also picked up the idea of Academy of Self-knowledge.

AA: The same things-

SFH: Yes, a correspondence course – and we had to answer back, and so forth.

AA: And he had so-called facilitators.

SFH: Thousands – all over the world.

AA: How many were his followers, would you say? Hundreds of thousands?

SFH: In America there are 400 centers…

AA: What are they called?

SFH: Chinmaya Centers... Chinmaya Mission – it's one of the biggest chain of centers.

AA: Did you encounter one in Kuwait?

SFH: One of the biggest – at that time it was not in America.

AA: What was the most noticeable thing about the way the course was taught? If you were to distill it, what was the core of his teachings that stuck out?

SFH: It was what I came across soon after meeting him – the teaching of Ramana Maharishi – 'who are you? You are not who you think you are. The self is an illusion; it's your fantasy; do not deny it but acknowledge the ultimate One.' It was really the One – there is only One.

AA: It wasn't overlaid with Hindu symbols and mythology?

SFH: Not with me. The other people did it – the celebrations and all. He never once took it in any way as of significance. So you don't need to change a thing. He said, 'Sonny, you don't change anything. It's already there. You don't change anything. It exists in Islam, it exists everywhere ... don't change culture, don't change language, don't learn Sanskrit...'

Leaving Chinmaya to Discover Sufism

AA:...and he pushed you back into Islam?

SFH: He pushed me back to Islam, towards its soul. He said, 'Find your Sufis'. I said, 'Where? Who?' He said, 'Find them.'

AA: What was your understanding? I mean Sufis were not the most celebrated people in Iraq.

SFH: Also for me, I didn't know them. I had no option. And he just weaned me off. He said, 'Don't see me any more.' I knew he was serious in that –

AA: He threw you out?

SFH: Not physically. He said, 'you have done it. You've got it. Now find your Sufis.'

AA: You got it in the sense that now you have shifted – your consciousness has shifted.

SFH: More or less, 'You had taken enough from whatever it is from me – now you need to put it on a path that will fit you culturally.'

AA: You connected with the traditions of *Tasawwuf* as being parallel to, similar to his own traditions. Parallel lines –

SFH: All connected – totally, totally.

AA: And he pushed you back into the culture you were more familiar with.

SFH: Correct.

AA: He thought that the culture would facilitate, encourage and hasten your progress-

SFH: It was as though the software was there – now 'he needed the hardware. Now he needed to dress it up', and I had to come back to the structure of Islam.

AA: He pushed you into a religious framework?

SFH: Into a more humanly, earthly, referable framework.

AA: He knew there would be major problems if you renounced Islam and moved into Hinduism, were you prepared to do that?

SFH: I was prepared to do anything.

AA: If he told you from now on you had to become a Hindu?

SFH: I was prepared to do anything. That's why my mother thought I had become a Hindu.

AA: That's how I first came across you.

SFH: She would be weeping at night –

AA: It became common knowledge that you'd become a Hindu.

SFH: I didn't hear it like that, nor did I care. Even my mother's weeping, I only learned through Zainab and others.

AA: So what would have happened if Chinmaya didn't push you back to Islam, would you have stayed with the path of Chinmaya?

SFH: No, but I was reaching a cul-de-sac.

AA: and there was nothing more to learn?

SFH: It was *Haqiqah*, but there was no *Shari`ah*. Mecca but not Medina.

AA: Did you acknowledge or notice that there was a gap here …?

SFH: Not overtly – subconsciously, maybe. I trusted he knew best. An incident happened one day. There was this man who sold all his farms land during the last years of his life and came to the Ashram. So early morning before *Fajr* I was sitting with Chinmaya, he comes – people come to greet him – and he said, 'Can I stay another week?' Chinmaya said, 'No'. He said, 'I've done everything.' Chinmaya said, 'No, you leave today; that is our agreement'. So about 10 in the morning I saw the man carrying his bundle about to leave – it's a long way to the gate. So I quietly ran after him and asked him, 'Are you content after this morning?' He said, 'Yes.' I said,' Why?' He said, 'I'm sure I needed to be kicked out. I trust him.' So there were incidents like this that reminded me that I had to trust – he knows better.

AA: He told you or did you ask?

SFH: No, he just turned to me and said, 'Sonny, I think it's time now for you to discover Sufism. Go and find your Sufis.' I said, 'Where?' He said, 'Go to Iran, go to North Africa. You'll find them.' So I came back to England – I knew that was it.

AA: How did you feel after leaving him?

SFH: I felt terrible. It was the biggest shock. So, for few weeks I reeled ... until I came across a connection with the Prophet Muhammad and Shaykh Abdalqadir.

Chinmaya – *The Spiritual Being*

AA: The whole thing seems a bit fuzzy Shaykhna; you were based in England and you have business going on in Sharjah and you're spending most of your time with Chinmaya.

SFH: Not most of my time – a quarter of my time, I guess. Quality time.

AA: Didn't your partners object? What about your family?

SFH: I didn't care. I didn't ask them. I really didn't ask them.

AA: Something that was driving you-

SFH: Passion, complete passion.

AA: Consumed you?

SFH: Absolutely!

AA: If he asked you to do anything you would have done it.

SFH: I would. Absolute obsession.

AA: Because he saw the light …

SFH: I said, I can't live with myself…

AA: I would have thought that the authenticity of Chinmaya is in his expelling you as it were. You could easily have stayed there and become his right hand man – taken on the empire – so he was not in the business of building a spiritual empire.

SFH: None whatsoever –

AA: Did he have charisma?

SFH: Mmm – Charisma, it contained an ocean, without it being sparkly – all these years with him, I did not spend a penny on him or on his behalf – not a penny – I was his guest. And everybody else thought, 'here he has latched on to somebody' – rubbish, rubbish.... He never asked for anything.

AA: Were you the only Middle Easterner there – the only person from the Middle East?

SFH: No, there were two or three other people from the gulf – there was the second son of Al-Ghanim in Kuwait, [an important business family], Qutayba; I think.

AA: Now he is in San Francisco –

SFH: He was one of his followers; and there were one or two from Bahrain, and one or two others. I didn't know them.

AA: You didn't go through the rituals of yoga, meditation – any of these techniques Shaykhna?

SFH: No I didn't...

AA: And breathing techniques?

SFH: Yes, I naturally was in a fairly good state doing that.

AA: And he didn't instruct you?

SFH: Not at all.

AA: And throughout the whole period, you were just immersed in this –

SFH: Absorbed his heart – it was his heart – companionship.

AA: When did he die, Shaykhna?

SFH: I think between 1980's or 90's[29]. It's strange also. I was travelling to Spain from England. I don't usually buy papers and things, and I went to buy a newspaper and got the Independent. I just opened its obituaries section and saw a huge, half a page, piece on him. He died in California, lecturing.

AA: Was he an ascetic in his daily life?

SFH: Who?

AA: Chinmaya.

SFH: Absolutely – abstemious – surviving on a little vegetarian food, clean, emaciated, thin. I never caught him asleep, ever.

AA: So he was on a spiritual path.

SFH: No doubt, absolutely. I would leave him sometimes, at midnight, very tired, exhausted, and I would come at four or five in the morning – there was a pile of letters he had answered, books that he had written. And I enquired if anybody had ever seen him sleep.

---

[29] He died in 1993.

AA: When you joined him, was he at his peak, would you say?

SFH: Health-wise, he was given only a short time to live. In his letters to me he said, 'Now I can spend more time in my ecstatic meditation, no teaching, and I will leave everything behind.'

AA: But his state – his *haal* – was constant?

SFH: Absolutely – his inner *haal* was constant.

AA: He didn't go through various evolutions?

SFH: No – he was already cooked, he was already done.

AA: A constant state?

SFH: Yes. And that was his teacher, who was called Topoban staying in a little hut above Rishikesh, right on the snowline. Chinmaya went and found him – as he told me – he said, 'When I met him I knew, this was my man.' He said, 'after several days hovering around the hut, the man wouldn't talk to him. He was just sitting' – so eventually he told him, 'If you want to talk to me, go and learn Sanskrit and come back.' So after a year he comes back. He stayed with him for several years. Eventually Chinmaya's inner way – he was content with his inner and outer – so he tells his master, 'I want to go and teach the Vedantas to the public.' He said, 'No, the public doesn't deserve it – not worth it.' So he insists and after a while his teacher tells him, 'You can go on condition that you walk from here all the way to the tip of India, barefoot, with no provision. If you've done that, then you can teach.' And he does that. I've seen pictures and details of that visit. Six months, he walks barefoot and people gather around him as they go and it becomes a larger and larger group. And Chinmaya told me that during that trip, so many places they went to, they were despised, because they were in saffron robes and people didn't trust them and scorned them. He said, 'And in many, many places people would not give us anything, not even water, and other places we were welcomed. I saw it all. If there was anything left of my ego it was thrashed out on that trip.'

Interconnectedness of Spiritual Experiences

AA: Extraordinary. Would you say that this experience is recommended to others? Or it's not your concern?

SFH: I don't think anything ever repeats – '*Kulla Yaum Huwa fi shaan*'[30] – we never know-

AA: But this theme of an apparently chance encounter that turns your life upside down is quite recurrent.

SFH: Correct.

AA: So therefore, there is some kind of thread that connects all these stories. And the thread is what?

SFH: It is where the subconscious suddenly comes in in the conscious – it is where a quarter or third or much more of our so-called being-ness suddenly comes out, though it's not always evident. That is where again physics and metaphysics meet. So it is like that – always, it is like that. We are clumsy, we are gross and always look for the cause and effect and the obvious and 90% is not obvious. So we don't know. There are energy fields and patterns within patterns we can never discern. So I learnt to really accept this: Here is the sign, read it and follow. Otherwise, why and who – I don't care.

AA: But the consequences are dramatic. Therefore it is intensely interesting.

SFH: Of course, of course…

AA: So, have you developed any kind of understanding of the significance of the current spiritual phenomenon?

---

[30] "Every day He is bringing about a matter." (Qur'an 55:29)

SFH: The only thing I can say in that respect is that there is a relentless drive in the whole of the world, the whole of the universe, towards higher consciousness, towards God realization, towards knowing the One. And if you are on that path, you will see much more of that. Somebody told me very recently, 'Look at George Bush's father. He pulled Saddam's teeth, then he gave him the leeway to go and clobber the Shi`as and do whatever he wanted. How would it ever be imaginable that his son would have to come and destroy Saddam? Who would ever in his right mind do that? What interest is it to America? In a crude way, we don't know, who is playing what – *Allahu Ghalibun `ala Amrihi*.[31]

AA: But just a rather crude simile. We have a foot here and we have a shoe. And in the entire cosmos this foot and this shoe come together – so it is a cosmic event in many ways.

SFH: Everything is a cosmic event.

AA: Of course, everything is a cosmic event, but the dramatic aspects of it are cosmic too…

SFH: Dramatic is only visible. The visible is insignificant – that's why I never took to the outer drama – whether it's politics or economics or whatever – they are all insignificant to me.

AA: So Shaykhna, you are in need of a teacher and guide and along comes this guide – if you reflect on it, it's an extraordinary occurrence.

SFH: Yes, it is.

AA: It's not that you were hungry and some guy brought you a plate of food.

SFH: True – No, I was hungry, and I didn't know for what, and somebody was exuding – a banquet arrived. It is the other side of the coin.

---

[31] "God always prevails in His purpose." (Qur'an 12:21)

AA: But if you were five minutes late at the airport you would've missed him.

SFH: Fine.

AA: If I didn't go to the fifth floor of Foyles…

SFH: No, I see more and more of *'alim al-ghaib* – I've been more and more sensitive to the unseen – *Alladhina Yu'minuna bil ghaib*[32] – we've missed that. The entire business is taking refuge and certainty in *ghaib* – it's all about that.

---

[32] "Who believe in the unseen." (Qur'an 2:3)

Sufism

Finding Sufis

AA: Shaykhna, so you had followed Chinmaya's instructions to leave the Ashram and leave his company and go and seek your future path with the Sufis. When you said that, you said that you had no knowledge of the Sufis, except incidental. You were 'shattered', to use the expression. How did you internalize that? How did you set upon finding a Sufi you were able to relate to?

SFH: I trusted him and I didn't trust anything from myself. I trusted that his judgment is right – he knows and I don't. And I had to remain in my not knowing, so I accepted this drift – very painful – and it didn't take very long – I think it was two or three months before I ordered a car to travel to find the so-called Sufis, a sleeper Volkswagen type of thing so I could go into the hills and so on. And in the meantime I came across Shaykh Abdalqadir's book, and contacted his followers. It was two or three weeks before a response came and I met him and I felt this was as good a next state as ever could be. He gave me two orders; he wrote them and gave them to me: Number one, take the first opening that comes to you. Number two, do not concern yourself with what doesn't concern you.

Chinmaya's Familiarity with Sufism

AA: Did you know anything about the Sufi orders – his ideas of Sufism, I suppose, were the groups in India you may have been familiar with – Chishtis and so on?

SFH: I think he had a very good idea. For example Vivekananda was taught by Sufis and others. So I think he knew that that was the equivalent of the nearest with what I had benefitted and come to know.

AA: And basically he pushed you into, as it were the spiritual dimensions and inner language and spiritual tradition of Islam.

SFH: Correct. Absolutely.

AA: Seeing that there were some points of continuity between his and a position with which you were familiar.

SFH: Knowing sameness in origin. He knew that in terms of the root of it, they are all the same. It's all about the Infinite, the Absolute, the Unseen and it becomes more and more cultural and ends up being different to the way it started. So he knew all that because there had been occasions when I had seen him talking to people from different cultures and religions – in interviews – and I could see his referencing all the time to the Oneness and Essence.

AA: But there was no particular teacher or guide within the Islamic spiritual tradition with which he was familiar and passed that knowledge to you, like information.

SFH: He didn't mention anyone in particular. He trusted that I should find my own flavor and do my own work and be weaned. I was totally dependent on him. I was taking energy and whatever sustenance, stability, balance, from him.

Leaving Chinmaya

AA: To use your own metaphor, did you feel that you were 'ejected' from the womb of the ashram?

SFH: I felt the severance, but I knew it was good. I knew it was good for me. It was a pain that I had to accept. I accepted it. No resentment, no anger, but the effect upon me was devastating.

AA: He cut off all contact with you?

SFH: No. He asked me to cut of all contact with him – he knew I was courteous enough to do so.

AA: You had no contact with him afterwards – apart from incidental?

SFH: Quite a bit. Incidentally, I wasn't going to be any more 'back to mama'. That is for sure. But there were a number of connections when I sent people to him. Eventually also, the last time I sent Batul and maybe one or two others to meet him in Houston. You can ask Batul – she had a very good time with him, and he warned her that I mustn't enter into this community '*ummah*' business, or conventional Islam.

AA: But you had no physical contact with him –

SFH: No.

The Search

AA: So here you are, you've left the comfort zone of the circle of Chinmaya. Why did you not look for Sufis within your own geographical world? Why not look for Sufis in Syria, in Turkey and Irfanis (*'Arifin*) in Iran?

SFH: I was going to. I was based in England. I had no strong affinity or connection with people in any of these countries. I'd been completely on the side in an oil type of industry, business, isolated, western, and Chinmaya was my main *qibla*, mother, father, all. So I was going to look for Sufis. I visualized my self in this van going up and down the mountains of northeast Iran. I remembered the connection with my father's uncle, who was a great Sufi master of his time. He was the grand master of the Namatullahis.

AA: Your great grand uncle.

SFH: Yes, the one who I also bring out in '*Son of Karbala*' as having told Reza Shah that he would be a powerful future king of Iran; yes, that's the man.

AA: He was a Nimatullahi.

SFH: He was Nimatullahi. He became the head Nimatullahi Shaykh.

AA: As you know, Sufi traditions in the Shi`a world are very rare.

SFH: Correct.

AA: So there was that connection –

Connectedness of Shari`ah-Haqiqah

SFH: Strongly. Also, I remember the story where my father was very fond of him – of his uncle – and his uncle came to Karbala – this happened before I was born, my father told me this story. And my grandfather didn't want to meet him. He was a very prominent man, and also a *marja'*, so he didn't want to publicly meet him. So he [my father's uncle] came to my father's house and met his brother, my grandfather, and he said that after two hours together, they both said that they were the same; *Haqiqah-Shari`ah* inseparable. So my father was very, very pleased for being the intermediary in having these two really returning back to, if you like, each other's bosom, and connecting with each other. One of them was very much into *Shari`ah* – steeped `*alim*; the other one was from his youth, very much searching for the other end, and they found they were really the same.

AA: I suppose your grandfather overcame the deeply rooted prejudice against the Sufis that the *Shari`ah-minded* people have.

Seeking a Spiritual Guide

SFH: Oh Yes. Correct. No doubt about it. But again there are exceptions. So I had that link, but it didn't occur to me. I thought I might go up and down the mountains of Khorasan. Then I thought, maybe I also had to go to North Africa. Whilst the van was being prepared for me, I made some deposit to get this car. So I was at the beginning of that process when Shaykh Abdaqadir appeared.

AA: So you don't see seeking a person as a spiritual guide as necessarily outside the traditions or the geographic area of the Middle East and North Africa.

SFH: No, I thought it would be there. I actually felt it would be Iran, and maybe also North Africa because of the link I had with Shaykh Ahmed al-Alawi when I was travelling in North Africa. And I had no other notion of Sufism. I trusted, and I believed that it would unfold for me.

AA: You were just waiting for the signal.

SFH: I was waiting for the signal, the means, the car, this and that. I was drifting with good expectations.

AA: So one can't say that you were a person who had basically discarded the linguistically specific culture of the Middle East in order to seek a guide who was more steeped in a different tradition – say the Hindu world, or some other spiritual tradition.

SFH: No, no. I had never been by temperament that type of a person. I would not totally discard the Middle East culture, but I would have a priority. I would move more towards something. I would never be able to discard. Whatever exists I believe has its purpose and it may touch me also. So I was never that severance type.

AA: You say your primary language was English or Arabic?

SFH: I would say more English, because I'd be writing and communicating in English – but my Arabic was also still kept up in a way – and a bit of Persian too.

AA: And the social circle you were in Arabic?

SFH: Absolutely, very much in Arabic. I would be at home in Arabic.

AA: Then you came across this book, which came to you actually, according to what you said earlier, quite abruptly.

SFH: Yes, it really popped at me.

AA: Where did you pick it up – at Foyle's?

SFH: Below my apartment in Queensway there was a bookshop, smallish, general bookshop. At the end of it there was a section on spirituality or religion. So I went straight from the entrance to the end. This book was the only one I picked – it's called *'The Way of Muhammad'*.

AA: I think it was his second book?

SFH: Yes, I think so.

AA: Something about the 'Book of Strangers'. That was a novel. There was a book called "Root Islamic Education" also.

SFH: I think it came later. Anyway, I picked it up and it opened on the profile of Muhammad. So I said, 'here it is, I am looking for the same thing and Chinmaya was right. I must find it in my own culture – it's familiar, easier. There's no point to uproot. It's all there.'

AA: If you look at that book – I came across this very early – it jumps at you, it's great in terms of its descriptive power, very appealing or compelling to a person who is trying to immerse themselves in this tradition. But re-reading it on several occasions after several years, it doesn't have that effect any more – it seems to have been designed for people who are just embarking on the path. Would you agree to that?

SFH: I hardly read it – a bit of it – a third of it. I looked for the man.

AA: So what jumped at you?

SFH: The profile of Muhammad. There was one page describing the profile of the Prophet – the Prophetic Profile. I said, 'This is what I want.'

AA: Here you are reading a book by Shaykh Adbalaqadir Murabit – I think that's what he was called then – and wondered who he was. Did you know him?

SFH: No, I didn't know him at all – none whatsoever. At that time I mentioned it to Hosam. I said, 'Look, I found this.' He said, 'I found the same thing' – something else he had found.

AA: Shaykh Hosam also for a spiritual guide?

Meeting Shaykh Abdalqadir

SFH: Yes, he was also looking. When Chinmaya met me he [Hosam] was also looking for spirituality, and we were cross-referencing. So I sent – I think the address was in Berkeley – I sent a telegram saying that I wanted to meet this man, and in about two or three weeks' time, I had a response. I was at that time living in Sloane Street [London] – on the sixth floor – I had a large apartment there. Somebody was at the door – two, three weeks after that – an Englishman, who looked like a very well dressed Oriental – European person, as though he'd just come back from buying carpets in Samarkand. An Orientalized European. His name was something Woolf. His father was a very famous psychologist – Abdulrahman Woolf, his name was. He came up to the apartment, very polite, Etonian type, and he said, 'Yes, Shaykh Adbalqadir has had a very bad accident, but he will see you soon within two or three weeks.' So I was very reassured. I had a nice chat with him – I liked him. I was about to go to the Gulf, Sharjah – I had a house there on the beach. So I suggested to Shaykh Abdalqadir that if he liked I'd get him a ticket, he could come; he welcomed it. I was in Sharjah when he arrived. He came on his own, bent – he'd had a major car accident, very ill. He came and stayed with me for a few weeks.

AA: Your first encounter with him was in Sharjah?

SFH: No, I'd briefly met him before for an hour or so – somewhere he was staying – very ill – lying on bed. Then I left. But when he came to Sharjah, that's where I really came to know him.

AA: Your first impression of him was what? He was the author of this book.

SFH: No, my first impression was that this man was as good a Muslim version as I could come across, who would give me the direction, the threads and indications. I knew there was something very genuine and authentic about him.

AA: So you looked at the person, not his context.

SFH: No, not at all. I knew he knew. And I remember the way Shaykh Abdalqadir was, and the way he behaved with people, was not at all to my temperament. I remembered Chinmaya's instructions, 'Do not concern yourself with something that doesn't concern you.' It was not my business what he said to other people.

AA: So you don't see the actions of a Shaykh with his community or disciples in any way reflective of his true character?

SFH: But it has to be that way.

AA: Why?

SFH: It's nothing to do with me. My reflection on him was that it's not my business. Whatever he does with the others is against – what I feel – the humanity or something else. But it was a question of flavor; also, he was not well. It wasn't my business. I was there for a specific reason. And even though the years that I was strongly connected, there were a lot of things going on that I was not in any way content with, it was not my business.

AA: So you think that a person can reflect the *haqq* in the sense of what you want to take from that person, while at the same time, maintaining a contradictory private life.

SFH: Not contradictory, but not necessarily on the same frequency. Not contradictory. I didn't feel any contradiction to the way of Muhammad as I knew it but I found the style or the flavor not at all to my liking. For example, one day he comes back and tells all of his *murids* – there were seven of them with families – divorce, all of them. So I thought that if he told me even a slight hint of that to me, I would not stay there for a second. He never did. It's not my business. These people were British. He knew what sickness they were in; he was putting them through some major therapeutic treatment. Not *haram*, but unpleasant.

AA: I can understand – I've heard that many times in the past from you that one should avoid what does not concern one, to stay away from things that don't concern one. But that must be only restricted to matters of understanding the actions of the One, the *al-Haqq*. It can't be in terms of the actions of that person – on creation.

SFH: True. Also, it depends on the stage of the person. I was in a stage in which I had to be in my own life's very narrow tunnel. Now, I would not follow that.

AA: A person who talks about all the aspects of *tawhīd* and oneness – that there is no reality except the One – and then he abuses an animal, or hurts a dog –

SFH: Unacceptable.

AA: But does that reflect on his capacity to reflect the Truth?

SFH: It will undermine the wholesomeness –

AA: Therefore, spiritual credibility can be discounted by personal conduct.

SFH: Correct. No doubt about it. For example, if it was even twenty years ago, I would never have invited Shaykh Abdalqadir to come for a talk, because of some of these things he did, their side effects, if you like. But in my stage at that time, I had to be completely narrow and focused on what would bring me back into that cultural rooting with the *Haqiqah* –

AA: So you basically blotted out everything that didn't concern you or was not conducive to your spiritual quest.

SFH: Absolutely. In a way subconsciously, I think I had no interest or expectation of being in a way more illumined by the *Haqiqah*. It was really the *Dīn* and *Shari`ah* which was missing.

AA: I'm trying to figure it out for myself.... what your views are on the kind of person through which these lights are channeled and reflected. For example, you can be a great physicist or chemist, say Shockley[33], but still be a very nasty man and racist and so on. If you were a seeker of knowledge in Physics and electrical engineering you'd go to Shockley, irrespective of the fact that he was racist, because you wanted that particular knowledge. But would that hold for people who claim the kind of contact with universality and the spiritual realm?

SFH: I have no interest about his claim or non-claim –

AA: As a general principle?

SFH: No, in principle, I would go for what would satisfy my particular need. If I were looking for the *Insaan al-Kamil*, I would have run away. But that was not my particular need.

AA: Going back to this example of Shockley, he was a world-class physical chemist, who won the Nobel Prize. But he was also a great exponent of eugenics, the hierarchy of races and so on. He probably

---

[33] A Noble Prize winner with controversial racial views.

would not have got a job now. But in the 1960s he was one of the founders of Silicon Valley, but an objectionable person.

SFH: True.

Spiritual Package

AA: So what is the answer when it comes to the science of the soul?

SFH: I wasn't looking for the science of the soul. I was looking for a more Islamic or cultural version, a package that I could taste and enjoy, similar to what I loved with Chinmaya. So I was just trying to find the equivalent of that Indian Hindu path, but in the Muslim or Islamic sense.

AA: But I'm sure Chinmaya was an impeccable person.

SFH: Absolutely!

AA: I mean you cannot fault him –

SFH: I could not one bit. But he maintained only totally and exclusively the highest referencing to *haqq*, higher consciousness. He never got himself concerned with communities, people, apart from services to the real needy, like eye clinics and hospitals and so on.

AA: So would you say that *adab* or courtesy is essential to the qualities of a spiritual guide?

SFH: No doubt. For completion of that. For wholesomeness.

AA: In terms of *adab*, is it restricted in the sense of only the *Haqiqi* definition or *Shari`ah* definition. Or does that also include cultural norms?

SFH: It will include all. The only thing to bear in mind – I can say that now – is that the *Shari`ah* part of it has to have a certain measure of flexibility to be strong; otherwise it will be rigid and brittle. In other words, –

AA: to reflect *adab*.

SFH: It has to reflect *adab* and accountability and correctness. Asking: why are you doing this, or why are you doing that? Being totally accountable. Not trying to slither out of it.

AA: We'll discuss that later. We'll talk about the character of a guide – but at that point when you encountered Shaykh Abdalqadir, you had no evidence that he had a complete spiritual package; you took from him what you wanted. Like basically going to the supermarket and picking the item.

SFH: Not so much supermarket, the only market; there was nothing else. The first door that was open.

AA: But you didn't seek to be part of his community.

SFH: Not at all, never. I never liked any one of them. From beginning to end. I had not the slightest attraction. In fact most of them repelled me, actually repelled me. And I asked him, 'Who are these idiots? Half-witted; Broken?' He said, 'I went to the dustbins of Europe and this is what I could find.' I would not have liked to be around any of the characters around him for more than five minutes, not even two minutes. To the end. But it wasn't concerning me. That was really the turning point back to the fullness of Islam. Having done Mecca in a way, Shaykh Abdalqadir pushed me into Medina.

AA: So Shaykh Abdalqadir showed up in Sharjah after a near fatal accident to recuperate, and you wanted to be in his company in order to imbibe what he had to offer. What happened in that period?

SFH: He made me read a few things, we prayed together; we had a very pleasant time; he was beginning to recoup.

AA: Was that when you started praying again?

SFH: I may have begun sporadically before. I don't think I stopped completely.

AA: Did Chinmaya encourage you?

SFH: He never encouraged me or discouraged me. He accepted me as I was and he somehow reminded me of my Muslim heritage, especially in the last few years, by always saying *Bismillah, Allahu akbar* – that sort of thing.

AA: I find this man remarkable, I wish I had met him.

SFH: Most remarkable.

AA: The ease with which he guided you.

SFH: Total ease and confidence. Generosity beyond limits. So then he [Shaykh Abdalqadir] wanted to go to Pakistan. A few of his American *murids* were already there; he had sent them to Karachi –

AA: Is this 1978?

SFH: '79.

Tasawwuf in Pakistan

AA: So in 1979, you moved out of the Chinmaya circle and into the orbit of *Tasawwuf*?

SFH: Correct. So he had a few of his *murids* – Americans – studying *Hikmah* or whatever...ism in Karachi. He wanted me to take him to Karachi. I had by then travelled to India maybe 30, 40, 50 times. Never ever thought of Pakistan. I always found it abhorrent with their beards and *kurtas* and so on.

AA: Why is that? – it's a common feeling.

SFH: I know I had that feeling earlier. But you know, I found these people not living at that time. I found the separation between the rituals and their meaning and imports so wide, I didn't want to be anywhere near them.

AA: And here you have a country of 100 million people that was off everybody's radar, so to speak, because of this commonly held feeling that this was an incorrigible place – so you went to Pakistan –

Re-Entry into Islamdom Through a Cemetery

SFH: So I took him to Pakistan to Karachi, and I had wonderful experiences. The second day – we were staying in the best hotel in Karachi – I don't remember its name – and he went to his *murids*, and I went to Thatta cemetery an hour or two drive from Karachi, and I wanted to stay there in that cemetery. I had amazing encounters with some of the dead/alive. I stayed there all day –

AA: Can you please elaborate, if you want to?

SFH: Yes, I went to this cemetery – there were a lot of early, early Muslims and I had this feeling towards Hyderabad. It's famous, the earliest cemetery of the Muslims who came there. I remember resonating with quite a number of the deceased people. I would sit on the shrine under the shade, do the *Fatiha* – have a bit of an unseen encounter with them. Sit with them, get a bit of a flavor and move on. Within an hour or two, a man arrived from nowhere – it was desolate.

AA: Who was with you? A driver?

SFH: A driver who stopped near the car. I said, 'I don't want you near me.'

AA: Shaykh Hosam?

SFH: No, he wasn't there.

AA: Shaykh Abdalqadir?

SFH: No – he went to his *murids*. I was alone. And then this man – with a beautiful face – arrived. He said, 'I came to greet you – I know you're at home here.' I said, 'Not just at home – I don't want to go to that miserable town. That is where the dead people are.' He said, 'Yes, I live here,' – a shack somewhere within there. 'I just want to welcome you and give you a little gift.' He gave me a silver coin. He said he had just come back from Hajj. He had walked – he'd been a few times – walking all the way to Mecca and back. Never on a wheel. It takes about 6, 7, 8 months. He said, 'this coin travelled with me all the way there and back and I want to give it to you.'

AA: He walked through Iran, Iraq …?

SFH: Yes – it was a beautiful little silver coin – Maria Theresa or something like that. Maybe smaller. And he stayed with me. And introduced me to some of these dead people. He said, 'this fellow had a more *Jalal*, more *Jamal*'. More this and more that. So after a few hours, I really completely lost sense of time and space. It was for me like a big carrot to be with the Muslims, to come back to the *dīn*. Very sweet. I was very resentful going to Pakistan, and this really opened up for me. I said to myself, 'Look at the saints who are here!' And then he came with me to the car late afternoon. So I went back. Very reluctant, reluctant indeed!

AA: So your re-entry into the realm of Islamdom, as it were, was through the cemetery.

SFH: Exactly. Absolutely. And later on I learned when Junaid said, 'the Muslims are in the grave, and Islam has gone to the books.'

AA: You actually lived it out.

SFH: It was really incredible. And it left such a sweet taste within me. I can never forget it. It was one of the nicest, most blessed, intense days I'd had.

Meeting Shaykh Abdalqadir

AA: What did Shaykh Abdalqadir do apart from giving you a few books? What kinds of things did he prescribe to you?

SFH: The second or third day when he was in Sharjah, he said, 'I know everything about you. This afternoon I had an encounter with Chinmaya. I know how much he loved you, how much you loved him and I think you have done the right thing and he has done the right thing, and that now you have to get on with your life and your *dīn* and move on.'

AA: So it was just verbal exchanges and a few books?

SFH: Ah – something else happened. In Sharjah soon after he arrived, he said he wanted to meet Sayyed Mehdi Hakim, who was there. So they had a wonderful time together.

AA: How did he know about him?

SFH: He must have known about him. He must have asked about the Shi`a notables or whatever, in order to connect. So he was very pleased that I knew him and I respected and loved him. He was re-assured.

AA: You knew Sayyed Mehdi Hakim?

SFH: I knew him very well. I'd met him a few times, helped with whatever I could and he trusted me and I respected him.

AA: He was based in Dubai? Imam Ali mosque.

SFH: He was based in Dubai.

AA: We'll talk about him later Insha'Allah. So you had some contacts in Iraq with the Hakim family?

SFH: I didn't. I knew about them from the household but I didn't have any contacts with them.

AA: So where did you meet him?

SFH: It could have been in England on a visit. But I respected his family, and I found he was authentic – much more than the others. Now then what had happened – the third or fourth day in my house in Sharjah, Muneera, who was working in Dubai – I knew her because she was in the same business of shipping – her best friend was a Greek shipping magnate who had Ro-Ro's coming and going, and I was in the same type of business of containers – so she was in Dubai, representing the Maris family and a few others; so she came to the house to help with supper, and I knew her through work – shipping, she would come to the offices of Gulftainer a few times.

AA: Was that your main business in Sharjah?

SFH: No, the biggest business was the health package, supplies and this and then, and there were a three or four other businesses, including the agency of Budget Rent-a-Car for the whole of the Gulf.

AA: I came across one of your companies – PDC.

SFH: That was a holding company. So she came to help with supper. She had embraced Islam three weeks before – I think she had been to the Masjid Ali. Years ago she was in Lucknow, she was very much touched by the Shi`a. Sayyed Mehdi had give her the Qur'an of Murtaza Pooya – it's a good *tafsir*. He had given her that as a gift. So she was beginning to learn about Islam. Shaykh Abdalqadir knew that. After two or three days, again, Sayyed Mehdi came to the house – Hosam was there then – he had come. So the two of them said, 'There is this fine lady who has embraced Islam. She is living here, you are living here – the rest of the time she lives in England. Why don't you marry her?' So I told them I never thought I was the marrying type. I didn't want to have these encumbrances – I had some other serious interests. So they said, 'Look, you are here, you have the means.' Suddenly the two of them connived. Sayyed Mehdi asked her, 'where is the Qur'an that I gave you.' She had it. He said, 'Do you mind giving it back to me as a gift?' She gave it to him. So he said, 'Here, this is your dowry. Shaykh Fadhlalla, would you accept marrying her?' There and then. Hosam was there. Without any pre-meditation.

AA: No preparation?

SFH: No preparation. So I asked Shaykh Abdalqadir. I said, 'Look I have a wife, children. How would I break the news to them?' He said, 'Leave it to me. I'm going back.' So in Karachi I suddenly began to realize what had I done. This stupidity. One is bad enough – I end up now having two! Again he said, 'Leave it to me. I'm going back to England. I'll meet your wife and I'll tell her,' which he never did – never happened. He saw me having doubts. He said, 'Look, you have to stop the doubts. Keep to the situation you have accepted, or get out of it – divorce. You can divorce anybody, this is clear, you must admit.' So I realized that the man really was quite decisive and was very helpful to me. I too had to become decisive at a certain point – to eliminate doubts; it doesn't help much. So anyway, we stayed there three or four days in Karachi and then returned to Sharjah. I think he stayed a bit longer.

AA: But it wasn't – no *khalwas*, or particular teachings?

SFH: Not at all. I felt this man was trying to resurrect original Islam. I felt deeply that he was trying to live as near as possible to the Muhammadi version. At that time also, he was very much in love with the *Ahl al-Bayt*. Ali was on his tongue all the time. Ali, Hassan, he would weep any time Hussain was mentioned.

Western Counter-Culture

AA: Did you know anything about his background? Professional background?

SFH: I asked, and I came to know that he was with the Beatles – and George Harrison was one of them – and he was a reviewer. I wasn't interested in it, and it really didn't matter. I was indifferent. I was indifferent to any of them.

AA: Were you ever affected by what was going on in the West in terms of counter-culture and all of that?

SFH: I was aware of these things.

AA: They didn't affect you, and they had no meaning to you?

SFH: Not really. I was aware of it, but I had no great respect for the Western highly secularized culture. I felt all along that there was something major missing in their lives, which was that window towards the higher. And I knew – I had worked it out – that for a few centuries they had allowed the more spiritually inclined people to go to the monasteries so they backed up the monasteries partly as guilt, partly to keep them isolated, and I knew that phase was over. They had reduced the whole thing to a monoculture: Either you can do all of this and be in the battlefield of money, or you are completely out.

AA: I suppose that was the conventional form, but the whole counter culture of the 60s and 70s was to do with the discovery of spirituality, in their own warped way. You can make a case that a lot of people who emerged from that period, who then became *Shuyukh* as it were, were more of a product of that Western counter-culture movement than any genuine immersion in traditional spirituality.

SFH: Yes, but there was also genuineness about it anyway, but no, it didn't affect me. I was aware of the flower children and that but I wasn't much interested in it.

AA: Going to Morocco at that point in the 70s, was quite normal for the seekers of spirituality.

SFH: That is right.

AA: Not only because of the cheap drugs but I suppose they wanted to find what they thought they were looking for: a form of *Tasawwuf*.

Shaykh Abdalqadir/Tasawwuf

SFH: Sure, Shaykh Abdalqadir was on that way, at the forefront of that. He was a part of the movement towards *Tasawwuf*; in his coming to Islam he owed a lot to Raja Mahmoodabbad. He loved, trusted him, was with him, and followed him. He really found Raja Mahmoodabbad an incredible being. I think that influenced him immensely, and he would talk about it often. And in the last days of Raja's life, he sent several of his *murids*, whoever were around him, to look after him, particularly one man – whom I met quite a bit; his name was Hajj Isa [Idris?]. He kept close company to Raja until his death.

AA: Pakistani?

SFH: No, he was English – European. Most of them were Europeans. There were hardly any Easterners around Shaykh Abdalqadir. Raja had nobody around him except a few of Shaykh Abdalqadir's people. It was after that, I think, he came across Shaykh Muhammad Ibn al Habib –

AA: Yaqoob Zaki ...?

SFH: Yaqoob Zaki was with Raja. Yaqoob Zaki had helped me a lot actually. He spent two or three months teaching me about Islam in Andalus – I benefitted, and learned a lot from him – in that sense – historical.

AA: So, basically a good man.

SFH: I hired him to give me a series of talks and lectures on the beginning and the end and ups and downs of Islam.

AA: But he wasn't with Shaykh Abdalqadir?

SFH: No.

AA: So there was none of the traditional entry, as it were, of a *murid* to a Shaykh in your relationship with Shaykh Abdalqadir.

SFH: No, absolutely not.

AA: He took you outside of convention –

SFH: Outside, inside – that's why I was the only aberration – everybody else revered and looked up to him. I only took what I could and I was his main financial backer and supporter, unconditionally.

AA: Were you resented by his people, by some of the *murids*?

SFH: Maybe there was some jealousy. The same thing with Chinmaya. I didn't care, and it didn't affect me. It didn't touch me. I didn't consider them to be worthy of anything.

AA: Or if they were, it wasn't your business.

SFH: It wasn't my business. I just went with the flow.

AA: So Shaykh Abdalqadir didn't immerse you in these various practices, which a person is supposed to engage in prior to his formal entry or initiation to a Sufi order.

SFH: Really, no, not at all. He really in a way was forceful in my coming back to the *dīn* in its fullness.

AA: I'd like to come back to that, Shaykhna, because if you look at the practice that was being offered with Shaykh Abdalqadir, it was greatly influenced by Shaykh Muhammad Ibn al-Habib, but also by the West. It's a Western version of its manifestation; you can deconstruct it that way. You find a lot of counter-culture aspects – existentialist philosophy, Heidegger, Neitszche, things like that, and the fact that nearly all of the people came from a Western cultural position made that point of entry more accessible than being in a classical form, Arabic form, Persian form or Turkish form. So you did not take that at all?

SFH: Not at all. And he always pointed out to me and gave me books or references that were steeped in the old Islamic Khorasani type of culture and others. For example, he insisted that I should really imbibe Suhrawardi, al-Maqtool, things like that. So with me, it was mostly feeding me material and stuff to really see the links of wherever I had come from with the Hindus and my own home background – Karbala – to its roots. He really encouraged me in every way, culturally, practice-wise, Medina-wise to get back to that origin. And to the Alawi way, Imam Ali and the *Ahl al-Bayt*.

AA: It was like a tailored program for you – that program was not used by others.

SFH: Not at all.

AA: It wasn't the North African flavor.

SFH: Absolutely. I was his friend, junior partner, and I had nothing to do with anything else whatsoever.

AA: So spending all these years with Chinmaya, you had no need for *khalwa* …

SFH: I did. I'll tell you what happened there. Then at the latter end of the period, I decided to be in America, and it is there that after two or three years, he had his nice *zawiya*. I bought for him a place in Tucson, Arizona – he called it the Rabat – it was a normal house with a tower type of thing, 5/6 bedroom house, big house, few hundred thousand dollars type.

AA: A lot of money.

SFH: He made it as a center on the edge of Tucson; I was staying in a small apartment in town, very pleasant, with Muneera.

AA: Why Tucson? Did it remind you of Karbala? Desert landscape?

SFH: He went there. I followed him. I felt I should stay in America for a few years. By then there was reasonable income coming from my work in the gulf. I wasn't that happy in England – the weather and other things. I was beginning to discover North and South America and felt I could do something – perhaps work in South America.

AA: What was your relationship with him? Was it the way it was with Chinmaya? Did you call him for advice? Take counsel? Did you consult him before you made decisions?

SFH: Rarely. I took hints from him – not that different from Chinmaya. I regarded him as a senior friend, somebody I could look up to like an elder. But I was not totally dependent on him on day-to-day things whatsoever. I only took hints from him.

AA: Not enthralled by him? Or is that the wrong word?

SFH: The same way as I was with Chinmaya. I took him as a man. I saw humanity and divinity connected in both of them. Some aspect was more on the humanity side, which didn't interest me very much. The aspect, which was much more on the divinity side, interested me much more.

Political Power of Muslims

AA: I find it interesting, I must say I am curious that you would be associated with a person whose sense of community and power was far more established than yours. It has a lot to do with political power of Muslims – Rabat, the choice of name for that place, and a lot of it to do with building communities.

SFH: Correct.

AA: Murabitun, and all that – things that you basically are indifferent to, or in fact, disdain. Isn't that curious?

SFH: Absolutely. Not just disdain. In the early days with Shaykh Abdalqadir, I knew that, essentially in him, there is that wish to create a major world movement.

AA: Power – *qudra*.

SFH: Power – I was completely the reverse. I knew this would not be the time for it, and I've always, as I've mentioned before, had the right intuition as to what is not on. And I knew this was not on. The timing was not right.

AA: Did he choose his name – Abdalqadir? Was it chosen for him?

SFH: He chose it.

AA: *Qadir* says a lot about him.

SFH: I don't know who chose it.

AA: *Qadir* – it says a lot in the choice of word, which means, power.

SFH: That's his choice. His interest was to create a world movement and he thought he could do it, but from day one I knew it wasn't my business.

AA: Did he see you as a partner in this?

SFH: Not at all.

AA: He didn't see you as a kind of *khalifa*? Right hand man?

SFH: Not at all. He knew I wouldn't be his *khalifa* – he was intelligent enough, intuitive enough to realize that.

AA: You were not that type.

SFH: He relied on me on many, many aspects of movement, people. He asked me about what I thought of others because there were some Arabs coming to him and so on. And I found his judgment was always colored by his desire to create this world movement; Hosam had with him some major disagreements, one of which was that Shaykh Abdalqadir wanted to go and be with Saddam. The embassy had been after him in London and they told him he could come and stay a few days. So he was willing to do anything. Hosam was very upset with him, and he told him that. I was there once on that occasion when Hosam said to him: 'You can't go and be with someone who is so blatantly a criminal and unjust.' But he was still willing to do that.

AA: But the idea of talking to people with power ...

SFH: ... desirous of taking over Iraq, whatever – being the power behind the throne. He did the same thing with Gaddafi; he did the same thing over and over and over. And he mentioned to me that if a man of the ultimate, the higher, meets with a man of the *duniya*, then the potency can take the world. I had from day one, said this is not the time – the winter is not yet set. The time for the movement is not on. The whole thing has to die out and the original version of *Shari`ah/Haqiqah* has to emerge, and what we are living on is something which is dead and cannot be resurrected. And every now and then Shaykh Abdalqadir would again come up with 'it's about to come! The great Naqshabandi Shaykh has come to me and we are now together.' When the Chishtis came to me, he said 'I wasn't sure whether the Chishtis would come to you or to me, but now that they have come to you, it will happen.' These things never appealed to me one bit. In my own heart from day one, I knew that our paths would not be the same, because I read the future as that this global world movement of resurrection of Islam as a world religion will not be on that stream. That stream is stinky – it is dead. You have to allow it but the original light is there. That has to be discovered in a different way. After a tipping point it will come. That is why I am temporary, from day one.

AA: But, as you have said, some of these elements, at some phases in your life were quite important, for example, probably in the late 80s, 90s, you could do a great deal of good, if you had a person in power in the company of a spiritual being, and you have such an example, like Ahmad Chalabi is a case in point. Even Saddam, if he had moved from the dark, as it were, to the other side, a great deal of good could've come.

SFH: Correct.

AA: But you never thought that this could lead anywhere?

SFH: I always thought it could be a big thing but I didn't think the timing of it was right. I didn't think the atmospherics were right.

AA: Some of the leaders in the Middle East, not just in the ME, but throughout the Islamic world, did in fact do that but the result was darkness. They became a *Shari`ah* minded people, like Zia ul-Haq and so on.

SFH: I knew it was too late from that stream and too early for the new hybrid that was coming up. I also knew deep down in my heart that the Muslims had not lived their *dīn*, so it couldn't suddenly come like this, and there was no alternative. They had not presented an alternative way of life to the Western totally, utterly monetaristic, materialistic system. It wouldn't work. So it would be a nice example but would be extinguished.

AA: Would you say that this insight was because you were disconnected, decoupled for 20 years?

SFH: I don't know – I wasn't that decoupled; I could read the time. From childhood I always knew what was not on. And I knew this was not on. In terms of principle if somebody like Saddam turned truly to Allah Akbar rather than being on the flag, in his heart, great things would happen, but he would be extinguished. The West cannot allow it.

AA: You were not interested in events per se, but in the principial aspects of events.

SFH: Yes, I think that's fair. I knew deep down where the poison was, and knew that the healing would come, and it was the West that had to begin to accept and turn things around. Once I knew the West was beginning to be tolerant, especially the Anglo-Saxons of the eccentric or spiritual types, I knew that there was hope and it would come globally. It would not come locally. It would not come from a local Islamic version of takeover or *Khilafat*, a new *Khilafah*. So when he produced his book on the *Khilafat*, I really thought this was ridiculous; I really felt this was done completely through the extreme end and nothing would come out of it.

Inner Reality/Insaan al-Kamil

AA: Going back to the inner and outer aspects – the *ma`na* and the form, it seems to me what you have been talking about is that the *ma`na* – always the meaning, the essence, principle, whatever you want to call it – has always been of far greater concern to you as an individual than how it's manifested.

SFH: Absolutely.

AA: Therefore, when you see any issues, conundrums and so on, contradictions, you try to relate them to the movement of the essence – the *harakat al-jawariyyah*.

SFH: Absolutely.

AA: So you were in the *harakat al-jawariyyah* before you knew what it meant – correct?

SFH: Absolutely. No, I only wanted to get to the ultimate light of lights and all of the other manifestations I took cognizance of, but didn't interest me. I left it. No concern. I was really totally, utterly inwardly focused, determined on not just knowledge, not just experience, but total immersion of the *haqq*. I wanted to be such that I would feel and know the presence of Imam Ali and Muhammad and Isa with me; that was really for me the most absolute passion.

AA: Did you see them as archetypes or real beings? Say, Imam Ali for example, you were not in any way interested in the outer aspects of power and Shi`aism.

SFH: No – I was interested in the embodiment of *insaniyya, ruhaniya*.

AA: So they embodied for you the meaning of …

SFH: *Insaan al-Kamil*.

AA: The Prophet.

SFH: Absolutely that.

AA: Were these notions also within the Chinmaya tradition?

SFH: They were there in him implicitly. And I saw quite a considerable aspect of that in Shaykh Abdalqadir as well. And later on in the great people, especially Sufi Barakat Ali, and a few others I met.

AA: So this period between '79 and '80 was a kind of transition from you being immersed, as it were, in the world of Chinmaya and the traditions that he represented, to a different world, a different construct, different linguistic forms in which they were expressed. Did you ever use expressions like, *tawhīd*, *Insaan e Kamil*, and *Imamate*, before?

SFH: Very little. I went for the taste, I went for the smell, I went for the *haal*. I had very little interest in the structures, in the specific borders, layers, control etc. – I was interested in the *haal* of it.

AA: So it was a form of migration (*hijra*) from one construct to another for you.

SFH: No doubt – in a sense it was a major *hijra* towards the sanctum – the years with Chinmaya – and coming back to Medina, acceptance and knowing that Mecca is in Medina. Otherwise there will not be a Medina.

AA: Did you enjoy going back to the traditions? If Chinmaya had told you to go and find a Zen Buddhist would you have done it?

SFH: I would have done it.

AA: But you would have had to learn that tradition.

Islamic Traditions/Sources

SFH: Yes. But this one was familiar, and there was also the love of the Qur'an. I really trusted the Qur'an. Always. And I knew it. I could understand the layers of it, the meanings of it – I could feel it gurgling from within me.

AA: You trusted the Qur'an, but in terms of your engagement with it you saw it as a whole, and didn't try to find the apparent contradictions and flaws in it?

SFH: Not at all. I trusted it.

AA: To you it was a seamless, integrated whole.

SFH: I trusted it, and I only took the positive side of it. I wasn't there to analyze it, to compare, to theologize, to do an academic study or whatever. I was totally focused on my state.

AA: But I recall in that period you were very much engaged in the revival of the Shi`a mystical tradition. You had books translated at your expense and you commissioned people to print obscure texts. Why was that?

SFH: All the time. True. It was a bit of, if you like, nostalgia towards what I thought there was and had been lost. And I hardly read them.

AA: Completely unrelated – *Kitab ul-Mufid*, it was done by Howard. What has this got to do with your quest?

SFH: I didn't actually do that myself. It was the Muhammadi Trust. I encouraged them.

AA: Did you finance it?

SFH: Yes, and I financed many other such things as well. I never read them. For example, *Misbah al-Shari`ah* (Lantern of the Path) was for me something special, and works like that. But it was really paying homage to these people. I somehow knew them deep down in me.

AA: Or was it to help or assist what the Muhammadi Trust was trying to do?

SFH: In a way also, but it was like a bit of a cry, to say, 'Look people, you pretend, say you are Shi`a, but this is your heritage. Get back to it.'

AA: These people must have been quite shocked – I'd say shocked – because suddenly you were back into this tradition. For example, the Muhammadi Trust people, Commander Hussein, they were very fine people.

SFH: Very fine.

AA: What was your experience of him?

SFH: He loved me implicitly. He lived for me. And I liked the man. I enjoyed being with him and I would say anything to him and he would accept it. Nobody else would accept everything from me. He took advantage of any opportunity to be with me, any time. And I trusted him and I knew he was the most authentic being. We had the best of times, and I knew he was lonely, and disappointed that the Muslims had ended up there. So I shared a lot of that.

AA: Were you introduced to him through Abbas Gokal?

SFH: No, through an exhibition on Islamic books; somebody brought me a copy of the first book that they had published – something about the Shi`as. So I said I wanted to meet him; it was through someone else.

AA: Did you know the Gokals when you were in England?

SFH: No. I knew the name.

Re-Prioritization of Life/Inner Wealth

AA: But you were not involved with them. So now, you have re-channeled your energies and decided to move to the United States. Why was that?

SFH: I felt it was a fresh country; for me it had far greater horizons. I felt if I were to teach authentic original Islam or whatever, the grounds there were much more fertile. I felt there was hope, there was possibility. I really didn't know the control mechanisms; the entire ethos is really…

AA: But your experience of the U.S. was pretty limited…

SFH: It was.

AA: And did you just want to get away from Europe?

SFH: Yes, but I also found that the people there were simpler, friendlier, more positive, and generous, in a way, also naive. Europe has now changed; it has all the usual stuff that a young person finds in America. I never thought I'd stay there; I thought this was a temporary phase.

AA: And you disconnected yourself from business at that point?

SFH: At that time I disconnected from the Gulf, maybe in the mid eighties.

AA: You went to the US in '83?

SFH: Yes.

AA: This change from a life that had a very significant part of it to do with business, commerce and matters of the *duniya*, the world, to abandoning it – that process is certainly not common. I think it's one of the key characteristics, I would say, of your passage. I don't know anybody who has done that. People may be different but they do not disconnect entirely, and then move to a new path, the switch, the re-invention of your self.

SFH: It was much more re-prioritizing.

AA: That's true. If you were 80% commerce and 20% – let's call it seeking – you can reverse it and say 20% commerce, 80% seeking. But in your case it was 100%.

SFH: That has been the case for me. It was for a few years like that. It wasn't overnight. There was a period of three or four years when it was 60% seeking, 40% business and then 70-80% seeking – it was gradual. It was two, three years. It wasn't overnight. It was gradual over 3, 4, 5 years. I just lost the taste for it, lost the appetite for it. I knew I would coast along, I'd be all right, I wouldn't be materially, totally destitute, nor would I be wealthy. I lost interest in it. I wasn't up to it.

AA: But you were obviously very successful at it.

SFH: Sure.

AA: Many people would know you as a successful businessman in the 1970s, early 80s. I knew you then.

SFH: It was the frontier, mainly again on promotion work, introducing what was needed in a new area, developing with oil money and what they needed. Obviously it was clear that health would be an important issue. Infrastructure would be another one, and education, and so on. I was aware of these things. I played a little role in that, and I knew I could be much more successful in it, but it just didn't appeal to me. I imagined myself having much more work and thinking what would I do with it?

AA: The process of accumulating material wealth was incidental to you?

SFH: Not just incidental – an anathema. I considered that this was the ultimate sin.

AA: While you were doing it? Not afterwards? On reflection?

SFH: No, there was something in me that was against that. I thought this was now going into the *Shaytanic* field and it would absorb me and burn me. So I wanted to limit it.

AA: What you used to call WDBC.

SFH: Wheeling, Dealing, Bribery and Corruption. At that time that was paramount, because there was nothing else to do. There were no operations, no production, only that. Finding a project, knowing government is paying for it, knowing who is who and getting your fee.

AA: Extraordinary, how one can walk away from these things. Didn't you see wealth as a kind of important enabler?

SFH: No doubt, but I considered inner wealth far, far more important. I considered from those days that this business of poverty eradication is a myth. Poverty is both outer and inner. It cannot be just outer eradication. No matter how much you try – I found even in India, Pakistan – villages were sponsored in Sri Lanka – we have had dozens of such projects. The more they take, the more they want. It's human nature. We're greedy for light, for knowledge. But there is a switch from the outer greed to the inner. If this doesn't happen, nothing will. So I knew my inner wealth was increasing.

AA: You didn't mind being exploited or taken for a ride by various charlatans.

SFH: If I was aware of it, I would not like it. But I allowed it, on many occasions, not to take revenge, not to be vindictive. My own inner thing draws me far more towards that goal than trying to clear the arena and going against those who were taking advantage of me. My inner wealth, or the taste of it, basically *tawakkul*, gave me such greater significant reliance and trust. I remember once in America with the Turkish Shaykh, Jerrahi, I was with him in New York, somebody brought him something, a gift, and I knew he had wanted it, or thought of it.

AA: He was a bookseller?

SFH: A small bookseller in Istanbul. Whatever it was, the gift, I felt it was his desire and he held it as if it fell into his hands from heaven. He put it on his head, expressing gratitude to the sender and he thanked the fellow who brought it incidentally as a messenger – he went ecstatic – there were incidents like this that showed me there was another way of living, and gratitude and wealth than acquiring it myself and being in control. From about the age of 40, I began to see more and more the Controller. That I wanted to control started to fade, and I began to shift my emphasis more and more towards reading the Controller's Will. 'Let your *irada* be under His *irada*, without denying my *irada*, suffer for it every now and then.' That was for me ongoing, something I could always tap into. As a reference it was there. *Iqra'*, read, read.

AA: But you have to read it with certain glasses.

SFH: With inner sight – with the heart.

AA: How do you know the *irada*.

SFH: Not with the *nafs*, with the *qalb* – out of the *nafs*, out of mind. No identity, no thoughts.

AA: In these business settings when wheeling and dealing and bribery were taking place, and you had this other energy, how did you communicate?

SFH: With more and more difficulty – I tell you one example. They were developing a club for investment and real estate in America. Because I was there, they recruited one top European real estate operator and they wanted a kitty of $40/$50million. I was one of the participants. This fellow came to me in America and I guided him. He was very arrogant and I knew it would not work. They bought many properties. The only one that worked was in San Antonio, which I bought. All of them failed. They were going to put another kitty, and I was there discussing it in the gulf. What was the name of the Iraqi man, the minister of oil?

AA: Abdullah Ismail.

SFH: He knew me and I liked him, although he was a gambler...

AA: A good man...

SFH: No, no decent man. They were discussing the next pot – the names of people, and who the investors were. I was sitting aside. When my name was mentioned, he said, 'He's really out of it. He's not interested.' I was so pleased. Had I not tipped already onto the other side, I would have considered this an insult: 'why are they excluding me? I am the founder.' But I took it as a gift from Allah. So I was excluded. I was not interested... I was no longer a player.

AA: You were involved in Intoil which went belly-up. I think you lost interest in it.... investment in oil companies... they ended up buying something called Arapaho Oil.

SFH: Hamid [Jaffar] was in the business .... his drilling and so on...

AA: You brought in Abdulamir Taqi. He ended up saving that company.

SFH: He was the best – brilliant. Our friend. Hosam and I were very close to him.

AA: I tried to bring him to Iraq.

SFH: I know. You called me. It was too late.

AA: He also was not well.

SFH: He's recovered health wise. No, it was too late.

AA: The only thing, Shaykhna. You must have known that once you'd amassed this fortune, that all kinds of people were hovering around you including those with a 'religious' aspect. I'm sure you saw through them. You still provided them with money. Why?

SFH: You know Allah endowed that for me so *"Waamma assa-ila falatanhar."* [34] It was on that light. I really lived the Qur'an. Don't say no to them. Give them something.

AA: But you told me about tens and 100s of such people.

SFH: It's all relative. I had much more. It's all relative. Just now, two weeks ago, somebody from England from way in the past sent a message wanting some money. I had very little in it. The first time I didn't answer, but the next day I said, 'no I have a few hundred pounds. Share.' It is that basically. I have to be accountable.

---

[34] "and do not chide the one who asks for help;" (Qur'an 93:10)

America

AA: We'll talk about your community – their actions. Again, you moved to America. There are certain rules for moving from one country to another. For example, what was your passport? Iraqi? So you could travel to the U.S. You went on a business visa and stayed on?

SFH: No, I applied for and got a green card. I wanted to stay there for a while – wasn't sure for how long. I went through the normal channels.

AA: Did Shaykh Abdalqadir play a part in your decision to move to America?

SFH: Not at all. He was there already, so that was an attraction.

AA: So why did you choose San Antonio?

SFH: I wanted a bit of a desert environment. I went to the East Coast, Miami, and then to California, which was very appealing. I wanted an environment not too softy, a bit like White River (South Africa). I wanted to be not too cushy.

AA: Arid.

SFH: Semi arid, but self-supporting – lots of sun. I didn't like Dallas. Too big. Also, there was a tiny little village called, Medina. So I saw a few signs like this, but I felt it was out of the way. I thought I could do something different. I could have an outburst – I felt there was this version of Islam, but, deep down, I knew it wouldn't last, that it would only be 3, 4, 5 years maximum, and then I'd be out.

AA: Did you have any followers at that point?

SFH: Yes.

AA: And when you were in England before you went to America?

SFH: No, the followers came after my *khalwa* when Shaykh Abdalqadir and others declared I was a Shaykh.

AA: You had a *khalwa*?

SFH: Yes, in Tucson. I was about to leave him when that happened.

AA: He had established a center.

SFH: Yes, his *murids* – a few of them were really good friends of mine by then. Many of them also came to me or were introduced by me and I passed them on. I was about to leave towards the east coast to look for some place, something –

AA: Who was trekking with you? Were you by yourself?

SFH: Muneera and one or two Iranians were with me. Other Muslims would come and help too.

AA: People who knew you personally.

SFH: Also, I knew some as teachers.

First Teachings

AA: Were you teaching?

SFH: Yes I was.

AA: When was your first discourse?

SFH: I think it was '78. In '79 I began to give discourses.

AA: Where? In Sharjah?

SFH: No, no – in America.

AA: But you were not teaching.

SFH: No, not at all. In UAE I did. Shaykh Ali from Hadramaut was a wonderful old man whom they all respected – every now and then Hosam and I would sit with him and enjoy. Shaykh Ali one day caught me and he said, 'today you do the Qur'an', and there were 60, 70 ladies. He said teach them the Qur'an.

AA: Where?

SFH: In Dubai – in his place. He had a house/*zawiya*.

AA: So your first teaching was in Dubai?

SFH: No. The first teaching was, maybe, in America.

AA: Did you have any experience in public speaking?

SFH: Not at all. I never liked it, I never imagined teaching – Who to teach? What to teach? – No, I resented all of these names, titles, roles, totally.

AA: So you did not set out to be a Shaykh.

SFH: Not at all, whatsoever, in fact I joked about it.

AA: So you ended up in Tucson with Shaykh Abdalqadir.

First Khalwa/Disappearing into Divine Names

SFH: And I was about to leave and he called me and said, 'No, you can't leave; I'm about to put you in *khalwa*.' I said, 'I don't care, what is this *khalwa*?' He said, 'No, it is important.' I said, 'Look, I am all the time in that state. What are you doing?' He said, 'No, from tonight please stay in your apartment, and be alone. I'll send you somebody to feed you once or twice a day.' I said, 'Fine.' So Muneera moved somewhere else; I stayed where I was staying. And they brought me breakfast. The next day I really broke down and I began to weep incessantly.

AA: How did you handle the isolation?

SFH: I was used to it.

AA: So why did you break down?

SFH: I suddenly began to see colors. I began to see myself stepped out of my own self, as it were.

AA: Did you have *dhikr* to do or did he give you something else to do?

SFH: No. *Khalwa* was very simple, the same thing as I do now for anybody else. Be thoughtless, do *dhikr* if you want, make sound, whatever it is to make you thoughtless. Don't be yourself. Get out of it. Die. I wasn't given any detailed instructions – it was easy for me.

AA: You'd had, I suppose 8 years of experience with Chinmaya.

SFH: Many. By natural disposition I could be thoughtless any time.

AA: When you were young, did you seek solitude?

SFH: Very much. I enjoyed solitude as a kid.

AA: Are you a solitary man?

SFH: I'm happy with myself. I was never ever more happy with others. Never.

AA: You prefer the company of yourself.

SFH: Not really. I don't mind the others either. But the company of myself is the first.

AA: Much more interesting – solitary, but not lonely.

SFH: Absolutely, never lonely. I was very sociable. I loved people.

AA: This is a predisposition.

SFH: So – I experience shock after shock. And then I had endless visions of the Prophet, Ali, of the family, all of them.

AA: This is a very important incident or event for me and those who may read the book. You were put into *khalwa* without any specific instructions, but you knew generally what you were, and were not, supposed to do.

SFH: Only *Salaat*.

AA: No Qur'an, nothing else.

AA: No books?

SFH: No books, no reading nothing other than the basic minimum requirement of *Salaat*.

AA: And to be in a thoughtless state as much as possible.

SFH: And if it helped me, I was allowed to visualize the name ALLAH, as well as other Divine Names.

AA: Did you choose to visualize the Divine Names?

SFH: Yes, he gave me something.

AA: Shaykh Abdalqadir?

SFH: Abdullah, this African American, brought for me the Divine Names written on a big thing, which I still have – I gave it to Muna – it's blue.

AA: Shaykh Abdalqadir gave it to you? Was it in the Maghribi script?

SFH: No, normal script. He said, 'die into it.' He said, 'visualize this, die into it, disappear in it, let it take you over. Whatever you do, so as you go into the next zone.' That's my understanding of what he said consciously. And that's what I did. And it was easy for me.

AA: Can you describe to us the various stages?

SFH: I sat visualizing the Divine Names on the horizon so that my thoughts become less, aware of my breathing – that is from India also. Breathe in, stop for a second, breathe out, stop for a while; breathe in and visualize this light emerging, growing, growing, growing – nothing else. Initially it can be colors, later on it becomes without a color; it becomes a diffused, foggy type of light and it expands and expands and expands, and you lose any sense of boundary and identity. It becomes so big that you are lost completely in it. Not a small being but no being. And you hold it there. And repeat, repeat. Sometimes when I am a bit mindful or whatever, I will say it aloud ALLAAAH and I'd paint it with a small brush, big brush, colored brush – ALLAAAH – and I disappear in the sound and the illusion of the form of some sort of light.

AA: Were you conscious ....?

SFH: I don't know – conscious to begin with but then you disappear.

AA: Did you have to exert effort?

SFH: It had to be easy – if it is difficult, it won't work.

AA: Once you emerged from the *khalwa* – how long was the *khalwa* for?

SFH: Three days.

AA: It wasn't the usual forty days?

SFH: No. I don't know about the usual, but it's traditionally become forty days, willing to do it for that length of time.

AA: Would you have needed more time if you were not already immersed in a form of retreat that Chinmaya taught you?

SFH: I don't know. May be I would have needed more bouts – not on one go – because it would be counter-productive, you know – if you get constipation, because it's in a small confined space, not moving, not walking. I think it has to be gauged at this time and age we're in. People have to be treated individually, and gauged closely as to whether there is a benefit. Otherwise it becomes a battle or an exercise in putting up with an inconvenience – I don't know, I was indifferent.

Takhliya/Tasfiya/Tahliya/Tajliya

AA: I suppose *khalwa* is a process of emptying out – it can be in very different physical settings. If you are able to filter out as it were the extraneous influences. Prison can be a *khalwa*.

SFH: Yes – no doubt. My understanding of it, which came over time, before and after, is that the crossover of consciousness from personal consciousness, conditioned consciousness, survival consciousness, to the other side of it, where the identity is diminished or negligible and the ego is almost banished – the crossover requires *takhliya* – emptying out. And that's a process that can span over several years. Emptying out – your assumption of your self, your illusion of your image – *takhliya* – empty out. Then *tasfiya* – have a clear mind and pure heart – and then *tahliya* – sweetening. Sweetening comes with the shine and the beam and the delight of the *ruh*, and if there is no *takhliya*, there is no *tasfiya*, then *tahliya* will ruin it. You're putting honey on muck; it won't work. That's why there are so many of the great masters who objected to the teachers constantly trying to make it easier for the people. Don't make it easy – don't put sugar on something that is mucky. Let the muck take over and suffer and be sick, you can't just say never mind, no you're all right, you're a decent fellow, whereas the fellow is a hypocrite and – don't make it easy. It must burst – it must be a dark night of the night.

AA: Dark night of the soul.

SFH: Exactly. So there has to be *tahliya*, after *tasfiya*, after *takhliya*. Then comes *tajliya*. Looking back I think I was at that stage – *tajliya* – not a big deal.

Spectrum of Consciousness

AA: Is there somewhere, Shaykhna, in the model of the self, moving from one state to another, or is it the self in its purity as it were, recognizing the *shahid* and the *qarin* and all of that. What is the *qarin* then – is it part of the self, or is it extraneous?

SFH: I look at the *qarin* as the companion self.

AA: With no reality of its own?

SFH: It has a reality like many of these different layers of consciousness; *qarin* is the part of me that witnesses me more. It is an aspect of *ruhaniyya*, but it is closer to the *nafs* and it allows the *nafs* to act, and if the *nafs* looks at the *qarin*, then it knows that it is hiding, it is camouflaging.

AA: What is generating it?

SFH: It is generated from the *ruh*. You can use the word *nafs* to imply all of it. In order for us to have a slightly better differentiation of this mapping, I say that is a spectrum of consciousness. One end of that spectrum is the *ruh* itself, or the Supreme Consciousness, or the Divine Consciousness, or God Consciousness – call it what you like. That is the same as the *ruh* before it's been encumbered. The other extreme is the first shadow that rises with the baby – the beginning of the identification and separation. You and I and he and she are within that spectrum. We cannot deny the fact that I have a bone and I may have pain, but all that is totally dependent on the original extreme of pure consciousness. The more the so-called 'I' – and this thing 'I' is my self – the more the lower 'I' of me, the survival 'I', the conditioned 'I', the personal 'I', refers to the higher 'I', the more I am in balance. That's all it is. There is nothing more than that.

AA: But, Shaykhna, you studied chemistry and all that – there is something called catalyst. Is the *qarin* and the *shahid* a catalyst?

SFH: They can be, of course.

AA: I mean going back to the *khalwa* side, because in the *khalwa*, you are going to empty out. Empty out of what? There must be something that's going to trigger this process.

SFH: I wrote to Chinmaya after I came out, thanking him, and I said, 'Now what was very obvious to you, and I took on trust, has become obvious to me. That's all I'd like to say.' That which was obvious now became obvious to me – by me disappearing for a while. That's all.

AA: And the soul sees that the self is now prepared and sends out emissaries?

SFH: I can't say that – I don't know. It's only one. You are one, the creator is one; the essence is one; the beginning and the end is one. I don't know. I am not too concerned. I have never been on the overall detailed dynamics and the mechanics. All what I know, and it's clear to describe is that there is a spectrum, and within that spectrum, there are countless levels and layers of forces of patterns of design. I have never been interested in the details of hierarchies, or which is which. I know that within me lies sacred consciousness, divine consciousness, *nur* of Allah. Also within me lies the ultimate shadow of separation of the 'I-ness' of the ego. I see all this is from the Divine. I don't denounce one and announce one – they are inseparable, they are seamless. All of this business of the *nafs* denouncing, I listen to it, but I cannot accept it. If it was not for the ego, how can you realize your *ruh*? So what is what? Which comes first? It's all a matter of our *duniya* and growing up with the arrow of time.

AA: This has come first.

SFH: No – I think actually you are more logical if you put it the reverse – Al-Qur'an tells us: *alladhi Khalaqa al-MAWTA wa al Hayat*[35] – death was first, end was first – then *hayat*. It's like an architect going for a design – you know the use of it – putting the end of it first. So I am not able to give, if you like, a useful description that is going to be a good prescription. It has to be based on taste and *dhawq* and experience.

AA: Going back and listening to the past – a lot of what you're saying now reflects your current condition of the self, and you wrote a book on this – 'The Sufi Cosmology of the Self'[36], where you went into great detail with various elements of the self. So the hierarchy of the mapping of the self, or a form of mapping, that is useful to people who want to follow the teachings, did these things emerge in those days or not?

SFH: I accept what you say. At the stage one is in, one can find beneficial teachings, descriptions, prescriptions – I do not deny that whatsoever, but if at the same time those descriptions and prescriptions do not constantly refer to the ultimate, then they also become demigods – they become the idols. So 'I have this – our *tariqah* has this, and your *tariqah* has this…'!! I accept the need for handholding, I accept the need for all of these things, I don't deny them one bit. If they do not refer to the ultimate negation of *La ilaha-il-Allah* and the affirmation of *Il-Allah*, then, as I said, the danger is that they become a *tariqah* God.

Becoming a Shaykh

AA: And then you became a Shaykh – you were inducted into Shaykhdom by Shaykh Abdalqadir – did any of the other *tariqahs* approach you at that point?

SFH: Not at that point. When I came out, I couldn't give a damn whether anybody was going to call me a Shaykh or not. And also, it took Shaykh Abdalqadir a few months before he came out publicly to announce that I was a Shaykh. I couldn't give a damn; I was not at all interested or impressed with the other *tariqahs* – no, it took years, later on in my journey. In the beginning, I was not interested in *tariqahs*.

---

[35] "[He] who created death and life." (Qur'an 67:2)
[36] See "Cosmology of the Self" by Zahra Publications.

America

AA: I'm sure you're not seeking a title but I'm just asking as matter of record, were you given the title of Shaykh?

SFH: It was in America that the Rifa`is came to visit us a few times, and Shaykh Asif [Durakovic] befriended me – he was one of the six well-known Rifa`i Shaykhs. At that time their most senior one, called Shaykh Jamali, came for a visit from Bosnia – they came to the center in San Antonio.

AA: You became a Shaykh in Tucson?

SFH: No – San Antonio – but he became a Shaykh in Tucson, with Shaykh Abdalqadir, in the Shadhili order.

AA: You then must have assumed a certain structure – you produced the *Wird Al-Haydariyah Ash-Shadhiliyah*.

SFH: Though I was working on the *wird* at that time, it took, may be, 8 years from the end of my time in America to complete it.

San Antonio Center

AA: Tucson was 1983, Shaykhna. Then you left Tucson to find your …

SFH: to find a place. I was attracted to San Antonio.

AA: Why did you want to start it?

SFH: I had nothing else to do. I didn't want to go to the Gulf; I didn't want to do business. I was attracted to sharing, not so much teaching or lecturing.

AA: Why didn't you just go to Los Angeles or Chicago?

SFH: Maybe I should have, I didn't.

AA: You wanted to start something that…

SFH: You know I wanted a place, which was more of a sanctuary; more of a place that serious people could come for two or three months, gain whatever then could gain, and go. It was really providing a haven.

AA: Not for you.

SFH: No. For whoever was seriously interested and I could find some affinity to help them. But not for me.

AA: I had asked you some time ago about this and you said, 'it was all about me.'

SFH: Mmmm! But my tendency, my orientation was not to benefit me.

AA: I don't think benefit – in the sense of having people around.

SFH: There is only me. There's only me in existence; if the 'me' disappears, I don't know anything about existence. From that point of view, it was an aspect of me that had reached a point of fulfillment that could only enjoy by overflowing and connecting and resonating with others.

AA: Were you sort of propelled by this Mecca/Medina paradigm? 'I've been in Mecca, now I'm going to Medina?'

SFH: Not really. There was no such mental construct. I felt, 'Here I am in America. There are a lot of decent people, a lot of people who are inwardly and outwardly impoverished.' Most of the people who came to me were outwardly impoverished, for sure. But also they had a certain inner tendency. So I thought I should provide something for them. You have the means, the ability, so enjoy it. It was that. I didn't follow a model that 'I'm going to be Mecca/Medina.'

AA: But there was a certain structure – it wasn't haphazard. There was community dining and so on.

SFH: Sure, sure. I was aiming to have two or three hundred people who could live there.

AA: The idea was that you would be there permanently?

SFH: No. I never thought like that. I was doing it as though it was on behalf of someone else, and I'd be leaving after setting this up.

AA: Were you encouraged to do that by anyone?

SFH: No, I was not encouraged by anyone.

AA: Who did the designs for you?

SFH: A local architect.

AA: Supervised by you?

SFH: No, paid and supervised by others.

AA: So what were his working instructions, to set up the community?

SFH: No, we had sketches, – I wanted to have a residential area, teaching area – a bit like a *madrasa*. There were three different courtyards. A big one with 30/40 rooms, each could accommodate 3-4 people – lots of bathrooms in between, and another courtyard the other side, and a ladies' courtyard. In total I think we could accommodate 2 or 300 people. And there was a communal kitchen. Two or three other areas of kitchen, offices, and a nice big sized mosque. And the entrance, I had deliberately had them installed very big doors, hardwood, nice doors with ALLAH inscriptions on the top. Next to the doors on the left hand side was a morgue. As you entered the place there was a place to wash the dead bodies. And we had a cemetery. So I did it deliberately – you either enter this door or that door – it's the same. And then I also put a big teardrop on the entrance, before the entrance – a plantation, a circle. I said, 'this is why I dropped a tear in America for also the wasted opportunity here.

Helping human beings to emerge in fullness.' And we had two swimming pools, we had lakes on the land – a fairly sizeable land.

Moving Community/Sanctuary

AA: It seems to me to be a kind of planned community.

SFH: It was an attempt to have a community, but much more of a moving community, rather than 'come and be a resident.' It was a *sanctuary*: I used that word repeatedly at that time.

AA: And you didn't expect people to emigrate or migrate there?

SFH: No, no; I hoped people would not stay more than one or two years, maximum.

AA: It wasn't like the idea of a new town or a village?

SFH: No, no – that was another idea, which we had a lot of architectural drawings for. You remember, it was called Safa City. I felt all of these were idealistic and had a strong sense of nostalgia and romance in them. And I wasn't interested in that. People were asking and I said, 'here it is.' We did it with a fair amount of detail.

AA: But it seems to me also that people who went there were looking to you for guidance and instruction, rather than generate the sinews of a spiritual community by themselves. How do you then square that with the instructions you got from Chinmaya to stay away from building a community?

SFH: I didn't follow it. I fell into the trap in a way. I wasn't building a community *per se*; I was trying to share that model of human being-ness with whoever came. So my ultimate objective was not to create a community as such. It was really to be available to whoever came as companions, friends or students, and move on.

AA: More like a resting place.

SFH: Again, as I said earlier it was more like a sanctuary.

AA: *Mawqif?*

SFH: *Mawqif* – much more of a *mawqif*, much more of a temporary refuge, for somebody to take a breath and be amongst people who are supportive and have free lodging, free food, take what they can and go. We ended up having a lot of ex-prisoners coming, because there was no place for them – thousands and thousands – people would go to prison and embrace Islam.

AA: Nowhere to go.

SFH: Nowhere to go. And then one man who was one of the very senior ex-thugs. This man was an exceptional being and he had organized huge things in prison. So he came out and joined me. We created a haven for them and we called it New Light City. And there were two or three hundred of these prisoners, and we set it up as a Halfway House. So many prisoners would come there for a few months, get what they wanted, and then move on.

AA: And you fed them and housed them?

SFH: Fed them, housed them, everything. Also, we had a big program from the center that was entirely for the prisoners – a correspondence teaching course, and there were at one time about three thousand prisoners on that course. I had about 10 people in the office managing that program. And I visited these prisons a few times. I think it was the biggest prison movement of education at the time. And then we bought that company called, 'Books on Islam.' So we had the largest Islamic bookstore by mail order.

AA: I recall also about this period; you said it was all about the Qur'an. You were immersed in it, taken over by it, dissolved in it. How did that express itself?

SFH: I was asked regularly to give some explanation, or some talks on different *suras* and *ayaat*. Most of it was new to me in a formal sense. For example, there was a serious request by some of the Muslims round San Antonio to do *Surat Ya-Sin*. So I read whatever I could from the existing publishers in those days, and then I let go into whatever came to me, reflecting upon it several nights and then giving discourses on it. So for over three years, almost every day, 2 or 3 hours in the morning, and many be 3 hours in the evening or at night, we did that, covering aspects of most of the Qur'an.

AA: And you were the one doing it?

Guidance from Qalandari Baba

SFH: Yes, I was doing it. And every now and then a few Arabs or Muslims came with their usual critical eyes and things. And then there was a growing number of these *tafaasir* to refer to. Some of the people there were coming to the point where I wasn't sure whether I should talk about the Qur'an, because they were rushing upon me. I wasn't sure whether it was allowed or not; so I wanted a reference, somebody to advise me if it was okay. And then I used to visit Pakistan and India at least two or three times every year. On these visits, somebody in Pakistan said, 'we saw your *doppleganger*,' and it was a man called Qalandari Baba.

AA: I have seen it – we went to his shrine.

SFH: You're right. So I felt that this man could tell me where I should stop. So we went to his grave – he had just been buried there. There was somebody with a charpoy sleeping there, fine looking man. There was a contractor who took to this Qalandari Baba, determined to build a shrine for him – he lived with him the last two or three years. So I asked him, 'Ask Qalandari Baba...' He said, 'every morning he sits on my charpoy, he comes at *fajr*, and we talk.' – I said, 'Ask him tomorrow, to what extent can I share what is coming to me about these expositions and these Qur'anic *ayaat*.' So the next morning we phoned very early, Abbas is the one who phoned. That man said, 'He came to me earlier, and without me asking, he said, "tell that man to be more restricted or he'll get into trouble. Don't say much." ' So I got my answer and, as a result, I put much less in the Qur'an commentaries than what came to me.

AA: We discussed in that period systematic readings of Ibn Arabi or Mulla Sadra.

SFH: Not systematic, never systematic, as and when. Then I had quite a number of people, maybe up to 20 people, reading for me and summarizing, and I hired quite a few people, some full time, some part time, to give me packages to catch up with my own education.

AA: In that sense it was systematic. It wasn't all over the place.

SFH: No, no, it wasn't all over the place, and we bought whatever book we could, in triplicate, quintuplicate – I ended up having maybe five sets of *al-Mizaan* of Tabataba`i, maybe 10 sets of the two volumes of Ibn Arabi's *Tafsir*, whatever it was called.

AA: *Tafsir* of Kashani…

SFH: Yes, absolutely.

AA: You also had the *tafsir* of Mulla Sadra.

SFH: Very much so. Whatever there were of the Qur'an…

Changing Outer Situation

AA: Then when you again framed the outer forms of the *dīn* which were framed, first as I understand it in the Maliki Tradition, then you moved to the Shi`a tradition.

SFH: Not at all, I never had the Maliki – I was never touched by it.

America

AA: I had the impression that after you left Tucson you followed the Maliki *fiqh*.

SFH: No, not with Shaykh Abdalqadir, I never took anything ...absolutely not.

AA: So you followed the Ja`fari *fiqh*.

SFH: Whatever,.... I was born as a Shi`a. I took that as an accident of birth, happy with it and didn't have any need to change anything.

AA: Why do you think people were attracted to you?

SFH: Miserable – misery, and they see somebody is having a good time, and want to experience it too.

AA: I'm sure you were having a good time, Shaykhna, but what about the prisoners and the halfway house?

SFH: I liked them, I enjoyed them and also ...

AA: Were they mainly African Americans?

SFH: Most of them – quite a few ex-Vietnamese soldiers. They caused us a lot of trouble – every morning at *fajr* with their fatigues, 40, 50 of them – they'd go out on a drill – the neighbors would said, 'what is happening here?' So we were sued left and right and center by the neighbors.

AA: It was the other side of America.

SFH: There were endless quarrels, particularly with one neighbor the other side of the lake – we had two lakes on the property – and he was very jealous that we had all this money and so on. So one day they did a survey and took some stones, which could have been on the border between us and them, and he claimed that these were antique walls and sued us for millions of dollars. So there were a lot of quarrels like that.

One day, his wife comes across and says, 'I know my husband is a rascal,' she was a young lady and she says, 'He's constantly trying to shoot people – I've got photographs of him, and I'll give you all of this evidence – I'm leaving him; I want to embrace Islam.' She embraced Islam, stayed with us for a while, then went to Tunis, and became a teacher. So there were quite a lot of such dramas. And between the dramas, suddenly you see Allah's hand.

AA: Then it was all abandoned, as it were.

SFH: Yes.

AA: This seems to be a kind of theme.

SFH: Definitely.

AA: You start, and then there is a halting point and the caravan moves on. Is that it?

SFH: Not the caravan; I moved on – I found it difficult to stay.

AA: When you move on you carry people with you.

SFH: Not really. I never carry people. A few people follow in the wake. It's really much more in the wake. No, I've never had that inclination to have a caravan and people and an entourage – it never was like that.

AA: You don't reflect on all those years?

SFH: I remember them, but I think they served a purpose and the time suddenly comes to move on. You know I remember writing on my table, and as I was leaving the pen I thought, 'this is the last time I am using the pen.' I left like that. It came to me. I could almost see the picture – the pen left there and I am gone. It happens to me regularly. Suddenly, my intuition tells me this is the last time. In England it happened the same. Yusuf, Asiya's husband, who is here now, from England, he remembered distinctly, he said, 'In Luton one day, I was sitting there and told everybody, we've had a wonderful time,' I never thought of it…

AA: Never pre-meditated.

SFH: He suddenly turned round and said, 'you know this is the last time I am seeing you. I just know that's it.'

AA: But once you assumed the attributes of a Shaykh, whether you sought it or not, the obligations that go with it. Did you feel that there were obligations?

SFH: I never did.

AA: And those who follow you were aware that they should have had no expectation?

SFH: No, I think they do have it – they think they own me or control me – I am never obligated. I don't feel obligated. Except to my own self, I am inwardly accountable – I'm not obligated.

AA: What about the courtesies of a Shaykh?

SFH: This is not discourteous. I am more courteous to my *ruh*. I'm not courteous to my self. How can I be courteous to that?

AA: So you don't evaluate it as such.

SFH: It exists, but not for me. It's perfect in its own way. Perfect to enter, perfect to leave.

AA: And others should have moved on.

SFH: Everyone is accountable to themselves, within themselves.

After America

AA: Then what happened Shaykhna? You came back to England?

SFH: I had a house in England.

AA: What about the Pakistan episode?

SFH: Pakistan, India, both – Pakistan, more so as time went on – visiting Pakistan was a regular feature in my life, two or three times a year. I liked the people, the culture, the love for the *dīn*, the Qur'an, so I enjoyed very much being there, visiting them. So out of England, I would visit more often. Then I had a place in London, in Talbot Road, where four days a week I would have a bit of a *majlis*. That's where I learnt a lot about our history, that's why the people like Bahr al-Ulloum[37] were visitors from the East coming for medical training or whatever. I would see them on a very pleasant, if you like, quality basis – there were many of the well-known characters in our culture.

Living in the Sea

AA: I remember that period very well. But at the same time you were travelling quite a lot – you went on a cruise, not cruise but on a ship. I was supposed to join you.

SFH: I bought a boat and stayed more than half the time on it for four years. More than half of my time. Just going from one place to another. At that time I had no passport, so I had to be a seaman. I took a Panamanian seaman's passport, having to pass exams and so on. Very good Panamanian – very useful, and I lived on it.

AA: Were you allowed on shore?

SFH: You're joining a boat as a Panamanian seaman.

---

[37] A known *`alim* from Iraq.

AA: You counted on your Panamanian passport?

SFH: Yes, that's right.

AA: How extraordinary. I thought you had another passport.

SFH: No, not yet. That was a bit later.

AA: So the late 80s, it was between the sea, Pakistan and Talbot road. What were the defining moments of those years, apart from re-learning the history of Islam?

Learning about Human Heritage

SFH: Really learning much more about human heritage, origins, the drift of history, Islam, early Islam, wherever I could. That's why, for example, I had two or three months of tuition on Andalusia – it really saddened me, I was really depressed – I went for a long visit.

AA: Tuition from somebody…

SFH: I had Yakub Zaki; I went to Andalusia for a month visiting all of the sites and relishing how the flourishing of high quality of civilization deteriorates, and also how the *nafs*, the lower self, sets in and more or less the same people rise and fall. You have the Murabitun come in and destroy everything and in 100 years the Muwahhidun come in and destroy the same thing. I began to really see how if humanity didn't lead to the individual taste and experience of divinity, it would never work; there will only be discord. So I was convinced that Allah's work was done – the rest is a matter of time and evolution – a thousand years, ten thousand years, fifty thousand – so I was convinced that there was no way out (*inna Allaha balighu amrihi*[38]). It doesn't matter who it is, or who they are, individually or collectively, they have to accept their humanity, limitations, the air, water, companions, acknowledging the joy of the limitless…it's clear to me. There's no way out – it may take a few

---

[38] "God achieves His purpose." (Qur'an 65:3)

hundred years this way, a few hundred years that way. Every individual must, if they really want to redeem themselves, have to acknowledge, in the outer sense, humanity, limitations and mistakes, but they also have to take that which is theirs, which is the *nur* of Allah. Without Mecca/Medina, as I began to realize that this was really the symbolic meaning of it, you will not be in balance.

Timelessness/Spacelessness

AA: Would you then say that the meaning of time is timelessness?

SFH: Absolutely. Timelessness is the origin of time, the root of time. Infinity is the origin of finality, and limitation. I consider *fitrah,* which is the crack, space and time, to be the prison of Adam. Symbolically, metaphorically, he was in the infinite, non-space, non-time zone of *Jannah* – how can you know what it means unless you go to its opposite, and its opposite is limitation – so we fall into this and we suffocate and become desperate – this is actually the tiny little veil on that which is infinite. Once that veil begins to be less and less, than hard and less depriving you from seeing that light, the more you are hooked by that which is beyond wealth, beyond power, beyond all of the attributes. So your will become only that – to realize the original will. And I think this is easy to get. It doesn't need a great deal of theology or a great deal of years of suffering. I really think it's easy. Provided there is the impetus, the desire for it, and the passion for it.

AA: One of the things that puzzled me initially but later I became more attuned to it, in my encounters with yourself, this curious lack of interest in chronology, days and decades and centuries beyond, really seem to merge when you discuss things – you're not really interested in the sequence of time, of events, which means that obviously you see things from a different perspective. So when you just talked about the history of Andalusia, it is really history of the movement of *al-haraq al-jawariyya*[39] rather than any specific time and place; the whole thing could not hold

---

[39] "The movement of the essence."

together – it was going to collapse anyway. The way that collapse manifested itself, whether it's in a day or a millennium, is in some ways immaterial. Would you agree?

SFH: I do. There is a couplet from I think Shaykh Muhammad ibn al-Habib – '*Innama al-kawnu ma`aanin qaa'imatun bi s-suwar*'[40] – it has been one of the driving things in my life. *Inna ma al-Kaunu ma`anin*[41] – they're all meanings appearing as forms. I don't deny the form.

AA: But this is really, I think, the two most significant ways of reconstructing the mind, which doesn't understand that the sacred is time and space. Time is much more than that and is difficult to reconstruct.

SFH: True.

AA: The sacred, time and space. So modern man is really the slave of time. Do you agree that it is essential to reconstruct the meaning of time, through timelessness?

SFH: I do. Unless you face timelessness, you are a prisoner of Chronos.[42] Timelessness is stopping the mind. First, stop identity – *takhlia, tasfia, tahlia* you know it is really timeless – your origin, your essence, your *ruh* is timeless. So then you realize that the only thing you are being gifted, the only asset you have, is time, which is timeless. A few hundred years here and there – what difference does it make?

AA: What about '*naseebaka mina addunya*'[43]?

SFH: You do that – I've done that –

AA: I'm not thinking about it specifically, but generally.

---

[40] "Truly created beings are meanings set up in images." ("Withdrawal Into the Perception of the Essence" – *Path to Light* – Zahra Publications)
[41] "Meanings set up in images."
[42] Chronos is the personification of Time in pre-Socratic philosophy and later literature.
[43] "Your share of this world." (Qur'an 28:77)

SFH: Everybody has to do it.

AA: How do you deal with the illusory arrow of time?

SFH: Everybody has to be honest and real with it. Otherwise, they'll be disappointed, they'll be blaming. To give you an example. A man who is earlier on in my quest – he is still quite significant in America. Earlier on, he was influenced by Shaykh Abdalqadir, and I saw him here on a visit a few years ago. He came here and said, 'Oh you too like me, were hit badly, bitten by Shaykh Abdalqadir.' I said, 'No I wasn't. I benefitted a lot from him.' This fellow, he took it as though Shaykh Abdalqadir betrayed him. I said, 'No, I enjoyed him, I benefitted from him by being with him.' Everybody believes whatever they read. He said, 'No, but he denounced you – he denounced the Shi`as.' I said, 'but I benefitted a lot, I am grateful to him.' So *'naseebaka mina addunya'* – you must at the same time .... otherwise, you will sit back and lament. Why haven't you done it? Do it, suffer from it and then you have to live the moment. Otherwise, going back and forth in time is horrible. Biographical re-evaluation and blame and claim. I've been fortunate not to do much.

AA: It's clear from our discussion so far that you are not really bound by the imperative of chronological order, apart from some ways that are irrefutable, like biological time.

SFH: No, I accept it; it exists but its existence is almost like a passing cloud on a permanent sky. I don't deny it. I have been very much caught by time – there's a date to attend, plane to catch – and I know that. But I am less and less, if you like, caught into its finality or formality. And that's why I leave it to others who are more competent than me – when they arrange something, I say to them, 'you take me, arrange it and I'll come.' You know time moves on and one's own inner tuning moves on. I'm far more in a way attuned to the timeless space-less zone. I am in that *barzakh*, and I enjoy it. So I can't see why, if I don't have to for any reason, be sent back to the fixation of this exact second, this calibrated entity – so I don't deny that time exists, I don't deny that most people have to do it – I wish them good luck – it's their life.

AA: But as a teaching Shaykh, you obviously want people to be near or at your state; otherwise why impart this knowledge?

SFH: Well, I have never liked to be called a Shaykh from day one; I tried many a time to renounce it. And also even teaching, it is sharing; and the other thing is that I know it is not by acquiring other's teachings, it is by giving up what they thought is their crutch. It has been a useful crutch, but you move towards something more, then you have to throw it. So it's by giving up that you will know what is up, not by constantly acquisitive – 'I like to be like you.' There is no 'you'. No 'me', there is only *nur* of Allah. It's in every heart. So I don't feel in that sense that obligated to anyone in these things. I am quite happy at any time to be denounced as a teacher, a Shaykh, a failure – wonderful!

AA: But the question is somewhat different, Shaykhna. It is to do with how you impart rather than how do others view the quality or effectiveness of your imparting.

SFH: As I have just shared – get rid of your mind; get rid of your identity; stop time; totally utterly stop your mind ticking. Use whatever techniques you want. Breathing, standing on your head, parachuting, inner technology – whatever. Stop your identity. Stop the illusion that you are this separate thing. And you have a birth and a death. You do have that, but it's so insignificant. And the other thing is, be able to stop time regularly, entering the zone of *sajdah*. That's really all that I can teach. Lose your identity, stop your mind, stop time. Everything else is fine. That which is within space and time is easy. Not a problem. You are being trained all the time; you have your *fitrah*, you know you can deal with it; you can move your hand. I think it's easy. I really feel immense affinity, empathy, sympathy, love, affection, passion for Muhammad's way. And I think Muhammad's way was somehow made by us lesser creatures into this religion, let alone the *dīn*. And more and more it became a ritual without any meaning, without any use. It won't last. And the essence of it was that: 'Your sickness is generally by you; your healing will come from you by stopping the sickness.'[44] ... 'you

---

[44] A famous quote from Imam Ali.

think you are a tiny little stupid microcosm, and within you is formed the entire universe.' I really believe that. I know it.

AA: I think all the great spiritual traditions share that.

SFH: Correct.

AA: Microcosm and macrocosm.

SFH: Absolutely.

AA: Ultimately, it's to do with the treatment of time.

SFH: Absolutely. Now you mentioned something that is very brilliant: the most difficult thing is the time issue. Space and time are inseparable – space/time. Space, we have almost managed to kill through instant connection. That's Connection. The next one is Continuation. Connection is easy. Continuation is difficult, timelessness or the infinite. Now I think the next bout in the world will be ways and means to stop time. I wouldn't be surprised if there'd be biofeedback techniques where people could plug in some electrodes easily, and for five minutes, completely stop the illusion of time, and get replenished. But the patenting or legal aspects of that may be a hindrance, because it may affect neurons, or people who are on medications, especially psychiatric medications, but I think the next thing will be Communication, and we will have more or less stopped space by communication via phones and satellites. We have not made any attempt to stop time. And we need help; we need some outside help – some electrodes. You go there, put electrodes for two minutes, and you are completely neutralized, re-energized, and you come back and face the mayhem that is waiting for you in the day-to-day rubbish.

AA: The inevitability of space doesn't affect one's material existence. The fact that the universe is a gillion miles wide, but time does threaten the illusion of space.

SFH: Correct.

AA: So the whole thing is about time. Would you say that ultimately it is that?

SFH: Yes. Time is the biggest issue because it's immortality. It's ongoing forever-ness. And also, as we know, there have been, over the last twenty, thirty, forty years, a quite a lot of information coming out on this, whether it is the issue of life after death, or all of these other phenomena and numerous ways to describe them, for example, out of body experiences, makes you see the continuation of life in front of this existence. In fact, I think if we do not have this notion of infinite time, our civilization will collapse. You have these two possibilities: one of which is that there will be no fertility, no future offspring, end of the whole thing, or a big catastrophic thing that will end life. Most of our activities will cease. You know, you won't move, you won't make clothes, you won't develop – so we're implicitly assuming timelessness. Our life is based on that – we are concerned about what the future generations will say, what will history say. We are hooked to that.

AA: If you look at Ibn Arabi's writings and *tarteeb* on the names of Allah, then the name *Al-Qayyum* ranks higher than *Al-Wasi`*. Do you agree with that?

SFH: I do. *Al-Qayyum* precedes that.

Siyaha/Breaking Habits

AA: Space, I think was an issue before, there were spaces that were not yet encountered – continents, oceans, poles and so on. Coming from time to space, we come to the realm of *Siyaha* – if you will allow me, I'd say that the decades of the eighties was the decades of Shaykh Fadhlalla, the years of *siyaha fil ardh*.

SFH: You see, you have to change the immediate environment in order for you to have a fresh look at the whole thing and re-evaluate it. *Siyaha* is that – you move into other cultures, other realms, so you take away the refuge of comfort and ease. It's important to have comfort and ease. The success of the international hotels 40 or 50 years ago was due to that – you want a comfort zone, stay in good health, and yet you want to poke your head out and go to the local strange bazaar or whatever. We are like that. We seek safety, security and exploration – it's a drive. One of the biggest drives in us is to explore, to discover, you can't stop it. And that's where the intelligence gets, if you like, more and more focused. So *siyaha* is that – getting out of habits. Habits are the killers. The ultimate habit is striving for constancy. I again found two things in the world, in our lives. You need constancy, but constancy is the *ruh*. Once you begin to know there is constancy in you, then you relish change – anything changes, fine. The entire uncertainty – everything is based on uncertainty. I want certainty. But I'm looking in the wrong place for the right thing. I'm looking for certainty in a zone that by nature is uncertain, unreliable – the *duniya*. But I want certainty. Certainty is my *ruh*. So ride on your *ruh's dīn* and go to the zone of uncertainty – that's fine.

I was often surprised and pleased to see people wanted to put themselves through experiences, for example, extreme sport, on the edge. Erton Senna, the racing driver, was asked, 'what is it that happens to you in this peak experience of your driving beyond the limits?' He said, 'I feel I'm sitting in the lap of God.' Where the inner certainty of the light of the *ruh* almost governs. So we are all like that. Why does a person like to be next to a huge mountain? So that he feels small. Why do we like to feel small? Everybody wants to be ego and big? Because you know intrinsically that the lesser the ego the greater is the greatness. You want majesty, facing a huge wave or being exposed to danger – you want to be small because the ego is not even small, it in fact doesn't exist. It's a lie. It's just a little shadow, not even Plato's cave. If I am seven years old, I say, 'this is me,' and I say the same when I am twenty years old. But by the time I am 40 and I don't begin to crack my ego, it may be too late. Without denying the shadow – this is my ego now. One of the first descriptions I heard, which again later on I found it's with us, like Ali and Muhammad, is that their inner state is exactly the same when they are denounced and when they are praised; there was hardly any ego left. You appreciate that this fellow is admiring you, and the other is denouncing you. You know what is what, but it doesn't affect your heart. Your *ruh* is paramount – there is no shadow on it. Both of you are right, both of you are wrong. Sometimes I am wrong…

AA: So Shaykhna, as one goes into the reduction of the significance of time, ... *siyaha*, unpacks space, which means unpacks culture, civilization and people, and therefore shows their ephemerality.

SFH: *Jum`a, Jama`* – gatheredness, oneness, the original, impossible to fathom, compactness, the original *kun*, the dot of the *bismillah*. Also look at the *ayah*[45]. After *Salaat al-Jum`a*... spread out, go to work. Another thing I found was most of the spiritual paths is about breaking of habits – most of them. Don't stay in the same place. I have tried most of my life never to sleep in the same bed more than three weeks maximum. It happened sometimes that I did it more than that but it was usually for three weeks: move, sleep somewhere else, so as you are a bit more jolted, and realize that everything is temporary. You are an exile in your body, and an exile on this earth.

Looking for a Base

AA: Shaykhna, when you were in the UK in the early 90s you were in a general state of discontent with being in Europe – am I right?

SFH: I was never content with being in the West, nor did I ever think that I'd be very content in the East or in Iraq or the Middle East, which was undergoing major turmoil, which I was aware of. I had a few periods in the East, as well as in the West, which were very, very pleasant. In the East, I remember in the Gulf, I had some wonderful periods for a few months at a time. In Iraq also earlier on I had wonderful periods. In America I had a wonderful time, travelling a lot. Whilst based in Texas, I travelled all over central America, South America, looking for a base again, looking for a home, like most of us go through. Displaced people are always looking for a new base that encompasses whatever in their perception was the best of their days and what gives them more at that

---

[45] "Then when the prayer has ended, disperse in the land and seek out God's bounty." (Qur'an 62:10)

time in their lives. So I travelled a lot whilst based in America, all over Brazil, Argentine, Central America. I liked Costa Rica. I set up a base there for two years. A lot of people embraced Islam. I didn't know how to back it up. I had two American Muslims based in Costa Rica, doing *da'wa* so to speak and we had many people embracing the *dīn* – but I could not find teachers. I remember some years before then asking Seyyed Mehdi Hakim, saying I wanted teachers. He said, 'I can't send you any; you won't accept any of them.' I said, 'you're right.' He came and stayed with us for a long period, once I think, for two months in one go. At *Bayt ud-dīn* he had the best of times.

AA: He participated in the activities?

SFH: He was teaching day and night, every day. People loved him. And he knew I wouldn't accept anybody unless they were really themselves illuminated. And for a shorter period of time, his brother-in-law, Dr. Khalif Tabataba'i, came for about a month or so and also taught very well. In any case, I had to abandon Costa Rica. In England I found the place, the people, the country, the politics as good as you could ever get it in a worldly sense, but I knew it wasn't for me. I thought: 'I can't stay; I'm not happy here.' It was very good for the children for schooling, but I was waiting to get out. And I thought maybe if I made a base in Pakistan it would work. I bought land there, in fact way before that I went to Sri Lanka and bought a most beautiful piece of land on the beach, 20 minutes north of Colombo. I had about a kilometer on the beachfront with coconut trees, and I designed a center, a home for myself, teaching place etc., and there were a lot of floods and minor tsunami, so quite a bit of the front went down into the sea. I took that as a sign not to do it. Soon after that the civil war began. Also, Aladdin Gilani[46] advised me not to do it. He said, 'this is dangerous. You won't last there.'

---

[46] Iraq-born Qadiri shaykh based in Pakistan.

It's All About Oneness

South Africa

So I wanted to get out. I said Pakistan would be a good place, and we built a place there in Malir. Abbas Bilgrami's father, a year and a half down the line, came to Britain. He said, 'you won't survive. There's a lot of kidnapping there and you will be embroiled in day-to-day survival. So I advise you not to come.' So I didn't go to Pakistan. And then, in 1992, I took my first trip to South Africa. I came with Hosam and Ali Bilgrami, maybe also Muneera and one or two others. We toured the country for three weeks or a month, and it was quite clear to us that Mandela would be released and things would change, and I thought this would be a country that was undergoing change, that they would tolerate anybody who really had no political or business agenda. From there on I knew I just wanted a base to settle in. I didn't want to be involved in any activity – I wasn't going to teach or preach or anything. So within two years from then, in 1994, it was quite clear to me that South Africa suited me. The few of the children remaining could do school and university there. My mother could have something; and the weather was good for me. So I wanted out of Britain. I really had been trying to get out; I never thought I'd stay long in Britain, although it had all the amenities. I'd gone past the interest in social connection, contact and had realized that it had served its purpose.

AA: You left a lot of people who were missing your presence.

SFH: I think so. I felt that would come. The place I would have loved to stay would have been Spain actually – would have been Majorca where I had a beautiful home – but it was not suitable from any other point of view; suitable for me, but not for the family, the children, language difficulty. I had to abandon that idea. I felt all along that I had touched hearts and many hearts touched me and there would be people, as you say, missing me, and so on, but I had never in my life really felt obligated to, if you like, human sentiments. I was always concerned about the spiritual side, and I always responded to these people when the call was spiritual, to do with *haqq* and light. But whenever it was personal, emotional, family-based, there was often very little I could do. By the early 1990s I was in a position that in my own heart, I could really not respond to human dramas or crisis. I found them all to do with, again, mind, identity and the illusion of time. I knew I was no longer able to address it. So soon after that I ended up knowing that people would not refer to me any more on their personal difficulties, family quarrels, husband/wife disagreements. It was really from my own heart that I would tell them, 'well separate – get rid of him, or whatever…' and they knew that I wasn't really going to listen to all their miseries and commiserate, to gossip. So on the human level, I felt there were people who would likely have continuity.

AA: I was one of them.

SFH: I never felt otherwise – I really felt you were so contained, content and moving on your own wonderful trajectory.

AA: You left a void and affected a great number of people, especially the Luton crowd; they felt to some extent not disconnected, but marooned.

SFH: One other thing I share with you. This has happened several times in my life. But I also felt that I had fulfilled my obligations in every way. For example in the Luton case, I remember telling people in London – in the early days of Luton, 'all of you, if you really want to have a bit of a semblance of community, all of you, move to Luton.' Property at that time was a third of what it was in London, and only a few of them moved to Luton. It wasn't until ten years later, that some of them finally wanted to move to Luton, but it was too late. They didn't listen to me ten years earlier when it was the right time. So I never felt in any way that I had not fulfilled my obligation. I often have this premonition and I also have a reason for it. In the case of Luton, it was very clear – there were two or three indicators. Even if you are working in London, Luton is accessible – property price, other prices – but they didn't move. So I don't feel obligated – even here.

The same thing here, with this center.[47] I told them, 'you must transcribe all of the talks that have happened – you have the entire *dīn* packaged for you here and it is not sectarian – you remain Hanafi and all of that.' And it's too slow. So I never feel in any way that I have not fulfilled my obligations as such. And those who actually moved and did things – always a few; and it's always been a very, very small percentage – I remain very strongly connected with them. But the rest of the people, you can't lift them up. *'wama anta `alayhim biwakeel.'*[48] This has happened with me several times in my life. It started with the things I have already shared with you. I told Zainab – when she was in Kirkuk and I was in Baghdad – to leave. I said to her, 'If you don't come within a week I'm leaving,' I apologized, and then I was gone. So I had to follow my heart and my heart really, my inner heart, my *fu'ad* – the heart can be really sick – there are 9 different sicknesses to the heart, as in the Qur'an – but not the *fu'ad* – there are 4 *ayaat* on the *fu'ad* – it's clear. The inner core is never wrong – it's correct because it's *haqq*. I know there have often been people who would have liked it slightly differently and so on. But there are a lot of social, cultural, religious practices, in a way, and it's understandable – we all want the familiar.

So I came here, looked around. I liked the Cape area very much and I put it in my heart that I wouldn't move unless there were three signs. The first sign was Aladdin Gilani – he told me, 'go as far as you can;' the second sign I thought I would go to one of the *walis* of Cape Town. During my first trip I was visiting somebody who was with me at work in England, who would be now spending half his time in winter in Cape Town – there were quite a few people, about a quarter of a million. He invited me to his house in Constantia for supper and, as he was driving towards the house, he said, 'you know it crossed me one of the three most visited Sufi masters, and maybe you'd like to go there – the house is right across – come back with us. So I went there in a very serene shrine – his name was Shaykh Mahmoud, so I opened the creaking door – it was beginning to be dark. I discerned there were a few people sitting, in a little *mastaba* with the shrine in the middle, so I sat next to them

---

[47] Rasooli Center, Pretoria, South Africa.
[48] "…And you have not been appointed as their overseer." (Qur'an 6:107)

quietly and did my *dhikr*, I went into *muraqaba*, trying to connect with the soul of the deceased. And after about ten minutes I heard the man sitting next to me in a voice – I noticed he was under a cover – he lifted it, turned to me and said, 'If you come to South Africa, you will have the best of times, people will respect you, love you, your life will be in every way comfortable, happy. Come!' And he went back under cover. So after a while, I left and waited for them outside, and he came out apologizing and said, 'I come every week to this shrine with my daughter, who is not well. My son is a doctor, but she only gets a bit of peace and tranquility when we come for this visit.' And he said, 'I never give in to this sort of thing. I don't know what I said to you, and why did I say it.' I didn't say anything. So I took that as a clear sign. He even invited me to his house; a very prominent Cape Malay man, very respectable, connected with these Sufis.

And the third sign was the finding of Highwood. I made some conditions. I said, 'If it doesn't come my way with ease, I won't look at it,' and it did. So that is how it happened. It took about a year and a few months to adjust the place to my needs and build on it, and the move happened. It was a bit difficult uprooting everyone, the whole family, to an entirely new environment. And I didn't know anyone.

AA: I came with you on the second visit. We saw an estate up there, not Highwood, but elsewhere. Shaykhna, I remember also, you were saying that there were other factors, one of them was in your days as a Panamanian sailor, you sailed up and down East African coast and felt some affinity with (SFH: strong affinity) Africa, and the other thing is when you saw the Rift Valley, where it cracks open, where original man, homo sapiens emerged from there. And the third factor I thought Shaykh Abdalqadir suggested that you went to South Africa.

SFH: He did call me when he first came to South Africa, which was 5, 6 years before I did – he called me from here several times during the early months after he came here. He tried to induce me to come but it wasn't the right time. So he was by then very well established in South Africa, but by then our relationship was hardly any. He did plant the seeds. There were a few other indicators. There was one man who was from a very prominent Zulu family, a chief, he was visiting America, part of a South African dancing group called Ipitombi, with lots of drums, and he was the chief drummer, very good. So out of the blue this head of Ipitombi phones me in San Antonio. He says, 'I've read your books. I want to come with my wife. I am a chief drummer in this band.' I said, 'come.' He came and stayed with me for years. He embraced Islam, and his wife became one of the ladies who looked after the children – her name was Yasira – she was also a Swazi princess. She couldn't bear children, and they bore children, three of them, born in America, healthy and they are here. They are connected with me. So that was a very strong South African link without me even knowing what South Africa was. So there were a few such signs.

AA: What about Africa – the primal origin – or was that just a passing matter?

SFH: Yes – I was curious about the spread of Homo sapiens from a historical anthropological point of view. So I began to find out more and more that really this area was the earliest of that cracking of, if you like, that physical, literal, biological, physiological, openings, and I just took it as part of the earth's Gaia, that sort of thing. As it happened, what is considered geologically the beginning of the Rift Valley is just two three kilometers from Highwood. There is a mountain there and this is the beginning of it, and it's still used by local sangomas[49] every year for a celebration. And I think that's the beginning of the whole crack and it possibly ends up somewhere near Jerusalem or thereabouts, beyond the Red Sea. So these are points of interest and curiosity.

AA: But they were not a driving force for you to have moved to South Africa?

SFH: No, not at all. No I would have liked to have more signs. We always want to read the unseen and translate it to the seen. But a lot of it was for practical reasons, such as schooling, universities, a bit of healthcare for my mother when she needed it. Not too far from these

---

[49] African shamans.

facilities. And I also wanted to be near nature; I felt I ought to be not too far from wilderness and wild animals, so I also bought a bush house almost right in the middle of Kruger. Earlier on I would be there once every two weeks for two or three days, and the animals were all next to the window. It was not protected. As time went by less and less people of my own family were interested to come. The last two three years, it's hardly used, so I gave it up. I sold it. So there was a call of wilderness and it always reminded me of something very primal within me. And also, by observing some of the animal behavior, I realized that I, as a human being, as a *ruh*, contained all the other *arwah*. So these were very interesting observations for me, on the line of meditation and submission.

Rasooli Center/The Four Journeys

AA: It was like an enabling environment...

SFH: Immensely enabling environment. And then it was really by chance that I think, a year or so after I had been there, a few of these people here, especially the Ravats, met me. There was a link with Majida Ravat – on my second or the third trip here, some people came to know me, and I was not happy where I was staying, so they asked her if she could find a suitable hotel or accommodation for me. So there was a link with them. A year or two after I was in Highwood, they wanted me to come and give them a bit of a talk on the *dīn*, because they confessed they hadn't got a clue. So I came to the gathering and sat in the middle of carpet and had a bit of fun, a few more visits followed. It took three or four years before Ibrahim and others decided (there were 5 or 6 of them at that time) – to build a mosque. I told them, fine but provided I made for them a charter as *adaab* for the mosque to hang there. No sectarian accusation etc. Then slowly by slowly the other buildings were constructed, and the ASK (Academy of Self Knowledge) program came about 12 years ago. So it began to develop, and I began to have an affinity with these people. I felt that I was at ease with them. I didn't have a lot in common, neither culturally nor dietary, but I found ease with them and they were well meaning and tolerant – so it began to move more and more, and somehow within my own heart I thought, 'let them have a bit of exposure internationally – let's have an annual gathering with different themes.' And from early on I thought there'd be fourteen of these gatherings, and every year we had a theme and everybody enjoyed it, and a lot of goodness came out of those.

This year is the 15th, even though I've said, 'no more; I'm not going to have any more gatherings,' but they are still having them, and I'll participate. But after 14 years I'm not going to be in charge. I want to do more of my own writing. I also felt deeply that my own writing would come on the line of Niffari[50] – as I mentioned it to you some years ago – it will be wonderful if we have a few weeks together, so I will redo a Niffari. And that's how it began about two three years ago, in the form of short stories, different vignettes, and poetry. A lot of poetry began to come out. They've recently been put on a map of the four journeys. Some of the poetry is running away from creation, and wanting to escape duality, drudgery. Others are just expressing the absolute: so that's the second. And the third one is coming out from the absolute, saying, 'how are you, how people are missing their life.' And the fourth journey is with your hands in the muck, like most great beings, great Prophets, that all of them go through, who try to do whatever they can with humanity but their heart is also at all times connected with the unseen.

AA: Do you think you went through the arc of these four journeys or is it just a schema?

SFH: No, I'm sure I have.

AA: In this sequence or some other sequence?

SFH: Not with a very clear cut-off boundary – they overlap, and if you look at it in a macro sense over the last forty years of my life, no doubt about it. But there has been a lot of overlap. In other words, for example, the third journey, which is coming towards creation, I have experienced

---

[50] Muhammad ibn `Abd al-Jabbar ibn al-Hasan al-Niffari, an enigmatic figure and mystic of 9th-10th century Iraq (d. 965 AD).

and tasted it much earlier also. So there is not just an overlap, there are also flashbacks between them. It isn't very clearly delineated.

AA: It's not a state that's maintained, and then discarded and move to the next one?

SFH: No. Except for the fourth. I think the fourth journey is much clearer – you can't do it unless you have been through all of the others. Especially if you are truly involved deeply with the human drama. Unless you have been through all of the others, it can overwhelm you.

Viewing Creation Through the Eye of The Truth

AA: But Shaykhna, looking at this schema of the four journeys, the last journey, which is with creation, but with your head in the skies as it were and your feet on the ground, from Allah with creation, requires also dealing with creation, interacting on their terms, on the terms of creation, within the framework in which human beings have ordered their societies and relationships. So you take that as basically a fixed point, and you deal with it with the eye of the Truth. So you see the creation from the eye of the Truth. What does that imply in terms of the extent to which you have to modify your actions to fit within the scheme? When you say that you are now with creation, but seeing it from the eyes of the Creator, it requires that you have to deal with creation on its terms. Is that correct?

SFH: Yes and No.

AA: In the sense that you have to deal with society, family, government, politics –

SFH: Yes and No – it depends again on personal situation. In my case, I am not one of these people here – I don't belong to them. This is not a Quraysh, not an Arab – neither will they accept me as one of them in roots, nor can I. I am also not one of them in terms of my age and my state. So whereas, totally being involved and one of them and yet holding onto the rope of *haqq*, was much more for me in America in the center there. On and off, with several hundred people and their families. At that time with my energy and my youth, I think it was quite clearly there. There was quite a bit of the fourth journey.

AA: So you had already gone by the fourth journey? Or just re-visiting it?

SFH: No doubt about it. Re-visiting it with new lenses of prescriptions, descriptions and remedies.

AA: One of the reasons why I picked up this book of yours – one of your minor works, in Foyles in 1980, I think it was, that's what popped out. The man who's speaking is the man who's on the fourth leg of the journey. So 20 years before you came here, you were there. But what I would be interested in – it's a kind of engaged indifference – let's call it that – the correct expression.

SFH: Brilliant!

AA: It's engaged indifference – it also requires that you have to deal with what you're engaged with your best capability, and give it your best shot. You may not be very good at it, but keep this balance. Don't you find it incredibly difficult to maintain this balance? It has to be a conscious decision not to be magnified back to one.

SFH: I've been fortunate since I came to South Africa that the issue of being energized by the One, immersed into the Oneness, has been the most consistent, most persistent referencing, touchstone and calibration for me. The only thing I can say is that occasionally if I did get involved a bit more with the humanity side, with the *nafsi* battles, and so on, I suddenly had to stop, withdraw a bit, to preserve my energy, my inner state. So I have not in any way been affected or afflicted. I know there is an inner mechanism that will kick in and I immediately say, excuse me for an hour. So I've never been able to pre-plan it or pre-judge it – I have really been at all times on autopilot on these issues.

AA: Would you say that the commanding feature is the stance of compassion – this engaged indifference is a reflection of *Ar-Rahim*?

SFH: I would say it's from both *Rahman* and *Rahim*. In a way it is indifferent in the sense that it doesn't touch my heart. It is caring without being overly concerned. There is a care there.

Seeing no Otherness/Engaging with the World

AA: The care that comes from compassion.

SFH: The care of seeing the sameness – there is no otherness. I see the sameness, but there is a limit. And some people need to have months or years to go through the same thing over and over again out of that groove. There have been cases here where people have expectations from their families, and this and that, and they can't get out of that attachment. And I feel myself repeating that issue – my mental construct – 'who do you think you are' – 'how much your brother has to support you' – it is your own expectation and you suffer from it. And I know that they need a longer time. One example here I give you: Yunus – he had a brother who is ten years older than him, nice man, decent man, but in terms of religion and spirituality, dead end. Just superficiality, structure, using head instead of heart, mosques, and all of that, with money, but no sensitivity. Yunus was trying and trying. My advice to him was, 'you can't help him; just be available to him.' He went through a period of two or three years of being very angry with the brother, almost enmity. And then, for his own sake, he had to make it up with his brother. I knew there was time needed, so they made it up, he yielded and now the brother is beginning to listen. It took probably the best part of twelve years. I've been through quite a number of such experiences.

AA: Indifference comes, not from not caring, but rather it comes from knowing that whatever outcomes are, they are superseded by a much greater reality.

SFH: Absolutely.

AA: But you still engage with it in order that the others see your involvement with them in their own frame.

SFH: Also, still being in this world, so I have to still act in this world. I do know that none of these things that we think are important, are of any importance. I know it. It's not a question of believing it.

AA: But I don't understand why anybody would come back.

SFH: It's not back. It's not back and forth. So long as I mentioned that spectrum – supreme consciousness and personal, individual and conditioned consciousness are still there. Which means that my *ruh*, which is supreme consciousness, is still in this body, which is personal consciousness of life, and therefore survival. So as long as that is there, I have no option other than addressing that a bit: there is still a bit of a *nafs* and ego. It can never die until literally physically I leave. So I accept that. This is what I understand by *'la tansa naseebaka mina ad-dunya.'*[51] I don't deny it. So I take a little bit of it. I enjoy my visits and company or walking and so on.

AA: But you don't take pleasure in the outcome. You said that if somebody gave you a million dollars, you would not take it.

SFH: I won't take – it's not pleasure, but it is pleasant. It's all right. It is not also dreadful; that is, it is not displeasure. It's as good as it can come, so long as I am in this body. There is no thrill in it. The only thrill I have, which repeats many times during a day, is again seeing how the seen and the unseen connect. We left today without looking at our watch, without checking when Hisham is coming – I don't know what time it was. We drifted to Rommana[52] for our lunch. And there was this thought in my sub-consciousness: 'I hope he'll arrive before we eat.' As we sat I saw him. These are the things of how the Governor governs it all, to His perfection. I just have to witness it, see it. And even they may be minor issues like this one, they repeat – these are the thrills.

---

[51] "Do not ignore your portion of this world." (Qur'an 28:77)
[52] Café at the Rasooli Center.

AA: The constant discovery of the constant manifestation.

SFH: Brilliant! Absolutely! *Hadhrat ar-Rabbaani*.

AA: And the *nafs* is only when there are breaks in this continuity.

SFH: I am very fortunate in that sense that I have been for years now, suddenly alert when the *nafs* is coming – it's there – every now and then suddenly one of the animals may put its head out of the zoo. It's awareness, and that awareness itself makes it go back again, because I don't want to suffer. I want to taste, experience, touch that magnificent offer. That is now, if you like, my habit, my norm.

AA: Habit in the sense of the 'garment.'

SFH: Absolutely, the garment that I'm wearing.

AA: The habit of the monk?

SFH: Exactly. This is what I enjoy. There are always those thrills but it's not due to my having a very, very special baklava; I enjoy it, and I think it's wonderful baklava, better than others, but that's about it.

AA: It doesn't go seeking the perfect baklava.

SFH: Nor do I – the pleasures, so to speak, which often are balanced by displeasures, are hardly there any more. It is the joy of witnessing, the occasional joy of being able to help someone, warn someone, and when it opens up, and many other subtler ones – someone I thought completely crazy and completely away, suddenly, they come back and – these occur quite regularly amongst people... So there are constant reminders of the arc of ascent for every human being.

AA: You see them at various points on the spiral…

Connecting with the Higher Consciousness

SFH: Various points – I also see it in animals; there's a rabbit that always comes here, I call him Abdullah – incredible.

AA: The animal has really no choice.

SFH: Right. But I can see how they respond to energies, how they want to have proximity to the higher consciousness – their limited consciousness is attracted to higher consciousness; as it is in domestic animals – cats and dogs, especially horses. So I see this all the time. It's what really makes my life rich.

AA: Signs?

SFH: Constantly – signs upon signs – my heart smiles when I see these signs.

AA: ......so it's not thunder and lightening – the blossoming of the almond tree.

SFH: ... Exactly-

AA: Do you actually get consumed by it Shaykhna?

SFH: No.

AA: Then you see manifestation and just take it the way it is – this is it?

SFH: Not only this is it: this is the only thing that is IT.

AA: How do you not become consumed?

SFH: I think I have been consumed in it for over so many years that I take it in my stride that this is life. I've also felt it in my life, seeing other people. But really there are two stages of life: One is personal, same thing as consciousness, survival consciousness, identity-based consciousness, and once you cross over to the other zone of pure consciousness, then you don't lose the early consciousness, but it doesn't cause you any of the usual past distractions and dramas any more. So I am burnt out and already fully consumed by that which has it all, does it all and knows it all. So there are no more surprises so to speak regarding this lower consciousness, earthly life, without denying it.

AA: A constant low intensity involvement?

SFH: It is true.

AA: But to calibrate the intensity requires time and experience.

SFH: Without a doubt. Earlier on, I'm sure I would have been screaming with joy about this and shouting *Allahu Akbar!*, but not any more. All of it is Allah *akbar*; the truth is Allah is *akbar*. Allah is greater than we can ever imagine, and we connect with Him. So it is all Allah. I can also gauge into people's *haal* and *maqaam* by what I see, hear and sense. After meeting a person, I can tell the inner reality of that person.

AA: Do you see their inner state and station?

SFH: To a certain extent.

AA: I don't meaning in the clairvoyant way –

SFH: No, I see that some people are more illumined. To me illumination is an expression of the state of clutter within the heart. My cosmology is very simple. The *ruh*, which is *rabbani* and is the holographic representation of the absolute, resides in the metaphoric heart, and the metaphoric heart is that which connects that light with all of the other factors, including of course what we call *nafs*, the shadow, or the self. And of course that energy also goes to the body and the organs, and the interlink fully is called mind, the center of the inner senses, outer senses, memory. So I have this very simple model. Somebody's face and so on to me is the sign that the heart is not too tarnished, not full of pus and darkness. So that whatever you call *ruhani* for me represents the extent of the mind, the ego, the body, and the organs are energized by the *nur* of the *ruh*.

Virtues and Vices/Outer and Inner Dimensions

AA: But you don't see the virtues and vices of people being an indication?

SFH: No, also I see that it can be changeable. A vice can be the best key to a virtue and I see a virtue can fall into the worst possible vice. I see all these dualities as linked, interlinked, and for a child I would encourage them to have a virtue. But for a mature person I try to show them that they are totally interlinked; don't ever ascribe a virtue to yourself: it can be worse even, and I find that very obnoxious. Religious superiority, spiritual superiority, rank pulling – I find that really despicable.

AA: We talked about virtues. Are there any vices that are incorrigible? Take envy, for example, what sort of good can come out of it?

SFH: Wonderful. envy, jealousy; they are wonderful. Covetousness, greed, nothing better than greed. Greed for what?

AA: But I mean greed in its material manifestation.

SFH: Terrible – we suffer from it. It burns you. But greed for Light that has no beginning and no end – that is my drive.

AA: There are no human vices if the focus is Allah SWT. There cannot be.

SFH: Well, Allah is beyond non-duality, so this duality of virtues and vices doesn't exist, it's past that discussion.

AA: No, I'm saying you cannot have these attributes if you're concentrated on Allah SWT.

SFH: Sure, you go past them. It is definitely past good and bad.

AA: It is not through the virtuous life?

SFH: It is through virtuous life. For a child, I divide life into three sections. The first section is developing: earning, learning, the *dīn*, the courtesies, the *adaab*, the Qur'an – all of this – and the ego is developing and the identity is there. The second half is in between; we begin to have glimpses of the higher. So you are in between, and every now and then a bit more of the lower self, some other time a touch of the *ruh*, inspiration, intuition, whatever, a hunch. And the third part is more and more perfecting the higher the subtler, the real you, the *ruhaniya*. So in that third section, towards the end of it, you are fully aware of the need for virtues, the need of grooming of the self for the child. And you don't deny you know it, you understand it, but you are no longer concerned about it.

AA: The Prophetic saying, *Al-dīn kullahu akhlaaq*[53].

SFH: Exactly. That is for the first section also. You have to embrace your *dīn*, to live your *dīn*.

AA: The outer forms of the *dīn* have to be garbed in virtue as well.

SFH: All of it has to be. Also *al-dīn kullahu muhabba*[54].

AA: But not the inner dimensions.

SFH: The inner dimension comes in a bit later. You have to start on the outer, until the inner begins to kick in. At the end you find the inner and the outer are inseparable.

AA: So you really can't exercise virtue towards Allah.

SFH: No, virtue is grooming the lower of you, so that the higher in you will lead you.

---

[53] "Religion is all about virtues."
[54] "Religion is all about love."

AA: Will then rise up like a Phoenix.

La Ilaha

SFH: Absolutely – it is no – *la ilaha* to the *nafs*, to my greed, my lust, whatever I want to acquire, my status, my being 'closer to God' and all of these fancy ideas, until such time you find you don't really exist. It's a figment of your own imagination that you were born and have got more years, and you have a CV. Boring stuff.

AA: You use that word quite a lot! Boring –

SFH: It's boring! Because it's repetitive.

AA: Do you see it as trivial?

SFH: I find it actually destructive. I mean boring in that it is even sad. Because you're wasting time on something that has no substance.

AA: Immaterial.

SFH: Yes, immaterial, and yet you are giving it value. I use boring in that sense – in that you have given it a status, you have given it a certain value, and you are mistaken. It has no consequence.

AA: Would you universalize what you have said? Is this true in all cases and conditions?

SFH: I think so.

AA: So the philosophers' way is doomed to fail.

SFH: I think it's a very useful arena to enter, a very helpful, if you like, zone to experience, and I think it's very important to get out of it too.

AA: Philosophy, theology, psychology...

SFH: Helpful, useful, but if you don't transcend it you are caught into that web. The whole idea is to be web-less, beyond limits, to be inside *Ka`ba*, not knowing whether you are inside or outside or who you are.

AA: What would you say to a psychologist who says these are all techniques to avoid facing the inevitable, the inevitability of your demise?

SFH: He is also right. From this point of view I accept you're right. But I know I have no demise. I don't have anything; nothing belongs to me; neither the material, nor the esoteric nor the energy side – nothing belongs – there is no 'me'. This is a construct that has occurred because of the confluence of so many of these forces, so I have identified myself with this so-called 'I' – birth, identity and so on. And that is why as a young man, I really resented to be photographed, personally, until I was with Chinmaya. He couldn't give a damn. Absolutely not! Because this is deeply ingrained in you – it's not really you, so how are they going to freeze it? But when I saw Chinmaya laughing, he said, 'Sonny, what does it matter? They want it, let them – fine.' So I didn't care any more.

AA: What's the point, then of all these '-ologies'? Psychology, anthropology, sociology –

SFH: There again, all part of the pigeon-holing that we try to control the universe and make sense out of it and try to contain and give these things a boundary. We want to stop against space and time: give it a boundary in terms of space, and its discipline – but as we know in the last 20/30 years, all that polymathism is coming, which is wonderful. I see *tawhīd* is beginning to sweep to us. In my first years in the oil industry, the geologists would hardly speak to even the paleontologists, let alone to the reservoir engineer. But now, there are lots of points of crossovers. It's wonderful.

AA: But it would seem that all these crossovers are at what one would call the horizontal level. They haven't gone beyond that. If there is a consciousness of *tawhīd*, it will come from people being exhausted by trying to find the truth and not finding it. What do you say?

SFH: I think that's correct, but I also think that once you are into those disciplines, and their rigors, there is such an attraction, because you are still within a zone that is delineated. I doubt very much if many of those people will be exhausted.

AA: But it's a constantly moving target. (SFH: that's true) Psychologists –, if you look at the old school of Freud, psychoanalysis, 20 years ago, 1960s at my university, it was seen to be practically gospel truth. Now it's the butt of jokes. So all these generations of psychoanalysts, dying out now, mercifully, and the god that they worship turned out to be faulty. It is true for nearly everything, including so-called hard science. So wouldn't that exhaust the constant attempt to nail down the truth? Like nailing jelly to the wall.

SFH: It's true. Brilliantly put. I think you're right. But I also think people get so absorbed and time passes and they get old and they want to have the anger of youth, the impetus to get out of it all, to be exasperated. They become like: 'yes all my life I worked hard, but I didn't get anywhere near where I thought I would.' I don't think people will wake up so much, if they have been very much in such disciplines. I think it needs a bit of wildness; there is a need for that wildness, or rebellion.

Explosion of Outer Knowledge

AA: One of the things that I was going to say, and ask you to comment on that, is the extraordinary explosion of outer knowledge and the misery and sourness on the faces of those who were its proponents and then have reached the tail end of their scholarly careers. There's nothing in my mind sadder than that; because they have spent a lifetime trying to pursue their version of the truth, and see it superseded by subsequent work and research and events, and all they have contributed to the growth of knowledge. But they know in their heart of hearts that this is not the case. So how do you comment on this growth of outer knowledge and its lack of transference to inner knowledge?

SFH: I am pleased to hear it from you because you have been exposed to it at a very high level in the academic world, which I have not been. I have always guessed that there will be disappointment and they will be –

AA: It's visible, manifest –

SFH: I didn't know –

AA: They become sour, dispirited, and angry.

SFH: Because it's unfulfilled – the outer is not balanced by the inner. And the *Awwal* is not balanced by the *Akhir*. We are universal beings, so you have to encompass the totality of it. You must again shrink space and the illusion of time.

AA: But what is it in their construct? These are supposed to be the most accomplished minds.

SFH: The *nafs* knows it is not happy; the *nafs* knows it doesn't exist, the *nafs* knows it must yield to the king of kings, which is the *ruh*. The *nafs* knows it has no sustainability. Early on it tries to assert itself, and so on and so on, but the time comes that the individual who is made of the *nafs* and the *ruh*, will fully realize the disappointing, if you like, cul-de-sac. He knows; everybody will know. They did not allow themselves to face it earlier on; they were too engaged in the battle of proving themselves, establishing themselves, competing with publications, or this and that. They did not step aside to reflect. The whole thing has accumulated, and in the end, they're smashed. The same thing with wealth.

AA: Fame, celebrity –

SFH: – and worse – I have met people I was with, you find they become much more miserable than they were thirty years ago because they know this is not it. They try to delude themselves with all the paraphernalia and reminders of their glory and photographs and the trophies – it's not real.

AA: I'm not asking in a self-congratulatory way: 'we know the truth, you know the truth, and they don't', but why don't they explore the last available avenue for knowledge? Why is that door shut? Why is the door that they transcend themselves shut for them?

SFH: Too late, too late – they don't have the attitude any more.

AA: And the *nafs* is locked and the key thrown away?

SFH: No, it's too late: everything had become so structured. The cells, the mind, the memory – it's too late. It's fossilized in a certain direction. You can't retrace it – it's too late. If you had not had doubts, uncertainties, crises in your youth and always referred to that difficult time it becomes too cozy, too smooth; all that matters now is survival and comfort and ease. Too late.

Passage Through Time

AA: It is too late for a lot of people. In some ways it's the ability to look at adversity in the face, and move on without it destroying you. To look at set backs, loss of position, money and really truly feel that this is just a passage, a point that you are passing, and with no reality.

SFH: People are fortunate if they have a serious crisis and total uprootment; they are the lucky ones. And the rest are just coasting along: 'all is well *Alhamdulillah*; we made more profit this year. My daughter is well, my son got married.' But asking the purpose of life, the end of it – death – is difficult for them; they need to ask themselves, 'Am I happy to die now?' I have been fortunate in that, from a very young age, I would ask myself, 'Are you ready to leave?' if the time comes. Of course, it was a bit of a blind type of *tawakkul*, but for many years now, I really think any minute the air goes in it may not come out. Or I'm going to live much longer. So I have not been in any way party to that amazing orchestration – I just don't know. I trust it. I have always been better and better and better, so I trust – He who knows all who has shared has allowed me to have a little bit of a glimpse of that – so I trust it will come in its own perfect way. There are numerous *ayaat* in the Qur'an that suggest that when some things are taken away from you, and there's goodness in your heart, Allah will give you better than what you think has been taken away from you. It's a question of evaluating: is that thing material? Is it power? In my own life there were periods earlier on that I could control a lot of stuff, and as time went by I am beginning more and more to see the magnificent Controller who enabled me to control through other means. Other people come and help and do and they're happier for it. They want to do that. In my younger days I didn't want in a way to have anybody doing me a favor, but now, when people serve me, I know I am doing them a favor, without any arrogance. It's a complete turnaround. And I don't feel that the giver is me. I don't see it that way. And if they don't do it I am also as grateful. No anger, rancor, say *bismillah* –

AA: So where there's sadness and sorrow…

SFH: It is for missed time, missed opportunity, not seeing it.

AA: *'likaylaa ta'saw `alaa maa faatakum walaa tafrahoo bima ataakum.'*[55]

SFH: Exactly – a huge prescription; it's for discipline. Do not ever regret that which you have done – we all have thoughts like: 'if I had done that, bought that property, now I would have had this or that.'

Sorrow

AA: So what is sorrow then? Is it real?

SFH: Missing the *ruh* – the *nafs* now, the *shaytan* in me, says – 'I didn't do anything wrong.'…. Iblis says, 'I didn't tell him, he did it.'

AA: So there's no *huzn* for loss in material terms.

---

[55] "Do not regret what has passed you, and do not be joyful by what has come to you." (Qur'an 57:23)

SFH: If you live the moment, none of these things arise. If you live the moment, the moment is forever. None of these things would worry you because they are all to do with the mind going past, and the past doesn't exist.

AA: Even when there is a great tragedy?

SFH: Again, tragedy is a sense of loss. Sense of loss is a big thing in our sight. It is to do with the *nafs*. The *nafs* wants to accumulate. The *ruh* has no loss. The *ruh* has it all forever. So who is experiencing the loss?

AA: But there is something called sorrow.

SFH: It is the ego again, the *nafs*; the lower side in me. No doubt about it. The lower side in me is there, and it does feel sorrow and gets upset and worries, but the extent of it depends on its state, which determines the length of time he is going to be upset and the depth of it. Some would say, 'yes, of course, we lost that, I'm sorry, let me weep for a while and then move on.' While others would feel the loss so much that they would feel their lives are over.

AA: Do you believe the story about Imam Khomeini and the loss of his son?

SFH: I think so. If it is not real, it is apocryphal. Yes I do believe it.

AA: And it would be real because it applied to him.

SFH: Absolutely – I think he was a man, a being who was a man, and he was a *ruh*, and therefore, as a man he appreciated that it was one of the inevitable things. Also, he must have felt, 'I am in exile, they are chasing me...' So I do believe it.

AA: Have you seen a sorrow-less but still a real response to what other people would consider to be a major catastrophe – calamity?

SFH: No, I think the *awliya* that I have met in my life, whose notes you have been sent, I think most of these people would have been like that. Ahmed Ibn `Ajiba in Morocco, and several others whom I have met.

AA: If someone buys your biography 300 years from now it will hopefully be based on these conversations, but it will be embellished.

SFH: No doubt. We love to embellish things; we love to exaggerate the *awliya*, people whom we know. We exaggerate the power of the people who are close to us. We want God, we want *Allahu akbar*, so we do it – it's natural. I can say I have met at least 20 people in my life, whom I knew, were aware of that and would say it as it is. There was the *Wali* of Behleil, who I visited a few times, and I asked Zainab and Muna and Aliya to go and stay with him. He had a daughter who was staying with him. The first thing he told them was, 'Don't give her any money, don't trust her, and don't leave things lying around.' She was the only person who looked after him, and the way he said it, there was a tinge of sorrow, but what can you do? This is it. There was no bitterness in it.

AA: So there is no tragedy in it.

SFH: No tragedy.

AA: There's no word for it in Arabic; there are various suggestions including Arabized version of 'tragedy'.

SFH: I think you're right.

AA: It isn't in any of the classical languages of Islam.

SFH: There isn't.

Living in the Now

AA: But these are such powerful sentiments around which entire cultures have been built – sorrow, love, passion and the sentiments that seems to dominate the psyche of post-modern man has no reality in the one who connects things to each other and then to the transcendent. How would you comment on this?

SFH: The now, the power of now, deal with the now – the instant – *hudhur*. The past is an illusion; the future doesn't exist, also another illusion, and all of it will be revealed at the point of death. So if I live in the now, I transcend death. Death is the ultimate conclusion. All of these were constructs of energies that have met in me with my senses and I gave them, if you like, their substance, I made them as idols. Sorrow is that; hope is that; all of these. If I live the now my future will be as good without the paraphernalia of all the baggage that I am carrying – sorrow, expectations, fears – and therefore with very little effort my existential side will improve. I won't have all of the muck that we are creating in the world, how we ruin the ecology. I think the tragedies are at multiple levels.

Human Qualities

AA: What would you say then to a person who says all the human qualities you either refuse or reject – you don't have them, or when you have them, you do that because you are on the fourth leg of your journey. What is your future? Why do you consider yourself to be part of the community, since you don't share our sorrows, you don't share our joys, and you're disconnected from our concerns.

SFH: I am aware of it – I share it with...

AA: I'm saying that in general.

SFH: It is a small share. I accept it, I understand it, I respond to it. It is the extent of it only. It is the quantitative side.

AA: But I'll say that there is nothing human about this – to be human is to have these qualities.

SFH: You can say that, but I consider the journey of humanity is the balance between humanity and divinity. And divinity is of such power, because it is the absolute, that it renders the human side almost insignificant. What you say, I think, is also a very valid question.

AA: So human beings are basically incidental and only achieve a reality when they acknowledge their yielding to the One.

SFH: To Divinity – absolutely.

AA: So they have no qualities of their own?

SFH: No, there are qualities, but these qualities are if you like, like traces of divinity. The Qur'an calls them *Sibghat Allah* – the colors of Allah, the virtues of Allah. Goodness, Generosity – all of these are there.

AA: You are turning the world on its head. For the last five hundred years it's been going in a different direction.

SFH: I know it's turned on its head – let me first turn myself – I think you're right – in that sense.

AA: You're not at all angered....

SFH: Not at all…no, I think if somebody tells me, 'you're inhuman', I say, 'maybe you're right! Good luck to you! Excuse me. I don't think I can help.'

Shaykh/Murid

AA: But from a teaching point of view, this type of prescription requires a massive enhancement of the ability to interact with people. And if you're not able to interact with them then it becomes an impossible task. Am I right?

SFH: Therefore, at this level – you're right – I am almost a redundant teacher now.

AA: So the only person who can benefit from your teaching is the person who is truly committed to re-positioning the authority of the soul over the self.

SFH: True. Or, they are accomplished in every other aspect of both humanity and Divinity.

AA: Then you have very few people!

SFH: No people! It's true. I don't want to put myself in the position of Shams At-Tabriz or – nor do I care …but Shams clearly says, 'I have no *murids*, I don't want to have any *murids*. Even Rumi is not my *murid*. I can only deal with people who are beyond the beyond. They will be my *murids*,' and that I think was genuine, real. I'm not putting myself at his level, but I feel the same. That's why, I can't lecture any more, or teach. I can't do it. But I still have the humanity part, socializing, connecting – I don't deny that either.

AA: I thought it was a mistake when I asked you the question; it seemed to me that one of the most difficult aspects of the *Shaykh/Murid* relationship is that paradigm.

SFH: True.

AA: It is – at some point – utter inhumanity.

SFH: Yes, all right! – at least the higher potency of the higher consciousness and much less of the lower consciousness.

AA: But it is inhumanity, not in the sense of being aggressive or anything, but it is also humanity in the sense that it is a state or relationship not experienced in society.

SFH: It's true. Well, I mentioned to you that, as of more than 20 years ago, I was spared listening to people's human crises – there were many cases I can cite.

AA: But this goes beyond that.

SFH: I know. But if somebody phoned me and said: 'I have a problem with my wife, and so forth,' I'd say, 'Kill her, kill your self.' So within two or three years, people started to think that I was useless. In a sense it's like that – you are useless as far as the humanity part of it is concerned, but most useful as far as the divinity part or spirituality is concerned, presumably.

AA: So ergo, the only effective Shaykh is the one who has flaws.

SFH: You need different Shaykhs at different stages in your life – like again going back to the story of Rumi – I'm sure he needed a Shaykh who helped him very much with the Qur'an when he was younger. A Shaykh who also reprimanded him for not reciting well and so on – and then as a genius at that young age of about 40, he obviously needed to have transcendence, and then this fellow arrives – Shams. So you get the Shaykh you need at the time you're in: there is that resonance between the seen and the unseen. So in a way what you say is right. You need earlier on a Shaykh as your aunt – somebody who loves you, puts up with you, and not really accomplished in the inner sciences, maybe a Shaykh of the outer. *Akhlaq, Suluk* and all of that.

AA: Looking back at the journeys of Mulla Sadra, the fourth leg is the Shaykh who knows the essential humanity of the *Shaykh/Murid* relationship, but transcends it in the interests of being with creation – am I correct?

SFH: Correct. Again, the fourth journey is all personal and circumstantial; it won't be for everybody; not everybody will touch you. When you talk about humanity, it is not in the global sense of humanity, it's individual human beings – it's like lighting somebody's candle – taking your candle to light somebody – it's like that.

Sorrow Has No Existence

AA: But sometimes it could be a powerful jolt, if one had a personal tragedy and he's seeking succor from his/her Shaykh. The response is get on with it. It's in some ways a kind of devaluation of the notion of sorrow.

SFH: There is no devaluation. Sorrow has no existence; it has no value.

AA: Devaluation from the personal point of view. It becomes one that is…

SFH: Sorrow is rubbish; we are the ones who give it a value; there's no such thing as sorrow. It's nothing other than counter-productive at every level – except commiserating with a little child because of pain in their toes. Now there are two ways in which a child cries – one is physical, literal, and one can sympathize, and the other one is because they've lost their toy, or something – horrible. And it continues: 'I've lost my contract – come and commiserate with me.' I'm afraid I cannot at this stage in my life have any sympathy or empathy with that. But I understand it, it's there and they need that sort of a palliative care – they can deal with it – I don't dispute that. But it's not my domain.

AA: It has no reality –

SFH: In its own sense, absolutely, it has no reality. It's fiction, and this is the cause of, if you like, degrading of humanity. All of the other functions, so much of our activity – sending this card and that, congratulating, all pampering to the *nafs*, degrading, degrading the human value.

AA: So the *nafs* can only bloom in its fullness to the extent that it reflects the light of the One.

The Withering of the Nafs

SFH: The *nafs* cannot bloom; the *nafs* will wither; the *nafs* can never bloom; it is the black hole, the downside, and a shadow of the *ruh*. It needs to grow naturally the first 20/30 years, stabilize and then wither. If it doesn't wither, then it is the worst poison. When it becomes clever, then that is earthly wisdom – Mu`awiyyah wisdom – it's about how to manipulate, without it moving into spiritual wisdom. There are two sides of wisdom: earthly wisdom, which is cumulative, clever, and conniving, and it's about how to play politics; whereas, spiritual wisdom is liberating, free to be, honoring and being the offspring of Adam, being Adamic.

AA: So the perfection of the *nafs* is through its withering.

SFH: Absolutely – through its withering. Early on, grooming it, disciplining it, restricting it, developing virtues. So it limits it – that is the path, the *Shari`ah*. But later on it has to be completely annihilated. The test of it again is where that person in his heart, with real emotions, is the same when there is censure and when there is praise. If neither of them affects you, then the *nafs* has become very, very thin.

AA: But the celebration of the *nafs*, which is part of what you wrote in the Sufi Cosmology of the Self, is related to the degree to which it is groomed so it reflects the qualities of the soul.

SFH: Abandoned to the soul.

AA: And then there is nothing to do.

SFH: It's all completed – you have almost completed whatever there is to complete, so you are now soul. That's it; the purpose of the whole thing, of existence is for you to realize you are not who you think you were and that what you think you were was a simple overflow from a Reality that is permanent, beyond space, beyond time, and that is your soul. You've done what you had to – now fun begins. After that point really, because you begin to have insight – you see the inner realities of things. This is where the thrill begins. Prior to that it will be pleasure and displeasure, a bit of this and a bit of tragedy, fear, anxiety and all of that – *khawf* and *huzn*. But once you are soul, you are aware of *khawf* and *huzn*, but it doesn't overwhelm you. You are aware of it – yes of course, it's sad, you said that, commiserate, that's fine. Resonate with them for them to remember that you are with them, but not totally engrossed in their state – so up lift them.

AA: The *Baqi* obviously is one of the cardinal Names – the name behind all the instincts to survive and perpetuate. You are asking the self, reflecting the *Baqi* to know that it is not *Baqi*; it's like a snake consuming its tail.

SFH: Correct.

AA: Again it's like the – mixed metaphor – like the Cheshire cat smile. The cat goes and the smile is left.

SFH: Brilliant, brilliant, absolutely.

AA: But this is a very profound form of subtlety – it's *Lutf* – it's one of the most hidden – in the colloquial sense – of Allah's attributes.

SFH: Yes, yes.

AA: So how do you make the hidden manifest?

SFH: It does it itself – it is a sliding scale, slow, slow, suddenly you find it's gone – then you smile at it, smile at yourself, and then you say, it is very good that I had a *nafs*, very good it bit me a few times.

AA: But if truth be told, these are incidents that occur, maybe once or twice in a lifetime – how can this incident – you've said that many times – you want to freeze it and make that your *maqaam*, but it's so rare – a rare occurrence, even for relatively accomplished seekers, to have it sustained as your end product. It can never be an attainable goal except for the very, very few. Therefore, shouldn't the process be not getting to that, but rather striving for it.

Awareness

SFH: What you say is correct – striving for it, but I also look at it differently. I think even that striving becomes sweeter, easier and more, if you like, effective, if I am simply aware: if I'm aware that now, I'm impressing you or not impressing you. If I'm aware that I'm a bit upset because of something, just the awareness of it will make it all disappear. Simple awareness without judgment. Just be aware of what you're doing. It will fizzle out. It will – and the *nafs* will have served its purpose, done its job, just awareness of it. The more I condemn it, the more it generates self-defense and the more it denies, and makes it impossible to catch it. It's not exactly a shift, but just awareness of it, and you become totally immersed in the Presence, in the dot of the 'be' of the now. And then from that you are also aware of the past, a bit of the present – you're not totally devoid of the existential side or of the conditioned consciousness side, but you are now totally, utterly connected directly to Supreme Consciousness by that awareness.

AA: *Muraqaba*, I am sure, is not a difficult condition to be in, nor *muhasaba*, to use your terminology...

SFH: Brilliant, it's essential.

AA: It's like a grounding.

SFH: The only thing is that if there is insincerity it won't last that long. What I find hypocritical – and it is the case with so many of the so-called *'ulama* – is if someone, who has been at it for all these years, comes and says, 'You must forgive me, I am a real sinner.' I'd say to him, 'Go away, you have become professional now.' So, do *muhasaba*, but it should be gone after a while. However, if you do *muraqaba* regularly, after a while, you *become muraqaba*.

AA: So, 'I am a sinner – I have transgressed.' I've just put a comment for you Shaykhna. Transgressing, does it mean the destruction of harmony?

SFH: Anything that goes against the ultimate, if you like, cosmic harmony, cosmic peace, is counter-productive. Allah is Peace, beginning with nothing other than peace, so the so-called movement change/existence is another zone – it is this zone, the lower zone. So it is, transgression is not being present in connecting with the different realities with least disturbance or no disturbance.

AA: ...harmony.

SFH: That's why the definition of the being that is awakened is: 'he who puts the things where they belong at the time they belong there, and without any pretense, without any *takalluf*.' *Takalluf* is one of the worst things. It's natural – 'I want to do it, but I'm tired now...'

Being/Becoming

AA: Going back to being and becoming. Usually it's juxtaposed as being like this old debate – superior to existence and all that. If there are two conditions, *being* and *becoming*, why can they not be a continuum? Visualize the formation of a huge wave: you, Shaykh Fadhlalla, would be at the crest; somebody else can be riding it without necessarily being at the crest, but knowing that there is a crest, that circumstance which is more modest, let's say, less ambitious, less spiritual, also has a reality as well, also has a being. So the condition of *becoming* towards *being* is true and valid.

SFH: But inseparable; they are inseparable – I am still becoming – to the extent that I am – again I go back to my model of spectrum. The more you are awakened to your *ruh*, the more you are energized by Supreme Consciousness in you, by Pure Consciousness in you. It doesn't mean you lose consciousness of your toe or your hunger or your excess drinking or whatever. So I am aware of my becoming all the time, but the being-ness side of it in a way is so overwhelming that the becoming doesn't overwhelm me. For a young person, who is ambitious, who wants to achieve and become this and that, the becoming is their god and so they also go up and down with the waves or signals they receive of failing, succeeding ... so it is success, and failure is to do with becoming, whereas victory belongs to the Being; victory belongs to Allah. *Wa la Ghalib Illa Allah*[56] victory belongs to my *ruh*. Success and failure belong to my *nafs*, to the becoming side.

AA: I'm trying to get back to the validity of this. If you look at it as a topological map rather than an ideological situation, the process of where you are now, you had to be somewhere else by the end of your twenties, and you had the first stage, as it were, and it has never left you. And the first stage – I should ask the question rather than make a statement – I'll re-phrase it. Many people come to you and to others, and say: 'I've been at this for forty-five years and I haven't experienced my *ruh*, what shall I do?' If there is sincerity in the process and this multi-dimension topology of *becoming* and *being*, if you are on that carpet, what does it matter if you are there or not?

SFH: You are right. You've said it simply, brilliantly. 'I' as a person with my habits and my language. I would say: 'You' said you have been – Who is 'you'? – you are forty years old now – the 'you' is of your own concoction – that's not you. So it may be five hundred years and you won't get anywhere. The real 'you' is your '*ruh*' and it's already there anyway. We are now an admixture of the two. So the less there is of the so-called 'you', the striver, the becoming, the more there is of the real you. It's a displacement.

AA: There is validity to the process of *becoming* without experiencing the state of *being*.

SFH: *Being* is the source of power and life and light to *becoming*. But also, there are two zones. One of them is the zone of Pure Consciousness, Absolute Consciousness. The other one is the zone of

---

[56] "There is no victor/conqueror except God."

discernible consciousness, changing consciousness, so *becoming* is that, and whilst I'm in that zone of *becoming*, let me now and then enjoy *being* –. why do people enjoy, celebrate the end of a project, or any success? Because they have touched *being*. *Becoming* is when someone says, 'I'm getting a job!' Now suddenly, he's got it. So for five seconds we celebrate, open champagne and so on. That is *being* – it's no-man's land. It's in between. I don't have a project then. And the mind cannot rest still, so it wants another project. So I'm back again into the *becoming* cycle, until such time I begin to displace it into meditation, service for its own sake – giving, giving without expectation – so that I'm moving more and more into the zone of *being*. Then the rules are different. The rules of *becoming* are earthly, worldly, and measurable; the rules of *being* are different. In the *becoming* the more is less, but on the *being* side, the less is more.

AA: Yes, but I think I must have misconstructed the question. If you conceive of *being* – very difficult to do that, but let's conceive the approximation of *being* as a topological field – it's a field, it's not a point. Although it is a point, but one of its expressions is a field, and this field has in it a topological high. You may not be near the topological high, but you're still in the field of *being*, so it can include in it the process towards *being* (SFH: correct), which I call clumsily *becoming*. (SFH: fine). You can very well not go beyond that field, as that could be sufficient for most people. So this sufficiency of being in the field of *being* is for those who want to be in this core is an unattainable objective, except for a very few people. However, to be in the field of *being* is a much easier achievable objective. Would you agree?

SFH: I agree. The issue is identification. If I have identified myself with my CV or my becoming, then-

AA: You have left behind all of that.

SFH: But once I lose that identity the field of *becoming* and *being* are inseparable.

Field of Certainty

AA: So, can I go to the next question? In the field of *being*, ambiguity leads towards uncertainty. The uncertainty points to certainty.

SFH: Absolutely! Uncertainty emanates from certainty.

AA: It's not the uncertainty of "I don't know what's going on!"

SFH: It's the uncertainty that has emanated and erupted from certainty.

AA: So it's truth in ambiguity…

SFH: Absolutely, totally.

AA: *Alhamdulillah wa shukrulillah*[57].

SFH: Totally, all of it is. If you ask me what is your conclusion in my life, I'll tell you one thing is that I know that I don't know, but I know that there is a field of knowledge that encompasses me, and it will give me from itself a *being* that I need to know at a time that I need to know it. That's not my judgment. It knows when I need to know.

AA: But in this topological field you are the realized person who – though you don't like that term – stands at a higher topological peak. It may not be real but it is within the field.

SFH: Absolutely. That's why I say, it doesn't take many years – the quicker one abandons oneself into that uncertainty, the more the certainty will access one.

AA: You know that there is an ultimate *rahma*, and you may not have experienced its full potential, but you know it's there.

SFH: I know it has encompassed me, and therefore, nothing else matters.

---

[57] Praise be to God, and Thanks to God.

AA: Including ...

SFH: Absolutely – the `adam is again another construct. It is that which is an illusion again. It's another zone – it's conditioned consciousness.

AA: I think we've strayed a lot from South Africa!

SFH: Bring it to a point that you're happy.

AA: I think this took us from your days here in South Africa to a very, very powerful exposition of the essence of parts of your teachings. So although I may have re-worded it, I am sure you might not agree with the way...

SFH: Brilliant, I enjoyed it. It's been very refreshing for me as well.

AA: I want to – not extract it – but to have the confirmation to add to the other teaching, which I think is the mapping of the self, or what we know of it.

SFH: I think it's brilliant; it was also very enjoyable for me. I add a little bit of a footnote to that. If I am to assure anybody, I say, 'just learn to give in, you are in that field – that zone is the only zone.'

Jumping Off One's Illusion

AA: It's like a flying carpet. Would you say that? Jump on it!

SFH: I must jump OFF what I saw as my horse or my carpet. That carpet is already there. The universal, all-encompassing, totality of it. I need to jump off my own illusion, I need to give up that; I need to really declare *Allahu Akbar*, even if it is forced to begin with, slowly by slowly the sound of it begins to absorb me; slowly by slowly I know it is the ONLY reality. So if *Allah is Akbar*, what significance do I have? Give that up, and you'll be amazed by the Presence of the Significance, the *Hadhrat Ar-Rabbaaniyya*.

AA: You have to switch off the apparent light of knowledge.

SFH: Totally. All of it is destitute. All of it is actually not there, they are totally redundant. Not again for the child. Not for the basic lower rungs of the *dīn*. It's perfectly correct. It's an evolutionary process. They have to accept that knowledge, those skills as paramount, to compete. But if you're talking about a zone of awakening or zone of enlightenment, or zone of whatever, then all of that has to be discarded – it's a handicap. The more of that, the less of this.

AA: Then the structure of religion has no part.

SFH: No, Absolutely (*Wa thiyabaka fatahhir*[58]) – take off what you thought was helpful or useful or protecting you or your identity – take it off – there is only the sacredness. So when we have given up the idea of sacredness then woe to us – we have given up the idea of it – how are we talking about it – it's the only reality – all of it is sacred. Where is it that He is not? Where is it that the Light of the One is not already in it? In the darkness?

AA: That's the unwinding of real human knowledge – in contrast to its rewinding.

SFH: Brilliant, brilliant, brilliant!! *Allahu akbar*.

AA: We have to thank Descartes for that.

SFH: In a way, yes.

AA: He also played a part to make people think.

SFH: It's true, no doubt.

---

[58] "And purify your outer garments." (Qur'an 74:4)

AA: But I think the Cartesian essence was there before… It was with Muawiyya… And before him Abu Jahl… [The glorification of apparent knowledge.]

AA: So I think this will end the biographical side.

SFH: That's wonderful – we can go to the more spiritual.

Other Sages and Realized Beings

Shaykh Abdalqadir

AA: Shaykhna, we have been talking about the biographical and spiritual biography of Shaykh Fadhlalla as it unfolded in space and time and ended in South Africa. One of the things which has always interested me – and I'm sure would interest any person who is tracking the path of a person such as yourself; for the lack of a better word, I'll call him a grand master – is the encounters with other sages and realized beings, spiritual masters of the time. I recall once you said that for a long time you went 'Shaykh-hunting', which spread across several regions and countries, and with no particular chronological order – we heard about Shaykh Abdalqadir, and his influence on you, and of course Chinmaya. But going back to Shaykh Abdalqadir – his path, the apparent one, diverged dramatically from the one that you have chosen. He seems to be more of a Shaykh of the outer, a Shaykh of communities, of the outer forms of Islam. Would you concur with that? What are the qualities that you see in him that marked him out as a person?

SFH: I found him as a Western model of an early Muhammadi awakened being. When I met him, I imagined him being one of the earliest followers and discoverers of the Prophet Muhammad (*saw*[59]), and someone who had dived into the Qur'an without having been through the formal training – Arabic grammar and all of the other things that go with it. But his *haal* and his heart and altogether his life were fully into that. He was exuding love of *Haqq*, truth, and the inner core of the message. But deep down, because of his own life, I could detect there was always love for numbers and communities and movements. He would often refer to some of the gatherings – there were so many, hundreds and thousands. And this from an earlier on stage left a mark on me – this was not my flavor or my direction, but I felt all along that this man had been in the infinite void of the empty/full cup – he had tasted and touched, if you

---

[59] *Sallallahu Wa `Alayhi WasSallam* (Peace be Upon Him).

like, the zone of the infinite. And that was his reference. This was my meeting point with him. This was the period that I was with him. He was all the time looking for the possibilities of a big movement, revival of Muslims, Islam and so on. Within a year, I could feel deep down a certain measure of sadness that I wouldn't be with him. But this idea of awakening the Muslims was completely alien to me. My own stand was that the Muslims had died before they were even fully enlivened; that Islam was announced but was not lived. It was derailed before Muhammad had died, and so on. This was a very strong feeling in me – that to try and revive that which has got some aspects of that make-up, but without the fullness of it, without it being Mecca in Medina, would not work. Whenever he mentioned the Medina model I cringed, and I couldn't take it. The Medina model is like Jerusalem, 'God is with us' – it's a mental concept. We're heavenly, we want to return to heaven, so we concoct things, such as *Khalifa* or the Mahdi. To my mind they are all mental concepts; some of them quite good concepts, but it's a romantic thing – promises something that it cannot deliver. So from early on I felt deceived of these things. Then I maintained my link and back-up for him; but then the idea of joining in with a man who had worldly power and felt that, if you had a man of the inner and a man of the outer something big would happen, confirmed that. His priority was to create a movement, to leave a big mark – without an egotistic ambition. I mean he was driven – he had immense drive, immense capacity – but it couldn't touch me. I felt it was out of time, out of place, it was not the way I felt the 'Medina' would come.

AA: Would you say he was a person who had reached a degree of maturity and fruition in his inner condition, but expressed it in basically a non-valid form in terms of action? I have not met him, so I know him mainly through his writings, so I'll pose a few observations and see your reaction. First of, to summarize what you've just said, it would seem to me that you recognize his 'shaykhliness' as it were in terms of his elevated station, but you don't necessarily recognize the validity of his outer actions.

SFH: It is the fourth journey that I disagree with; his prescription or his remedy in his fourth journey: being with creation but referring to the Creator, I found is inappropriate, it won't work. My interpretation is that people have to suffer more, individuals have to awaken, there has to be thousands of awakened people and the atmosphere and environment and hegemony of the world situation, being totally Western capitalistic and so on, has to be modified and changed, before Muhammad can be rediscovered, before the Qur'an can be re-lived: so I disagree with the remedy and the prescription.

AA: As I said earlier, I know him only through his writings, and from what I hear of him, and I see him through the prism of political philosophy, (SFH: yes) and without mincing words, I'd say he is probably one of the most original political thinkers of modern times. Not recognized widely, but he is really a remarkable thinker, with some extraordinary insights. If I look at him through my own prism, I see certain things that are highlighted. One is the desire, or the belief, that shocking the Muslim system is one way to awaken the Muslims. You shock it by creating communities that are self-identified in a kind of chivalrous condition. Then you shock it by dinar/dirham business; whether it has any significance in practical transactions is another matter. But it's a series of shocks. The other thing is this: I think his political philosophy is to do with connecting with some of the more, I'd say not forgotten thinkers, but the more quixotic thinkers of Western tradition – those who were always on the outside, the margins, but nevertheless had insights that only became evident years, sometimes centuries, after their deaths. So it seems to me that his political philosophy of an invigorated, re-charged community with chivalrous men leading and women supporting from a spiritually fortified citadel. In some ways it's a romantic vision, but in other ways it has a certain reality in terms of shock therapy – would you agree with that?

SFH: Absolutely. I think you have summed it up better than I have heard it or even thought of it myself. The idea of the *ribat*, coming out of the *ribat*, Murabitun – I think you're absolutely right. In fact, I think if you are interested, he would probably very much enjoy meeting with you, and for you to have a good encounter; I can arrange that for you. He is going to be more and more in France in Toulouse.

AA: I know some of his people – a man called Idris Mears, a very fine man and I have become friendly with him. From time to time I send out feelers as to whether he would be interested in entering into a philosophical-political discourse, but to be honest I am a bit concerned about his dogmatic anti-Shi`aism.

SFH: You have picked up on something that others have not. He is underestimated, undiscovered, and that in itself is rare.

AA: The works that he has done are really profound political thoughts. If you look at modern political thought – in the Western tradition, because we don't have much, frankly; in the Islamic tradition we do. For example, he is very close to the Scottish Renaissance of the 18th century, Ferguson and so on. And he has a very heroic perception of history, and the role of the heroic man, who is generally but not necessarily Wagnerian. There are certain figures that are on the margins of European society in literary and political life that are only now being re-visited. Sometimes people who were sort of fighting poets – Gabriele D'Annunzio, a heroic figure in World War One, fearless, led a most ridiculous attempt to seize Trieste after WWI and claim it for Italy with a small band of people. The emphasis that Shaykh Abdalqadir gave on people like Malaparte, who was also – used to be a forgotten writer of that period, but now rehabilitated – borderline. So this world as it were of Wagner, Germanised, Nietsche, Heidegger with his concern for *Being*, and it seems that he is trying to unite a political tradition – that is mainly Western – with, trying to draw out of the Qur'an and *Seerah,* a political core that merges the two at the level of the Unseen.

SFH: He found a resonance and unity – if there is anyone that I know also who sees that connectedness and unifying factor, which you have described, I think he has it. And I don't think anybody has been able to draw it out of him. Idris Mears, is he about my age?

AA: Yes.

SFH: Nice man – his father was in the oil industry in Bahrain. He was born there.

AA: I think so, yes.

SFH: One of the few whom I also like.

AA: I met him through one of the finest beings I have met, about 40-45 years old, an Egyptian with a German mother, Tarek Diwany... who I think is one of the world's authorities on – not Islamic banking, but the meaning of financial transactions in Islam – he wrote a textbook on that and he introduced me to him we were discussing the issues of dinars and dirhams.

SFH: It really touched my heart very deeply – you will enjoy it and he too will be rewarded. I pray for a meeting between you two for a day – I'll put it in my heart.

AA: I'd be very pleased, though I am a bit concerned about, not the form, but the layer of people around him. So wouldn't it be a bit unsettling for them to have a Shi`a coming to him?

SFH: No, you go straight to him; as I said, with me, he is apologetic and he feels guilty; he always wants to actually clear this past.

AA: In fact I don't think he is – every time I come across it – I don't think it unbecoming to discuss minor matters...

SFH: It won't come to you; I don't think any of that will arise.

AA: But politics does – seeking out the political philosophy – but he has the heroic figure – (SFH: Definitely), which stand against – I thought that being in that context that his idea of the historic figure would be the person of Imam Ali.

SFH: No, but... because of the schism and so on. Have you seen his main volume of Ian Dallas collection?

AA: No, I don't have it. I have nearly all his works.

SFH: No, this is the European version – you will enjoy it – all his collection of work in the Western sense.

AA: There is this element of shock and...

SFH: You summed it up well.

AA: A kind of outrage, outrage with the leaders of Muslims.

Return of Caliphate – An Illusion

SFH: Return of the Caliph.

AA: The first *Khilafa* – they have a reality that can only be understood in the context of the *Dhahir* – the outer forms.

SFH: There is a theatrical element of absolutism. You summed it up exceptionally well and I think there is value in that. To me this proves my childish but innate *fitri* idea that you cannot revive that which has been stillborn. I have followed just my *fitrah* – it is stillborn. You can't revive it. Re-establish, move as you did, you can't think that somebody, a king or a ruler, will come to lift it up to a global scale – it won't work.

AA: But I think the kernel of truth in that is the revived religion – individuals voluntarily grouping with other individuals, like the knights of the round table.

SFH: It won't happen any more. That is again horizontal. I think that has died, that luxury is no longer; it now will come vertical, individual, thousands of them, and then they will see eye to eye; in fact it will happen with people like yourself and others. You will be seeing eye-to-eye; you will know the extent of their *iman* and that is the point of trust and connectedness, without calling it brotherhood, sisterhood, *futuwwa* – none of those. It will just be, I know this man I can trust, one to one...

AA: If we act we act together.

SFH: It will happen in a different way – it will be vertical, not horizontal.

Shaykh Bashir Osman

AA: You and I both don't want to discuss the polemic side of Shaykh Abdalqadir – why and when – so this will suffice on Shaykh Abdalqadir. There is another person whom I have never met, never read any of his work – a man called Shaykh Bashir.

SFH: Bashir Osman – he was a Somali, presumably very highly respected like the chief of a tribe, someone in Eritrea or Northern Somalia. He was involved early on in his youth for some sort of unification movement, political movement, and established the first newspaper that provided political expression in that country. And then he began to move more and more with people of light. I think in his early thirties or forties, he ended up with people who had immense power and access to jinn and talismans. So I think by his early fifties he was perhaps regarded as one of the greatest beings alive, who knew those worlds and had access to them. And then for some reason – I forget the details – he ended up living in Medina and being closest to a very great Shaykh, Bukhari, also of Somali origin, a much older man. So they were more or less the connecting point of most serious, sincere, spiritual religious people from the horn of Africa. And he used to visit me regularly, wherever I had been. In England he used to come once or twice a year. The person most close to him was Hajj Mustafa – he loved him and would accompany him. As he arrived in London, Hajj Mustafa would be there holding his hand. And he had people who loved him and followed him all over the world. In England there would always be 20-30 people. And I was a host. I was never really taken in much more than knowing the man as a significant being. And he was very keen for me to be with Shaykh Bukhari, and meet him, which I did. I went with Shaykh Hosam to meet him in Medina. We were supposed to get there by a certain flight – we didn't make it. Four days after that flight we ended up in Medina without him knowing. So Hosam and I went to the hotel nearest to the *haram*[60]. After twenty minutes in the room – there's a bit of a courtyard in the hotel, four or five stories, modern hotel, my room was on the first floor – within twenty minutes I could hear some loud voices in the lobby. He was asking about me. They didn't have my name, but he was asking where was Shaykh Haeri, Fadhl – I didn't know who he was asking for, my passport might have had a different name of mine. So there was quite a bit of confusion – but he said, 'No, I know he's here.' So I looked down and saw the man arguing, he said, 'he is here'. They said, 'No there is no such person,' and I said, 'Yes, he is here!' – So there were dozens of such encounters with Shaykh Bashir Osman. Anyway, he said, 'get ready, because *Maghrib* is here and Bukhari is waiting.' So we quickly went with him, with the usual crowd.

AA: Wasn't he connected with Ahmad Zaki Yamani[61]?

SFH: Maybe. It didn't occur to me, maybe. So we get to the *haram* and he says, 'Shaykh Bukhari is waiting for you. He has space next to him – it's for you.' And that is the nearest possible to the shrine of the Prophet – 2 meters. So I could barely get through the crowd. I didn't see there was room, but when I got there, there was room for me. So we prayed and I really felt his presence, I felt blessed, I felt good about it. So we had a bit of a conversation – nothing frivolous, very high level. So eventually I asked him, 'give me one advice.' He said, '*La ilaha-il-Allah* is enough for you.' And he looked at the rack of books of Qur'ans and *du'as* and said, 'you know all of these don't weigh a thing, even an iota of dust in balance of *La ilaha-il-Allah*.' I really felt there was a transmission in that for me to be more in *Tajrid*.

Lack of Concern with Solomonic Qualities

AA: But you're not really much concerned with his Solomonic qualities, are you?

---

[60] Reference to Masjid Nabwi in Medina.
[61] The former Saudi Minister of Oil.

SFH: No. In fact this lack of conern helped me a lot because in America I was for a period of six months under heavy pressure from the neighbors of the center – attacks and court cases from them – and I wasn't really up to that; I used to say, 'what am I doing here? I'm not here to fight humanity, to create a movement.' So there were two *jinns* who were all the time coming to me: I could always feel those two energies on my right hand side, immensely powerful, more or less waiting for me to give them an order: 'do you want us to destroy this or that?'

AA: How did these presences manifest – they were just there?

SFH: I could feel energies. I still feel them. I talk to them as though they are still further in terms of time and distance... they were there beckoning. I thought I'd wait until Bashir Othman came. And they would say, 'Today, look there's all this going on, we can make a fire. Finish it all.' Of course I was tempted – it's wonderful to have big powers. But I restrained myself. I said, 'no, I know Bashir will come, and I have to go through the door – I can't just jump into the courtyard.' So Bashir came and he knew, and said, 'you are tempted,' and I said, 'yes'. He said, 'Avoid it.' I said, 'I am under a lot of pressure.' He said, 'Avoid it,' and I did. I took him as a man of authority on that. So I never had been tempted. And there were many such incidents with him; numerous amazing incidents, and he would be a very special type of a *hakim*. He would do a lot of what is called in the sub-continent, *kushte*, mincing and burning the thing and keeping it on fire all night, repeating and repeating. If you don't mind, ask Batul on her encounter with him.

Unseen Realms

AA: I'm interested in the aspects of the encounter, more in terms of significance for your spiritual development, your own condition; for example, did Shaykh Bashir, because of these Solomonic powers, access more completely a realm that you knew was there but might not have had the same degree of access to or authority over? So how do you view these realms? Is it part of the seamless hierarchy of the heavens – *malakut*?

SFH: They exist, they are there and many people have access to them, many have the right entry, if you like, courtesy of connectedness. I was not that tempted, except mainly in order to overcome certain obstacles or difficulties. I was never tempted to show off these powers.

AA: You had a utilitarian access, to benefit from them?

SFH: Yes, only for that, but I wasn't in any way infatuated by that.

AA: What are these worlds? These worlds are real in one sense but they are also unapproachable in another sense – there are dividing lines and divisions between various kinds of creations.

SFH: Yes. I had followed intuitively before even Chinmaya told me: 'Do not concern yourself with what doesn't concern you.' It is not my concern. I am *insaniyya* and I want to be completely in body in the infinite boundless, timeless *ruhaniya*. So I consider these distractions. I knew Shaykh Asif had been in that since his childhood. I knew – and he still is – appearing in three or four places at the same time, and people vouching for that, until now. It never touched me. I considered this as being a handicap, an obstacle. I considered these situations as the *Rifa`i* path in a sense, of shock and awe. 'Look at this – the sword has gone in me.' You know, that encounter with Shaykh Jamali with Abbas's father, I have shared with you. He was very skeptical about the sword going in someone's belly. Shaykh Jamali came right in front of them and did that in the *zawiya* in upstate New York. You could see the whole thing, and there was a touch of blood as he hugged Abbas's father. You know after this, when he hugged, a touch of blood dropped on Abbas's father.

AA: A mark of certitude.

SFH: Yes – it never concerned me. I was not of that orientation.

AA: But I recall you saying that the things he passed on to you – which you are now using – was the final element of concluding the *salaat*, with a recitation of the last ayah from the Qur'an from Surah *al-Hashr*[62].

Other Sages and Realized Beings

SFH: Correct. He gave me a pile, which I still have, of special invocations, for different things, Jinn and others, without me being Jinni oriented – you know, for this, for that – he passed several things to me, one of which was crossing borders, crossing countries. Same as Imam Ja'far Sadiq's *du'a* and I've used that often, and it almost freezes everything, but I have to enter into that *haal* – it isn't so much what I say, it's about my heart. So I enter into that zone of oblivion, no animosity, no fear, anxiety, and say, *'Allahu Rabbana wa Rabbakum,'*[63] and I suddenly go into that *rububiyya*, that encompasses the entire cosmos, and then I do what I can and you do what you can, there's no warfare between us, no animosity – so it's *tawhīdi* – that's one thing he gave me and also this *du'a*. And a few other things, which I can't remember right now. But there were quite a number of things that he parted with. I must have been with him a total of nearly 20-30 times, each time for a week or a few days, or a bit longer. I left him to his devices – he had his own circle, his own thing. A year before he passed away he went to Pakistan, collecting a lot of very eccentric type of remedies, including venom, snakes and things. Seyyed Ikram also helped him a lot with these things in the bazaar and Abbas was telling me he ended up with a huge suitcase of this stuff. How was he going to get out? In the morning he was to go, the Saudi consul general in Karachi turned out to be one of his followers. He said, 'Come, I'm taking you inside the airplane.' He managed it. So he was like that. And every night he slept with his shroud, as though he was dying – Hajj Mustafa will give you some wonderful things on him. But I was never concerned with these things. I was never intrigued. I just took it that, 'whatever is my destiny will come to me.' I had no concern or anxiety. There wasn't any more, if you like, the quest for the unusual.

AA: You were not amazed by the world of the jinns and wanted to know more about it?

SFH: No – I wanted to be in the infinite Presence, you know. I was never tempted, except for the example with the *jinn*. But I waited – actually I

---

[62] *'wahuwa al-'azeezu al-hakeem'* ("He is the Almighty, the Wise" - Qur'an 59:24)
[63] "Allah is our Lord and your Lord."

had this innate gift of watching myself, my *nafs* – it wants to be king of kings, but there is another master of the world – be His `abd and you are better than the king – I had this innate contentment.

Shaykh Asif/Traditional Sufi Way

AA: I'm sure you know Shaykh Asif better than I do, but he had certain defining features that would have left, I assume, certain traces on those who were within his circle. One is the regular commitment to *tariqah*, which implies all the physical hardships that are part of it; and the other one is a kind of immersion into, let's call it, the ethereal world, in which he spends time, enters and exits very often very frequently. What is appealing about him is the rigor of *tariqah* and the belief that it is not pointless, it is not for nothing. There is a certain purpose to it. The other things are incidental. Would you say this is correct?

SFH: Correct. Absolutely. I think you have summed it up better than I could have. But again, my own personal thing is that we are hundreds of years too late for any of that. I considered from the earliest days that *tariqah* was over, that traditional Sufi way was over, though it still has a purpose. It still has like some value like formal religions, but that is not the way that human beings will discover their true unity of humanity and divinity. It will still benefit many people, it will continue, but I could never subscribe to it. He came here, helped a lot to establish this place also and started it by saying that everybody was considered a *murid*, they must sign up and give 10% of their income. So of course these people were all after money, so they resented it. Then one day, they asked me what do do, and I said, 'I'm not Shaykh Asif. I'm not interested.' I knew there'd be no such commitment, I knew they would wriggle out of it, cause a lot of havoc. So I knew the whole thing was over before it began. What he had done helped many people, and was attractive and seductive for many people. I could never in any way subscribe to it one per cent.

AA: But his entry and exit into this world, the various realms – are these qualities that are available only to a few or anybody?

SFH: I think anybody can – potential is there, the *ruh* has got it all, the potential is there, but I still consider all of these are distractions and diversions. I consider the most important thing is for everyone to truly know to the point of no return; know that they are not who they think they are. I give the metamorphosis: you must move on from being the caterpillar.

AA: Like the chrysalis.

SFH: Absolutely, and still say I am enjoying it, fabulous.

AA: You start from the practices?

SFH: Yes, as you told me...follow instructions. I am very compliant.

AA: Do I detect that Shaykh Asif to you is a Shaykh in terms of a person who has seen the full panoply of the *nafs*?

SFH: Not so much. You know I can't define a Shaykh in such easy terms. I define it in the spiritual sense for this purpose: 'somebody who has been pulverized, burnt out, has touched the Absolute.' So that is it for me, yes.

AA: So his behavior and so on may be outside the norms, but whether it's of benefit or not does not detract from this inner quality.

SFH: No, he is an illumined person, an enlightened person. But I don't think there is anybody I know who has a better and full understanding of the cosmology of the self than what Allah has given him.

Shaykh Nazim

AA: Shaykh Nazim, whom I don't know at all – all I know is that he has many followers – a huge number – I've recently in preparation for this watched a few YouTube talks of his. I find them beguiling. He seems to be rooted in a highly traditional form of *tariqah*, like Shaykh Asif.

SFH: Most of the Shaykhs adhere to conventional paths.

AA: Outer garb, the courtesies ...where people sit, *amana* is established, silence and so on – very much part of the Ottoman official Sufism tradition with all of its benefits and problems. You can probably visualize a great figure in the latter part of the Ottoman Empire – consulted on and brought out with other *shuyukh* and *mawlawi* on state occasions.

SFH: Two hundred years ago. Correct, I think your evaluation is very correct.

AA: I see aspects of Shaykh Nazim's movement as presenting the worst aspects of *tariqah* in the sense of this rigid hierarchy, the role of relatives and in-laws, his entourage... but at the same time I see him floating over it.

SFH: He can: I tell you again; there is no real knowledge of the *nafs*. He himself has lost everything – has no vanity – he is clear of that – but he belongs to another era, he says things which are completely out of context in this time, such as a whole book written on the healing power of kerosene, for every ailment you drink kerosene – things like that. So the largest numbers of people around him are disappointed in life, failed in life, maybe two-thirds of them are women who found their husbands in Egypt and are miserable – they flock across to him – so it is that. I think these people have touched the thing, but the connectedness, the overall aspect of looking at the Adam of thousands of years ago, and Ibrahim and then Muhammad is not there. The perspective is not there.

AA: I cannot comment, because I find his writing impossible to grasp.

SFH: No, no discrimination. My last time with him – we had about an hour together and there were lots of rubbishy people coming and going – he turned around to me and said, 'You know Allah has given me the worst, most impossible situation in this life. I don't want to tell you more – you know who is my son-in-law.' So he confided in me. Good luck to him. He wants that position. I had deeply, deeply ingrained in me the dervish-y, the *malamati*[64], the pre Shams i Tabrizi touch, and that has been often if you like, my line of rescue from all of these movements, gatherings, *tariqahs*. I never ever paid any attention to any of them whatsoever. Titles, garbs – I could not care less.

AA: So all these types, which have been manifest, have little effect.

SFH: The effect has been much more on *La Ilaha* rather than *Il-Allah*.

AA: I don't think you'd say the same about Sufi Barakat Ali.

Ahmad Ibn `Ajiba

SFH: No, I wouldn't. He is the exception that proves the rule. Nor would I say that about Ahmad Ibn `Ajiba – not the one who lived 200 years ago, the living one. He is there –

AA: I didn't know.

SFH: He is one of three brothers. Again, Batul can tell you more about him. I stayed with him a few days in his little *zawiya* in the middle of nowhere – in a cactus field outside Tangier – an hour and a half drive. He was a living being – the most unusual being, not well and had a *zawiya* and students, typical Shadhili type of thing – Alawi and Hasani.

AA: Is that the *zawiya* in Tangier?

SFH: No – an hour and a half out of Tangier in the middle of nowhere, very near where his great grandfather and namesake is buried. Several tombs, beautiful white tombs and green fields. He was a remarkable being.

AA: *Qalandar*?

---

[64] The Malamatiyya or Malamatis were a Muslim mystic group active in 9th century Greater Khorasan. Their root word of their name is the Arabic word *malamah* "blame". The Malamatiyya believed in the value of self-blame, that piety should be a private matter and that being held in good esteem would lead to worldly attachment.

SFH: No, he was a Shaykh of a *tariqah* and – no paraphernalia – simplicity itself, walking barefoot – simple. And the day I was there with him (I may have visited him more than once) but that day was a very full day – a very wealthy Saudi came in his private jet, because his daughter was paraplegic. He had been all over the world, including America, and couldn't find the cure. So he had heard about this man who was a healer. He turned to me quietly and said, 'what does he think I can do?' And the Saudi was very angry; he said, 'he's not immediately giving me this and that, I've come all this way.'

He was another being – light upon light – great – and his wife got on very well with Batul and they had a lot of good confidences.

Shaykh Ikram

AA: Shaykh Ikram, whom I know but I never could really be on the same wavelength with. Maybe because of his archaism.

SFH: No, I was the same, not that different from you. But I knew of his *batiniyya*, his immense power. And I am a balanced being. I am a worldly being, heavenly illumined, or whatever, but I knew that this man was not the same as anyone else. And his inner effect upon others was immense by *Nadhr*.

AA: But I think he's a person, whom you have to have been in his cultural milieu, as it were, to take benefit from him. The kind of Hyderabadi, Pakistani…

SFH: No, not necessarily – or without a mind, or intellect or reason; being able to enter that zone, then you connect.

AA: What type of benefit did you get from him?

SFH: The benefit that there is another being who knows the immensity of what you and I may call oblivion or no thingness. He experienced it; he is in it. He refers to it; he calls upon it. He also used it whenever he was doing his medicine – he was an unusual being.

AA: A *hakim*?

SFH: Very much so, that was his main thing. And the way we met was a most amazing thing. It was one of the miracles of miracles. The way we met.

AA: How did that happen?

SFH: I wanted a place to save myself from the American Muslims, somewhere in a Muslim land where they could at least hear the *adhan*. Where was it? I couldn't find it in any place in the Arab world. So I thought of the middle of the Punjab, Ahmadpur. I had a few people with me there, such as Khalid Iqbal, so we found a place very near Ahmadpur; we bought land and built a place for these people to go for a few weeks/months to imbibe something. I can't remember the details – it was very intricate. Seyyed Ikram was practicing in Hyderabad. There was a man who every now and then appeared in their culture, and who had died 800 years ago in Syria, a *Qalandar*. He would appear every 10/20 years giving someone instructions and disappearing. A man from Ahmadpur, from that area, had a son who became sick, so he dedicated the son and said, 'I will make this son a Hakim for Allah's sake.' He does Istikhara, goes to Mecca and forgets about it. The son goes to *madrasa*. One day the son, a teenager, becomes so sick he can't even walk on the road. He goes under a bridge and there was this man, the *Qalandar* who is dead, tells him, 'Go and tell your father to keep his promise. There is a Shaykh Ikram in Hyderabad. He must go to him and be his student.' This is the story. So the father takes the son to Seyyed Ikram, saying, 'he's your apprentice.' His name is – the son in Ahmadpur – Akhtar. So Seyyed Ikram had a link with Ahmadpur: that's when I arrived. He said, 'I've been waiting for you the last two years; I've been making *du'a*. I want to meet somebody who has got the flavor of the Shadhilis, a Shadhili *shaykh*, as I'm missing them. We are too Eastern – I want that Western flavor.' It's amazing, the way we met. The encounter with Bashir Osman, with you, with Shaykh Asif and *jinn* have all been amazing.

AA: I can't think the other *shuyukh* – unless you care to mention them. I don't know anybody who comes to mind.

Sufi Barkat Ali

SFH: I'll talk about Sufi Barkat Ali; he was the dearest to my heart of all.

AA: Because of his singularity…

SFH: He was far more universal than all of them. That's why he would put the names of many of the *tariqahs* after his name – some, I had no idea. I don't know if you have seen them – two or three lines after his name – this and that – it was like a holy joke – I'd think, 'what's he talking about?' He would say, 'I am one of those.' Also, whenever he met someone he would say, 'you are also my *shaykh* – you are the real teacher' – and on and on and on. So he had gone way past all of them. When I met him, it was just a carry over of being in this body and in this life... and he had been fasting for thirty years. And of course with me, he would just laugh and talk and converse – that's why the few people around him thought I was very extraordinary and special, they would run after me all the way to Karachi and every where else; they had seen in him behaviors – for example one evening there were forty, fifty of these fellows with big beards, really genuine followers, and he would say, 'I am the *shaykh* of the buffalos so follow another *shaykh*…' So they all said, 'where is he, who is he?' *Maghrib* came and somebody called the *adhan* in this huge place with rooms where all the chiefs of Qur'an would come. And he would say, 'now we all have to pray behind the real *shaykh*.'… there were a number of incidents like this. The people around him realized this was odd. Of course I wanted to stay with him..... So I think in terms of real love and total unison, I knew him and he knew me, and we knew nothing except the source of knowledge…a holy fool... a more evolved being, a more illumined... he knew it inside out, had access to it. "He told me I was once there with him and this man, who is now Prime Minister, Nawaz Sharif. He was in Faisalabad, half an hour drive. He wanted to come and see me. He asked, 'can I come now?' There was nothing I could do for him, nothing he could do for me. Why was he wasting his time?" He was beyond wisdom beyond.... and he operated at all of the levels of consciousness…

AA: He was a former air force officer?

SFH: He was in the army and I have a number of letters from him: he called me his inspector; he used to say, 'Fadhlalla comes to me as an inspector. .... I had lent him one of my Qur'ans; so he comes even with a general to inspect' – and he said he was discharged because his officers found him God-intoxicated. I had immense love, connection, affinity, for him – he was a father, a brother, and he knew that. And he hid under the Prophetic character, the Prophetic profile; he wrote a lot on that; and he was surrounded by people who were at another level... really peasants.

AA: Did he withdraw completely from society?

SFH: No, he was fully in it – he had a huge compound. He had four sons; later in life he denounced them all. He walked away from that huge center, for Qur'an; that center was on an enormous land, with buildings like a Versaille Palace. He used to put together Qur'ans from pieces; that was his mission. He would say, 'if you find a piece of the Qur'an, bring it to me.' He had three or four hundred children sticking these pieces together, thousands of sheets of Qur'ans, compiled and put together.

AA: In order?

SFH: No, not in order,... and there were Qur'ans that were written on grains of rice, Qur'ans that each page was about 6 meters – four people had to turn the pages – it was extraordinary, extraordinary – and whenever I was there he would open up all of them... he used a number of these... and also he had the habit at the end of the day: no food nor provision would remain in the center. There were about 10 large rooms, huge halls... going up. And in one of these halls he had six or seven piles of rose petals on the floor that he would use for healing. And not far from it he had 20 or 30 piles of his clothes from last year, the year before – he had two sets of clothes, the same; they were full of holes and were worn out. These were his past. Somebody asked him why? At the end of the day everything would go out. So at the end of one visit, I gave him a list of 7 things to be taken to his place – a sack of rice, a sack of this and that. There was the director of a college of Islamic Studies – a Pakistani who also came to America with me, with his assistant – nice people. So I gave them money and said, 'go and get all of these and take them to the center of Sufi Barkat Ali.' They arrived there at about *maghrib* time. One of the big sacks was of flowers – I had asked for flour, and they took him flowers. So Sufi Barkat Ali said, 'It's too late, it's after *maghrib* – none of this will stay here, it will be distributed.' Secondly, he allocated two or three of his men to put these people in the *mihrab* and throw these roses at them. He said, 'Idiots, how could Shaykh Fadhlalla do this?' So there were a number of such wonderful incidents.

AA: Interesting anecdote!

SFH: He said, 'How could he send me flowers?' He was an extraordinary being. I went to see him a few times with some Swedish people, with Ali Bilgrami's wife, and he would be running between the orchard and his house and he would have a *tasbih* of I think 5000 beads – two or three people had to carry it behind him – and he would deliberately go around a tree and confuse them.

AA: Mischievous!

SFH: Mischievous – wonderful. He would show his sense of humor especially for me. For example, if someone said, 'he is not here,' he would say, 'of course he is not here! Who in his right mind would be here?' That sort of thing.

Seyyed Hossein Nasr

AA: Shaykhna, the other people I am interested in are the Hukamas, sages or philosophers; also the pious *'ulama* – I'm sure you came across – (SFH: Many) the ones who came to mind – for example, Seyyed Hossein Nasr; what is your opinion of him?

SFH: I think he was an earlier hybrid of what was to come – a typical well bred, well brought up, educated young man, of western orientation, infatuated with western thought, science, with a great empathy and sympathy for the tradition. He wanted to be the introducer of the inner lights of Islam, or *Tasawwuf* or Qur'an, to the West – I think he took that role upon him. He was a great example of what was beginning to sprout 40, 50, 60 years ago; he wanted to introduce, in a way Tabataba`i's[65] thing to the West, to be that link – that channel – take on the young Chitticks[66] of the world. I think he was very hopeful that he'd play a big role with the Shah's wife – he became her personal secretary. And he was taken by those roles. I think it was commendable. I felt pity and sorry for him. When he came to England during the revolution, I was there, and I met him a few times, with Commander Hussain. He was given an exercise on writing a book on the life of Muhammad, *The Man of Allah* – that's the title I gave him. Nice people. But I also felt sorry for the man. A man in that position – he'd not had a penny in England; he'd come with three suitcases, mostly clothes, to go to Japan as the Shah was invited to Japan. The Shah couldn't go because of troubles ... so they appointed Nasr to go. So he came with 3 or 4 sets of clothes, formal clothes to go to the imperial palace. The suitcases were useless as he couldn't go to Japan. Anyway, I really felt sorry for the man.

AA: You wanted to help him, relaunch him.

SFH: In a way, but without a great deal of inner affinity.

AA: Are his teachings, his research, in any way usable?

SFH: Very much so. I would recommend them to anybody, at any time. I find most of it boring though.

AA: But you would recommend them anyway, right?

---

[65] A well-known *hakim*, and philosopher.
[66] William Chittick is an American student of Nasr and later, a major scholar of *Tasawwuf* and ibn `Arabi.

SFH: No doubt. I recommend them all the time. I'm one of his big advocates.

Sayyed Mehdi Hakim

AA: What about Sayyed Mehdi Hakim?

SFH: Again, as good as you can get out of that theological background – he had *tawakkul*. He had that innate reliance on Allah, always. When he came from Dubai he was under threat. I was sitting with him at one of the cafes in Kensington High Street. Two people came from the CID in England and said, 'you know you are being shadowed, we don't recommend you stay here.' So he turned to me and said, 'I'll never defend myself, I won't run away.' I said, 'Since we are being given this advice, we should move somewhere else.' And he really relied on his *tawakkul* – I respected him, I loved him, I learnt a lot from him regarding *Shari`ah*; he had light, he had honesty, no pomposity, vanity, not much of self. I trusted him, I loved him, and I learnt a lot from him, in short doses also – half an hour, an hour. There was no delight; there was no ecstasy; for me humanity and divinity, when they are balanced – on the human level, you are concerned, you do what you have to do, but on the divine level you are beyond all that. That wasn't there; nor did I expect it. But with me, we had an impeccable time – the last time I met him, in a house that he bought for my sister – Kensington Mews or something – he would often make Iraqi tea for me. I would go there quietly and after about an hour when I was about to leave, he would come to the door, very courteously, so I'd say – as usual, Iraqi stuff – 'Is there anything I can do for you?' He said, 'Yes.' Surprising as usually there is *tatt'aruf*. I said, 'what is it?' He said, 'Pray that I will join my brothers who were martyred.' I said, 'I never pray for these things; time is not in our hands – it's in Allah's hands.' He said, 'But didn't you ask me if there is anything you can do? Then pray for me. I want to go.' The next day he went to Sudan and the day after he was killed. I was not surprised one bit. It was his inner desire. This man's connection was deeper than ordinary. So there were quite a number of encounters with him.

AA: He never broke the balance?

SFH: I don't know.

AA: What you saw of him –

SFH: What I saw of him was that he was a man living on *tawakkul*, trusting in the One.

AA: A man of virtue.

SFH: A man of virtue, accountability, *akhlaq* and *suluk* to the hundredth degree.-

AA: Unconcerned.

SFH: Total concern and devotion and ready for martyrdom. This was obviously his *qibla*.

AA: The best of the clerical, `*ulama* tradition.

SFH: Absolutely. And also, yearning to be in that stream.

Ayatollah Imam Khomeini

AA: What about the encounter with the person who may have connected the two – Ayatollah Imam Khomeini?

SFH: No doubt. He was an exception that proves the rule.

AA: You saw him?

SFH: Yes.

AA: And you perceived that?

SFH: No, I knew that before I saw him from the incidents that I heard – there were a number of strange incidents. Somebody from Najaf seeks me out in London at a bookshop. Out of the blue. I even forget the name of the man. He comes and says, 'I know you know and love Imam Khomeini – I came to tell you something – I was there the morning after his son had died, so I used to go every morning to pay my respects – 8 o'clock in the morning. His man brought tea, and I said, "doesn't he know that his son has died? This morning!" He said, "Of course he does." I waited – the Imam was discussing something with his students – their income or something. I went back to the man who was serving tea – I said, "How come? Where is the *janaza*?" He said, "You know as you go." That man told me, "You say you know him. It turns out you don't know him at all. If you knew him, you would know that he carries on doing whatever; he will attend to his son and it's not the end of the world." ' He said, 'I wanted to tell you that – he was like that – obviously he took it to heart, but in his outer conduct, he carries on.' So I had a number of such incidents coming to me. For example, I went to visit him in his office in Jamiran –

AA: During the Mu'tamar – the conference in support of the Iraq opposition.

SFH: Yes, the Mu'tamar and ... there was Baqar al-Hakim – all jostling with their robes to sit in a position where they could be noticed – and I didn't want to be noticed because I had no passport – and they'd renewed my passport, and the fellow who renewed my passport told my cousin that this fellow was suspect. He was with the ambassador – they gambled together. He said, 'I'll renew it for you, but watch out!' So after we arrived in Tehran this fellow who made my passport phoned me to the hotel in Tehran, he said, 'Look you didn't tell me you were going to Iran – the ambassador just phoned me. Several of your people with you told them.' So I said, 'Please excuse me, you didn't ask me.' So I didn't want to be noticed.

AA: Avoid the limelight –

SFH: Yes, I wanted to avoid the limelight. Anyway, I end up sitting somewhere, he [Imam Khomeini] comes and sits one meter in front of me. Between us there was a blue cotton roll of rug – probably from India

– and on the edge of it was written the word, '*'Irfani*', in big letters. Between him and I there was this word '*'Irfani*'. So I looked up to see where the sentence began – it said '*Waqfa*...something something, *Jamiran, 'Irfani*' – this cloth is donated for the thing, for *'Irfani*. And the way he looked at me – more or less he said, 'What are you doing here?' Also, when he was in Paris, I thought of going back to the East, and the message was: 'You don't belong anywhere here. Stay in the West, it's much better, more important. We don't need you.'

AA: So you don't see him through the prism of *Hukuma Islamiyya*?

SFH: No, incidental, accidental, and he responded only. None at all –

AA: And it was his vision – divine inspiration?

SFH: Totally. I think it was again that when human beings begin to awaken they have to choose leaders who have led themselves. Therefore this is my interpretation of *Vilayat al-Faqih*. I don't think there was such a thing; the same thing I hear about the biographies of the Prophet, that he plotted – strategic planning and all that rubbish, as we are taught nowadays in MBA courses – so we try to impose that. I remember him saying, 'I had no idea what's going to come. I thought I was just there with a small little preacher – I didn't know I am holding the tail of a fighting bull', meaning Iran. I don't think he had any pre-conceived ideas about how to run Iran.

AA: Things just unfolded.

SFH: Unfolded, and he responded – I think he was one of the greatest ever...

AA: ...and have you changed your view?

SFH: No. In terms of what we see in a way of a sustainable movement, that again is not his judgment – he went along. It wasn't sustainable, because it was euphoria, mass hysteria. What can you do, but let things unfold? If you unleash something what else can you do?

AA: What would happen is that other, more scheming and cruel, people would take over.

SFH: I consider these as part of little cycles along the path of rise of consciousness. Yes – and I think he carried that along, saying he was taking the cup of poison with them – because I know that he asked them to stop the war with Iraq, but the others were all full of feisty and all that and said no, no, no. I investigated that and I found that the second year of the Iraqi war, this was his wish, but they didn't follow him. So he took his `abaya* and left. So they carried on for seven years. Why? Take a cup of poison – what does it mean? He said, 'You people poisoned me; you are the people who don't listen, don't hear.' I think he was one of the very few who had the seen and the unseen connected, and he was in both and neither.

AA: All these were just chronological incidents…

SFH: …and many people read in them what they want to read.

AA: They had no intrinsic meaning for him.

SFH: I don't think so – I think he lived the moment fully.

Reaching Luminosity

Knowledge from Books

AA: What about Shaykhna, knowledge that comes from books, not by knowing people but knowledge that comes from reading, not *'Irfani* but other scriptural texts, poetry, the Mathnawi for example, Western wisdom traditions – did they ever have any effect on you?

SFH: No doubt. Early on in my life they were like little openers, little teasers, hors d'oeuvres, early on. Later on, much more, they confirmed what I had already experienced. Even more useful. Far, far more useful in that I suddenly read something I already know, and I see that it's now been verbalized.

AA: I ask you a question that is asked in 'Desert Island Discs' – you are on a desert island and the only books that are there are the Qur'an and the collected works of Shakespeare... what would be your choice apart from these?

SFH: Nothing. I'd say, take them all away.

AA: The Mathnawi and …?

SFH: Nothing. I won't say I don't need them. But I don't want any books; I can read my own book. Where is it that I look and it is not the book?

AA: *Nahj al-Balagha*?

SFH: Part of it, maybe due to emotional reasons or something, but I wouldn't take anything.

AA: Qur'an? Nothing?

SFH: I would be reading the Qur'an, reciting the Qur'an, in my own heart, in my own voice.

AA: Are you a *hafiz* of Qur'an?

SFH: No. But I have been given I think enough of the fabric of *Qur'an bil Qur'an*. I think if you give me any *ayah* I can almost tell you either the completion or the meaning of it.

AA: So you don't need to have a written copy of it?

SFH: No I don't. I really have come to the point of a blooming desert.

AA: …and the Upanishads…?

SFH: No interest – none, I say, 'please, I don't need it. If you leave them there thank you very much, I respect you…'

AA: It's your choice?

SFH: No, I have no choice. Somebody brought it, I have no choice. 'Thank you very much. It's not my desire.' I really see myself as a real *faqir* – doesn't mean that there isn't much in my hand of my provision. But there is nothing in my heart as far as deep desires are concerned.

AA: So they are of no use to your present state in terms of reference?

SFH: Not at all. I have no reference. There is no *ayah*. I really don't see the *ayah*. No referential, no differential – no…….. I respect them, I acknowledge them-

AA: Wouldn't you be interested in, say you are in a certain *haal* on a desert island, don't you want to have a reference/idea as to how someone like Ibn Arabi might have experienced in the same condition?

SFH: Not interested – Ibn Arabi or anyone. If you give me the Qur'an that was written by Ali himself (AS) by his own hand, I'd say please take the top copy. Don't leave it here, it'll get sandy.

AA: Your library will be bare...

SFH: If you want to leave it, *Bismillah*, but be the keeper of it, I'm not around.

AA: You will not open it?

SFH: I doubt it. I really doubt it. I have not opened any books. I have collected books for 30, 40 years, some of which I have not read at all, they are still there –

AA: I will hoard the books!!

SFH: Good. "Each one does as one is".... I respect you, I love you, I adore you – *Bismillah*...

AA: I will ignite it for a fire if the temperature falls below zero.

SFH: You are at the cusp of realizing that the Light that caused the energy that caused all of that output is in you. Tipping point. So I'm not concerned. You still impress me that you are a hoarder, but I don't think you are not a hoarder, so don't try to convince me!

AA: No, I'm asking rhetorical questions Shaykhna, provocative!

SFH: You are not provocative, you never provoke me.

AA: I must say, I cannot imagine that if somebody offered you the Qur'an, you would say, 'leave it there. I may return to it.' May be…

SFH: I live by it. Not that I may return to it. But if it is written by Imam Ali (AS), don't waste it there, because others will reveal it and –

AA: What about memory, Shaykhna? Supposing your memory fails and you want to read the Qur'an.

SFH: Terrible. I don't want memory – it is the biggest handicap.

AA: How would you do your *Salaat*?

SFH: Don't do *Salaat* – if you can't do *Salaat*, don't do *Salaat*.

AA: But is it not obligatory on a desert island?

SFH: It is obligatory, but if you don't have a mind, it is not obligatory.

AA: But *Shari`ah* ...

SFH: It is obligatory as long as you have discrimination and a mind – if you have no mind, then it is not obligatory.

AA: But there's no one around you. There's nothing there. And provisions are dropped from the sky...

SFH: I will send you an email when I am there...

AA: But I'm talking about *Hayy ibn Yaqzan*[67].

SFH: Everybody has a *Hayy* in their heart.

AA: So every question I ask, you respond to it in relation to your luminous self or non-self.

SFH: There is only that. Everything else is secondary and dull.

AA: Therefore from non-self Hayy and Mickey Mouse are on the same level.

SFH: No they are not.

---

[67] The Arabic philosophical fable *Hayy Ibn Yaqzan* is a classic of medieval Islamic philosophy. Ibn Tufayl (d. 1185), the Andalusian philosopher, tells of a child raised by a doe on an equatorial island who grows up to discover the truth about the world and his own place in it, unaided—but also unimpeded—by society, language, or tradition. Hayy's discoveries about God, nature, and man challenge the values of the culture in which the tale was written as well as those of every contemporary society.

AA: As written works.

SFH: As written works, yes, but as depicting different zones of life or consciousness, no. One of them appeals to my childhood, and a bit of silly childhood fun; the other one is telling me that everyone has to go through that zone of trying to save the world; when you go to the mosque, suddenly you find that you can't save the world. Go back and let them try it; it's a revolutionary issue; it may take another thousand years before *Hayy* is called back again.

AA: But as I understand it, non-self and self are the same – two sides of the same coin, of no inherent meaning.

SFH: Non-self implies somebody who has done the work that was expected: live the self, be the self, don't deny the self, but transcend it. Transcend it. I never deny the self – I love the self, I love the ego – I think it is sacred. But equally, I have to transcend it to a zone where neither the sacred nor the profane have any zone.

AA: You're satisfied then with what is called.

SFH: Totally…

AA: …The Beatific Vision.

The Absolute

SFH: There is only that – the only vision – everything else is division.....can I take a break?

AA: Yes, as we come to the Absolute now.

SFH: There is only the Absolute.

AA: Shaykhna, there's so much talk about the Absolute, Transcendent, Non-Manifest, as a way to illumine the human mind and try to understand this Infinitude. We're not talking about what lies beyond that

– I don't think it is either appropriate or correct to talk about it. But why is that? Why can you not talk about the essence of the Absence? Is it simply unknowable?

SFH: What I see as a clear pattern is that of duality emerging from unity sustained by unity, returning back to unity. So the whole thing is an illusion of an occurrence or an event or creation. It's an illusion, and we delude ourselves that this has got some sustainable reality on its own, that it is independent. There's no such thing. My own personal conviction and experience is that the less we try to look what is beyond, the better, because you and I and he and she have been trained to think rationally through the mind: this leads to the other side of the coin: causality, rationality, logic, reason, justice – and the Absolute is the cause of it all, the mother of it all, the father of it all. It's before it, within it. *Awwal, wal Akhir, wal Dhahir, wal Batin.* So we are infatuated by one thing, what we know as this limitation of space and time, or *fitra*, crack, to continue forever. It doesn't work. It's another zone. What I see again is the duality of consciousness. I'm conscious of my personal awareness of life in me, pain, anguish, comfort, zone, trust, not trust. This is the realm I am in. I want to extend this realm to its origin that is beyond space and time. It's absurd, it will never work. It's absurdity itself, stupidity itself.

AA: So why talk about it?

SFH: Because they are absurd, they are greedy, they are presumptuous, assuming that I, this so-called limited being with its space and time, birth and death, I can now jump into the other zone. Rubbish. Unless I accept and submit to my limitations – and Islam is nothing other than that.

The limitless may or may not show itself in its own way – I don't know. Otherwise it's presumption, spiritual materialism; it will lead to nowhere except academic debate, and to a nonsensical barrenness.

AA: Nearly all the people who one can say have reached the point of this kind of luminosity, they usually reach it at a certain point, after which they go into silence, for example Aquinas, who wrote the greatest theological work in history of any culture. In the last month he was about to finish his Summa, he said he had an experience. His scribe said, 'Why have you stopped?' He said, 'because what I've done is just straw,' and he kept quiet, the same thing you can say about the last months of Ibn Arabi – worthless, who also went into silence. You were asking about the Prophet in his last months – but these are the final stages of complete erasure of any barriers... but before that Shaykhna, there's a period when these things were the stuff about which great beings spent a lot of time, and very valuable time to try to come to grips with. And it is in that context I'm asking about the Absolute Essence.

SFH: Well I can't comment much on that. The great being is the One and Only Being, who by some mysterious reason or cause or effulgence, some impossible for us to imagine – that great Being has bestowed that spark of the *ruh* in every other being. So I don't really have that much great reverence other than in a traditional way for great beings – there's only One Being. All of the rest are hindrances. It's good for the seeker, earlier on to find this is greater, this is finer, this is more ..... until such time all of that falls off and there is mindlessness. Entering into silence doesn't have to be literal – it can also be metaphorical. Those who know cannot convey it because that knowledge is not conveyable – it's absolute. You can only talk about this is slightly better than that – then there is relativeness and comparison. Good, fine, until such time that you are exhausted from that *mizaan*, scale, going up and down. *Saorhiquhu sa`uda*[68]. We have to be so exhausted that you submit to it. The greatest thing we have actually is the name of Islam – surrender to it. Otherwise the other side, discussion and all, takes over. I personally know that this is a realm in which you have to enter with another set of courtesies. There's a courtesy in discussing reason, logic, theology, philosophy in this realm, but once you are at the edge of *Ka`ba* then *ikhla na`layka* [69] – you cannot in any way any more allude to anything. So you must have inner sight. And that you find is there – you find that in truth there is nothing other than Reality – capital 'R'. Every other reality with a small 'r' is deriving its nourishment from that Supreme Consciousness – that's

---

[68] "I will exhaust him as he tries to rise." (Qur'an 74:17)
[69] *fakhla` na`layka* ("Take off your shoes!" – Qur'an 20:12)

all. And then there is nothing more to say or do. Other than whatever is a bit of a habit. You still have to maintain the body, eat, relate, thank people. That's about it.

Knowledge/Two Zones

AA: So all subsidiary knowledge in relationship to outer knowledge is really like straw in the wind.

SFH: No, but straw has a reality in the realm of *duniya*. I again say there is nothing possible in this existence except it is one of two. There is this *duniya* and there is the *akhira*; there is this world and earth, and there is heaven; there is *nafs* and there is *ruh*; body/mind and there is *ruhan-ruh*. It has its realm; it is part of the plot of Allah – I can't deny it. But if you want to extend yourself to the other realm with your feet and your heart and head still in this, it's a waste of time. From that point of view you have to abandon it, submit to it, say no more.

AA: But Shaykhna, as pathways to reach this kind of knowledge, surely this discursive reasoning, this speculative thinking, all these constructs are very insignificant aids on the path –

SFH: They're useful to the door. After the door you have to "Take off your shoes," you have to get rid of all.

AA: But as processes some have more or lesser reality. Some are good, some are misleading.

SFH: I accept. Some of them are misleading, correct.

AA: And in this construct in the classical cosmological scheme of things, could they have any reality as doorways to the Doorway?

SFH: No doubt. There are two zones – this realm, which takes you up to a very high sublime subtle thing, and then there is the other one, which is the Absolute. And in between there is a *barzakh*, there is a no man's land. So they'll take you to that no man's land, but from that point on you're on your own. And there is no 'own' – you are not alone – there is all one. So you have to accept it, revere it, thank it, and leave it – now you are into the in-between state. Then you are between the fingers of Rahman – *bayna asabia al-rahman*[70] – that's it. You don't know what comes. You have access to some reference to that from a person or from Qur'an or from Muhammad's life – great, but otherwise you are there, hanging between nowhere and everywhere, until such time as you know that you don't know. I mentioned to you that I wrote to Chinmaya after my *khalwa*. I said, 'The obvious that you constantly told me, now is obvious, there is nothing other than the Obvious…'

AA: Then why did you spend thirty years, Shaykhna? Writing?

SFH: Stupidity – this is life – I've been given hell, I've been given friends like you – no, nothing is waste; this is relative. Nothing is ever wasted. Everything is energy increased.

Spiritual Hierarchies – A Big Handicap

AA: I can ask this question from a personal point of view; I see these as rungs, as steps on the ladder – I know they don't have a reality; they are only pointers or indicators, useful incremental tools, useful concepts, ways of thinking, but they have a value because they point in this direction. You are more likely to engage with these questions in a constructive way than if you spend your time watching TV.

SFH: One of the issues of Sufism, which I have also found very distracting, is that the teachers – even some of these great Sufis – do not say, 'this is now for the novice.' And, 'this now is for the mature novice,' and 'this now is for the one who is at the door of *Ka`ba*'. I saw myself as having shed a skin and now I'm taking a piece of stick and looking at the skin. It's useful for others who have not shed their skin, but for someone who is at the door of *Ka`ba* I'd say forget it all. You

---

[70] "Between the fingers of the Merciful." (From the Prophetic saying: "The heart of the believer is between two fingers of the Merciful.")

must be mindless. Stop thinking of books and writing. So it depends who you are talking to. So…

AA: I'm not talking specifically about you – I'm talking about you as a person who wants to transmit and transfer the experience rather than the actual condition.

SFH: No, I cannot be the agent of transmitting or anything. All I can say is that every human being has a *hajj* in front of him – he has to move from the earliest awareness, which brings about individuality, separation, individuation, the ego, to the root of that awareness which was their beginning. So this business of path or journey I think, for people who are mature, can become a big handicap. I say ignore it. There is no beginning, no end, there is none other than the One. Stop this. Otherwise, 'I am now moving more' and the rung of the ladder. Boring stuff! It can actually be a big handicap. How far are you on the hierarchy?! And the Sufi traditions of having five, six, ten different hierarchies of people close to the Shaykh. Forget the Shaykh! Go to the light of the Shaykh and you'll find there is only that Light.

AA: Am I allowed to agree, Shaykhna?

SFH: Agree or disagree, it makes no difference.

AA: But before that …. and I can tell you reading this in preference to that made me reach the *"I shall exhaust him as he tries to rise,"*[71] quickly and easier.

SFH: Really? Brilliant! I accept that.

AA: So if some people ask you, 'can I read this or that?' What would you say Shaykhna?

SFH: Same – I'd say go and listen to Ali; he is better than me! I really mean it. I say I am at a zone that I may confuse you more. Don't come

---

[71] Qur'an 74:17.

near me. I feel I'm like the burning bush. You are either going to burn into dust and be nothing or you're going to be illumined. So be careful. Don't come near me. It all depends according to your *niyya*. '*Wa `ala niyyatukum furzaqun*[72]' – according to your intention. If your intention is really to give up your so-called 'you-ness', and 'I-ness', then you'll be illumined. If your intention is to test me and try me, you'll burn. Don't do it.

Nur of Allah

AA: This knowledge – is it absolute confirmation or can it be false?

SFH: I won't call it knowledge any more.

AA: This state.

SFH: This state is the only early first effulgence from the *nur* of Allah. It's the *Muhammadi nur*.

AA: So you cannot experience it falsely?

SFH: No, because it burns everything else. You have to be first, having done whatever during earlier stages – you have to do the *takhlia* – emptying out: *tasfiya*, purifying, *tahliya* – sweeten – you know the sweetness of the *ruh*. You know the ultimate sweetness in existence is the *nur* of Allah, the bliss. If there is any thrill, it is that – everything else is frivolous, at a lower, lower, lower level. It becomes pleasure and you have displeasure, which becomes duality then. So then it leads to *tajlia*. All what is left every now and then is just polish. *Inna Lillahi wa Inna `alaihi raji`un*[73].

AA: It can't be false.

SFH: At that level it cannot.

---

[72] "You will be provided according to your intention."
[73] "We have come from Allah, and are returning to Him." (Qur'an 2:156)

AA: Can it be experienced without that?

SFH: It's the only experience – every other experience is non-existent.

AA: What about what is commonly termed as insanity?

SFH: Well, they are very close at that time, because you are beyond mind anyway. You can't approach that with a mind. It has to be with the *ruh*, with your *qalb*.

AA: But this process of *takhliya, tahliha*,...

The Map

SFH: It is getting rid of the *nafs*, getting rid of the mind.

AA: It's done consciously, not unconsciously.

SFH: To begin with it's consciously; to begin with you're sick of your self, you're tired of the duality of reason. Then you move on from that – watch your *nafs*, put it in its place, laugh at it, express it. Say, 'Look here, my *nafs* thought you were going to be revering me today. There were not two thousand people as you promised, there was nobody.' Laugh at it initially. Until you find that it was leading you. The *nafs* is the agent on one side, the agent of your *ruh*. And the other side of it has to have its own independence because it's *duniya* related, and the *ruh* is heavenly oriented. You find the whole map is so simple.

AA: Undeniable.

SFH: Undeniable. Surrender to it and you will not only see the map, read the map, it will read you.

Kufr al-Khafi/Shirk

AA: So what is the '*kufr al-khafi*'?

SFH: It is *Shirk*. When they asked the Prophet about *shirk*, he said, "the Qur'an says, 'And most of them are *mushrik*'[74]", meaning most of the real faithful believers – people of *ihsan* are *mushrikun*: '*Wama yu'minu aktharuhum billahi illa wahum mushrikoon* [75]' You are associating because you are there – you are associating with you. There is a 'you-ness' within you. So most of creation, the best of them, still have a trace of *shirk*. Because there has to be in creation a slight element of 'you' still being in creation, and that is *shirk al-hafidh*. And so they asked the Prophet, 'What is it?' He said 'it's like trying to catch a black ant creeping on a black rock in the middle of the darkest part of the night.' So there is still, as Ibn Arabi said, there has to be an aspect of the *nafs*; don't deny it. But it is, as the Prophet (SAW) said, when she asked him, 'what about your *nafs*?' tells her: 'it's your *nafs* speaking now, Shaytan?' she said, 'What about your *shaytan*?' He said, 'Mine is *aslam*, quietly sitting in his cave.' You know you want to be god, you want to be the ruler, you want to be the king of kings. Everybody thinks if they are given the power to rule a country, they can do better. If you don't know that, then you are not really qualified to rule. If you've not governed yourself how can you govern others? There's no otherness. It's a fantasy. That is why most earthly ruler-ship, leadership or governorship is miserable. It is because of that.

AA: With your permission I'd say that I find this far less interesting than the opposite, which I've never heard of but I'll say *at-tahqiq al-khiz*, that is, denial, affirmation of denial is in itself a confirmation of reality.

SFH: Correct. Absolutely correct. 100%.

AA: And in this age it's not the *Shirk al-Khafi* which ....

SFH: Absolutely – right, and this has also been said repeatedly classically. I'll try to remember, there is a couplet – it will come to me later.

---

[74] Qur'an 12:106.
[75] "And most of them will only believe in God while also associating others with Him." (Qur'an 12:106)

AA: So it doesn't matter what you do, what you say, how you act, you're ultimately dragged kicking and screaming.

SFH: Absolutely. Denial of that which is illusory is conclusory – denial of that. There is a beautiful Arabic classical saying …

AA: *La ilaha* – the *Shahadah*? *La ilaha* by itself – is it a form of *Shahadah*?

SFH: It is the foundation of *Shahadah*. Without denial of illusory – it has to conclude, it has to balance, because it's half of two – duality. It has to be concluded.

AA: Even though you don't acknowledge it.

SFH: Acknowledging is by work, by words, even though you don't acknowledge it. That's why people like Shams and others said, 'those who consider themselves to be *kuffar* are far more in essence surrendering to it.' That's why if you say somebody is atheist, he is a theist, with that 'a' added to it.

AA: Refusing to reason.

SFH: Absolutely – it's another theism. The word is *idraak* – 'the exasperation that you are not getting it is itself getting it' *Wal' ajzu `An `al-idrak, idraku*[76] – giving up – is having been exhausted – 'I'm not getting it' is *idraak*, because it has got you! That's why I said this existential thing, constantly, from this zone you cannot jump to that zone. This zone is a little pimple having emerged from the other zone. We don't deny it; do it, take it, leave it – it comes upon us when you are about to jump into the ocean, take your clothes off. Jump. Even if it's a bit of a taste. But denying of that is the misery that we are suffering from universally and destroying the environment. Ecology is sacred, sacred expression, and our ruining the ecology is based on that. So it's scratching us from that point of view. Great. Allah catches us from

---

[76] "The inability to really know is knowledge."

every way. Collectively, we are ruining it, we have ruined ourselves; we have ruined the possibility, the potential.

Spiritual Realm

Spiritual Process

AA: Shaykhna, we have been talking about the Absolute – the various manifestations – does the Absolute require – not the Absolute – this is a very hackneyed way of posing the question – but this whole process – doesn't it require a form of preparedness, *ista`daad* or predilection?

SFH: No doubt. Potential is the first, most important thing, an intrinsic *fitri* potential; there is *ista`daad* – this *ista`daad* is within the sphere of the relative. I must exhaust the relative; I must have seen it all, tried to get it all, control it all, be the king of it all – that is *ista`daad*. Once I've tried every possible which way – where is the way, where is god, who is he, how can I get to him, who will show me? And when I am really truly exhausted, that is the *ista`daad*.

AA: If we postulate that *ista`daad* is available to all, in equal, higher or lesser measures, it still requires this leap, for, as we know, why you still haven't reached the end of the process, that if you embark on it you're going to end up in self-destruction, or at least what appears to you to be theoretically illusory at this point, has not yet been realized. So one of the great obstacles to the actualization of *ista`daad* is that when you recognize your *ista`daad*, your preparedness, you still have not yet reached the point where your self is annihilated. You're basically embarking on a process where you – it's self-destruction. So why would anybody do that? Isn't the element of fear critical at that point? Don't you have to overcome this fear? By much greater hope?

SFH: They become so close that you don't know whether it's fear or hope. Hope and total and utter despair become one. Self-destruction and self-resurrection become one. Self-destruction and soul resurrection become one. There is no 'you' anymore. You are lost beyond loss. Initially I don't want to lose. *Nafs* wants to be the king, wants to rule the world, to control the whole world. Clever. The mother has clapped for him, so it is natural and understandable. As you grow, you become more and more defined and confined, so you say 'No, I can't win or...' so you specialize, until the point comes when you find the death of the self is the resurrection of the real 'you'.

AA: But surely it's not only for those who have the means.

SFH: True.

AA: Is it fair to ask people who do not have the means ... because they know they will be thwarted?

SFH: It will be a fool who asks those who are not ready – you don't ask, you read – *Iqra'*. This lady that came today now – she was ready, absolutely ready to take flight in her *sajdah* – it was quite clear to me. It's obvious – '*`ayn al-basirah*' – the girl has been following this, doing this...

AA: Isn't it people toying with the idea of the process, because they somehow feel they would be at a joyous end, but when it actually comes upon them, the knowledge of the elimination of self – they shrink away from it, and go back to old patterns.

SFH: Always. Go back and never come back.

AA: And never leave the circle – of blame and regrets.

SFH: It can be – it happens a lot.

AA: In nearly all cases?

SFH: No.

AA: I don't want to put a statistical number – it's a very high number of people.

SFH: Only at an earlier stage. It's like skiing – the early slopes – anybody can jump in and jump out, but once it has caught you and you become an addict; once the passion has caught you, there's no way out. And that is less and less. As you get nearer the peak, there are very few people left.

AA: Like a finite amount of self whose fuel is itself and as the level goes down, panic ensues. Isn't that correct?

SFH: True – a nice allegory.

AA: At the point of panic – most people will panic.

SFH: True.

AA: It's like a person who says, 'I'm going to hold my breath if I don't get what I want', when their face turns blue, they panic.

SFH: Earlier on, very early, you find many candidates, everybody says, 'I too.' Once the race begins, once it moves again, then you find more and more doubts. And there can also be mass departure from it and as time goes by, and only those serious people with that obsession remain – we're all obsessed, all human beings have obsession. The reason for that thing which we call obsession is to be obsessed with the *ruh*, give up otherness. The only obsession we have deep, deep down is to avoid otherness, and be obsessed with Oneness.

AA: The Qur'an says, *wama yulaqqaha illa dhoo hadhthin `adheem*[77], implying very, very rare people hold the course to the end.

SFH: It's true. I think it's also an evolutionary thing. A time will come when it'll be more and more or less and less unusual.

AA: Wouldn't you say it's the reverse? It was more common before than now?

---

[77] "And no one achieves this except those of great good fortune." (Qur'an 41:35)

Spiritual Cycles

SFH: It depends on the time scale you look at. I'm convinced there is a .... (AA: from the rise of homo sapiens) – if you look at 5-6000 years then you find the little up and down cycles are really local – in other words there is an arc of ascent. But within that arc of ascent there are small little loops going down.

AA: Eddies.

SFH: Eddies. And we give it more momentum. For example, if we consider our age now, dark compared to 4-500 years or a 1000 years; it may very well be that from that darkness small sparks will generate enormous light.

AA: Is it the age of Kali Yoga (SFH: I really don't know) the age of darkness at the end of which a new age will arise?

SFH: You know, I am sure if we look at human history for the last 4 or 5000 years of recorded history, you find quite a number of possible loops that happen, maybe 4, 5, 6, so you hear a lot of people saying *qaht al-rijal* so few and I am sure in relative terms it was, but it will rejuvenate not in the same way that we had thought or expected because we are culturally in a way biased.

AA: ... this has always perplexed me, and I'm sure it might have perplexed you – this is so self-evident..... why is it so cumbersome? Why is the utter simplicity so inaccessible in actual terrestrial life?

SFH: Because terrestrial life is terrestrial and we are talking about terrestrial succumbing, giving in, surrendering to the celestial. Nothing wants to surrender: anything that exists wants to mimic continuity, eternity. Of course, it doesn't want to give up.

AA: But I'm back to the point of Allah's justice or *`Adl, Rahma*, if it's equally dispersed – why is this aperture only available to a few?

SFH: It's part of the swing of nature. I think it implies that – it doesn't mean it is rare, it means you're fortunate if you've managed it. The emphasis is for people not to be too disappointed early on. At the moment your hub is not there, carry on. In a way it also implies within it a certain encouragement.

AA: But isn't that the nature of evolution? It was one ape that stood up, not the entire world of apes. So the one ape that stood up is the progenitor of humankind. Is that the same?

SFH: In a way. I don't think it was one ape – may be quite a few spread out over a period of a few hundred years, thousand years and then it happened.

AA: But not the common world of "apedom."

SFH: Of course not.

AA: So limiting it to the very few is an essential element of the ascent of the genus.

SFH: Correct.

AA: And man, as a spiritual genus, can only express it through a very few.

SFH: I agree with that for the time being as we are, because I think we are in the middle – in historical terms, evolutionary terms and I think it will open up more. I think what is rare now will be less rare in maybe a thousand, two thousand years. I think there is an acceleration.

AA: Have you seen that in the world of space and time?

SFH: No, I haven't seen it in my lifetime. I am part of the cycle of inner decline as seen by the outer measure.

AA: So we are moving to some kind of Shangri-la down the line?

SFH: Could be – I wouldn't use these terms. What I know is that the *rahma* is there, continuous, it has its own pattern. I measure it from my own life cycle, birth and death, cultural decline, other things, so I'm biased. I can't read it well. So I am certain if there is an individual Shangri-la for me by disappearing from the darkness, which is the only way, by negating all that which moves or changes, or is subject to space and time, if I personally tasted it, maybe only a glimpse of it, or an occasion of it, or longer term, if I have tasted it, so it is there. But there needs to be a critical mass for it to happen. Then it will be contagious, because we have a herd mentality, we would not have survived had it not been for, if you like, preservation of the species; if it had not been for selflessness for the species, not just selflessness for me. We are ingrained with that. So I am totally in every way, not just optimistic – I see the pattern and the program, but can't read the small print of it. I can see the overall macro trend of it. But it is about the ultimate, the Absolute and the Absolute resides in me, and if I don't touch upon it then I am lost in the lower me, and I've not yet been, if you like, sparkled by the real me, which is the real, whatever, wherever you look.

Presence of the Absolute

AA: If you say that the knowledge of the Absolute is universally and equally distributed, but knowledge of the Knowledge is not, then you could also say that the rewards, as it were, the just rewards, are also differential.

SFH: I wouldn't say the knowledge of the Absolute, I would say the presence of the Absolute is Absolute Presence, but to gain the knowledge of it, I must stop the illusion and the mental construct that I have some knowledge. I must stop all of that. Its presence is there, but I will never get to know it through what I have assumed and learnt in the terrestrial realm to be knowledge. This is hacking away, this is being clever, a mental construct.

AA: If you leave terrestrial knowledge as ephemeral, only useful as a product of reason and logic and move to knowledge of Allah, whatever you call that, is that…?

SFH: The Presence that reveals itself. The Presence itself reveals itself. I can never access it in any way except by negation of anything else. That is where the big problem arises. The *nur* of Allah reveals itself by itself. I cannot ask for it. I cannot demand it, or pray for it. All that I can do is stop everything else in order to be able to receive a glimpse or a flicker, or spark of that. Once that has touched me, more than once or twice accidentally, then I have no option, and I don't think anyone is spared that – that's where the justice comes. I think everyone, every human being has been given enough knocks, enough shocks, enough questions, but they don't read it. They blame somebody else – the opportunity, the exchange rate changed, or my boss was horrible, or my wife cheated me, or whatever. No one is spared the mercy of challenges and difficulties. No one ever! But how do they interpret it? The *nafs* is so strong and so big it interprets in a way to preserve itself even more.

AA: I would say that the system – if you don't mind me calling it – is only valid at an individual level, and only then valid where the person has already removed all these obstacles to realization; at the collective level this is manifestly not true; it's like a light, a sun available to all, but some have visors on and some have dark glasses on, some look at it and go blind, it's only the few that are able to gauge how to acknowledge and experience the Absolute.

SFH: It also works on the collective level. It does. If they have trust, love and faith, then there'll be a rise, in the same way as there is mass hysteria in a negative sense; there'll also be spiritual uplifting in the other side. It does help if you believe, connect and trust, if you resonate, it grows much more. In other words, at a collective level if the collective allows the individuals to flourish and shine and be given if you like, the proper, non-asked for influence, the thing will move much faster, evolution will grow much faster.

AA: That is so, but that requires society to organize itself in ways whereby the self is de-agitated.

The Karbala Model

SFH: True, but it is contagious. I remember as a kid, my model of Karbala was very skewed but it was real – there was peace, there was harmony, no police, no courts – as I mentioned to you, the second world war, we didn't feel it, and our household was not amongst the wealthy traders; it was in the economic sense middle-class – people were living modestly – I wouldn't say it was an ideal situation, but there was a formally differentiated hierarchy amongst the teachers, the mullahs, the traders and they would sort out things amongst themselves – there would be an arbitration of disputes. When they had a serious problem, they'd ask somebody whom they trusted. So it worked, it had in it, if you like, healthy ground rules, and therefore many, many of the simple people could rise higher along the arc of ascent. The atmosphere, the environment, was healthy. There was a lot of generosity even though people had very little money. And there was a lot of exchange of goods without it being called barter. Every day in our own household there would be 10 or 15 things arriving to the household from neighbors, and also from the house whenever there was a good supply of harvest from the farm to be distributed. There were no refrigerators, you couldn't keep food. If there was a sheep sacrifice all the neighbors had it. It had a big influence on a positive side, and that's what I imbibed really as a kid.

AA: Did sharing and caring exist?

SFH: Very much so.

AA: Probably existed in all other places in the world as well.

SFH: True – sharing caring, but there was a recognition of a spiritual, if you like, hierarchy as well, and as I mentioned to you, authorities would come, if not every day, every other day, and would quietly confer with my father on various issues, like: 'What if we opened that road? What if this or that?' So there was a lot of acceptance of authority that was not purely rational. And no one was superstitious of reading the future or the unseen, because spiritual wisdom is based on earthly wisdom.

Absolute Revealing Itself Through Shari`ah

AA: Does the Absolute then reveal itself to the collective through the *Shari`ah*?

SFH: *Shari`ah* is the primary, essential qualification order to get away from the highly relative, towards the more durable. It's about durability and sustainability.

AA: Which is a pathway for the collective to create a better quality life.

SFH: In a way, absolutely.

AA: There is no other purpose to it.

SFH: A better quality life at the level of the relative. You can't progress much if there isn't a certain measure of certainty or time – the time is continuing. There's not going to be another revolution next week. You won't go and do anything – life will be frozen unless there is a bit of that. So it brings about that stability – ongoing-ness.

AA: I think social democracy does a better job.

SFH: Sure. Really, I am not against that. Absolutely.

AA: But social democracy has no pretensions that it is reflecting the will of the Absolute...

SFH: I'm not sure that *Shari`ah* has that potential.

AA: But *Shari`ah* is *Shari`at ul-Allah*, the way to Allah –

SFH: Everything is the way to Allah – I don't consider that is the only exclusive absolute way. It was for its time and the way it came, there was nothing better. I agree with you now – social democracy or whatever, if it can curb the excesses of controlled mechanism of capitalism and all of that spurious financial – if it can curb those, then I think it's as good as any, if not better.

AA: But in the sense that it doesn't prescribe any devotional requirement on the collective – hence the *Shari`ah* – and the *Shari`ah* is social democracy plus, the way I understand what you are saying – social democracy or a form of economic welfare, plus a strong commitment to truth.

SFH: Because it was a package and they were congenial, there were the two: if you want *Haqiqah* then you need to accept *Shari`ah*. If you want for example, inner joy, then you have to accept outer regulations and laws. Not that different.

Haira

AA: Would you say that as you move from this pointedness of a few individuals – this absolute focus, down this pyramid of spiritual cognition, those in the middle and upper layers must be overwhelmed with a sense of *haira*.

SFH: *Haira* is a big thing and prominent for a long period. *Haira* is the same as uncertainty or doubt.

AA: Did you experience *haira*?

SFH: Constantly. Perpetually. But *haira* in my case now is much more in the moment as it unfolds. Shall I go or shall I stay? That sort of thing. It's not so much *haira* in the classical sense; it's more about finding a better of the two of whatever choices there are. *Haira* in the spiritual sense, for me, is more like the no-man's land in between. When one is leaving more, if you like, the zone of terrestrial balancing and dualities towards that which is of another realm, then *haira* is very serious.

AA: Would you say it's not knowing where to hide from the gates of the Divine.

SFH: Could be. I've not given that thought.

AA: A kind of metaphorical understanding.

SFH: Could be. I have personally found in my own experience that *haira* can also be to a great extent reduced in its negative impact, bewilderment, so to speak, if there are some references even at the basic level. For example, I would find people like Sayyid Mehdi Hakim very helpful to me; although he was not in any *maqaam* or any station, I found just his company to be useful because of his certainty and total reliance on what he knew. That in itself was a good *haal*, a good reference. It was attractive, and I share it with you that, during his lifetime, I really regarded him as a decent and reliable person – as good as they come. I knew the moment he was assassinated because I suddenly had a shock at that very moment – it was two days after I met him in London, and he went to Sudan. The day after he died, I had a dream of him – he came as though from a very cloudy, misty sky, and he greeted me. He said, 'you never really thought much highly of me in a spiritual sense when I was alive.' I said, 'No, I didn't.' He said, 'what do you think of me now?' 'I think you are in a higher station now.' A week later, he came to me in a dream again and said, 'today you must go and invite' – I forget her name – he had a wife in England – he had married somebody – you know that, and he said, 'Please invite her today for lunch at your house with Batul.' I said, 'this is what I have, do you mind calling her?' He said, 'No, go to her house. Invite yourself to her house, with Batul.' So Batul called me and said the lady was shocked that I invited myself, but she said, 'I will do it.' So I came and we went. She sat weeping. She said, 'Today I was preparing to gas myself. I had everything ready, the shelves are empty. I was going to put my head in the oven to gas myself.' Strange, isn't it? There have been a lot of incidents like that. Again, I am susceptible. I am not after these things, but I have had enough such cases that I have no *haira* about them.

AA: *Haira* in this sense, not knowing what to do –

SFH: No, I understand.

AA: A sense of being overwhelmed – overwhelming perplexity.

SFH: It happens, it's natural for everyone to go through that, and with more *tawakkul*, more trust, the duration can be shorter, longer – there are no two people the same. No two paths are the same. I have been fortunate in that with a natural propensity of being personally within my own self, fairly secure, maybe again to do with babyhood, upbringing, being loved, so it didn't really affect me a lot. There were a few people, especially one person, who had really gone very speedily through *khalwas* and things, but I felt his *haira* could destroy him unless he had companions, and it did – truly destroyed his life.

AA: He's around?

SFH: Still alive, but he really is in complete utter –

AA: Confusion.

SFH: Danger. Dangerous.

Layers of The Absolute

AA: It seems that at a certain point one has no need for the unseen, the *ghaib* – no point in knowing these realms. They also have no reality, like the realm of what they call the '*mulk*', so the *malakut* has no reality, to ultimate reality.

SFH: I have not had that curiosity. I am more than content with whatever is in front of me. Earlier on it has been far more '*mulki*', and as time went on, a bit of a *malakuti*, and occasionally *jabaruti* as well, but I really had no deep desire to pierce any of that. What I felt within me is enough for me. I had that natural contentment.

AA: To what then do you attribute this concern with the way which the Absolute manifests itself down these realms?

SFH: Again, this is our evaluation of 'down' or 'up' – it's our evaluation. The Absolute is absolute and the relative is relative, and between them there is this no-man's land, which is within me. Part of it is humanity; the other half, for lack of a better word, we call it divinity, and that's the Absolute. And I am both. Whenever I get a bit too frantic about the humanity side of things, and if I am able to witness that state of being frantic, immediately the little window of the higher, the Absolute, opens up within me, and it immediately, in a way, neutralizes all of that. So I am back again to say, 'all right, when you have the mind, anything you can do with it, do it.'

AA: So you don't necessarily need to understand these various spheres – in which various forces operate?

SFH: I don't. I've never taken an interest in it – maybe people around me, and with me, have had serious interest in it; they benefit from it; they teach it. I have not.

AA: Most of them seem to be focused on the spiritual world of spirits and *jinns*. I agree Shaykhna, it's of no interest, but what about further up?

SFH: It's a personal thing – I have not been tempted or interested in these things.

AA: In the world of archetypes –

SFH: I'm sure they are useful as models, as maps, some people have that propensity so why not? I can't say it's useless. To me they have no interest. Nor did I waste any time or effort on them.

AA: So you do not reflect on the Absolute through these layers?

SFH: Not at all – only later on-

AA: …. unfolding.

SFH: Absolutely. The *Hahut* and the *Lahut* – fine – so what – I am not interested. But for other people it can be very beneficial.

AA: Never interested?

SFH: No, never. Only because there are quite a number of people who benefit from them, and use them, including Batul Khanum. She teaches them. But to me it's not interesting.

AA: But you don't deny their reality?

SFH: I don't deny them, nor do I discourage them – if this is what people want, *Bismillah*, but it's not for me.

AA: If a person says, 'I'll take the bus, or whatever is convenient, as long as I get there.'

SFH: Choose what you think – or get away from where you are – I won't say 'get *there*'. My language on these issues is fairly consistent – there is no 'there'. The 'there' is here. And neither the 'there' nor the 'here' has any reality.

AA: Classical thought, both in Islam and elsewhere, posited the existence of these inner faculties as the way in which the unseen can be approached. By the 'unseen' I assume to have meant the Absolute. Is this still valid, do you think?

SFH: I think so.

Inner and Outer Senses

AA: When you talked in Sweden in the early nineties about the *Hiss al-Mushtaraq* and the *wahm* and the *khayaal* and ... I can't remember – the inner senses and outer senses, are these real?

SFH: They have some reality. These two phases are like under the ocean and above it. If I am under the ocean and coming up from the bottom of the sea, there is this map, there is some reality in it; As I am approaching the surface, I am now beginning to experience more light – the fish changes, so there is some reality in it. So, for me as a person coming up from 3000 feet below, the surface towards 10 ft. below the surface, it's helpful and encouraging, a bit of a sketch I can look at as a map, but if I don't refer this every now and then to the other reality which is THE Reality, then I have too much expectation of this. The teaching of the *Hiss al-Mushtaraq*, the *khayaal*, it gives me an idea as to how am I functioning – what is the nature of my memory, my heart, my *hafidha*, my *mufakkira* – great, but it's only a vehicle to lead me to a zone where no vehicle ever operates.

AA: A sort of chariot that you have to ride – you have to use your outer senses to deal with the outer material world.

SFH: I accept that. And there are also models of something else, some other kingdom, I accept that as well.

AA: But why are they not demarcated so specifically, as the outer sense has been demarcated?

SFH: There cannot be an outer sense without an inner sense: there are five outer senses and five inner senses and they balance each other. So my inner senses are much closer to my *ruh* or, if you like, my inner heart, so that is how they connect also. In other words, my *ruh*, my soul, my spirit, beams its light through a pure heart, which is a metaphoric home for it, towards the inner senses. So that is where if I want to have more and more access to the other zone, the Absolute, I need to have less concern about my outer senses, and less concern about my inner senses, my memory, my *hafidha*, my *mufakkira*, so that I am closer to that abstract light, towards the Absolute Light. So they are all part and parcel of the Oneness, which is me. I am a construct of the Absolute and the relative, a construct of divinity and humanity; I am a construct of timelessness and infinity and boundlessness and that which is bounded between birth and death and between limitations; so *Fabi-ayyi ala-i rabbikumatukaththiban*[78]; if I deny this, I'll be denied that.

AA: A kind of inverse relationship to the outer senses.

SFH: I think that's a very good description.

AA: It's something – as they say – 'use it or lose it.' If you don't use your sight, with time you lose it: if you don't use your *mufakkira*, with time it'll never arise.

SFH: Right. When I first had to have reading glasses, I was in the optician's room and I wondered, I said, 'where is the *rahma* in this case?' – I said, 'how come' in this case? As though a huge voice came to me, which said, 'But isn't your insight more now than it was ten years ago?' Of course the answer was yes! So I was so ashamed of myself. I said, 'shut up! Lose a bit more of the outer side, in comparison to gaining more insight.'

AA: That's a very significant statement.

SFH: It spoke to me instantly, and I really was so contented and genuine, not as to ameliorate myself, no, I was very happy. I said this is perfect, a very profitable exchange.

AA: But one of them seems to be on a sort of autopilot, the autonomic system of seeing, hearing, touching, you don't have to use your will to use it – the other one seems to require *irada*.

SFH: Correct, I feel both. Sometimes I suddenly find myself switching to autopilot, in an instant, and other times I'm not. It's about time, somebody has come, and you have to do something. And they are seamless. The Absolute and the relative are seamlessly connected.

AA: But one is, you have agreed, on autopilot and the other one requires a kind of fuel.

SFH: Sure. It automatically switches to the other.

---

[78] "Which then of the bounties of your Lord will you deny?" (From the 55th Surah – Ar-Rahman).

AA: And is it a fuel for igniting the inner senses? Time?

SFH: Sure. Absolutely.

AA: I think it's very strange to find a five-year-old speaking about *tawhīd*.

SFH: Yes of course.

AA: But it would be very sad if the person who is 70 or so doesn't think about it.

SFH: I think things go more gradually. People in their thirties, forties, if they are not speculating, if their intellect is not aroused, if they have not had enough training, they are dead inwardly. Really, by the time one is 50 and on, you know that somebody has another dimension in their trajectory, and you know that people, by the time they are 60, most of them are dead anyway. So there's very little one can do. Although, there are always exceptions. Suddenly something happens. But generally there is a trend, a tendency; it doesn't happen suddenly – there are telltale signs – it's connected.

AA: It's as if the door to the inner sense has a key and the key is picked up through your experiences, which leaves you nowhere to look except to say…

SFH: It is true. Here, I just want to add another issue. There are some people with a propensity of wanting to look into the inner, in other words the meaning of it – go deeper into the analysis of it. Where is it from? Why have I become angry? Why…? So the more one is on that search in a way, the more is the likelihood of going more and more into the unseen, into the no-man's land between the relative and the Absolute. There are these telltale signs. And that is why so many of the *awliya* and seers pick somebody in their twenties or earlier and say, 'Look, this child has a bit of potential. Keep an eye on them.' Implying that they have this supra curiosity; it isn't just a normal investigative thing. It's something else. Or their behavior also occasionally is not quite all the time for acknowledgement and – there is the beginning of some other element in them of *ruhaniya*.

AA: So you don't really think that the subtler qualities – let's call these inner senses – have been overwhelmed by the weight of quantity?

SFH: I think it's true. We have moved into that cycle. Quantity, outer material and reliance on technology – the quest for comfort and ease. You mentioned something very interesting about Shaykh Asaf, hardship, difficulty – I think that is a key element. No, I think it is correct. We have been numbed and short-changed.

AA: The actual potential has not been erased.

SFH: That's why suffering is more. If you allow people to express it, you'll find far, far more people will admit they are suffering than we think. But they put up a face and say, 'never mind, it's all right.'

AA: So what would you say to a person that in time the knowledge of the inner faculties will disappear, and therefore the potential of recognizing the Absolute through human beings will end, and therefore it is the end of time. In the sense that the human being's function is to relate to the Absolute. If that capability is lost, then the principal idea of the human being ends.

SFH: Yes, and it could end. I would not be surprised. The Qur'an alludes to that – '*He [Allah] will replace you with another people; then they will not be the likes of you,*[79]' not impossible at all.

AA: But you don't see it as –

SFH: I don't, no. I really have never had such curiosity. But I wouldn't say it's impossible at all.

---

[79] Qur'an 47:38.

Patterns of Energies and Their Interface (Barzakhiya)

AA: We come to this really critical aspect of this relational force, the *barzakhiya* – the force of the condition or the field, or the state, whatever you want to call it, that connects to Realities greater than the rest. What is the nature of this relational principal?

SFH: I look at these things as patterns of energies, and I can imagine all kinds of energies. I regard, for example, the so-called *Asma al-Husna*, or attributes, or whatever, all as energy bands. They dovetail into each other and they mix and connect. I regard, for example, generosity, as a field of energy. If I touch it by acting generously, then it will change my entire, if you like, cellular connectivity, neurons, maybe, and so on. So I regard *barzakhiya*, or in-between, in a way, as though the Absolute has its own domain of total utter absoluteness, which is not changing, not subject to operation, whereas the other one is all balance between the dualities and so on. Now, in between, you have some sort of, if you like, hazy cauldron of connectedness between the absolute of energy and the relative, and that is where *haira* also occurs, mostly. It has some discernible possibilities, explanations, and to a great extent not. Anything can happen in there and it is the most dangerous realm. In other words, ideally, one has to pass through it very quickly, if possible. You can't – that's why he [The Prophet] also says, 'there's no stopping place for the people of Yathrib.' For the people of Yathrib, there's a passage to the Absolute, so you can't stop there. Jesus says, 'Do not build a house on a bridge', and this life is that. So these are the meanings I get from that. It's a mixed bag of energy fields that are not easy to discern, and they can cause all kinds of eddies and currents and there is no discernible, expressible or exchangeable pattern in them.

AA: But there are relational forces.

SFH: Sure – but again –

AA: They don't have a function beyond that?

SFH: It is an interface. Something that's vast and infinite connects with something that is tiny and miniscule, that is our universe, one of, God knows, how many thousands and millions of multi-verses. So it's one of those – connectedness, it's a little bit of a glue, and it has a bit of the character of one side and a bit of the other side. That's how I see it.

AA: And you see it in relational terms.

SFH: I see it in relational terms. Also, I see it like coming out of a door and entering into a door – that sort of thing – it is a passage – and therefore it is disturbing.

AA: A tunnel.

SFH: It could be a tunnel but one thing leads to the other.

AA: You shouldn't linger.

SFH: You shouldn't linger; it's not meant for that – or return back to your relative state and stay there longer, until such time you are not even making an effort; you are suddenly thrown into it. That's why often, the awakening to the Absolute is referred to as a 'thunderbolt' – it doesn't come gradually – there has been a lot of gradual inclination, gradual taste, or allusion to it, but often that taste comes by avoiding that which is not. Then suddenly the Obvious is obvious; there is none other than that, nothing you can add to it, nothing you can subtract from it, nothing to say, nothing to do.

AA: As long as there is an atom of the self, the *barzakh* will always be necessary.

SFH: True. And also, I think as far as absoluteness is concerned, you are put into it, you experience it, you will be pulverized, you'll be burnt, thunderbolted, whatever, but then soon after that you come to the third journey – you realize that you have been created for something else, or the fourth journey also, you are with them – so the second journey is not subject to time, not subject to space and you've got it and you find there is a major change in you, in every way, cellularly and otherwise. And there have been, as you know, so many tests by monks and others who have had their brain scanned and this and that – they find there is a different change in them. They don't look at the world events and shocks to the same extent as the so-called normal person does. So there is a major change at every level of the being, their value system, their cellular system, whatever. In my own experiences in India, I have met people who have transformed and impacted physically. One person who woke up one day found himself in the Himalayas, and another man had a lot of hair, and he was totally bald the next day. Everything fell off. The Prophet himself says, 'I suddenly became white when *Surat Hud*[80] came upon me.' So the seen and the unseen meet; the relative and the absolute meet, but then you come back without being able to forget that, if it has been established, if it is not a *haal*, it is a *maqaam*.

AA: You cannot step back.

SFH: You cannot. Neither step back nor step forward – you are stamped – and that is where in the traditional sense, people say, 'he is a Shaykh of enlightenment.' That's all it means.

Rungs of Awakening

AA: I was asking about the rungs, which you talk about, of greater and greater awakening, which are facilitated or thwarted by the way the person deals with the *barzakhiya* phase.

SFH: Could be. My own knowledge, understanding and experience is that, if you are ripe, as I was actually described as such. I was described as a fruit that might be over-ripe, and just needed a prick, but other people might need to be ripened more by regular periods of reflection, so I did not have much of that experience of climbing up the rungs.

AA: Did you experience the *barzakhiya* through what are known as angelic forces?

---

[80] Surah 11 of the Qur'an – the name of the Surah is based on Prophet Hud.

SFH: Not really. I would use the word, 'oblivion', I became more and more oblivious, regularly and extensively, entering into a zone of no thing-ness, no thought, nothing, emptiness, and I began to practice by seeing light, like intense light, or darkness and sometimes I would exchange, sometimes with color, sometimes no color. Eventually, it became so easy just knowing, instantly, and that was very helpful to me when I was in business. Whenever I felt the thing was becoming a bit too out of balance, for 10, 20 seconds, I'd just go, switch off, and come back. Then I realized I was more and more excluded. So I can't say it was angelic or non-angelic; I've not been into those models.

Angelic Forces

AA: But you referred at some point to 'angelic forces', these fields of forces.

SFH: Sure.

AA: Not the lowest form but the most accessible form of *barzakhiya*.

SFH: Sure, no doubt – I can imagine that and there will be many other layers of them, but it wasn't my business; it was Allah's business, and I am at the receiving end, so I said whatever comes, fine.

AA: Also guided.

SFH: No. I never asked for it, I never looked for it. It's not my business. My business is to give up every other business. My business is one, to deny falsehood; one business; if I attend to that business, the rest is already there. So I never asked for any of these things, or even the *nur* of Allah, or the *anwaar*; I have no such interest. My business was to get out of the mire that I knew was there affecting all humanity, and me as much, and I just wanted to save me from me. I really was looking all the time at that which is not – *La Ilaha*. I was never really that curious. If somebody mentioned something to me that made sense, I'd take it; otherwise, it wasn't not my business.

AA: I take it; it would be interesting to know as a being engaged with this –

SFH: No, not in any describable overt sense. In the sense of feeling the result, or outcome of it, yes. I suddenly felt that I was stripped of all and was beyond the world of liberation into that total, utter, brilliant unfathomable, infinite view of singularity.

Religion

AA: Moving on, Shaykhna, do you see the function of religion as a way that human beings structure to understand the transcendent, or is it something that's bestowed? What is religion in your views? Are human beings hard-wired to be in it?

SFH: I think there is a very strong argument to say that we are hard-wired wanting to know the Absolute, wanting to go beyond knowledge, beyond the limitations of realities or relativity, but I think the *dīn* is there irrespective. It is us. The *dīn* is actually us. It is that I want to reach a stage where I am not feeling inadequate any more. Nor do I have a lot of fear and anxiety and concern about death. I am – you know what Abu Hassan Al-Shadhili said, 'Promise me two things, and I promise you you'll be liberated. One is no fear for your provision, and no fear of human beings.' I feel we all want that. We all want some sort of independence, but we construct it as material independence, physical independence, social independence, and emotional independence. It's not that; it is inner awakening that we are really looking for, but we think a bit of independence from other factors leads us to that. It could up to a point but it's not going to do it all. So we are all in the *dīn*, in the *dīn* of *islam*[81], so every reasonably healthy human being would constantly be in need or looking for a path, religion or a *dīn*, that gives the outer boundaries within reason, and the inner boundlessness. The two must go together, again, Mecca-Medina. If I have done enough meditation on the mountain and all that and so on, more likely that the majority of these people would still come down and say, 'Look, don't waste all these resources, all your time and so on.' So from Mecca, they've come to Medina; and if they are in Medina, trying to do whatever, they will say, 'who has come from Mecca? Tell us: "is it going to last longer? Is it going to be too frivolous? Is it just an election gimmick?"' – so they are

---

[81] The word, *islam*, refers to self-surrender unto the Reality that encompasses and permeates all other realities – an inner state; it's the essence of being-ness and of all revealed religions.

looking for Mecca. The last two or three weeks or months when Musharraf was the president – I was in Pakistan – the question was, 'we're going for election, how can we be better prepared?' I said, 'you must know your *dīn*, live your *dīn* – you are in a country which professes to be a Muslim state, and work from within.' Obviously none of them were prepared, but neither the President nor the Prime Minister was prepared. So we all want short cuts – it doesn't work, it has to be real.

Shari`ah

AA: So this legacy, as it's called, is linked to a process as a structure, the structuring of this process through the forms of religion – is that necessary for human salvation?

SFH: Altogether we are made of structure and a more amorphous intermediate thing, which is to do with electro-magnetic forces within us, and brain functions; and also far, far more subtle transcendental forces. I think the human being, the human journey, has to be based on the sensory, which is to do with structures also – feeling, touching, knowing, hard, soft structures, and the mental which has got its own construct capacity, and the transcendental. So I think structure is necessary. I am structured; if my bones are weak, I will not be able to function or whatever. The whole business of creation or existence is based on the unity of physics and metaphysics; this is the challenge; if I deny the physics, I am unlikely to be anywhere near the metaphysics. Also, with the *dīn*, you need some structure, but it needs flexibility – it can't be rigid and frigid, because it'll be brittle; so in other words, *Shari`ah* has to be there, the laws must be there – they may have been surpassed into something better even – fine. But it's a necessary condition for the outer sense, the relative sense, the existential sense. At the time of Muhammad, there were no such laws. Roman laws had fallen into disrepair, so it was the best of the best. And that's why they thrived. But without it being Mecca/Medina, and being constantly improved, it will atrophy; it will become a slogan as it is now.

Religion

Reckoning/Salvation

AA: I accept this sort of division between pre- and post-axial religion: the pre-axial ones really have no concern with the after-life, salvation; they are basically mapping the way in which the Absolute unfolds. The post-axial, of which Islam may be the last manifestation, is very much concerned with human salvation, so this additional aspect doesn't seem to be necessary. Why do you think it's essential to knowledge of Allah to know the limits and bounds and have some kind of accountings attached to it?

SFH: It's again to bring me now to my awakening. If I am accountable now, there is no account after my death. It's finished; I am doing it now. I am perpetually, constantly re-balancing my inner and outer; my inner intention and outer action. Zoroaster I think summed it up: 'Correct thoughts, correct sounds, announcement and correct action.' So you're unified. The question of time – I am timeless – my *ruh* is timeless, so the question of *akhira* is a flip to illustrate or exaggerate the fact that if I am not accountable to the Infinite now, I will be held accountable when I leave that which is not mine – the body and so on. So I think it is a good, important, if you like, addition to the model, to an experientially, experientiable metaphor as well. The Prophet also says, 'Your *qiyama* is now – *maaliki yawm iddin*,[82]' the Owner or Controller of the Day of Reckoning. What is *Yawm iddin*? *Qur'an bil Qur'an*[83] – it says, *Yawman* .... *'an nafsin shay'a*[84] – the day of reckoning is the occasion when you can't do anything to anybody, and nobody can do anything to you. So it can be now. Right now I know you can't add anything to my happiness or misery, unless Allah has decreed it by my own allowing it, also connecting with it. Then I'm in the instant of the *dīn* so it is the now. For most people they are too pre-occupied and say, 'All right I'll come to you later.' I remember in Karbala, if somebody was mischievous, they'd try to help or stop him; a point would reach after a while, I could hear

---

[82] "Master of the Day of Judgment" – Qur'an 1:4
[83] [Understand] the Qur'an by the Qur'an.
[84] Qur'an 2:48. The complete part of this verse is: *yawman la tajzeenafsun 'an nafsin shay-an* ("Day when no soul will stand in place of another")

somebody saying: 'Look, you can't help him, leave him to Allah.' Which is again a very practical way of dealing with it. He was not causing a great deal of havoc, but he was a cheat – so they said, 'leave him to Allah. Allah will punish him and show him.' And sure enough, they were sensitive enough to see how in his own life he was being reprimanded.

AA: So, the element that involves judgment, weighing, *halaal*, and salvation, can all be compressed into the now – those who have that capacity.

SFH: Absolutely. No doubt about it and everybody has the potential; every human being has the possibility if they really concentrate on it and give it the devotion and energy that's needed, of course.

AA: And inasmuch as there are only a few, therefore the structuring of religion together with the elements of salvation and transcendence are essential for the religion.

Habits/Religious Forms

SFH: *Dīn* is to be transformed into a full being – on earth, but not of earth. Otherwise, it's not the *dīn*. They've concocted religion. This is where they said, 'our forefathers were used to do this;' because we love habits. Habits give the illusion of continuity, and one gets the illusion of forever-ness.

AA: So what you're saying is that, at some point, you have to structure this method of experiencing enhanced awakening through religious forms?

SFH: It is living a life, personal and communal, and is at all times bringing more and more evolved beings who naturally will be looked up to, respected and so on. So, yes, in this case, the effect is overall. Otherwise, it becomes a ritual, with less and less, if you like, effective meaning and impact. It can atrophy.

AA: Religion has that function?

SFH: sure –

AA: In reality, religion is for that purpose?

SFH: Absolutely. It's for you to awaken now to the fullness of the real you. Otherwise it becomes a ritual without much meaning. The Prophet says: 'And for so many people the prayer becomes nothing other than tired knees. And for so many people fasting – there is nothing in it for them other than hunger.'

AA: But you still have to do it.

SFH: If you believe in that, then do it; at least doing it is better than not doing it. But there is a huge difference between doing it and being transformed by it, by seeing the inner meaning of it, and doing it but not seeing its inner meaning and not be transformed by it. Huge difference!

AA: But these particular forms, Shaykhna, are they essential? Do you have to commit to a particular form?

SFH: I find that in terms of particular `ibadat, any form that you are familiar with, happy with, if it is a complete form, will help you. In the case of Islam, it is complete – I don't think I can improve on it.

Islam – The Primordial Religion

AA: So this kernel of truth can be found in all major religious traditions – is there a primordial religion?

SFH: No doubt. And I think primordial religion is *islam*.

AA: I mean you can call it anything?

SFH: *Inna dīn Allah Islam.*[85]

---

[85] Full quote: "*Inna addīna `inda Allahial-islamu*" – "Indeed, the religion in the sight of

AA: But this is what the *dīn* is?

SFH: This is what the *dīn* is, precisely.

AA: So there's an element of primordiality in it.

SFH: Absolutely, totally primordial.

AA: So what are the contours of primordial religion? Just *tawhīd*?

SFH: It is two things: experiencing *tawhīd*, witnessing *tawhīd*, totally being at all times in unison with *tawhīd*, and that can only come as my soul and my self are in unison. My ego and my *ruh* are in unison. Then I am *in islam* – Otherwise *tawhīd* becomes a slogan.

AA: But isn't the Adamic religion?

SFH: I think that's all what the Adamic religion is, it cannot be anything else. The other thing is timelessness. I put these two legs. One is living *tawhīd*, the Absoluteness of Oneness, and the other one is knowing experientially that there is an aspect of me within me that is not cooped up in space and time, which is my soul.

AA: Then, as it moves along in the axis of history, it unfolds in different ways?

SFH: Sure. Then there is a lot of cultural impact, geographical impact; it will be different in terms of many aspects – it will be different if you are in Alaska than if you are in the middle of Arabia. The metaphor is there – all hell and fire and so on – in Alaska it would have been cold, cold, cold! So there is that. There will be quite a lot of difference in these allegories if the Qur'an had come down in Alaska.

AA: ... or Cameroon.

God is *islam* (self-surrender unto God)." (Qur'an 3:19)

SFH: That's it – the metaphors, the symbols all of that would be very different.

Prayer

AA: So what is prayer? – all the religions seem to have that.

SFH: Yes – it is a discipline for the self, the *nafs* and the body; prayer is nourishment for the body. Food is nourishment for the soul. It's the reverse of what we think. Prayer and surrendering, meditation – it's important for my body; otherwise my body has no reason. For my body's sake I pray; otherwise the body isn't there; it's in order for it to have a better connection to the sublime. Whereas food is for my soul; it's for my spirit, because without food my body will not be there, and my body is for the spirit; it's the home of the spirit, the exile of the spirit.

AA: The mule.

SFH: The mule of the spirit. Exactly!

AA: But you won't term the prayer as a willing acknowledgment of the Divine, constant formal acknowledgment of the Divine.

SFH: Yes, it is that also; stopping other things, distraction, stopping deviating, more this, more that – make one more phone call, one more purchase, one more this. Of course it is diminishing my fascination, greed, stupidity about the *duniya*. Yes, it has many factors. You can list dozens of good things about it. It's very inconvenient; suddenly a time comes, I have to stop everything and do that. Very inconvenient. Good! In a worldly sense, but it could be very convenient for my higher sense.

AA: It's fuel for the body.

SFH: Absolutely! Fuel for the body to be replenished – don't over do yourself –

AA: Re-charge your battery.

SFH: RE-charge your battery – brilliant!

Consciousness/Mystical Experience

AA: So when do you then get this shift in consciousness which is absolutely essential – you talked about conditioned consciousness and the supra consciousness or the higher consciousness.

SFH: I generally divide it into conditioned consciousness, personal consciousness, changing consciousness, evolving consciousness – because it's changing. I'm not the same person as I was 30 years ago – my consciousness has broadened, deepened and so on – so it's ever-changing, personal, conditioned, and it is only a reflection, an echo or a mirror of supreme consciousness, God Consciousness, Divine Consciousness, Absolute Consciousness, Pure Consciousness. We can give it any of 20, 30, 40 names. And the growth, if you like, of wholesomeness and well beingness, completing *insaan al-kamil*, is for the two to match. Which is the same as my ego becoming subservient to my soul. And the so-called 'I' becomes truly `*abdullah* and is liberated from being `*abd* of anything else; my whims, my biography, my desires and so on. So the more this lower consciousness is aware of its father, or mother, in Heaven, the more it is likely to regard anything it is going through as part of a process that's going back to *Jannah,* or to Paradise, or to salvation or enlightenment. And so it yields more, and it makes it easier.

AA: So this shift, or enhancement, of consciousness is what is commonly known as a mystical or religious experience?

SFH: Yes, at the higher end of it, yes. Earlier on, it is that: 'I am taking counsel with somebody who is more experienced – his consciousness in that realm is more.' I go to a doctor because he has got more experience – his consciousness of medicine or health is broader, deeper, more specialist than mine. So it moves on until I reach the point when the mystical side is really the No-Man's-Land, it is in-between. Because up to everything discernible in this consciousness, you can discuss, you can say, 'Look, he has got far greater wisdom and knowledge and experience; he has been five times the President of this country and that' – so it's obvious. When I'm moving to the other zone, its rules and parameters are totally different, then you can say it's mystical. It's only an expression that I don't know much about – mysticism, same thing as metaphysics, or the same thing as 'paranormal'. It's not normal, not something you and I can discuss. I personally don't find these terms that helpful, because they bring with them often some elements of superstition, so I don't find it that helpful, but you have to use it every now and then.

AA: But in some cases the experiences are a steady state and the shift in consciousness may have happened at some point abruptly or gradually – incremental.

SFH: Gradually.

AA: But in some cases it is not – it comes in one blast, in which case it is commonly known as a 'mystical experience', would you agree with that?

SFH: Absolutely, but it is more common that you have it gradually with more steps in it. Epiphanies happen – an opening of something more unusual, an opening, insight – it does happen. But there will be also one or two occasions that are very severe and render one quite incapacitated.

AA: It does happen.

SFH: It does happen. In my own case for 6 months I couldn't ride in a car. I could not sit on a wheel – 6 months. I couldn't; it was impossible; I wouldn't go into a car.

AA: Why?

SFH: I don't know – I found this so strange. Either you are above it or below it, or you are on foot. It happened suddenly. I mean I found it most odd. Impossible to fathom. I have not discussed it that much but it was frightening.

AA: Some people discard their own clothes.

SFH: There you are! So that happens. Each one of us is a special being.

Faith

AA: So, Shaykhna, it seems that if you are in a steady state, with perfect or near-perfect knowledge of the assuredness of Allah's mercy, what need do you have for faith?

SFH: It's useful at an early stage – but later on –

AA: Later on, what is faith?

SFH: None. I myself have no faith.

AA: Because there's no need for it?

SFH: Whatever it is, I have no faith. I just know there is none other than the One. But if you tell me you have faith, I say, wonderful, good luck! I respect that.

AA: So *iman* obviously is then restricted to those who have no faith?

SFH: No, but it remains there, but it hasn't got the same value any more. It won't have the same importance. It isn't that I don't have faith *per se* – I do have faith, but I don't rely on it any more. It's not there –

AA: You have certainty.

SFH: Yes, you know, I used to rely on 5 or 6 or 10 credit cards, 20, 30 years ago; now I don't. You come, and I say, 'pay for it,' and if you don't, I say, 'don't come any more.' It's not a question of trust or faith – it is that the right thing will come at the right time. I acknowledge it; I don't deny it – *Wa amma bini'mati rabbika fahaddith*[86] –.... knowledge.

---

[86] "And proclaim your Lord's bounties." (Qur'an 93:11)

There is no knowledge other than the One, no doer other than the One – *wa la fa`ila illa Hu, wa la maqsuda illa Hu wa la mawjuda illa Hu*[87] – so what am I discussing this and that and the other? *Bismillah*.

Function of Islam

AA: I'd like to continue on the themes of the function of religion; also to bring it specifically to the religion of Islam, both as understood historically, as well as understood from its inner knowledge. The self-definition of Islam is that it is the only manifestation of the *Dīn al-Hanif*. Do you accept that?

SFH: Islam, in the sense of not denying reality at all its levels – yes. The hard is real; the soft is real; my illusion is real – it has a reality at infinite levels – I submit to that – yes. Other than that, I don't understand.

AA: So you don't think of the package, that is normally called 'Islam', in itself as encompassing the entire meaning of religious truth?

SFH: In the way, it came down through Muhammad and practiced by him as a transformative program, yes. But once you take the unison of Mecca/Medina out of it, then it becomes much more of a structure that is begging for a meaning.

AA: If you visualize the *dīn* as a descent, an effulgence (*laylat al-qadr*) through a veracious *barzakh*, the removal of the elements of the veracious leaves what is supposed to be transcendent in the *dīn* bereft of truth and therefore almost by definition, it has to atrophy in time in terms of human comprehension.

SFH: Probably so, yes. Unless there is, because of the human primal urge and need, a renewal of it, from it, within it. At worst, the structuring of it has become so hard and brittle, then, that renewal is becoming, if you like, more and more illusive, and a time reaches when there will not

---

[87] "There is no doer but He… There is no objective but He… There is no existence but He…"

be renewal anymore. Like what I read now, to really try and return back to the origin, through understanding and the culture also of what the culture was, what the words meant at that time, the effect of those words upon every muscle and every cell. That's why I think if Islam is to become again an effulgent pathway, we have to go back to its origin, live it as near as possible we can, but in the modern time, it's a tall order.

AA: But how can you sort of roll up time and go back to a point which you can only conjecture about?

SFH: Correct.

AA: Therefore it is not possible to talk about perfectibility of religion after the removal or the death of the veracious element.

SFH: Except for most of the Meccan *ayaat*, it is possible.

AA: This is the Qur'an – so the ineffability of the religion as an unfailing guide can only be through the scriptural texts rather any prophetic action.

SFH: Right. It's more difficult because of that, more difficult to live with it, and because of the missing *Insaan al-Kamil*, missing that mirror.

Revelation

AA: So, what is then revelation in the sense of the process of delivering a heavenly message? What does that constitute?

SFH: My understanding of revelation is that it is a more direct impact of the Absolute upon living entities or the relative, if it's without much interference, without much noise factor. So revelation is not black or white. Revelation has got, if you like, different levels. The one that we talk about as Muslims, we imply it is the most direct, the most absolute in a sense. But it has in it also a lot of other echoes and a lot of other grades as well. Allah talks in the Qur'an – 'I revealed to the ants, I revealed to the honey bees.' 'Revealed' – the same word is used. We've become too fixed I think on some of the Qur'anic terms, and they've become enshrined into some specific cultural mold, which I think has caused us quite a lot of rigidity.

AA: But still, there's undeniable revelation, whether it's nuanced because the word itself has multiple meanings, but it's a process by which the Divine or the Absolute reveals intention to the relative. And that process is channeled through individuals.

SFH: Yes, fine.

AA: So all religious truth, therefore, must be intermediated or not necessary?

SFH: Not necessarily. But the ultimate objective is for the human being to realize and experience the total interconnectedness of the relative and the Absolute, and the seamlessness of supreme consciousness and personal consciousness. So it has to need that being, that intermediary.

AA: This issue of the *iha'* and the way that this kind of – because it can't be contained by human beings or material entities like rocks or mountains or whatever, if it descends in its fulsomeness, infinitude, cannot possibly be absorbed by the limited; it will consume it, it can't exist alongside it.

SFH: Correct.

AA: So revelation then is a form of *rahma*. Would you say that?

SFH: Yes, no doubt about it. Great *Rahma*. And not every being can take it. *Inna sanulqee `alayka qawlan thaqeela*.[88] Not every body can take that. Also full entry into the infinitude of the *ka`ba* is also not for everyone – not everyone can take it. You talk to even a mature person about reducing their ego, they become angry, let alone getting it out, let alone dying from it...

---

[88] "We shall load upon you a weighty matter." (Qur'an 73:5)

AA: But inasmuch as the Prophet had no choice in the content and the delivery, then in that sense he is basically a vehicle.

SFH: Yes, he no longer has the need or the requirement or the function of the normal human being. In that case, at that level, there is absolutely no choice. He has given himself up to the higher. *Ba`a nafsahu lillah wa sar*[89]..... I have the illusion that I have a bit of a choice. Until by choice I don't want to choose. Then I'm entering closer to that state.

AA: But obviously an individual person who has that highly developed personal consciousness, approaching higher consciousness, is not the same as the Prophet; the Prophet need not have any consciousness.

Qur'an/Religious Rituals

SFH: True, but you become more and more in resonance with the Prophet. He himself encourages people to have that – he says, 'first, read the Qur'an until you hear it as though I am saying it to you; until you read as though Jibril is saying it to you. Until it comes to you as though it's direct from Allah.' It's not trying to make such barriers. Just shows that there are different grades – not deny the facts of that. It's accessible.

AA: You once said also that if the forms of religious ritual were not perfected, you would not really follow it – the form that was brought to you by the Prophet.

SFH: Yes.

AA: And in a certain way, you have independently verified their aptness as it were.

SFH: Yes, I can't improve on them. So, therefore, it's out of the question. I really cannot improve on them.

AA: There's no point even looking at improvements.

---

[89] "He sold his self to Allah and became *`Abd Allah* (The servant of Allah)."

Religion

SFH: I don't. Exactly. For me it is that. There can't be one *raka`*. Although the principle is one, it's inadequate – I love it, I have to do the second one, to confirm it.

AA: So basically you have remolded what is obligatory, into something that is part of you, something you acknowledge independently.

SFH: Totally.

AA: And it just happens to be coincidental.

SFH: I don't know, coincidental or what, I don't know. I think I don't see any possibility for me to improve on the form, the structure of the *`ibada*.

AA: Because of its periodicity over one's lifetime, it has a certain completeness.

SFH: Yes.

AA: Daily, annually .... lifetime – the cycles are effective in and of themselves, not because they have been exercised in a way that was deemed to be correct.

SFH: I think they do resonate also; the question of exercise also comes into it and the repeated pattern and the familiarity makes it sweeter; it makes it much more homely, much more reliable, gives one security. There is that element as well.

AA: And would you say it's all to do with re-configuring the human being's perception of time and space, in the sense that if you look at the movement of the day naturally, and within the lifetime, there is a break of space.

SFH: No doubt.

AA: Is that part of it?

SFH: I'm sure there is that element.

AA: *"Faskh al-`Awa'id."*

SFH: Also, there are things to do with the whole structure of the planets and the earth and the moon. I mean *maghrib* is a big time, very important time, another *barzakh* time, separating two different zones, the day and the night. The birds go into their nests – other things, animals, go into another zone. So I personally feel at that time that I just want to be quiet, and disappear. So I think there are a lot of elements that we don't necessarily know overtly or clearly. Intuitively, I think that many people feel some connection.

AA: Like sacred rhythm…

SFH: No doubt about it.

AA: Spiritual.

SFH: Far more, if you like to connect with the celestial and other powers, like planetary movements, the personal changes in our own body – the body chemistry; all of these are connected with it.

AA: So a kind of terrestrial glimpse of the cosmic dance?

SFH: In a sense. We are dancing. The dancers and the dance in a sense are in unison.

Dīn of Islam

AA: Shaykhna, it is apparent that the way the *Dīn* of Islam is understood by you is in fact distinct from what we commonly or conventionally call 'Islam'. But if you see Islam as abiding by the outer aspects of the *dīn* – you perform your rituals and your devotion with your appropriate courtesies – it is the door of inner knowledge open to you through that – the gateway of piety, it's called.

SFH: I see unity in every aspect. I see utter, total, seamless connectedness between the outer and the inner, and the first and the last. *Awwal wal Akhir, wal Dhahir wal Batin*. I see seamless connection between the physics and metaphysics, the ritual and the meaning. The only issue here is to be given the map of this *tawhīdi*, utter absolute, reality. So a person knows that he is giving charity, he is serving, in order for him or her to get out of the illusion of constantly being self-obsessed and self-serving. The same thing with the ritual – outer movement, if it is pointing towards the *qibla* of inner stillness, then it is *in islam*. It is in submission to the reality at all its levels. Realities are infinite, all emanating from, sustained by, and returning to the One and Only capital 'R' Reality. From the One has issued, has emanated from, the effulgent, countless-ness: otherness is only an outer little flash from Oneness. Duality is based on Unity; multiplicity is nothing other than the outer peripheral of that which is singularity. So I accept you start with the ritual *wa thiyabaka fatahhir* [90] – start with cleaning your clothes, you end up trying to purify your heart.

AA: We were just talking a minute ago about this person who is really a good example of the *muttaqi* – who is pious, does his rituals, probably has a high standard of personal ethics, and sees Islam in the sense of as not just a religion per se, but as a kind of *Hudhur*, presence, good actions, good works. These people become in some way settled in this type of devotion, but they cannot be anything beyond that; they quote, for example, *Surat al-`Asr* – *`amilu salihaat*[91] – they say: 'I pray, I'm doing good works, good deeds;' they don't do the *ta'wil* that may lead them to explore other possibilities. Are these people cut off, not from salvation, but from any form of inner knowledge?

SFH: No-one is cut off – as I said, it is seamless. Supreme Consciousness and the first consciousness of life 100 million years ago were utterly connected. The question of these people who become habitual is because they want to perpetuate their habits – firstly, *wa tawasa'u bil haqq*[92] – what is *haqq*? *Haqq* is Absolute, so whatever you

---

[90] "And purify your clothes." (Qur'an 74:4)
[91] "Do good works." (Qur'an 103:3)

are doing is relative, and so it's an aspect of *baatil* – they don't read that. Secondly, *tawassa'u bil sabr*[93]. *Sabr* is timelessness, patience – have they tasted timelessness? If they have tasted timelessness, then they will not be at the altar or the idol worship of habits. Habitual, they are stuck; that's it. We like to be habitual; we like to perpetuate the illusion of foreverness. The *nur* of Allah is forever. How am I trying to perpetuate that? This is a mental concept that this is the only way. It's madness.

Framed in a Limited Culture

AA: While agreeing with you, it still poses the question that the vast majority of people, who are, let's say more amenable to unlocking the door to inner knowledge, have been framed in a limited culture, whether it's Islam or Christianity, or Buddhism, or even secularism or an a-religious or irreligious culture, but focusing on good works, a high degree of personal conduct and in religious traditional worship, there's an entire legacy of rituals and practices that sustains them, propels them and keeps them in what you can call a 'prison.' So the process of breaking out becomes much more difficult for those who see themselves as pious, see themselves as *muttaqi*. Do you agree with that?

SFH: Yes, but I'd slightly re-frame it. I'd say instead of breaking out, 'breaking in'.

AA: Breaking in –

SFH: Yes – accept the outer constraints, the color of your face, your shape, genetic or cultural – but go into the microcosmic way, the subatomic side of it, not to the astrophysical side. The two sides that end up in the infinite vastness, in this case disappear into the nothingness of the inner. I think, being framed is unavoidable. You are born somewhere, you've landed somewhere on earth, it's unavoidable. And I don't think it's a necessary condition for enlightenment, illumination, or any name you like to give it. I don't think it's a necessary condition that you should

---

[92] "And exhort one another to truth." (Qur'an 103: 3)
[93] "Enjoin on each other patience." (Qur'an 103:3)

'break out' or denounce or any of it; you can do it exactly where you are. Get out of the mental constructs, the mental habits; get out of the identity issue and the time issue. These are the three culprits: identity, mind and time. Just try and step aside from each one of them. Be without an identity. People who have a high profile identity, such as celebrity, do anything to be lost on an island. They go out of their way with all kinds of tricks in order for them to be anonymous. Same thing with time – they do anything to be drugged to be out of their time. Same thing with mind – they do anything to be mind boggled. So do it without any of these fancy unnecessary arrangements. Get the map, live the map. Easy. I also think, for young educated intelligent people, who've done a bit of practices, including things like TM[94] or yoga, or *salaat*, it's easy. Be thoughtless. If you can't do it, repeat. A bit of a breath, oxygen – do it again. I think it's easy.

Inner Technology

AA: In your earlier teaching you told me about the inner technology as a way to break down these points of resistance, break down the point of identity, mind and time, it is partly to do with practice. But within the rituals of formal religion, whatever they are, they do not push in that direction. I've yet to see a monotheistic, religious culture that privileges this kind of inner awareness.

SFH: Although the earlier you go, the closer you go to the origin, the more you find that the outer ritual was inseparable from the inner meaning. Even with our own path, you find, every few decades, one of the illumined ones tries to highlight the secrets of worship. Several of Imam Khomeini's most important works were on that. The inner transformative part; though he doesn't use the same language. It's all about you, even the book *Asrar al-'Ibadat* – and others and others – throughout the ages. And this has been one of the enjoyable things from my trying to look back into our culture. I found this business of trying to balance the inner meaning and transformative path with the outer form,

---

[94] Transcendental Meditation.

has been repeated in our culture. Same thing with all of the other traditions. I found it the same with the Hindus, the same with the Christians, to lesser extent maybe, but the outer and the inner are inseparable. If I want the inner, I am starting with the outer as a kid, I start from where I am, and I'll realize the inner was there from the beginning.

AA: I don't want to labor this point, but it is also a matter of technique and process. If you look at your own life's work and add to it the work of others, let's call them masters.....in terms the realms of quantity, the teachings are generally taken at the level of personal conduct, improving one's ethics, commitment and so on. But very, very few – and I'm not just referring to anything specific, but generally, very few people make that span the abyss, make the leap and find that there was no abyss and the leap was basically done. So the issue of the inner technology, the issue of techniques and processes, isn't this also fundamental? Shouldn't one focus on that too?

SFH: I do. I accept that and I have been, not just early on in my own self, but during my journey of discovery even now. I would re-define, in a way, inner technology as that subtle awareness of what is going on within me as self-soul dynamics: *self* being more lower self, ego, identity, separation, individuation: *soul* being that mysterious light which replicates, or holographic representation of that unknowable sacred totality. So, self-soul dynamics, watching which part of me now is responding. At the moment I respond to you through my ability to hear you, process that through my mind and then respond to it through the motor neurons, which result in my moving of the tongue. But at the same time I am constantly referring to my *ruh*, so that I don't deviate from that referencing, that calibration. Otherwise it becomes just chitchat. So that awareness is, to my mind, the ultimate purpose of anything like reforming the character, inner technology, self-awareness, self-criticism, all of these things. It's to do with the self-soul full integration. The self is the mechanical, physical, has to relate to the world, to otherness, and the soul is none other than the representative of Oneness. That is the inner technology.

Religion

AA: Would you say that the degree of resistance of the self to what you have just called breaking in becomes greater and greater and greater as you perfect as it were the outer qualities?

SFH: I don't know about the quantitative side – I wouldn't say it's greater – it becomes more subtle and therefore maybe more difficult. It's like learning to ski; when you're on the lower slopes of watching yourself, your ego, 'they admired me so I am very happy, or they didn't admire me, so I am now gloomy, or they didn't clap enough for me. I was not acknowledged or they didn't give me my full title, or whatever.' So earlier on, like on the ski slope, if you fall into that pit, it's not a big disaster. Later on it becomes more and more difficult. At the end, at the pinnacle, you really need someone who has been there and knows all the dangers of avalanches and crevasses and all of that. So earlier on you can take any teacher, it doesn't matter so much – although you need more – but, ideally, you learn one technique so you can keep to that. That's why often the Sufis insisted on one teacher and said that don't change them, like one mother, if the teacher is really full and genuine. But it is later on that the dangers are much bigger. That is why we have so many people who get totally disappointed – having followed somebody whom they found is not as complete, as full as prophetic as they had hoped. So later on the falls can be more devastating.

Dhawq

AA: Would you say the whole issue of process and technique and so on has no vitality – there is no *dhawq* behind it, no taste – if that's the case, what is luck, is it given in equal measure to every human being or in differential measure?

SFH: Differential for every human being according to their ability to be in it and touch it. *Dhawq* is like a field of energy – it's like the field of compassion, the field of love; it's a field, an energy field. Love is an energy field that unifies, connects diverse entities, things that you may not have thought they had much in common. Love connects them. That's why it's also called on the human side; human love blinds, because you are united with some other person so you don't see any of their faults; you just see the perfection of that oneness, the taste or *dhawq* of unity. So it's a field, *dhawq*. The more you taste the *dhawq* of presence, of that infinity, of that unfathomable thrill of Oneness, connectedness between the seen and the unseen, the more you are addicted to it. *Dhawq* is a field that you need to taste, but if I have my mouth full of other stuff, how can I taste something else? That is why inner technology becomes really meaningful and alive if you follow a program of *takhliya*, emptying out, and then *tasfiya*, purifying your thoughts, ideas, and concepts, And then *tahliya*, sweetening – if you sweeten it before you have emptied out, it's like putting a very high quality soil on poisonous ground or on rocks – it won't work. So, emptying out first, purifying and then sweetening, by reminding yourself that this is not what it is: you are moving into another zone – it is here also. That zone is not just in the Hereafter, that zone is present. Then you have *tajlia*, it becomes easy with constant reminder; it is not a hacking work.

AA: So *dhawq* is something that grows or reduces with immersion or lack of immersion.

SFH: True. It's a displacement. *Dhawq* of the higher, meaning tasting of the higher, is entirely based on tasting of the lower. You pay less attention to, if you like, the existential side, to the survival side. Then you are more and more poised towards arrival. It's a displacement. You're one person; you have one energy; the moment is only one moment. So if it is occupied by the outer skirmishes, trying to balance it, trying to maximize it, to take an opportunity, then you are not exposed at the threshold of the other side. There are two sides of consciousness. One is the limited conditioned human duality, relativity, and the other one is the absolute, and they are ever connected. If you are at the threshold, then the less you are concerned about the outer, the more you *may* have the taste and the understanding of the inner. It's for that reason we designate sacred places, sacred times, rituals annually, or monthly or whatever. It's a displacement. 'No' to this can give you 'yes' to that.

AA: Which is then *dhawq*?

SFH: *Dhawq* of the higher, *dhawq* is *dhawq*. *Dhawq* is also of muck, but *dhawq* here generally with the Sufis and others implies *dhawq* of the higher – tasting the Presence, tasting the ever dominant Light – Allah.

AA: So you wouldn't treat it in the way I would originally have conceived or constructed it. *Dhawq* is like a person who can't abide sour food – he has no *dhawq*; or a person who has the predilection for barley soup.

SFH: Fine, but it's for that moment. He may change later on. If he becomes very sick and finds barley soup his only healing or the remedy, he will love barley soup. There is no person, there is only that construct of the so-called identity and the mind and the time at that time. There is no such thing as a person, or a character. There's conduct, yes – change it, it changes. There's no such thing as, 'he is like this'; there are certain visible things that do not change. The 'spots' of the tiger may not change, but the character, the quality, the conduct of the tiger may change. Kill it, pull his teeth out, pull his paws out and it becomes a rug. The spots are still the same, but the tiger becomes a rug.

Modeling and Schema

AA: The way that you have replied in great detail and density is still in the area for what I call modeling and schema for your individual re-arrangement that serves your purpose. However, in your case I assume the vitalizing force is this stirring, this kind of highly subjective model and the schema tells you the 'how', tells you the 'what', tells you the relationship between the parts and the whole. But it doesn't necessarily transfer your vitalizing force to others. So most people understand the schema and the model; most people find it intellectually satisfying. It's rigorous, it's self-defined, it's not having any intellectual faults, but the vitalizing force is usually lacking in order to give this schema a reality. You are the architect and the engineer, but you are your own mason, your own builder. What most people would be vitally interested in is: how can they be the mason of their own edifice?

SFH: That energy to re-vitalize is there, but inadvertently I think most of us use it to perpetuate our old habits and to perpetuate the idea of ongoingness, because we are propelled by these two major forces: to connect end space, and to continue in time. So a lot of that energy that is available to the individual has been consumed trying to perpetuate what my concepts and ideas and mental constructs have been, so as I have an idea of perpetuity. If I denounce or get out or lose perpetuity, people will die, everything will die. The idea of ongoingness of life, and life hereafter is key to our survival, because it's vital, it is there. Allah's *nur* is forever, so we always want to hang onto some aspect or another, even though they may be subconscious. So to re-vitalize, to bring in life into this edifice, this structure or schema, as you called it, I think we need to stop; we need to start the other thing. As I said earlier, it's *takhliya*, that is, you have to empty out. Lose your identity. Use the concept of your roles; that's why there have been all of these practices throughout human history, especially their regularity, are according to the solar system – pilgrimage – going to a sacred place. Everything is sacred. Everything is from the One to the One, by the One. But we have designated some areas, and they are being imbibed with that human energy and regular visits, and it becomes a ritual. But you need that until you find out that, actually, the Light of the sacred is *in* you. So you become immensely respectful of what is in you. As a result you become very respectful of the same sacred in others. So you regard them as essentially the same as you. That is the foundation of justice. Injustice is the idea that I now can be independent – that's the *nafs*. But injustice begins with my birth, with my awareness of my awareness. The root of injustice is me, when I think that now, I can do anything. Who are you that you can do anything? You are here – a shadow of something that represents the source of everything. So how can you ever deviate from that *haqq*?

Gateway to the Dīn/The Mecca-Medina Model

AA: We'll get back to that later, *Insha'Allah*. This is of great concern to those people who call it the spiritual pedagogy of it and pedagogically nearly all teachers who have laid out this scheme, and with your permission about a year ago I asked Shaykh Saadi. But frankly, again in discussion with you, if you just throw people in at the beginning of the beginning, it still is to develop them so there is that kind of preparatory phase always missing in this process. And this *Insha'Allah* we'll discuss later. But going back to the *dīn* of Islam, as it were a gateway to the *dīn*, it pre-supposes in some way, knowledge or experience of the transcendent, a sort of Mecca before Medina. And you said recently that it is now all Medina, which implies that there should be a reverse *Hijra*. Would you call it that?

SFH: I wouldn't call it reverse – I think it's out of balance. Life is balanced between the physics and metaphysics, between the seen and the unseen, the relative and the absolute. I won't use these dramatic things at all – I think it's all there. The *nur* of Allah is everywhere at all times. It's just that we are trying to exaggerate the shadows and darkness. So all that is needed in Medina is to have that constant *Qibla*; instead of idol worshipping of projects or developments, this political thing or another, we should worship the Adorable passionately, that which is Infinite and ever-connected, where everything was gathered before its explosion into the Big Bang. So Medina needs to be in every way re-oriented towards Mecca, and then that's fine. You are both – Mecca and Medina. Finite-infinite; here, not-of-here; boundless and bounded. So it needs to be modified, and it can happen quickly. I don't think it needs a great deal of fanfare and *hijras* and all that. *Hijra,* meaning turning away from the extreme end that we have reached. 'Middle people', meaning that you see both ends clearly – one end of me is celestial, the other is terrestrial. I am in the middle and that is the spectrum of consciousness. One end of the spectrum of consciousness is the supreme and encompasses whatever you can ever imagine, and the other end is me. I am conscious of me; I am dying or living or tired or not. So all what it means is a slight adjustment. We'll be forced to that adjustment. There's no way out. The human make-up is that. The rise of Adam, the evolution of Homo sapiens is that – it was supreme consciousness. And once I even have the slightest orientation towards that which is most durable, most encompassing, I will automatically begin to adjust. So Medina must be towards Mecca. Mecca cannot exist on its own. It has to yield into a plethora of infinite varieties of existences. Medina is one of them.

AA: In other words, would you say that if the individual's *qibla* is Mecca, that is prostration and acknowledgement of the absolute Oneness, that suffuses all existence, and Medina is the social/collective image of that, or equivalent of that, then the *Qibla* of Medina has to be shifted. But it's not to do with the inner conditions of the individual, but rather the outer aspects of the collectivity, does that mean that you have to smooth the Medina, as it were, from its cultural specification, moving more away from nations and states and loyalties over and above the Meccan axis? Reducing the scope of the apparent range of the *Shari`ah*, and religious exclusivity – that is, go in the opposite direction?

SFH: It will adjust itself. Once I bring in even a speck of the Absolute into this, if you like, distraction or excessive one-sidedness or extreme sidedness, it will adjust itself. All you need is the constant reminder of, say, death, the end of everything. If you bring that element alone, every minute somebody has to stop for five seconds remembering the end of everything, it will bring in an immense calibration.

Prophetic Message

AA: Shaykhna, this idea of self-regulation and self-adjustment would preclude any need for outside agents, like a prophet or a sage.

SFH: The outside agent is a reminder of the inner agent, nothing more.

AA: So why does it stop then? If we need outside agents, like a prophet to remind nations –

SFH: What has stopped?

AA: The prophecy has reached finality according to –

SFH: There's nothing more to say. There is no *naba'* – there is no more news. What more news do you want?

AA: So how does self-adjustment do it?

Religion

SFH: Adjustment – the news is that there is only One and you are here only to get out of the illusion that you are separate from the One. That is the news. So there's no more news after that.

AA: It was always the news.

SFH: No, not so clearly.

AA: Finality is to do with the degree of clarity.

SFH: The degree of completion of the multi-faceted atlas of existence. There's nothing more you can add to that.

AA: I don't want to get into why it was done incrementally. I think it's really futile to question it. But at the level of this unfolding it was done incrementally – the assumption that there's a certain level of finality – this is it – human beings have not advanced any further intellectually or culturally to require any other Prophetic experience, as it were…

SFH: It's an evolutionary process – to the point that you are no longer primate – you reach a point where you no longer have of whatever was there 200,000 years ago. Suddenly, something happens within a matter of a few hundred years, 1000 years, this standing up of the ape or the versions of Adam – whatever symbolism or even biological change you want to bring into it – something happened that is not reversible – no more news to tell me that there is only One, and that One is beyond the limitation of the mind to fully comprehend. But that representation of the One is in your heart. You are here as a representative of the One as a *Khalifa*, as a vice-regent in order to act, play a little god in your home or in your domain. You are responsible for the ant. On *hajj* you mustn't kill even a mosquito. You are not a killer. It is part of nature. There's nothing more than that. *La Nabiyya ba`adi*.[95] No more news. It doesn't mean there are no prophetic beings. Everybody should be a prophetic being.

---

[95] "There is no Prophet bearing news after me."

Good News

AA: The direction of this event doesn't feel to lead to any...

SFH: I don't see it as an arrow – I just see it as a reality. We have reached a point in evolution that that's it. And I think science will begin to show more and more how true that is. Once they get out of this very limited thing of total verifiability at the physical level. They have become a standstill for the last 20-30/40 years—whether it's physics, whether it's medical sciences – they have to break out of that. They are beginning to accept other energy models, this model, that model. Fifty years ago, Chinese medicine would have been considered total quackery. But now it's accepted by most of the Western systems as part of the healing process. Until 30 years ago even the notion of death was considered to be an anti-social thing, until Elizabeth Cobbler Ross and others made it acceptable – so don't deny it. We are still very primitive. Simply because of a bit of technology we thought we had resolved everything! Man is a divine being on earth: he must acknowledge his humanity, limit it, contain it, care for it – whatever – so that there is a bit of order, and totally utterly be energized and thrilled by Divinity – that's the news.

AA: That is the news – it was revealed incrementally and intensively over a very narrow period of time.

SFH: True – 10-15,000 years – 10/15% of the rise of human consciousness.

AA: If you ask about the outer – even inner forms of Mecca 1,400 years ago, it's probably superior to the outer form of Mecca today.

SFH: I can really not compare – I understand. I can't say the past was better than the future or the present – I can't say that at all. There is qualitative aspect and quantitative aspect; they impinge on each other. The business of quality and quantity is the most intricate; there hasn't been much work on that, actually. There is a point in which a bit of a *barzakh* exists, where they interchange: a certain quantity becomes a quality – it changes.

AA: That's what Karl Marx said!

SFH: So it's an incredible situation. I can't say the past was better. It's a romantic notion.

AA: I'm not saying it was better; I'm saying that the problem is: there is oppression, disease, injustice, and idol worship to a greater extent now.

SFH: Worse. True. Also the population has grown a lot. Years ago, how many were we? 50 million?

AA: Probably half a million.

SFH: No, the whole world – 50 million? Look at it now; it's 7.2 billion! It's an enormous thing. Something else has happened. We don't know what that mass is doing. I do not think the situation is worse now in any way from my perspective. You can look at it from a certain angle and you find of course it's worse. From many, many other angles, I don't think so.

Field of Prophecy

AA: I ask from only one specific angle, which is the angle of prophecy: the angle of prophecy is that there is news delivered incrementally and it has now stopped. This is axiomatic. You're saying that it stopped because there's nothing more to say.

SFH: I don't think it has stopped fully. It's been embellished more, rendered more acceptable, in terms of language. Look at the language we're using now, with the technology we have. Transmission, reception, charged by batteries – all you said was not there 50 years ago. It's much easier now for me to actually convey what is in my heart than it would have been had I been here 70 years ago. It's much easier now. You say you have not received it; the message is in your tablet but you have not opened it up. Open it, unpack it – there is a whole host of vocabulary that has lifted us up from the Medina mire towards the Meccan lights.

AA: What you're saying, Shaykhna, is that the field of prophecy is still there but it's no longer necessary or useful for it to be focused on the individual.

SFH: You cannot deny the essential key importance of an individual. If there is no individual, there is nothing you can say, but it is not anymore, if you like, confined to a particular one person, or culture or people. It is now universal. I think there has been so much cross-pollination, cross-fertilization in the last 2-300 years, which we, as Muslims, have missed a lot of it, but it's been going on in the West, it's been going on elsewhere. We have missed it; we, as Muslims, are not reading people; we are not literary people. I as a youngster was horrified when I saw the huge proportion of fiction in bookshops, but I did realize that this was part of the culture of these people – their life's learning. To me it was an anathema – I considered it all almost *haram* – 'what is all this novel, novel, novel?' But within the novel there were so many creative things and we missed it – I missed it. So individual is important, but it's a transmitter. And I think the West, the rest of the world, will reach the same point, no matter who they are. But through more diffused ways. They reach the point that there is Oneness in humanity. Even in this country,[96] thirty years ago it was not considered as such. There were considered to be superior, inferior, lesser and higher, people. Until now they did not consider the children of Adam being One. Whereas Muhammad revealed it. All of us are children of Adam. So evolution has taken us 1,400 years for these Westerners to realize at least the basic foundation of sameness in human beings. So I think it's accelerating. I think the individual – going back to your question – is important as a pivotal point of transmitting. One of the Divine attributes which Ibn Arabi also acknowledges as one of the seven key *Ummahat al-Asma* is *Al-Mutakallim* – express yourself. We are not allowed expression in the East. Whereas the West, not having had a map, they ignored all the

---

[96] South Africa.

maps, threw away the bath water and the baby – they are beginning to allow the expression. The best of it will remain. Fifty years ago Karl Marx was taboo. Now he's being re-discovered as one of the greatest geniuses. And so on; so allow the expression – time will prove it – time is Allah, is Allah. Allah will prove it. Allah will prevail. It will come. I think the question of individual as a transmitter, disseminator is such that, that which has *haqq* in it, is more durable and sustainable, will remain. That which is not, will be local, fashionable, much more time-dependent...

AA: So basically, individuals will become in their collectivity, what the Prophet says about it: *Al-'Ulama' wuratha'a al-Anbiya'a.*[97]

SFH: Correct. No doubt about it. Not only *wuratha*, but I would also consider ....*sadiqa*, companion, no doubt about it.

AA: It's a far more satisfying explanation than usually given by those people who claim they are speaking for the Prophet.

SFH: Absolutely. I have met a few people, one of whom was the *wali* of Behlil, who had served forty *shuyukh* and had fasted for the last fifty years of his life.

AA: Was he a temporal ruler like the Wali of Swat?

SFH: No, he was *wali* in the *wilaya* of illumination.

AA: Not like Wali of Swat?

SFH: No, no – *wali* in the North African sense, of *wali* of Allah, and it was clear to me that he could not talk, he would not move unless he was in the Prophetic presence. You could almost feel the Prophet and other prophets next to him. So you become like that. You cannot talk unless your *ruh* resonates with the *ruh* of those prophetic beings.

---

[97] "The knowledgeable ones will be the inheritors of the Prophets."

Love/Heart

AA: What does love of the Prophet mean?

SFH: Love is unifying. Love is a field of unifying which is the beginning of the explosion of the dot. From the extreme density of singularity, the *haqq* is embedded in the fields of Love. Truth is totally, utterly in the middle of the cosmic vastness of this energy field called Love. That's why without love there is no life. It's a semblance of life. That's why people have to have some passion, some sort of utter and total, if you like, obsession. We are obsessed by the *ruh*. But we don't know it, so we become obsessed by power, money sex, until such time you know you are obsessed by your own *ruh*.

AA: Is love *muhabba* or *muwadda*?

SFH: No, *muwadda* is an aspect of it – a subtler form.

AA: Which is the higher?

SFH: I can't say, I don't know. I think *muwadda* is an aspect of *muhabba*. *Muhabba* is more intense. *Muhabba* engulfs everything and finishes everything. It ends up in *tawhīd*.

AA: *Muwadda* implies responsibility.

SFH: *Muwadda* can be between two different levels of entities; yes, it implies responsibility.

AA: But Allah is referred to... as *Al-Wadud*.

SFH: Yes, because he is beyond – the absolute is with Him.

AA: Creation with responsibility.

SFH: Sure, the absolute is Absolute. Allah is *al-Wadud*, but the Absolute cannot love; love has *emanated* from the Absolute.

AA: One of its manifestations is: loving itself and therefore –

SFH: Absolutely – there is only that.

AA: Assuming our mind understands what this means.

SFH: Absolutely.

AA: Or even our heart, I don't think it can.

SFH: The heart is not about understanding, it will know. It's no longer 'under' standing – it just knows. I don't know why but I know. I know that I'll be given what I need to be given at a time when I need to be given that.

AA: I have a little saying from Joe Campbell on this: it says, 'Allah (God) is a metaphor for a mystery that absolutely transcends all human categories of thought, even the categories of being and non-being.'

SFH: Wonderful – transcends all.

AA: Including the categories of being?

SFH: Yes, because they are categories of mind; they are mental constructs: becoming is me with ambition, mind, with a biography, an arrow of time. I want to become this great *`alim* or Sufi or master. It is an ambition. There is a separation in it. There is an 'I'-ness in it. Being is less of an 'I'. But that transcends it all. *Becoming* and *being* are all emanations from that.

AA: A metaphor for the absolute, unknowable –

SFH: I know, but it is inwardly experiential. As Imam Ali says repeatedly in his wonderful *khutbas* – it's not something you come to know, not something you can discuss, but you inwardly are certain of it. *Khalas*.

Expressing Universal Truth

AA: It seems you, Shaykhna, are living or expressing universal truth and realities that all lead to the truth and Reality, but encapsulating it within the historical devotional forms of Islam. At least, that's my experience. Why did you do that? Is it because of necessity or appropriateness? Why did you couch it in Islamic terms?

SFH: I cannot couch it, nor can I encapsulate it; it's not encapsulable. My background is this. My cells, my culture is that. The first thing I heard was some Qur'an and some *adhan* in my ears.

AA: Is it by necessity or…?

SFH: No, it is by nature. I can't deny that; it's an accident of birth.

AA: So if you were born in Tibet, you'd express it through their culture and language?

SFH: Probably, most probably. I wouldn't be surprised at all. That's what Chinmaya did – he said, 'You were born somewhere else; get back to where you were' – you don't have to learn Sanskrit.

AA: It is basically a sort of statement of fact.

SFH: Absolutely.

AA: I was born in a Muslim environment; so this is a culture; these are the terms that people use to discuss the unknowable.

SFH: Absolutely.

AA: So it's like: 'I want to discuss the unknowable; I want to live the reality of the unknown, therefore I will use these norms and terms to describe it.'

SFH: Absolutely. Here is somebody who has lived with palm trees. He can't live in Alaska. Go back to where the palm trees are... they already

Religion

exist there – that culture contains it. You don't need to change cultures. Use your culture and the fruits will come.

AA: It's a kind of natural –

SFH: Yes, if it has in it the full program of using the fruit. Because, as I said, if it is completely distorted – western or whatever, it doesn't work. You have to come and learn Sanskrit.

AA: Or if you were living in a sort of Christianized world, very few people around, maybe in South America, then you would express it in that culture?

SFH: Yes – it's an accident of birth.

AA: But the accident implies also certain actions.

SFH: Sure. It's an incidence, a natural incidence.

AA: Do you mean it would be difficult and probably inappropriate to express yourself in Hindu terms.

SFH: I was totally indifferent to how I expressed it or didn't express it to you. I was indifferent.

AA: You went on a teaching path; you have to use the language, you have to convey your thoughts.

SFH: No, I was teaching myself, the teacher was taught.

AA: So what about all those families who were with you?

SFH: Whatever it was – I was teaching myself. Rediscovering a heritage that to my mind, and to many others, was semi-dead. No, I was really rediscovering the Muhammadi Light. And I was always encouraged by some sort of Muhammadi presence.

Good Work and Piety/Khidma

AA: I don't know of any case where universal truth that is reflected in all the great spiritual traditions has been expressed and framed in this way. And has been able to overcome, or transcend the forms in which the peak of worship formerly took, which was piety and good works.

SFH: I think good work and piety have been the foundation to many, many of the traditional paths and religions. Christianity is embedded in that. So is Hinduism and all other religions. Zoroastrianism is nothing other than good speech, good thoughts and good deeds. Good deeds implying again, the beginning of getting out of separation. It's not just for me. There is no 'me', there is only the One. Through the grace of the One I have the illusion of the 'me' and for that illusion to reach its conclusion, I have to yield the so-called 'me' into the One, by serving the so-called otherness; to realize there is no otherness. It's only a manifestation, if you like, camouflaging Oneness. So I think there is a great deal of similarity between most of these human, if you like, heritages in the last 5, 6, 7000 years. Except in Islam, I think it's closer and nearer, and also because of that familiarity, we see a slight deviation, we exaggerate it. Two years ago a survey showed that there are about 22,000 different sects of Christianity in America alone. Here, amongst the Muslims, there are only very few slight minor deviations. But it's the human mischief that wants to exaggerate differences. It's nothing to do with the *dīn*. We are very fortunate. Qur'an is clear. The difficulty of the language of the Qur'an is that the cultural distance is vast. Many of the words meant something else 1400 years ago than what they mean now. And that familiarity actually is a barrier. So we need to stop thinking that we speak Arabic. Get back to what it meant then and you will find that it resonates in a different way with the heart. So I find altogether that discussing Islam, sharing a part of Islam, is very refreshing. But for most people again they get more security or whatever from their own habits. They resort back. It's a human tendency. Human tendency is to perpetuate what they have become familiar with. That is the lower self and ego and that's the barrier.

Religion

AA: How does one interact – you are now on the fourth journey using it metaphorically – so how does one interact in society and creation? How do you do it? Set up soup kitchens?

SFH: No, I'm no longer doing that. I'm only concerned about what touches me from the *ruh*. I cannot at this stage in my life, my age and whatever, really do the first rungs of the ladder of ascent, social services, etc., anymore. I acknowledge it, I encourage it, but I can't do it. When I see people stuck in their inner progress, their inner technology, their inner journey, I yield to that. So my *khidma* is far more subtle. When I see somebody, I hold them and sit with them, and then they will know. And a lot of it is by my intention. It happens on a daily basis many times.

AA: The *khidma*, which you mentioned is Allah's call to service, is to do with changes – your sense of *khidma* maybe 10 years ago was in fact doing work which somehow touched the collectivity, not the individual. Your sense of *khidma* now, because you are using this metaphor, is more to do with transmitting this energy to the individual.

SFH: Also, I don't see much of collectivity at the moment. I see a lot of diversity now. 15, 20 years ago I saw most people were grouping, but now I see much clearer layering and levels between those groupings. I don't see connectedness. Give me 20 people and I'll show individuality and diversity. In fact it happened five nights ago, here. There were 14 people. I spoke to them as a group. They were all from this land and had discovered their *dīn* and attached their hearts. They were together, almost like one hand. But they were diverse. So no, what you say is true, but also not true. I don't see groups because individuality exists.

AA: You said earlier Shaykhna that it's much more subtle. When you use the term *khidma* colloquially, it implies doing some kind of materially value-added service to the poor, the indigent, sick and so on. It's not seen as trying to ignite as it were the love of the One in the hearts of people.

SFH: Depends on the dictionary. Sufis use *khidma* entirely for 'moving the heart.'

AA: Your dictionary?

SFH: No, the Sufi dictionary.

AA: [With a smile] There is no such dictionary, Shaykhna, you gave that definition.

SFH: Sure. And I also did whatever I could for the subtler side if there was that.

AA: This is really just to map it out rather than to show why you are doing this? You did that [material service to others] before, but it's now irrelevant. So is this the *khidma* that is possible in this condition?

SFH: I only *respond*. I respond to what comes in front of me, and if nothing comes, I respond to my inner. I only respond. I am very fortunate in having less and less personal drive and desires as such. I see if a child needs something – most of my sweets and chocolate go to the children who come here at that level. But I respond more to that which others do not read. It's not because I am distinguished or something greater, but I find that is more important. And that's something I can do which many other people cannot. So I prioritize it.

AA: You used to say before that your heart goes out to the poor and the indigent people.

SFH: True. It is also because they are purer: either the very poor are the best, or the very rich gone beyond it. The in-between is the misery – those who are aspiring to have 6 cars and houses; it's despicable. I found the establishment middle class aspiration for that is the curse. I am not here on a rampage to destroy – it will destroy itself. They are destroyed already before they have reached there.

AA: I think we reached a kind of natural end here!

The Sacred

The Qur'an/Sacred Texts

AA: Shaykhna, I remember you once said that your entire life, spiritual life as it were, was ignited by your engagement with the Qur'an, you were so overwhelmed by it, when you started reading it with a different guise, with a different eye, with the eye of '*Haqiqah*'. What did you mean by that?

SFH: What I meant was that as a child I enjoyed the sound of it, it impacted on me, and I would recite it even as a 6/7 year old. I remember myself walking up and down to different houses, climbing up and down to the roofs and reciting the Qur'an. It took me to another realm, if you like. I would suddenly become like a bird flying with wings, and of course the meanings were to me the more obvious straightforward meanings. But when I came back to it, especially in the United States, where I began to look at everything in life through the lens of *Haqiqah*, it was a completely different zone and it began with some people asking me to make commentary on *Surah Yaseen*. So I had a very good library of traditional commentaries. So I looked at several of them, and after a week or two, we had a gathering for a few days, two three hours each time, for me to make commentary on *Yaseen* more accessible, based on what I had read and what I had begun to perceive. So I began to really see the Qur'an as the gathering of all the different realities with a small 'r'. In other words, the accumulation and the collection of all the different facets of life. I began to see the Qur'an as a basket of a universal weave that contains within it strands, any aspect of human life and experience, and I realized from early on a lot of it is to do with the sincerity of approach. If I approached it as a scholar, or as a talker, or as a teacher, it would be very different from if I approached it as a bereft being that wants to be guided, who wants to be led, or who wants to be admitted. In other words, with humbleness, no assumption, no presumption and no expectations. In other words, I began to learn that every time I came to it I would have to be in both outer and inner *wudhu*, outer and inner, if you like, dissociation, and the meanings of the Qur'an would come to me. And that continued for a few years in the States, and so I began not only know, not only realize, and not only believe, but totally, completely and utterly experience that the unpacking of this revelation was something monumental for human kind. And so I was in every way feeling honored that I was doing it for myself and others around me, for itself and its own sake. So it was an entirely new approach.

AA: And would you say if there was no Qur'an you would not really be in the fold of traditional Islam.

SFH: I can't say that really, because I was born into it. I can't really say that.

AA: So it's a pointless conjecture.

SFH: I don't know, maybe, I can't say.

AA: Have you come across any other, to quote 'Holy text', that had the same effect on you?

SFH: Well, certainly some of the unpacking of the Upanishads that Chinmya did, subconsciously it showed that it was in the Qur'an, consciously it touched me in a way it pierced through veils of thought and mind or personal perception. I certainly found that quite a number of such, if you like, discourses were taking you again to *Haqq*. I haven't read it myself, but they were unpacked for me. I'm not a great reader or a scholar. I just respond. But my responses to some of those were very electric.

AA: I have seen and read some of, nearly all the texts, of Christianity and so on, in fact I was taught it for years, and although it does encompass many of the themes of the Qur'an, the expressions of the Qur'an are far more potent, far more vital, which confirms to me their ever fresh nature as you said that it's to do with courtesy and approach and sincerity.

Sacred Texts' Language Barrier

SFH: I think the biggest obstacle between human beings and the so-called sacred texts is the language barrier, which is based on the cultural barrier. I think that's endemic, including the Qur'an. Much of it is also encased into a time warp because of the culture. I don't think people have realized that, or it's been looked at that way. So many, many of the terms we take it for granted that we know now what it means. What did it mean then, so I think this is huge barrier. The Qur'an is closer and nearer to the same original language, but being in the same language also has got its down side as many words don't mean the same thing now as they did originally. We assume Arabic has preserved it; no language is ever static, every 200-300 years most of the terms or the nuance change. We are stuck; people haven't got the courage to see it that way. They think it is sacrilegious to see it that way. It's not, Baba. What did most of these terms mean at the time the Qur'an was revealed?

AA: It seems to me when you read, you have no question, no issue that it is a package that is not humanly created, or humanly conjured.

SFH: I don't see the separation. I see unity of humanity and divinity. I think a lot of such historical arguments have never touched me or I have not entered them; I cannot really comment on that. How can it be other than humanly divine?

AA: You can say that about any text.

Connection Between Supreme Consciousness and Human Consciousness

SFH: Sure, the only thing is that in this case the connection between Supreme Consciousness and human consciousness was not interrupted by any other, if you like, noise factor. That's the difference, so it was directly revealed.

AA: That's what I meant.

SFH: Everything is revealed so finally I don't have no.

The Qur'an – A Highly Condensed Revelation

AA: Everything is not the Qur'an.

SFH: No, everything is not the Qur'an but everything is within the Qur'an, and therefore, everything you and I say has a touch of sacredness.

AA: So I can find sacredness in a telephone book?

SFH: Sure, there's only sacredness, yes. This is a highly condensed revelation. Condensed and taken out a lot of the other ramifications of it, so it is *Jami`*. That's why it *Majm`a*. That is why it's *Mushaf*. That's why it's *Kitaab*. That's why it's Qur'an – *Kara, Jama`*.

AA: It's the final proof.

SFH: It's very high voltage; very high voltage – the rest is diluted.

AA: So it has in it like a degree, let's say that everything is sacred. The degree in which the sacred reveals itself in a telephone book is nil, not nil but little. You can't make a religion out of a telephone book. The degree in which it is revealed in the Qur'an is extremely high, may be 100%.

SFH: True. *La yamassuhu ill al-Mutahharun*[98]. You must come out of the abstract, out of the relative, into the pure; then you can touch it, then you can enter it; otherwise, you can't even touch it. For the outer meaning of that you have be purified in the outer.

AA: So concentration, refinement, purity, is what matters.

---

[98] "No one can touch it but the purified." (Qur'an 56:79)

SFH: Immense, intense (*Maknoon*) is condensed and hidden and closed; so you have to end your identity in order to be admitted into this inner sanctum of it. I see it as a continuum. I don't see all this dichotomy; many, many of your questions have in them, 'it's either this or that; it's either black or white,' either I see seamlessness in oneness, or I don't.

AA: No, I'm trying to frame it as seamlessness; at some point seamlessness has no beginning or end, but for my mind to encapsulate it.

SFH: But the trouble is the mind, the mind encapsulates it but then what, you have to go past it.

AA: Then the statement that all is sacred infuses sameness to the degrees of absolute relativity and one is less and one is more, so it is less and more.

SFH: Fine, fine, but I'm not interested in measures. The more we try to measure the more we are slaughtered. You have to measure as a child, yes, 'this is half your cup, this your medicine, your food, finish it,' but the time comes when the whole thing is measureless from Him, to Him, by Him, unto Him, and if we don't refer to that constantly we remain in the realm of the relative, and its endless. The battlefield is endless.

Essence of Revelation

AA: But it is revealed in relative time.

SFH: But I also want the essence of the revelation that is within it. If I want the essence I must also forget time and space. All what drives us is to forget time and space.

AA: *wamaa ya'lamu ta'weelahu illa Allah.*[99]

SFH: If I forget myself then there is only Allah.

---

[99] "No one knows it but Allah." (Qur'an 3:7)

AA: True, but you're making statements, positive statements.

SFH: If I denounce or forget, or get out of my illusion that I was born on so and so date, or *Akiriyah* that I die, and all what remains is that, and that's what gives me the infinitive moment and the bliss of the ever continuous now. If don't taste that, I'll remain in the battlefield of otherness. Endlessly. That is why the miracle is that not everyone is fighting everyone else. It is not the miracle; the ultimate amazing thing is twoness; 'how can twoness exist?' 'How come not everybody is at the front of everybody else?' This is the miracle.

AA: We all partake, and you partake to a greater or lesser degree with the Absolute, greater or lesser degree of shadow, but you cannot filter a text that has made certain statements about itself, through that prism, because the state is the reflection; the text is the reflection of the Absolute, more so than either you or I.

SFH: Correct, true.

AA: We are all sacred beings, but to the degree of sacredness in the realm of absolute and relative.

SFH: No, I didn't say we are all sacred beings; I said there is only sacredness, and from that has emanated vast cosmos, and I am part of that cosmos. But with intelligence I am driven towards that inner sacredness, until a point comes when there is no longer a drive that will take me there. I am now in the no-man's land; that is where most people fail. You don't realize that the mind has to stop at a certain point; intellect has to accept its incapacity because it's within space and time. This is one of the biggest obstacles to thinkers. They become sinkers, they sink.

Limitation of the Mind/The Qur'an

AA: But even beyond that Shaykna, I haven't been beyond that….

SFH: There is no such thing. Again, you are trying to measure the *beyond* with your measurement, it is such an invalid comparison.

AA: No, even without measure there is still a duality because you are not the *absolute*,

SFH: There is no more 'you,' forget the 'you,' first, do that, and then let me talk to you.

AA: But then Shaykna, there is the physical, psychological and the mental and the spiritual that you are facing and dealing with.

SFH: Stop for five minutes and then we will talk again. Stop that for just two minutes, stop any of the physical and the mental; it's *your* problem, not mine, stop the psychological, physical, moral, spiritual, material, neuron, all of it, just stop it for two minutes, it's another zone.

AA: But you can't stop it completely because you can't stop time. I suppose *you* can.

SFH: Thank you, thank you, whatever, I don't know. But experientially, you don't experience anything else. You don't experience mind, the clutter of the mind, the clinking of it, everybody loves that. Why is it that the drug and alcohol and all these industries are the biggest in the world? People want oblivion, and our ritual is based on oblivion in the *Salaat*, in the *Sajdah*.

AA: But the times of differentiation and authenticity and so on, apparently have got no meaning in this zone; therefore, what's sacred or what is completely opposite in relative terms have the same reality.

SFH: That language doesn't apply anymore; after that point nothing applies, inside *Ka`ba* there is nothing, and that's what we are talking about.
    Before it we can talk about the first journey; after it, we can talk about the third journey, then the second journey, there is the absolute no-thing-ness from which everything-ness has emerged and is dependent upon,

and the less one theorizes and talks about it the better, because it then becomes a mental concept and becomes the biggest value.

AA: I'm talking about the Qur'an Shaykhna. The Qur'an itself, as a constant reflector and a warner and a guide, must have certain relativity about it; otherwise it's impossible to understand it.

SFH: Absolutely.

AA: In the realm of this zone that you are referring to, there is no Qur'an, there is nothing.

SFH: Most of it is metaphorical, symbolic and anthropomorphic; for example, 'God's hand,' what is 'God's hand', 'God's anger?' I don't respect a man who gets angry, but what about God when He gets angry? It is our own anthropomorphic, to make it accessible, of course; it is as you say.

AA: Well, that is the text I am referring to; that is the text we are discussing.

SFH: It is that.

AA: Which is non-manifest.

SFH: Therefore, it's like a ladder; you take the part from it, which you can climb.

AA: The ladder that I see in the Qur'an is the *muhkamat*, which are commonly accepted, and the *mutashabihat*. It is not to do with what is relative as such, but what is absolutely relative; therefore, it has built into it the moving essences; therefore it is changeable for ever, it's ever changeable, it's not changeable, so if it's ever changeable, then how can you drive immutable constructs from it?

SFH: That is the center of it, the ever changeable is *mutaghayer* but *Tajrid* is also a part of it. The ever changeable is the manifestation; it is the effulgence of that which is ever constant, which is *kulla yawmin huwa fee sha'n*[100], which is *Tajrid*, which is the absolute, absolute. The closest to it is the constancy of changeability.

AA: Can you derive ethical constructs from the Qur'an as guides of moral action between individuals?

SFH: I think anything that alludes to the essence of it can be used to derive ethical constructs and moral actions – the ethical thing is that which is disturbed least or interfered least by the human point of view in the natural passage of the situation. In other words, the more it is loyal to the divine names such as *Al-Salaam* or *Al-Wadud* or *Ar-Rahman*, the more it has got that color, the more it is ethical.

Ethics and Shari`ah

AA: Can I read you then this question? 'By attributing sacredness and normative in the *Shari`ah*, ethic becomes subsidiary to the *Shari`ah*. However, if we believe that the *Shari`ah* is the realm of the absolutely relative, then ethics are appropriate moral action, must desire from modeling action on implicit and essential meanings of the names and attributes of Allah, and not on the Prophetic model in the absence of the Prophet.' Do you agree?

SFH: It's too complicated for me; it's very much of a subtle, intellectual and rational construction. I really can't cope with it.

AA: Mulla Sadra said so.

SFH: I know, but I can't cope with this part of Mulla Sadra; I will leave it to him. I accept that, but all I can say is that all I can derive from my *dhawq* and my inner personal experience and that I reach a point of inability to, in the no-man's land, is that I approach it with the mind, with the highest discriminating intellect, then I reach a point where I must give up, and I find myself really inside the house. What you are

---

[100] "At each instance He is upon a creative act." (Qur'an 55:29)

talking about is that interface I have not been given the *dhawq* of that aspect of subtle spiritual philosophy; it doesn't touch me. I just say, 'sorry I don't know.' All that I know is that there is a *hijab*, there is a barrier, and the two zones meet at that barrier. One does not overcome the other, and how you experience the unity of those barriers is the *Rahma* of Allah. The less there is any identity – the less there is mental movement – the more there is an actual experience of that, without denying either.

Framing Questions in Terms of SFH's Current State

AA: I mean you trying to frame the conversation solely in terms of your, with your permission, solely in terms of your current state which is a state of no-thing-ness, but we have to have a conversation, and the conversation cannot be about no-thing-ness because then, there is no conversation.

SFH: Good, good, good; that's wonderful! Much better! Silence is far more of a voice than sound. I have no option but to be honest to my state.

AA: But I must pull you back, if you don't mind Shaykhna, into states you may not want to even acknowledge, so we can frame these questions in ways that they are answerable to people.

SFH: Fine, I'll try to remember, but there also is a limit to my memory; there is an average movement. If you say that 20 years ago, I said so and so, I'll say I must have, most of the time, and I'll try to be honest, and honesty is *Tawhīd*. So I must have been relating to my inner state then, reflecting also on my outer environment.

AA: It's been an interesting meeting and an interesting conversation.

SFH: Yes, yes, but I've also been trying to make a conversation.

AA: Trying to make a conversation; otherwise, we have no conversation; but that requires complete immersion. Conversation, if it is not punctuated by inner silence, it becomes very frivolous. I hope I'm not being frivolous.

SFH: No, No, No, I try not to consider it frivolous; it's me, not you.

AA: I am the questioner, so.

SFH: I am the responder also – I can only reflect my state now and I can also have understanding and some compassion or tolerance of what there had been before; I don't deny any of that.

Compassion for Other People

AA: And compassion for those people who are bewildered by you.

SFH: I'm not concerned; that's not my business, that's their problem. I've no concern; I'm not the creator, so I have an understanding of their state and bewilderment, and because I am basking in the absolute generosity, there is no doubt that some of that generosity comes out as a compassion. But there is care, but no concern; I have no concern, it's their problem, and who said that problem is bad. Problem may reach a point, a crescendo, and then there will be breakthrough.

I'm not saying I'm going to create the crescendo; Allah is the doer. Who am I to relieve somebody of an issue? Amongst the great benefits to me of these short sayings, some of the great ones like Ibn Ata' Allah: *Al-Faqat a`yad al-`Arifin*[101]. *Faqa* is an extreme catastrophic state; it is a celebration of those who know because it is beyond shock. It is a reconstitution, so who am I to… So compassion, now a days, means comfort and ease – it's dreadful; that's why we are sinking – the whole universe, the whole world, is sinking.

AA: So what does it mean, Shaykhna?

SFH: It means we have succumbed to our miniscule insignificant worldly side. We have become all nice, nice, nice, compassion,

---

[101] "Catastrophes are the feast days of the Gnostics."

compassion, you know all these sentiments; it's terrible. We have created monsters out of human beings instead of them being above angels. That's what it means.

AA: So it's a sentimental kind?

SFH: Sentimental, and also degrading to the human potential – and who said harshness is rife? Let people be willing to die, and then they will live. I am not the agent of that. All I am saying is that that's fine when others have expressed their needs. I try to respond from my own heart at that moment – no more than that; nor am I trying to be the agent of the Creator or the representative of the Prophet SAW. It is not my business. I have to be honest to myself, which is least of my ego.

Khalifah tul-Allah

AA: It seems that you refuse to be entrapped by Qur'anic one-up-manship. I was going to ask you what does *Khalifah tul-Allah* mean?

SFH: True. Absolutely *Khalifah tul-Allah*. It means there is no self, soul only. And the *ruh*, the *ruh* is *Khalifah tul-Allah*. It's the king representing the King of kings; that is *Khalifah tul-Allah*. So every one of us is trapped or entrapped, and we are all trying to get out of the trap. Entrapment is what we name ego self, lower self, *nafs*, that's what it is. It's like metamorphosis, you know, like becoming the butter fly – self disappears, only the sould remains

AA: You are saying that butterfly does not want to be reminded of worm like existence of the past.

SFH: It can't remember; I don't think it can, as it's moved into another zone. So it is also in *Shari`ah*; you are not allowed to dig the graves and cut the bones that a grave has, but we are also fortunate to have less memory. In my case, I don't try to forget consciously. No, something else has superseded it so much that I can't remember things, like pain in my toes 15 years ago. I can't remember it, thank God. The same thing with the movement that occurs in the inner most.

AA: No, you can't recreate your condition of 20 years ago, but surely you can recall the outcome.

SFH: Yes, I can recall aspects of it and output of it. Yes, no doubt about it.

Who is Shaykh Fadhlalla Haeri?

AA: Should people, not that you will answer, you probably will, but it depends on you, you will have to be honest with yourself. That's a good answer. I won't ask the question.

AA: [laughter] It does not make very good dialogue…..

SFH: No, go on; I'll do my best, ask it.

AA: I want to make it accessible to people.

SFH: I understand; I'll do my best.

AA: We can't understand SFH in his current state but may understand Rumi throwing off his cloak and dancing around like a clown – and this is their exposure to the realm of absolute love and absolute nothingness – and they see it in a packaged way, in a way that is appealing; although for me, I don't find it appealing. I find it terribly sentimental, so how does one approach SFH, taking this boring past and his self-definition.

SFH: I think again, through honesty, authenticity and loyalty. Everyone has to be loyal, which means an aspect of Oneness, to one self. In other words, one has to take what is digestible. For a two year old child, it's unfair to give them rump steak or something – they must eat something else. So I think one of the biggest camouflages of the ego is the curiosity of interest: 'What is there? What is it got to do with you? Take what is in front of you.' It is like somebody tried to be close to Shams e Tabriz because they knew that Rumi loved him, and so on, and of course he said, 'it's all one, it's all one,' and eventually, Shams got fed up and said, 'what's that got to do with you, it's all one, He's One, and there is only the One, and you are from the One.' In other words, some of the things I enjoyed looking at and benefitted me, were perhaps far, far more enjoyable than my present state. So go for that; it's not important to consider where is SFH; who is SFH. He is dead. He was dead before he was born. So take what is accessible – the teaching, again of Chinmaya, take the first opening that is suitable for you, and do not concern yourself with what is not your business; but we are all the time making the world as our business – the politics, this and that, the history, and you know, we need to be narrow to come across the infinite width.

AA: It seems like a 30-40 year detour, back to where you started.

SFH: Sure, there is no beginning and no end; no doubt about it.

AA: What was this all about, what was the journey when he was dead already?

SFH: It was that everything was there; Allah was there already, but I wasn't there.

AA: You were there with Chinmaya.

SFH: No, but I wasn't aware of what being with Chinmaya meant. What it really meant is that the state that Chinmaya had is accessible also through the Muhammadi light, and easier for me. That's what it meant. That's why he also reached the point where he said, 'you've had enough taste of light; now go and look for the shadows that indicate light in that culture.' That was it, really.

AA: Now you're no longer interested in it?

The Path and the Outcome

SFH: I am interested; it as a wonderful path, as a methodology, but I also have to differentiate that there is a path and there's the outcome. The outcome comes before the path. And if you are on the path, good luck and carry on, but don't worship the path, don't worship Islam. People begin to worship Islam, and they kill each other and their notion of what they are worshiping. This is the danger.

AA: It's in the very early stages that these things happen, but you're right, most people are stuck in that.

SFH: I remember as a kid in Karbala, when there were religious arguments, I thought it was like they were going to a garage; that is, they wanted to get to Baghdad, and, instead of getting into a car and going there, they were comparing different models, and kicking the mud guard, and so on, but never getting on the road to get to the city. The purpose of the path is to get you to your ultimate destination, which is ever present there in you, so get on with it.

AA: It's an awakening, a gradual unfolding.

SFH: Right. In other words, what I'm trying to highlight is that I do not deny the path, I do not deny the essential structures, I do not deny the importance of the outer, it's very important. But as a package, if we constantly don't refer to the ultimate purpose of it *Wa anna ila rabbika al-muntaha*[102], if we don't refer to that, then it becomes a cul-de-sac. I found so many people have their religion, and instead of it becoming a flying carpet, it becomes a suffocating dungeon. That is the difference.

AA: Most people in the West these days don't have a religion anyway.

SFH: No they have; they have the religion of confusion.

AA: Whatever they worship.

SFH: It's true. It's religion of finding an opportunity, exactly; they cannot be without a religion.

AA: The focus is on devotion.

---

[102] "And that to your Lord is the ultimate destination." (Qur'an 53:42)

The Sacred

SFH: Absolutely! We are sacred beings, encased in the material and too inseparable.

AA: I'm watching this butterfly, I'm trying to see if it[103] remembers or not, you say it doesn't, I say it does.

SFH: It may do. There is always a memory but it becomes so faint that you are not sure if you are honest and try to depict it, but you become hesitant because you're really not sure what it was.

AA: Nikos Kazantzakis talks about the chrysalis and the silk worm eating itself and the flying fish trying to be something else.

SFH: I know; brilliant I'm enjoying it, I read it last night.

AA: I think we have reached the end of this segment.

SFH: *Bismillah, Allah Akbar*. I respect that Ali. I respect you immensely; you're a treasure.

---

[103] This is a reference to Shaykh Fadhlalla Haeri and his spiritual metamorphosis.

Consciousness

Limited and Supreme Consciousness

AA: One of the most important teachings that you have evolved over the last few years, and I think is probably the core, is the soul and self-relationship, which we will talk about later. Now, I'd like to talk about limited consciousness and Universal or Supreme Consciousness.

The way I understand it is that human beings have evolved a consciousness that is conditioned by their experience, genes, predilections, and, in of itself it, is of limited, defined nature, and cannot really aspire to encompass within it the totality of knowledge and being. And then, juxtaposed against that is Supreme Consciousness, which takes on different names in different religions – God, Allah, Atman. And that Reality is when limited consciousness, or conditioned consciousness, dissolves itself through a kind of voluntary process, an awareness of its dissolution in which only Supreme Consciousness is allowed to be. Is that a correct approximation of the teaching?

SFH: To a great extent. I personally experience the situation as follows: The so-called 'I' encompasses a whole spectrum. On one end of it is Supreme Consciousness, impossible to fathom, the Absolute. The other end of it is this self-identity, and the arousal of selfhood, call it ego, or whatever. So this is the box that I am. One end of it is the beginning of that infinitude; the other end of it is the beginning of this natural drive towards the so-called Absolute. The so-called 'I' begins to experience awareness and consciousness by identity, by the sensory and the mental accumulation, and then comes to the point of wanting to go past that box. And that is where it begins to tap more into the realm of pure consciousness, which is all within this spectrum. So the so called 'I' is a spectrum, and the more I begin to taste that infinitude, timelessness, endlessness – that which is not boxed in space and time – the more I find the importance of lower consciousness, which is the social 'I', the identity of the 'I', and all of the other things that identify *insaniyya*, the importance of all of that begins to be of less and less importance.

AA: The model as I see it is complete, but, if I may, it seems to be a model where there are no verbs. If the only actor is Allah SWT, Supreme Consciousness, as you have always said, *La faa'il ila Hu*[104], and if the relative 'I' is really a shadow, illusory, compared to the universal 'I', *Inni ana Allah*[105]. So all 'I-ness' is His. Doesn't this require some active force within the limited nature of conditioned consciousness, as you call it, to propel it forward? It's either there as a force that acts on it, or it is autonomic; that is, the movement of limited consciousness towards Supreme Consciousness is inevitable from the perspective of Supreme Consciousness. But from the perspective of limited consciousness, there has to be an actor, a force. My understanding is that the actualization of that movement has to be acted upon. Is this correct?

SFH: Yes. I think there is both. There is a natural autonomic irrespective drive: even before creation that drive was part of that unfathomable reality – it was there, but there was no creation. So there is an autonomic drive. But that autonomic drive propels, if you like, the individual will, to want to close the gap of space, wants to end this illusion of separation and the illusion of being in time and death, both of them are there. In my own case, the speed or intensity of this drive of ending space or time, accelerated over the last 20-25 years, until a point was reached, a few years ago, that it pulverized everything, in the sense that I could really no longer attribute anything to myself, hardly anything to myself, except the most menial tasks – washing my hands or trying to change my clothes. Everything else I could only see that it is Allah's doing. Allah is doing it, not in its absolute sense, that absolute ends up being very relative, but that it is emanating from that. And the more I begin to see how that subtle hand is behind it, the more I am amazed at the immensity and the intensity of that Oneness. So there is both: that force by itself – Allah's will, Allah's *kun* – whatever it is that's part of that emergence, as well as my own will. I wanted to see the inseparableness of the celestial and the terrestrial. And so there was some will from me that propelled me more and more towards it and consuming me, in a sense.

---

[104] "There is no Actor but He."
[105] "It is I who am Allah."

Pulverization of the Self

AA: The Qur'an talks about *karaha* ... You are going to get there whether you like it or not. (SFH: That's right; brilliant) Most people will get there *Karhan* – the vast majority. I'm referring to the common people. You choose, if you will, to move your limited consciousness into the realm of Supreme Consciousness, knowing full well that that world is the world where there is no verb and no subject, or even an object. Therefore it requires pulverization of all the obstacles in the way, particularly the self, as it's constructed. Don't you find that extremely demanding if not impossible to expect from normal people?

SFH: True. Extremely demanding – and so-called normal people are very much concerned about their own universe: their body, their mind, their survival, that they are functioning. So, it's true; it is extremely difficult for them.

AA: And intellectually one can accept this model as a very good, extremely good approximation of what things are really like, but still be faced with the awesome fear (SFH: No doubt) of a world without action, without a verb.

SFH: I accept that. It is correct. I think it is most abnormal, unusual, that's true. At the moment in life, this is what I can concur, but it is not everybody's thing. I just want to go over the issue you mentioned earlier, to highlight it. It isn't so much moving towards high consciousness. It is being tired and uninterested in the conditioned consciousness. You find the thing over and over – it becomes boring, it becomes inconsequential. So you just turn more and more away from the limitations of conditioned consciousness, ego consciousness. It doesn't interest you any more. When that begins to dry out, then you have more and more of the vista – and the higher consciousness begins to show. It's a displacement.

AA: And this movement, as the classical doctor would say, is the form of, you say, borrow – it's like you pull yourself by your bootstraps. You *borrow* the power to eliminate your power.

SFH: It is true. You get tired of the so-called 'own power' or what you attribute to your will or your *qudra*. You're no longer interested in it. So in a way that bootstrap actually propels itself towards you. You live more and more according to this higher will, which is there, and you're constantly aware – *it's avoidance that gives you that access*. It's not so much the drive and the passion for it. That is expected; that is natural, but it manifests in fine, subtle observations, and awareness. Why should I do this? What is it? And that is really the outcome of liberation. Liberation is not the final answer. This move towards being in the ocean of infinitude is an outcome of liberation and so-called freedom, or enlightenment. There is no way other than being completely between the fingers of *bayna aydi arrahman*[106] – you have no option. It isn't a question of you *chose* it; but that you *wanted* it. You did *not* want that which was drudgery; that was constantly based on duality. That's all – you turn away from *that*.

AA: So it seems that the core of the teaching is for those who want to be like that – and if you don't want to be like that you don't enter into it.

Eliminating Duality

SFH: But we don't know what is 'that' – that's the whole dilemma; you only know it when you are in it. You can't know it from the outside. It is one of those, if you like, oxymoronic things. You can't say, 'I'm not sure if I want *that*;' all that you and I can say is, 'I am sick and tired of this ongoing cyclicality of duality.' So once you begin to lose interest in that, then I think it naturally takes you into the beginning of the other realm of higher consciousness.

AA: Still it's an issue of – of course I don't want to push this, because you've answered me – it's an issue of wanting to dissolve these irritations, because of their tiresomeness. The intellectual elegance of it needs to be founded into actual reality, and that coupling mechanism is what the teaching is about. Would you say that's right? (SFH: Yes.) So

---

[106] "between the fingers of the Rahman…"

those who cannot abide or stay or continue along this are basically spiritual grazers.

SFH: Good. That's a good description.

AA: You tolerate them; accommodate them.

SFH: No way out – there is room for everything. In this existence there are countless varieties and degrees of intensities or zones of consciousness, yes.

AA: Do you feel the need to share these experiences?

SFH: I don't feel the need. But again, it comes in naturally when there is a connectedness, when I connect with someone who is there. Today, at the end of the lecture, there was a Hindu, and I spotted him when I was talking for several times. He had bought a bag of books. I didn't know him but I went to him and said, 'you don't need any of these books.' He said, 'no I don't.' And we hugged. He said, 'No, it's actually for somebody else.' It was an incredible union with this man. He wanted very much to connect, so they gave him a connection. But we were already connected. He was at a very, very high subtle state of inner clarity, inner beingness, a very beautiful being. As it happened, he was also a very handsome man. I wasn't there to share, to care, just an expression of the One between us.

AA: That is what people see – that is what people desire, but that is what people are not prepared to go to the limits.

SFH: The price of it is death. Die before you die. None of you is left any more.

AA: It is actual death if you pulverize it – what else is it? One is metaphorical; the other is material. They both have equal existence, would you agree?

SFH: Totally.

Self and Soul

AA: Before I go on, I will ask you about self and soul. Is it special to human beings or is it available to all sentient beings? If you go back to the Qur'an – the *Jinn* had the Qur'an and they believed it. Did it imply that they heard the entire vista, the entire story, and considered themselves as part of this chain of life, and therefore they also have access to this – is it correct?

SFH: Yes, and no. I have a very simple notion of understanding the duality of the material meaning – or physical – and the inner meaning or sense of the soul of it. I have a very simple view of the world of *arwah* or spirits or souls. And there is no doubt some sort of a hierarchy, which is a bit like the Russian dolls, one inside the other. So the soul of a mouse is not the same as that of a primate. The soul of an ant is not the same as that of a lion. So I think that the soul of human beings is probably the most complex of the pinnacle. And it has within it the software of all other *arwah*. That's why we can understand all the animals and all the others. There is a clear differentiation between the soul of a rose bush to that of an apricot. With a rose you can have any cutting and it continues living. In fact you don't know when the rose that has been cut is going to die. If you plant it before a certain time it may sprout. It's not the same as an apricot. You can't grow it from a cutting, and it goes on and on.... it's far more developed, far more evolved. This is in the plant kingdom: the same in the animal kingdom, and also the souls of the mineral kingdom – the frequency of transmission and the complexities.

So I think there are infinite levels and layers and varieties of soul, including the *jinn*, including that of the angels and any other entities we don't know. But I think the human soul is the ultimate in its being the most complex, most evolved, or the true representative in a form of the ultimate spirit of the Universal Soul or Allah. That's why we don't know what this mechanism is. I don't know it. It is something like a supra-holographic representation, and it is *that* soul which is the *khalifa*. And the *khalifa* implies responsibility of being cautious, not to disturb the peace and balance and goodness and *baraka*. So man is, if you like the vicegerent, the steward. So how can I be steward of other souls if I have not been a steward of my own little kingdom, the physical, material, the body, my mind, and the vehicle, which carries the soul, my heart. So this is how I see it. I see the soul of the human being, the pinnacle, and it is directly connected to the Universal Soul.

AA: Which manifests itself as soul in different gradations, depending on the receptacle.

SFH: No, I consider all souls the same, the same capacity, the same potential, the same make-up.

AA: Can a plant then understand the...?

SFH: Sorry, no, I meant souls of human beings.

AA: I'm referring to the world of plants.

SFH: No, no, they are different...

AA: They are found in different gradations. A plant cannot relate to Allah.

SFH: Absolutely. That's what I said: the soul of a rose is not the same as the soul of an apricot.

AA: Would you say as a metaphor that the spectrum of Allah's names and attributes are within the human soul in their apparent totality?

SFH: Absolutely.

AA: While they are in a much restricted form in other forms of life?

SFH: Totally restricted – in other animals and forms of life.

AA: Mixed with *jinn*.

SFH: I don't know much about that, but definitely I follow the Qur'an in that – *wa `allama adama al-asmaa'*[107]. So the soul of Adam had been exposed to all of these fields of energy or beams of light which we call *asma'*.

AA: So the point at which the self acts, it obviously derives power to act, including thinking – that power is granted for that particular purpose at that particular point. (SFH: Yes) And that automatically the 'now' changes, as the 'now' becomes a factor in that (SFH: moves into the future) – taken back. So this is a constant process of actualizing action, which then immediately disappears. (SFH: superseded – yes) Everything is re-created at every instant, including human beings' capacity to act.

SFH: Exactly. *Kullu yawmin huwa fi shaan*[108] – one of the meanings is – one of the, if you like, experiential and directly understandable, interactive meaning is…

AA: And it never repeats.

SFH: It never repeats, but the principle remains the same: never repeats –

AA: No act of creation is ever repeated.

SFH: Exactly. And yet the Essence is the same.

AA: So human beings are really not appropriate, in your opinion, to themselves as the unique entity in the universe.

SFH: I think there's nothing in existence unless it is part and parcel of the will of God. But again, going back to the gradations or supremacy, or complexity of soul, the human soul is all-encompassing, to my knowledge.

---

[107] "And He taught Adam the Names." (Qur'an 2:31)
[108] "Every day He is bringing about a matter." (Qur'an 55:29)

AA: Essentially, this mapping is universal in the sense that, in all places and at all times, there is something akin to what you have mentioned .... will unfold, unveil itself, or reveal itself.

SFH: There are also some teachings I have been unable to give them their due attention, or reflection or meditation – teachings, in which the Prophet has said repeatedly that there have been many other Adams before, and there maybe even many Adams now in parallel universes. In other words, we may not be the only unique beings at this level of consciousness, higher consciousness. There may well be others, but we haven't been given their knowledge.

AA: Fruitless speculation.

SFH: Yes.

Good or Bad/Absolute vs Relative

AA: What do you understand by ego? Is it just the absence of good?

SFH: Yes. It is the other side. Nothing exists unless it has its opposite. No possibility in any sensory or mental understanding, unless it's one of two. It's only the transcendental, which is on the third level. Anything that I can perceive at the sensory or mental level, at the conceptual level, at the ideation level, is one of two. It's either good and better or higher good, or not so good, bad and then evil.

AA: Evil has no reality.

SFH: Neither has goodness and so on. It's relative. There is no such thing as absolute evil or goodness.

AA: It is not that our limited conception or consciousness is a doorway to Universal Consciousness, for the individual. Is that representing the Absolute as the good?

SFH: I don't think there is a door – it's two zones. But you have to work your way through the first zone to a point where the other zones meet. It's like coming up from the bottom of an ocean towards the surface. You have to get closer to that, but the surface is not a doorway. It is a separating *barzakh* between the zone of conditioned consciousness and boundless unlimited Pure Consciousness. So you need to rise from conditioned consciousness to slightly less conditioned consciousness, to be able to be receptive enough to the ever-present Supreme Consciousness, which is actually the mother of the conditioned consciousness, which is feeding the conditioned consciousness. The conditioned consciousness exists because of that.

AA: But Allah refers to Himself in the Qur'an as *Nur assamawati wal Ardh*[109] – (SFH: Sure). *Nur*, as a positive substance.

SFH: It is also Supreme Consciousness.

AA: So if you equate *nur* to the good, light to the good –

SFH: At that level there is neither good nor bad – Allah is neither good nor bad.

AA: But light is good.

SFH: Depends again if it is the origin of that light. *Nur al-Anwaar*... if you get close to the Absolute, then you can't talk about good and bad with the Absolute.

AA: I want to come back to this point, because the good obviously in human language has implications in it of appropriate, correct and moral conduct, and the root of ethics. There is good, i.e. good action, and there is bad, which is bad action; that is, one is juxtaposed to the other. And bad exists only in terms of its reference to the real. So darkness exists only with reference to light. It has no reality of its own. So evil action, as such, does not seem to have a reality.

---

[109] "Light of the heaves and the earth." (Qur'an 24:35)

SFH: It has a reality as the conditioned consciousness, at the human side, the *insaniyya* side, clearly. As the *insaniyya*, the *insaan* has to take on the colors of Allah, *Sibghat Allah*. One of the important aspects is that of harmony, well-beingness, stability, peace. So the good action is that which is durable in enhancing, maintaining peace, lack of agitation, animosities – all of the other things. So good and bad are essential for me as a human being, and the human being in me is essential for me to recognize the divinity, which is beyond good and bad.

AA: One of the ways in which the other monotheistic religions, especially Christianity and Judaism, have been attacked in modern times, is that their conception of God implies responsibility for actions on earth. They usually say, 'How can there be a good God if there is so much evil?' Your conception is that the Supreme Absolute has no personal features to it.

SFH: There is no personal to it. This is my idea of it. That is why even the Qur'an humors me, by being so repeatedly condescending, so to speak, by being anthropomorphic. *Yaad Allah* and *`Ayn Allah* – these are all in order to make that Absolute slightly more accessible to me. But once I start speculating or philosophizing, then I won't be able to say that any of these attributes are anywhere near the Absolute. Imam Ali has repeatedly said this, and he has some wonderful teachings on this. He said – they asked him, 'how did you come to know Allah?' He said, 'by taking away all attributes from Him.' Not possible. They are effulgences. They are manifestations; they are *Anwaar*. And there are more than 70,000 layers of *anwaar*. So if you say one of the great attributes of Allah is *al-`Adheem, al-Qawiy* – yes fine, it's an attribute. And I love that attribute. That's why I want that attribute, and all others. And these have been, or the meaning of these, or receptivity of these, has been passed on to the *ruh. wanafakhtu feehi min ruhi*[110] or *`Allama Adam al-Asma'*[111]. So I know that I want ability, I want knowledge, I want the ability to communicate, which connects, relates. So all of these are bridges, if you like, that will make me closer and closer to the zone of

---

[110] "And I breathed into him of My Soul." (Qur'an 38:72)
[111] "And He taught Adam all the names." (Qur'an 2:31)

the higher consciousness. Once you are talking about the Absolute, or the Essence, or the *nur* of Allah, then it's the original *nur*, and none of these things arise. It's pure *nur*. Inside *Ka`ba* there is nothing – no good, no bad, no-thingness.

Impoverishment and Intercession

AA: The Qur'an encourages people, and people want to have some handle on the Supreme Absolute, and they do *du`a* and they do *tawassul* and they plead, pleading to Allah – there's no possibility of –

SFH: No, of course there is, because you plead to get out of the illusion that you are separate. You pray and you plead and you cry and weep to get out of the mire.

Of course there is – all of this is valid. At a stage if somebody has to cry, you have to cry. Plead, cry, and express your needs. Wonderful. Otherwise how would you get closer to being the butterfly? It has to be. One little chemical reaction leads to another. It's perfectly in order. And there is an incredible complex chemistry and physics in all of this. You have to be honest. You know, we're all in need. At all times, as a human being, so long as there is humanity, so long as I am still breathing and I have a body, there is a need. I like to have that smoothness; I don't want that pain. So my needs will never, ever end, even though I know, I have experienced irrefutably that my truth is essentially *ruhani*, even though I still have a bit of humanity left. In other words, the ego does not completely disappear. It'll be just thin, and that's it.

AA: If you're a desperately poor person, and you plead to Allah to remove the poverty, is it to remove your material poverty or the barriers to your knowledge that you are poor to Allah.

SFH: It depends – if I am physically hungry, it is to stop the hunger, because the gross prevails over the subtle.

AA: But you'd say it's moving all in the same direction.

SFH: They all are, and once my hunger and my pain have subsided, then I have other needs. I want companionship, I want friendship, I want status, I want longevity, continuity. I want to be God's agent, to be this and that – it's endless. Continuous. My impoverishment is forever. And if I accept it and acknowledge it, then it's an honor. But I, different from an insect, I know that my needs will never end. *Wa anna ila rabbika al-muntaha*[112]. And *rabb* means *rububiyya*, when things are given their due. My body belongs to the earth. It's a material thing – has to return: the soul has to return to the level of energy, subtle energies – *al-Anwaar*, so *ila rabbika al-muntaha* – that is the time if you like, my expressible impoverishment, comes to a point of end.

AA: That's a very interesting, probably a unique take on the idea of impoverishment, the principle of it; what would you say about intercession?

SFH: Again, in the world of duality, you need intercession – there's only two, two, two. In intercession I see you more competent than I, in a skill, so I ask you, 'please help me with this skill – show me, teach me.' That's intercession. Then the skill can be more and more mental. 'Teach me the risk formulation – this is a complex thing in algebra for me.' And then I say, 'Look, I am doing my utmost in trying to groom my self, to acquire virtues, giving up vices. I am accountable. I am doing my utmost to maintain my ethical boundaries within *Shari`ah*, within this. Help me more in order for me to be liberated.' I don't want to remain all the time on tenterhooks – it doesn't mean that I will deny the breathing, or deny being *insaniyya*, but I want to reach a point where inwardly I know without being able to express it. In other words, help me to see, guide me, throw me into the deep end, so that experientially I know that there is none other than the One. All action, all energies, the whole universe has emanated, is sustained by the same One. So I use you to help me, and that the so-called 'you' could be the Prophetic light, could be the soul of the Prophet, could be his – whatever. So we all need that. Intercession is when a person who thought he is alone and can do it, find out that no, he

---

[112] "And to your Lord is the ultimate destination." (Qur'an 53:42)

needs some help. So the two of them together, somehow to get closer to the One.

AA: The only validity in it, the only reason, the only justification for it, is to remove all the obstacles and barriers that allow that person who is seeking intercession or supplication to reach those obstacles in his limited consciousness that are stopping him from understanding the true universality of the Absolute.

SFH: The original meaning, I think is to 'vouch for.' You are going to the king. He doesn't know you, so you go with a friend who knows the way to the king and he can take you and put in a good word for you, so as your needs, your fears, your anxieties – all of that is removed, as the king can do anything.

AA: Is it not a second-degree *tawakkul* – aren't you relying on human agents in order to get closer to Allah?

SFH: No. You are relying on a human agency and its outer form, but there is none other than the original Divine Agency. That is why also, people who were all the time having *tawakkul* and thanking Allah – the Prophetic teaching is that if you deny the *wasita*, you're denying also the origin. So you must thank the human being who's doing it. And that is what I would start with. Thank the person because it is more visible, more tangible. In an earthly realm it is more real. So if I cannot deal with or acknowledge what is appearing real, in a physical sense, how can I ever get to know or interact with that which is THE REAL but not visible. So I have to start with where I am.

AA: One of the stories, Shaykhna, I think it was Moses or Prophet Yunus – he sees this shepherd grooming his sheep, and portraying him as his god, and saying, 'I'll comb your hair this way, I'll cut your nails' – and one of them admonished him – I'm sure you know the story. How does that relate to human agency?

SFH: That is something different. It is according to his cosmology. His love and passion for Allah again had become so in a way materialized in a sense that anthropomorphically he sees God as the sheep. 'I'll comb you, and cut your hair,' again it is at that level of consciousness, and Musa tried to correct him at his level of high intellect and awareness and knowledge. That shepherd was in his own way expressing passionate love and service, and Musa also in his own way was expressing *his* passionate love and service at his level. So he was in a way admonished by *Rahma*: 'You can't do that' – the man said, 'thank you for telling me off...,' so he had moved also to another level of consciousness.

Two Zones

AA: We have talked about the two zones – which can be understood metaphorically, or it can be understood experientially – I think it's the latter, the way that you expressed it. I was pondering on this and what came to mind was this: *Bismillahi ar-Rahman ar-Rahim* – *Surat al-Najm: Laqad raa min ayaati rabbihi al-kubra* [113]. It seems that this zone – let's call it 'zone' is '*ayaati rabbihi al-kubra*[114]' and it is the zone of *Qaba Qawsain* the gateway to Heaven – and if the Prophet could not go beyond *Sidrat al-Muntaha*[115], I don't suppose any perfect being can do that and still maintain physical presence. But it would seem to me that you may have been given this *qaba qawsayni aw adna*[116]. And therefore it's an experience that is incomparable, unique to those who have reached that point. And that is the zone of inexpressibility. I understood what you have been saying all these years about the incomparability of the knowledge that comes from this spark, this presence, this *hudhur*. Although it can be approximated in a different and more clumsy way from another root to make it more understood, is that from *Shari'ah* we may understand bits and pieces of *Haqiqah*, but through *Haqiqah* we can understand what is really *Shari'ah* – what is really the relative understanding of *Shari'ah*, not in terms of its nexus of laws and rules, but in terms of a path, *shar`*; and it also reminds me of the image of a kite that has been seized by the wind, the breeze, and wants to follow the

---

[113] "He certainly saw of the greatest signs of his Lord." (Qur'an 53:18)
[114] "The greatest signs of his Lord." (Qur'an 53:18)
[115] "The Lote Tree of the Utmost Boundary." (Qur'an 53:14)
[116] "Two bows length or less." (Qur'an 53:9)

breeze and doesn't want to be grounded, and there is this poor fellow trying to hold it back. This poor fellow is the remnants of the self, trying to hold his kite. The kite's reality is to waft in the breeze. First of all, is this a correct description of your condition? And secondly, I now can see why it is absolutely essential to follow the precepts of such a person in terms of guidance.

SFH: You have a very interesting collage type of representation, which is beautiful and very flattering also. It is true that once we touch the inner *Ka'ba*, once you touch the zone of infinitude, these words and this language are no longer allowed or followed. *Qaba Qawsaini* or *Ayat al-Kubra* – none of these – they are only allusions to that. They don't arise any more. You can't discern any more. In other words in that incomparable state of absoluteness, you can't even talk about knowledge. Knowledge has to do with a bit of discernibility, a bit of express-ability – all the other things that we have been given. So what you say is, as I said, a very beautiful, and also flattering representation. You cannot have anything more exhilarating than that which is beyond freedom – it's no longer freedom. Freedom from what? And the idea that you are being held back and so on is also in a way true, but it is not, because everything is connected. So I cannot totally utterly erase the past. *Hal ataa 'ala al-insani heenunmina addahri lam yakun shay'an madkoora.*[117] I was at some time or another in some pattern, some design, in somebody's memory. I may not have had the memory. So there is a connectedness. And it is not – when it is real, when it is in true Islam – *Iman, Ihsan, Islam* – there is no longer resistance, whether coming back or going there, there is utter sameness in that state of incomparability – utter sameness. So within that *tajrid* there is always that comparability.

Realized Person

AA: I understand what you are saying, Shaykhna. What I am trying to understand is this intermediary phase where the person can use terms

---

[117] "Was there ever a time when human beings were not remembered?" (Qur'an 76:1)

like 'realized' or a substitute of it. The realized person who has tasted the inexpressible for a number of reasons to do with self, to do with history, to do with genes, *Rahma* of Allah, he still has this thread of connection with materiality.

SFH: May I interrupt you for a second... it's our language. There is no such thing as 'absolutely realized': there are *akhawat* within it and *maqamaat* within it. In other words, earlier on it is a lot of touch and go – a bit of burning, a bit of yearning, a bit of *fana'*, a bit of *baqa'* and a bit of *bala'*, quite a *bala'* earlier on. Because you are in confusion, you are in your mind, for years, or set to be able to be anchored. Suddenly you find that there is no anchorage that you can have any control over. It is here where a person really needs some companionship. You need a bit of someone who has already been a bit more there to reflect for you as a mirror. That it's all right. This is part of it. It may last longer or shorter; you may be more jolted, may be more tempted, and no two are the same. So enlightenment, self-realization, illumination, they are also steps, and this creates levels. And not all of these people also can return to the folds fairly intact. That's also rare.

Framing Questions According to SFH's Current Inner State

AA: It occurred to me last night, Shaykhna, that maybe the whole set of conversations – interviews should be re-done. The reason why I'm saying that is – it struck me last night that I've been framing the questions and engaging in conversation without really respecting your *haal* – dragging you down as it were into the realm of what is comprehensible to me and to others. That's really injustice to your state. It's necessary as a pedagogical process, but the questions from now on will be framed in another light, with full respect for your state, not with an intellectual or rational or self-serving extension of where you are. I now understand why you resist and reject the attempt to frame you or to categorize you within categories that have no meaning to you. And you are basically condescending to be with us. Maybe condescending is the wrong word.

SFH: No, I understand. It is not so much me, it is the respect of the *Ka`ba*, respect of the infinite – nothing to do with me. It's just that the absolute is the Absolute; when you get close to it, you'd better shut up and be blind and have no senses and die. And you'll be resurrected.

Haqiqah

AA: I'm being asked now to frame a question as to how does *Haqiqah* deal with materia, not being in *Haqiqah* –

SFH: *Haqiqah* is in you –

AA: True. Nevertheless, there are different degrees of it.

SFH: Not having lost fully what had protected *Haqiqah*. That is fine. You can say 'not being in *Haqiqah*' – I don't think there is anything other than *Haqiqah*. *La ilaha-il-Allah* – and I would only re-phrase it by saying that there is still quite a bit of protection which is *insaniyya* .... all of that, of *Haqiqah* – which is fine.

AA: One of the reasons why you've had this sort of reaction against hundreds of people you come across – or thousands – who've listened to you, bought your tapes, listened to your lectures, moved on technologically to CDs, MP3s, books and so on, and haven't really benefited, because of their structural inability to frame the question, and to frame their response to it, from that light. We ended yesterday's conversation – it's a kind of spectrum shift. Now that spectrum shift could never occur if you had not shifted yourself along that spectrum.

Three Levels

SFH: Again, I go back to the three levels that every human being operates at. First is the definable, the sensory, the physical, the material. So we are sensory – five senses, inner, and outer. So this is my first part of consciousness. Then I come to the higher level of that, which is the intellectual, mental, conceptual, ideation – all of that. Then comes the transcendental. So there is this natural shift in all of us, and we can't deny this, if you like, flow of this. So people get familiar when they are used to the sensory and the material, and the numbing effect of it, which gives the semblance of ongoingness or continuity: 'I've been living in this house all my life.' So that numbing effect actually makes the access to the transcendental almost impossible. 'I've got so much used to the illusion of constancy of "Allah dom"'. 'I have always done like this – I have always had my coffee this way,' 'I've always gone to Hajj, I've been to Hajj every year.' It gives the illusion of forever-ness, which is already in my heart. So my *nafs* becomes a mimicker of the soul – this mockery. That is why the worst thing is when religion becomes entirely ritualistic and so on. It becomes disgusting mockery. It's better without it. At least they can come to a novel form, something unique, something rare. You look for it – anything rare, you look for it – the only peace. You are the only person. You are loved by Allah, Jesus loves you. But when it becomes habitual, that's the problem; that's why they can't hear. *Waqrun fi adhanihum*[118]... already dismisses it. My eye will dismiss the room that I am familiar with. Nothing changed. But if suddenly the whole wall has fallen, that's something! So I live by exception. My life is driven by exception. The door has fallen; it is gone, so pay attention. I only give attention to that which is away from the familiar, not the norm, abnormal. My *ruh* is the most abnormal thing beyond *Qaba Qawsain*; words cannot connect it in terms of communication. It is the source of connection.

AA: It is really inexpressible, and that's why sometimes I feel that in some ways it's futile to engage in this conversation about the inexpressible. I am trying to fix it – how can you fix this kind of essential experience? Essential in the sense of its essence. I think that again another story: a kind of Columbus like figure sails into the unknown, and then actually goes into something that's inexpressible. Instead of reaching America he reaches some kind of infinite black hole, which has all kinds of marvels, and then pops back again on shore. And people come to him and say, 'where have you been? What have you seen?'

---

[118] "Blockages in their ears."

There are really three choices: one is to express things as they really are, which is inexpressible, but you have an audience that wants to hear what you are saying. Or you can keep quiet and withdraw into yourself or you can express it in terms that are astounding, amazing and astounding. Lights went off, magic, demons, paradise, rivers and so on. Or you express it in terms with which they are familiar, in order to get them to make this judgment. The point is that people are there on the shoreline, waiting to hear from this person who has gone on this adventure. So they'll ask: 'what have you seen? What have you done?' Or some will say, 'Oh it is all a figment, he went round the corner and disappeared for 10 years.' I call that the rational scientific explanation for each and every thing. These are psychological conditions, used to describe them as 'too much fruit at night' or something, nightmares and so on. This is one band, and the other band says, 'let's listen to what he has to say.' And if you really express what you have to say, you cannot say anything, because it pulverizes everything. So you're left with either explaining it in metaphorical terms, or express it in terms which affect people's conduct, like: 'I came back and I was given a tablet and the tablet says this', which means that the entire business of a Divine *Shari`ah* can never be more than that. Am I right? This is a colossal discovery!

SFH: Now I, in a personal way, with absolute genuine outer and inner openness, I can say that it is the raison d'etre of existence – it is the purpose, it is the direction, the ultimate destination; it is the ever-present destination, because it relieves us by exclusion of all the things that causes me on this earth, in this life, a desire to turn away from. Limitations, shortness, incongruities, ugliness, lack of affection; so once one is in that zone, the best way I can describe it is that none of the things that irritated you are there, none of the things that you are desirous of arise any more – it is a state of perfect, timeless, boundless bliss. That is why we love drugs; that is why we love deep sleep, why we love water – that state is our higher, inner, real state; that's the description. The rest are metaphorical, and also on the edge of it, the magical part. And that is why it is important not to be caught – you have concentrated very well on the *barzakh* side coming to it –

AA: that's what concerns people –

Four Journeys of Mulla Sadra

SFH: Yes, it's very important. That's why the four journeys of Mulla Sadra are the greatest, because the first journey is running away from that which is not: we do that all the time – I don't want pain, I don't want discomfort – so it is the most wonderful fundamental universal law. We want to avoid that which is not conducive – the push-pull. I want to pull that which gives me that ease, which is a semblance of bliss, and I want to turn away from that which gives me dis-ease. The second journey is – it's not a promised land – it's the only land, without a land, it is *Na Kujabaad* as Suharwardy says – it is the nowhere-ness which is perfect. *Abaad* is perfect, most orderly – *Kuja* is not a place. Then after that you are still alive, so you still have your liver sticking... so you come back and say, 'there is such a thing,' but it's in you, and I can't really help you other than being a brother, a friend or a mirror. But getting it, you will not get it by wanting it; you have to turn away from anything other than it. That is called passion for Truth. Love Allah beyond love, because He is emitting love. Language is helpful actually; I don't think it's that difficult. You must love it beyond love, you must be willing to die, now, and then you'll find that you have been alive forever, and that your *ruh* is alive. The fourth journey is the more rare in a way. It is much more prophetic. You are truly with what appears as humanity – in truth they all are harboring divinity. You can only be amongst them every now and then – a bit of a flash may awaken someone or other – but it's not in your hands any more. So you are here, but not of here. Within you lies the source of all bliss, the root of *Jannah*, eternal light, Divine Light itself, but outwardly you're in this life – if compassion touches you, fine. If your role is such that you have to go and cook for the poor, you go and cook for the poor, not a big deal. There are no these terms any more – vices, virtues, etc., they don't touch you so much. But you're aware of them. You're aware when you have been, if you like, admired, or admonished – you're aware, but it doesn't touch your heart. Because your heart now really is the abode of this infinitude, so it doesn't touch it. So the relative comes close to it, and just fizzles out, because it's no longer your reality any more.

Going back again to what I have said earlier, the state or this ultimate inner condition of utter unconditional, beyond discussion, knowledge of it, if you like – no longer usual knowledge, comes in bouts, until such time it becomes your real nature. I began with my real nature developing my own personality, a bit of ambition, a bit of drive, a bit of this, and bit of that, and then it switches on to the other zone. This is the nature of human beings. It's not abnormal. We have in a way collectively as human beings for the last few hundred years, if not 2 or 3,000 years, made it such that it is a rare thing. But it is in human nature. I think this is the Adamic rise, the homo sapiens rise, and if we don't do it, we are causing chaos to our own personal ecology, buddy ecology, mind ecology, and macro-ecology. And I am certain, looking at the whole arc of ascent and descent over thousands and millions of years, it will happen. And whoever attempts a little bit towards it, they will be the first beneficiary and what they think and do will last and will be sacred, because the whole thing is sacred. And they will be in time recognized and whatever, if they are re-discovered. So looking at it again in the micro sense of time and years and the macro-sense, it is not a question of sacrifice or *jihad*, it's a question of reading it – that the purpose of it is IT[119], which has no beginning and no end and can be only experienced, tasted and reflected. It cannot be given, because it is the source of giving. So I cannot give it; I cannot guide those whom I love. So it is expressible, expressible more as you're getting to *Ka`ba*, just getting your head out of *Ka`ba* – then *Ka`ba* becomes *Qaba Qawsain*. If what you're doing is correct and the methodology is right, I think your approach is correct, honest and will be valuable.

Dealing with the Interface/Guides

AA: Well, again going back to these four journeys, using them as a guide and an indicator, without necessarily being rigid, the fourth journey is really the most interesting, because – I'm speaking now in terms of the

---

[119] Inner Technology.

interface – the world of the *barzakhiya*; as long as you interact with others in any shape or form, whether you are realized or unrealized, there has to be some kind of mechanism, some kind of field or space where these energies are repeated, transferred, imbibed, rejected, absorbed or whatever. So I'm interested in the interface.

I will never know your reality unless I approach it or reach it at some point, but I can respect it experientially, rather than intellectually. We all know that there is a fourth journey – anybody who has read Mulla Sadra knows there is a fourth journey of the realized person in time and space. But to understand it experientially is another matter entirely.

So again it's *`Ilm al-Yaqin* and *`Ayn al-Yaqin* and *Haqq al-Yaqin*. So one can be at a stage where it is beyond *`Ilm al-Yaqin*, it is now *`Ayn al-Yaqin*. You're at *Haqq al-Yaqin*, again using these Qur'anic approximations. So the world of no-oneness, only Oneness, which implies no otherness, from the point of view of otherness, there is still the *barzakh*. There is no *barzakh* from the world of the Oneness, and this interface is really critical, because it, I think, causes confusion amongst whoever you interface, with; not Shaykh Fadhlalla, but anybody who is immersed in the realm of no otherness, cannot deal with the otherness of those who are no longer there – from their perspective anymore.

The first step, you can see it, I mean you can see it. So the first journey – I'm speaking now from the point of view of the interface – although there is no point of view, there is no interface, but at the relative point of view you interface with a person on that journey, has a personal reality for them – that this person who was buying and selling and making money and so on, packs up and goes off somewhere – ashrams or whatever – and people start panicking, and finally some are reconciled to it – some are not, but those who are interested in it – this is the only point at which the person on the journey is interfacing with others. Then that interface is cut because the journey becomes of the individual. In creation, then to creation, through *Haqq al-Yaqin*.

Then there is the fourth leg, there is the interface aspect to it, because, instead of disappearing, refusing to talk to people, minimizing that person's relationships, the interface emerges again; maybe it had never left, but it emerges again. If people are still in the frame of either the first or some kind of rationalization, some kind of expectations and so on, my assessment is that one of the reasons why people do not understand what's going on is because they themselves have not shifted in terms of perspective. So until, and unless, these people shift in perspective, there can be no possibility of benefit, unless it's done in a kind of rigid form, a kind of teaching, as it were. But teaching is never the intention of the person on the fourth journey; it's something incidental and probably ephemeral. There's no aspect to it, except as it relates to the awakening aspect. So how do you deal with an interface when you don't recognize the reality of this interface?

SFH: I hide under the cloak of Muhammad and *Ahl al-Bayt* and the Sufis, in that it is most, most, most essential at these stages, especially the interface, to have access to someone whom you trust as a teacher or as a coach, as a guide.

Now you follow the path, and suddenly, you leave for the forest with him and disappear, as it has been the pre-Zoroaster tradition with the Hindus. It has been a very natural tradition for people, who are endowed with quality of health and well-beingness, that, after being a householder in their thirties and they have a family, they leave it all.

When they come back, having attained a higher state of inner consciousness, they don't go back to the domestic setup of the past. They set themselves up somewhere, in a village square or whatever, and everyone, including their families, have access to them. But there will always be some intermediaries, who have been with them, wherever they go, who can also access the glue with a new face.

Guidance and guides and coaches for this zone where it is not totally discernible, mental, or intellectual, is essential. And here where we have to take a guide whom we trust – there isn't a question of 'is he absolutely authentic?' It doesn't matter. There was a program not long ago, on BBC a year ago trying to interview the top 12 international gurus who have got their television station and their jet flyers and everything, and the brilliant investigator, a Hindu lady of the BBC said, 'I am confused. I find each of these people have something to say which is very wise, very erudite, very spiritual, but I really don't know whether they are real or not. Are they real? Are they authentic?' She said, 'I now am going to ask them – one person who I trust fully to tell me that.' And it turned out it was the most senior Chinmaya man in Delhi, also a guru. She goes to him and he says, 'what do you mean "real"? You are sick, you need help; take whoever you feel is going to help you at the time. For you that was real at that time.' There is no 'real, real real'. Usually you end up taking someone who in your language is more real, or more realized or not.

So guidance, help, mirroring, friendship, based on trust that you know in this issue – forget other things – just focus on the issue at hand – that is what Chinmaya told me – he said: 'take what is relevant for *you*; take the first opening that is relevant for you, that touches you.' Second, 'do not concern yourself with what doesn't concern you' – there are all kinds of other things that go on, and it will distract me from my trust – it's not my business. I have to trust that I am on a quest, I am thirsty, I am in need, therefore the importance of a teacher, guide, a coach, a friend, fellow traveller is essential, essential, essential. Latter day Sufi masters, especially of North Africa, they repeat this issue; they labor upon it to the point of boredom. Take one of the best of *tafsirs* to my mind, the most enjoyable, most balanced is Ahmed Ibn `Ajiba's *Bahr al-Madid*. I don't think it's possible to read every two or three pages of it without you coming across how essential it is for you to have a teacher. If you don't, Shaytan is your teacher. Once you are in a new land, you need to have somebody who is a bit more familiar with that. And it doesn't have to be whom you find as the ultimate evolved enlightened being.

Shaytan is the Best Teacher

AA: Teaching functions are essential; it's one of the questions I was going to ask you. If no one has a Shaykh, Shaytan is your Shaykh, but sometimes Shaytan appears in the form of a Shaykh.

SFH: It's the best master – Shaytan is my *nafs*! I read Shaytan *ba'uda, shatana*, as my *nafs* – that's my Shaytan in me, and it is my best teacher – it is my Shaytan that shows me *Rahman*, so I owe everything to the One who created *Rahman* and Shaytan; and Shaytan was the first, because it gives me the illusion that I am the master and the source, so when I suffer I say, 'no, that's coming from Shaytan.' It's Shaytan that shows me *Rahman*. Shaytan brackets me; Shaytan has been barriers for me not to fall into the infinite abyss of self-destruction. So I do everything – Shaytan is my best friend.

AA: But you mentioned here, which I think is a really very important observation, is that there's this person in an infinite voltage state and here are these people expecting or wanting or desiring something, and they see glimpses of that, of filtering; I think a kind of 'nearly' realized buffer is essential to introduce what these people can still relate to on the issues of accountability and responsibility, and so on –

SFH: Correct.

Moses and Aaron/Shaykh Hosam Raouf

AA: In your own life and journey would you say that Shaykh Hosam Raouf plays that part?

SFH: Hosam played the biggest part in my life in reminding me of the shield of the sword, inadvertently. He didn't play that role consciously or – as he always reminded me – of *Ummatan Wasata*. I would have completed my task – I would have completely disappeared at a much younger age on possibly the beach of Kerala or some such place. Hosam was for me that soothing calming *raoufiyya* presence – that was for me the biggest gift in life. A reliable, decent, stable, authentic, and calming factor, in a genuine way without being anxious. Just there as a friend. So I have to seek him out as well; it wasn't just him mothering me – none of that – it was his brothering me that I benefited from.

AA: But looking at him as an archetype, you see one face towards you – the face that you mentioned – the shield, brothering, calming etc.; and the other face is towards those who might misunderstand or be consumed by this direct voltage. This to me seems to be a 'Haroun and Musa' kind of relationship – both realized but with different qualities of realization (SFH: Correct); so in the case of a person of high voltage, the other face – I won't say Janus-like – but these two sides – *wajhain* – is that itself a kind of *maqaam*?

SFH: Could be – why not? Yes – but I don't think we can stereotype that. *Ya'ni*, it happened like this in my case; I was very fortunate. In retrospect it looks as though it is quite a model, but I'm not sure how reproducible all these things are. In that sense it is a *maqaam* because of its intricate connectedness, as a model – no more, no less.

AA: Ibn Arabi tried to come to terms with it, that the forms in which what Mulla Sadra calls 'The Fourth Journey' – I don't want to use the term *Insaan al-Kamil* that combines all these forms – but the forms in which it is expressed take on 'Prophetic features'. So you are expressed in the form of this prophet or that prophet. Of course nothing is as discrete – there is a continuity to it – do you accept that these are manifested in different, as it were, the *relativization* of the Absolute Spirit through the first degree of prophet-hood at certain times emerged?

I mean you are a 'Mosaic' type, perhaps, but Shaykh, in terms of comprehensibility... '

SFH: Yes, I think these are useful guidelines, but once they become an 'archetype', or we try to pigeon-hole them, then I think they become counter-productive and they become less useful. I enjoyed the *Fusus al-Hikam*, but it really didn't touch me much, nor did it affect me, nor did it concern me. I think these were, if you like, expressions of gems that have been collected from around the mine that has no visible gem. Also, in my own particular life, none of these things impressed me, no matter what was said by anyone. Somehow, subconsciously, I know it is said; therefore, it is only trying to express that which is inexpressible. I had no interest. They never impressed me. I have collected all of whatever possible, Ibn Arabi's works – *Futuhat* and so on. And I found them a bit turgid earlier on and then some many years ago, I found them very easy. And many of them I find them useful. It's better to dive into these sorts of little pools than misleading ones. These have some reality in them. But I really genuinely have not that much use for any of them.

AA: But in terms of others observing – if I were a fly on the wall, I would say you have more of this quality and less of that quality – (SFH:

sure). You have probably less jovial qualities, and more Mosaic qualities.

SFH: Probably –

AA: You say 'probably' without much conviction!

SFH: I have not really looked at it. As I said, it didn't interest me.

Spiritual Architecture

AA: Do you think then this attempt to create this spiritual architecture is really intellectual exercise?

SFH: Not a bad one either – the danger is for it to become yet another idol.

AA: That is true. Absolutey. But the question insinuates itself, as you have to infer from the reading whether the person is in fact the fourth journey person or not.

SFH: Again, these journeys are not disconnected from each other; there is a huge interface between the third and the fourth journey. It's difficult to separate them – these have been taken as metaphoric things and as enjoyable samples.

AA: We deal with the end product, which are 300 volumes – in the case of Mulla Sadra, 50 volumes. Why do you think that these people felt they needed to express it in this form?

SFH: Because of the effect of the name *Mutakallim* – they had no option. The cat meows, the little stone transmits its frequency, the rose expresses its smell; the human being also, must say, transmits its reality – it's unity, it's *tawhīd* – it's a connectedness. How can you not be connected? The whole business of existence is based on connection and continuation. So you have no option other than exuding it.

AA: You can't reverse it, in the sense that you see all of this work; you read all of this work, whether it's Mulla Sadra or Suhrawardy or Ibn Arabi or whoever, trying to express themselves in the way that the rose bloomed or the almond tree blossomed.

SFH: But the reverse is also true, because time is on both sides. If you stop time, the reverse is the same as the other one.

AA: So a person reading your work with the right courtesy and an open heart, can infer-

SFH: Only if he reads in between the lines, not the lines themselves. The lines follow the arrow of time. If he jumps into between the lines, then he is in the no-time zone where there is no time – could be either way.

AA: There is no direct entrance, because it's not a structure where everything is linear. It's a field relationship.

SFH: That's it – brilliant!

Heart and Mind

AA: Infinite Axes ... the only thing that can understand it is the heart...

SFH: That is why I feel in a way driven at this age. Because we have reduced human beings to a monoculture – just mind, and incredible aged mind, through technology. It has altered everything in us. It has altered our way of life, our values: we have been conquered by the supra-mind situation; the giant universal computer, the nano- whatever technology. It has reduced us into some other creature. I don't think that will last. The heart has not been addressed; the children have not been taught from the beginning – it's both: heart and mind; the creative side has not been given to us. The West has had it even better in a sense, because of that creativity, that question of art – we have fossilized it. We have not allowed it in our structure; we have done ourselves in. No art, no music, no expression, no singing, no creative, no visual, no acting – everything is *haram haram haram* –

AA: And therefore highly developed rational intellect that dies in scholasticism –

SFH: And therefore our religion, our *dīn* becomes also totally rational, rational, rational – dead end. Where is the heart? We are like thalidomide children – we have been fed everything about the senses, but no heart, no arms. Out of balance.

AA: It's best to understand the heart in ethical terms. They have to understand it in this non-axial –

SFH: Non-axial – absolutely.

Reproduction of Elements of Consciousness

AA: I'll ask you a question – it's the stuff of science fiction and frankly I don't have much interest in it, but it seems to be of interest to others, which is the way in which technology is moving towards the manufacture or reproduction of an essential consciousness – so if technology moves in that direction, whether it's artificial intelligence or infinitely complex computers and so on, the element of cognition, of soul, seems to be redundant, if you can reproduce the elements of consciousness. Is that of interest to you – this kind of conjecture?

SFH: Only in what I have already personally concluded, in that it comes to a cul-de-sac, because what we are talking about is zone A, the other zone. It's not subject to any limitations in time or space. All what we are talking about is within time and space.

AA: So any constructed entity, irrespective of its complexity or –

SFH: It won't work – It's still only within time and space –

AA: It's unable ipso-facto –

SFH: Ipso facto.

AA: To generate the –

SFH: Absolutely. It's another zone. That is why we are also dwelling upon the difficulty of getting into it, or the *barzakhiya* – it is another zone that can only be accessed if everything else has stopped.

AA: Including the whirling of the dervish.

SFH: That's why I think early experiments, such as the double slit experiment are very vital-

AA: Michelson–Morley.[120]

SFH: The shooting of the laser into two slits-

Ego is a Particle, Soul is Like Wave

AA: Waves and particle?

SFH: Yes, wave and particle – the most apparently repeated experiment in physics. If you look at it now, we still don't know this puzzle; if we see it then it behaves as a particle; if there is no sight then it behaves as a wave. Now, I have seen so many cases like this in that – it is as though I am the same. My ego is a particle, but my reality or my soul is like a wave. If you look at me, define me, talk to me, it's as a particle – I'm between a beginning and an end – I'm within the space and time, if you like, constructs; but if you don't, then I may enter into that zone beyond my identity, beyond the limitations of the 'I-ness' and time. I'm awake. That is where I get replenished. That is why we know – more and more the last few decades, scientifically proven – those who meditate, who try to get out of this zone, have got a much better state of mental alertness, physical well-beingness, and, and, and.

---

[120] The Michelson–Morley experiment was a scientific experiment to find the presence and properties of a substance called aether, a substance believed to fill empty space. The experiment was done by Albert A. Michelson and Edward Morley in 1887.

It's proven that this getting out of the particle definition, it helps in one's well-beingness, health, happiness even. So many experiments have now been conducted, to prove it. That's why I say all of this business of the supra-intelligence or the ultimate computers, or the artificial intelligence; it's all within this construction. That's fine, I think, it's great. But the pity is that we have fallen into the fear of quackery, of not allowing something else to emerge. That's why there have been so many recent attempts to try and open up a bit science – towards those things as well – people like Sheldrake and so many others. But look, let it be within science – but be a bit more open. But with fear of quackery, which has been really a very, very bad thing, in human evolvement. Those who say it's taboo and all rubbish, I say, look at the effects of it upon people – it's helping them. Twenty years ago patients were not allowed in hospitals to have their pets; obviously there were also fears of pollution. Now that we know that a bit of emotion, a bit of a flow, it gives them life – encourages them to live; it improves them. The issue of emotion, the science of subjectivity has not been looked at.

Access to the Other Zone/Space and Time

AA: I think your argument against the possibility of any construction in time and space achieving the capability of assuming zonal access is impossible.

SFH: It is impertinent, discourteous, it is out of place; it is like somebody who is asleep – you ask them to give you some sort of a mathematical solution to something which is astrophysical – it's impossible. They are two different zones. This zone we have to respect, and it can be over devalued, can always be tested, and always be repeated. The other zone is not subject to space or time.

AA: Of course it can go either way – if you call it Zone A and Zone B. Zone B being the zone of creation, the zone of relativity, including all these hierarchies, whether they are distinct or not. You're saying that as human beings evolve, more and more, the capability of transferring the spatial, temporal, mechanical aspect of existence to constructed entities, you have more time, more spiritual leisure as it were to explore entering into the infinite. It can be the opposite too of course, in the sense that the more and more machines and technology assume, the more they reduce that function. So, rather than moving towards leisure, they move more towards sensory experiences and heightening of sensory experiences. So there are these two binary outcomes. You see it in one direction. Others probably see it in another direction, who knows which way is correct.

SFH: The problem is time, as you yourself said earlier; space is easier to grasp and shrink. Time is not – I mean we need aid, and we are so much reliant on outside agencies. Space is accessible to us instantly because we have an outside agency that allows us to end space. Before you say it, space is available to you, as are credit cards, and this, and this and that. Time I think is difficult to end, but I think it will also come. There are ways and means of helping us in being able for two three minutes at a time, to stop, and be re-charged. I think it is coming, through electro-magnetic aids and whatever; especially the outcome of decades of research that we have had of biofeedback technology – I wouldn't be surprised if it's already used to null pain in battlefields. I think the problem is commercial, legal and so on because people are taking psychiatric drugs and so on, and it may interfere with the neurons. I am certain, the next big things, commercially in the world will be aids to stop time. I could imagine people, specially the corporate world, every hour or so on, they would give them 2 or 5 minutes in order for them to get out and reduce the agony or the ego, the battle they've had with their boss or being downgraded or upgraded and so on, and then come back and suddenly, they're more functional. The question is time.

AA: Time and space are the extraneous factors on individual human beings. They also have to contend with their inner faculties, which also conspire if they're not directed properly towards creating the illusion of autonomy, reason, psychology, emotions-

A Danger of a Teacher

SFH: It's the need for a teacher. That is where the dangers lie, actually. It suddenly goes in the head that I am the person – through me you can be enlightened, without me you will not be able to – I was very curious about what happened to that Indian musician – your friend the Dutchman of the world Bank –

AA: Oh, Johannes Witteveen of the IMF.[121]

SFH: Who was his music teacher?

AA: ... Inayat Khan.

SFH: Why didn't it really become universal? I have pondered on that, because I like the man, I liked his music and I have met with the son and the grandson. Recently in their center in Cape Town, we had a wonderful night of music. It is a beautiful hall, very unusual, and for some reason I decided I was going to pray. They couldn't find any place, except a small little sanctum room and there was this big picture and the whole story came to me there. Under the picture it was his last will: he said, 'I tell all my *murids* – never despair, I am not dying. Although I may be dead, but I am ever alive. I'll come to you at night, I'll come to you in your dream – you are still my *murids* and I am your master.' Something to this effect. I knew that's why he's not livable any more. He's personalized –

AA: He died in arrogance – clear.

SFH: Not clear – instead of saying, 'you have it in you – the same light I have is also in you. You have to do it. I may be your friend. I may be your mirror, and be liberated...' Anyway this is the danger.

AA: This is the other aspect of ...

---

[121] Hendrikus Johannes "Johan" Witteveen (born 12 June 1921) is a retired Dutch politician of the People's Party for Freedom and Democracy. He was a managing director of the International Monetary Fund (1973–78). He also wrote books on Universal Sufism and economics.

The Map

SFH: He may not have been arrogant, I can't say – he had given them the wrong map. The map is not right. The map is that there is only One, and that same One is everywhere, but you can't see it because you are seeing something else; you are looking with sight. Sight is going to blind you. Switch off and go to *in-sight* and you may catch a glimpse of it – I can't give it to you. It is already yours, provided you stop everything else. That's it. Simple map.

AA: But only if – there is no 'but', but I'd say as a figure of speech: all these malevolent traffic cops of reason, emotion, psychology and finally the most dangerous one, the intellect. And that's why they always create a detour and you're going back in circles –

SFH: *Allahu Akbar*!

AA: You get out of one, only to fall in another one.

SFH: That's why I say we have done in humankind. The last few hundred years we have perpetuated the worst injustice upon us. It's all fine. I have no problem with any of the sciences, technologies, aids, comforts, ease, provided you have constant referencing. All of these are stage A, and you are here for Stage B. If you don't refer to stage B and remind the children from inception – when you have sexual intercourse, it's *Bismillah*, and she and you are inseparable, and there's only One, if you don't give her that which is not yours, if you have it, as she gives you that which is not hers, then there is no union. It's rubbish. It is a social construct and establishment imprisonment. It's deadly. That's why everybody wants to get out of the domestic rut because of it.

AA: It becomes bestiality –

SFH: It is bestiality....perpetuating 'beastiality'-

AA: Including intellectual bestiality – 'beastial'.

SFH: Of course, absolutely – subtler, more difficult to get rid of.

AA: But once you've recognized it, Shaykhna, it's horrible.

SFH: *Khalas*.

AA: In Iran, in my last visit, I wouldn't mention names – there was a man who was probably 2 or 3 in the hierarchy, so full of intellect, scholasticism, extremely high quality, scholasticism, intellectuality and ethics, but ultimately 'beastial'.

Ernst Jünger's Eumeswil[122]

SFH: Well, that is establishment for you. That is why you need the Anarch.

AA: But the real one also –

SFH: As a reference – doesn't mean he'll be the guide, the demi-god – no, at least he's a reference this is not it. It has a reality; we have to accept it at its level. It's giving comfort and ease. It gives the sick some sort of a palliative; it helps, fine, reduces agitation, fine.

AA: The Anarch of Jünger is ultimately to do with a form of solitariness, not necessarily aloneness but solitariness, and it seems to be essential to...

SFH: Essential – for everyone. You see, I think human beings were in a better balance and healthier because it was not homogenized globally. There would have been some villages somewhere, some of them would have had their own oppression, repression, dreadful rulers, but there would have been others also which had a bit of a respite. So to allow the

---

[122] Eumeswil is a 1977 novel by the German author Ernst Jünger. The key theme in the novel is the figure of the Anarch, the inwardly-free individual who lives quietly and dispassionately within but not of society and the world. The Anarch is a metaphysical ideal figure of a sovereign individual, conceived by Jünger. (From Wikipedia)

seed that is the human foundation, for it to take its own full expression. Fullest expression is *Duniya/Akhira*, human/divine, humanity/divinity; they are inseparable.

AA: Again, it seems that religious traditions have hijacked this capacity, and in my experience, as it were the technology, especially recently in the last ten years, many people outside of the religious tradition, have reached the same thing without necessarily describing it – profound and dark night of the soul and (SFH: Brilliant! I think it will continue) ... is one of them, which I have given you: Jünger, a person who understands, is intuitive, is as real as the person who goes through the cumbersome religious cycle. (SFH: I accept that) Why do we continue in this way?

SFH: Because it is a tradition we have – part of the growth of Homo sapiens; it helps some people in bringing certain stability, glue to society, ethics, and morality.

Religion

AA: Many people, especially in the European world, have abandoned religion – they think it's useless.

SFH: I think it has served its purpose. Start with the aspect of *Shari`ah*. As you said quite rightly, the question of current day legal systems have evolved, specially in the last 30 or 40 years – the social, liberal type of democracies and so on, served their purpose. But you must realize fourteen hundred years ago, at the time of Muhammad, what laws worked.

AA: We agreed Shaykhna, that this was only pertinent during his lifetime – did we not?

SFH: But it served the purpose for the next 3, 4, 500 years.

AA: Because society did not evolve fundamentally in a different way.

SFH: But the specificity of the laws has to reflect the society and what they want. Take the foundation of it – *La ikra ha fiddin*[123] – you can't force people. So it has to be derived from people.

AA: But you force them by training them when they are young.

SFH: So it is, that's why it won't work; it becomes too rigid and frigid and will crack.

AA: I'm not trying to extract from you whether you think religious traditions are essential to express this or are desirable. Are they useful, or neither of the above?

SFH: I'd change 'religion' – if you say '*dīn*', I say there is only that.

AA: No, but '*dīn*' expressed in temporal form with structures and guidelines, rules and so on.

SFH: I need structures but the structure will modify: everything is modifiable, everything is adaptable.

AA: Is it ever modifiable?

SFH: Constantly. Everything is moving; everything in existence is changing at all times. My mind now, the mind of a young 10 year-old person in the West now, is radically different to what it was 100 years ago. The language even is different. What they use in terms of communication, gadgets, aids for education – there are lots of changes and incredible adaptation of these changes.

AA: But they have become alienated from key symbolic terms (SFH: correct) the word 'god' – in Europe people shrink away –

SFH: Less and less. 30 years ago, if you were a scientist mentioning 'god' you'd be ostracized: Not any more. People are beginning to be

---

[123] "There is no compulsion in religion." (Qur'an 2:256)

more and more tolerant because they are going more and more to the metaphorical side of it; the other side of consciousness. If you mean by 'god' Supreme Consciousness, beyond space and time, then speak out. If not, stay quiet. So it's opening. As much as there is darkness I also see the potential of Light.

AA: Ever optimist! But we can also be in a form of yielding by being a pessimist.

SFH: Equally – in between is the 'holy fool'! (laughing) Everything has its truth as well.

The Teacher

Loyalty, Love and Sincerity

AA: I think we've covered most of these aspects. You mentioned loyalty many times. Do you mean this is a form of *Tawakkul* or do you see it in the form of *Ikhlas*?

SFH: Loyalty, sincerity – all of these are reflections of connectedness. If I'm loyal to you, my main interest is what I perceive, conceive, understand is the best for you. And the best for you is for you to really be the Higher You, the real you, the soul. So I will act and behave in a manner that is subconsciously going to help in you being the real 'you'. I'm totally loyal. Sometimes you may question me and say, 'why did you do this – I was going there and you stopped me, or whatever.' I say, 'I really thought if you get there, it'll become too big, you'll lose your head and become despotic or whatever, and I interfered. But I did it out of love.' Love is the foundation of loyalty, sincerity. Love is the universal glue that brings together what appear to be diverse entities to be unified. That's why it's the foundation of creation, the foundation of the universe.

AA: You can be essentially loyal, surely without being loyal to a particular person or situation.

SFH: Loyalty is a field of energy –

AA: Is it an 'either/or' situation?

SFH: No, but I am essentially loyal to my quest, I am essentially loyal to me being really me. And therefore that takes on other reflection of other people as well, because there is no 'otherness' in truth. So if I am really loyal, if I really love me totally, then I also love you and others. So it has a ripple effect. The same thing with sincerity, same thing with honesty – all these are different facets of that field of energy.

AA: But it is still the point, it's a comfort zone – there is the essential loyalty, for example, I might be essentially loyal to you, in the sense that where it matters, I will be sincere, I will be responsive, but not necessarily in the particulars. Why should I be loyal?

SFH: Because it's a spectrum; loyalty is this field that emanates from the Absolute, the inner *Ka`ba*, but appears and manifests in the relative. Your loyalty essentially is to that which is totally your essence, to Allah, but because you are also living in a relative realm, combining the two zones, so therefore, it appears as a loyal person. Loyalty is emanating from the Absolute, while sincerity and other things are emanating from that field, from the *Ka`ba*.

AA: In their essential forms?

SFH: Yes, they are – they are so-called Names of Allah, attributes of Allah.

One Shaykh/Rebelliousness

AA: But many *Shuyukh*, many masters, expect total obedience as a form of loyalty.

SFH: In order for the *murid* to move faster, not to be distracted, but it doesn't work any more. That technology does not work anymore in our time. *Al-fana' fi al-Shaykh* was very quick and very easy – a big luxury: stop looking elsewhere, just focus on this, it is your *Qibla,* and if he is the real *Qibla*, he will be your *Qibla* also, if he is not a rascal to abuse you, to obsess you, possess you. Possession and utter focus on one *Shaykh* is essential to take you to the One. And that is why, traditionally, it has been that if you have one teacher, you don't change teachers. The same thing with the Shi`a following a *marja`* – you have to have one *marja`*, you can't have two. You can't change your *marja`*. You can't follow a dead *marja`* either. It has actually taken some aspects of this *Haqiqah*, this truth that if you have taken one teacher, you have taken them all. But that one must be a real one in a sense. If you are young, it doesn't matter, it's not up to you, it is taking a step further –

AA: But the modern human condition rejects a teacher –

SFH: Correct. I'm all for that. I'm all for, if you like, the total rebelliousness, especially amongst Muslims. I see this is the class that will emerge. The people I have in Johannesburg are more and more that type, and I have relished them; I think they are the best.

AA: Loyal without being obedient.

SFH: No, they've seen something as a child that's not acceptable – the father and mother in Islam, a mullah, or a thing that is crippling. So they may give a bit of lip service because the parents want them to go to the mosque or the religious school; the parents haven't done it anyway; they shoved and shoved them into these madrasas; the children are completely rejecting it. But they're not bad people, they've been brought up reasonably well, but they become total rebels. Instead of going to the mosque, they go to the disco. But once they taste something else, they realize religion. So rebelliousness is going to be more and more the prevailing, dominating attribute of the young people, as against what it was a hundred years ago: obedience.

In the past they had no choice, it was survival, your obedience was because of survival. Because if you don't obey the village chief, you'll be thrown out and you'll die. So it was survival. But now they are rebellious because of arrival; there's no fear of provision. They can go and get a job. If you are rich and have the best factories, and have a son, and you want him to work for you, he will take half the salary and half the security, and will take a job down the road with someone else. Because we want that exposure, we want to explore the possibilities. Survival is no longer an issue. The refrigerator and industrial farming in a way have helped with that. It's *arrival* that they want. And we underestimate the *Haqiqah* need for young people. We still treat them as little kids. They may be kids in the mind, the intellect, but their heart is far more alive, but we can't nourish the heart. Parents don't have the technology of nourishing the heart.

AA: So where does *antum a'lamu bi dunyakum*[124] come into it?

Specialization

SFH: There is specialization in this world; there are all the time people who are experts in physical performance, skills, mental performance, knowledges – so this...

AA: It doesn't mean you know better.

SFH: No, you know better how to cut this tree than I do. But when it comes to referencing to what is durable, what is going to be in a way a glimpse of what is beyond space and time, then I know better than you; that's the issue. In existential matters, in matters that can be discerned, you are better than I because there are so many of you, and each one has got a specialization – I could not do that. That means time and energy and I don't know it. I don't know how to cut the tree, not ruining the saps and the area around it, and which trees are ... So you know better, you have been in the woods for many more years, so I follow you. You show me how to do it or you cut it. When it comes to using that tree for superficial luxury and thrones and so on, I tell you, 'Look here, this will go to people's head and some poor despot of a village in Africa becomes the imperial majesty – don't do it. Don't use that wood for increasing somebody's ego and arrogance. For that come to me, but how to make it, joinery, I don't know. What is its final use?'

AA: You see it in terms of technique rather than a course in life. Many people basically abdicate or return their relational responsibility to their Shaykh, and sometimes it leads – apparently – I say apparently – to terrible outcomes for them and for their families.

SFH: I accept that. I have seen more disasters actually, especially when the Shaykh begins to interfere out of compassion – again the fourth journey. It can only be done as a special case, not in every case. The general situation is that people have to suffer, to make their mistakes; the

---

[124] "You are more aware of the matters of your world." (A Prophetic saying)

less there is interference from the Shaykh, the better. But in special cases it is then valid, when there is a real outer, inner and in between *bayah* – then you have no option.

AA: I think that's where you get the Aaronic qualities, you get the Harun.

SFH: That's right.

AA: It seems to be essential (SFH: absolutely) for those people who are compelled to express their compassion in ways that may not transfer properly or appropriately into modern conditions.

Shaykh/Murid

SFH: In our time I know – especially one of the *Shuyukh* I know – when people really come with true desire to become their *murids* – and of course you know, they go through euphoria – the atmosphere is good, so one of them says, 'I'm going to be a *murid*.' So he makes them write it down, give a portion of their salary and so on, but come another month or two or a year, he discovers – 'No, what have I done?' So the whole thing in a way becomes counter-productive, and bounces back badly. That is why many of these people have had some of their *murids* writing books against them, because of that. In that case I have been fortunate from Day 1 not accepting the usual norm of Sufi teacher relationship – I said, 'No. If you want to be my *murid*, you accept it and you follow, but I am not going to in a way, follow that formal structure; the more I see you, I know you, fine; it's much more of a friendship. Times have changed. Because also, as a master or a teacher or whatever, I cannot protect them; I cannot establish a structure – because the Sufi master or Shaykh often acted as a little king in his village – I can't do it any more; I can't protect them. Issues with wives, problems between spouses, and so on, what can the Shaykh do? It's a laughing stock. You sit there and you see these people coming to you with their problems; no, I can't do it – times have changed. The horizontal way of connecting is now beginning to become vertical. It's between you and your Creator now. I am at best your friend. Come to me if you want when you are at ease or difficulty, I may be able to do something. I may not be.

AA: It seems to be a minefield, because human beings want to congregate, they want to mingle with each other.

SFH: It's a minefield, a minefield – it doesn't work. I followed Krishnamurti for many years: I benefited from it, but I had to leave eventually.

AA: And you followed the teaching?

SFH: I followed him physically and did everything. In Ohio and other places in America and Brockwood Park in the South – dozens of times. I followed him diligently for 8/9 years with the encouragement of Chinmaya. At the end, I saw the minefield he was in Brockwood park: a lot of emaciated homeopathic people, eating jacket potato in the miserable weather of England - it wasn't for me. But the man was authentic, a loner – everything around him was a minefield; not a single person could emerge; but I benefitted a lot anyway. I enjoyed his presence. I asked myself at the end, as I was leaving that minefield, 'Describe in one sentence, what he really taught,' and the answer was: 'Have no self-concern – go beyond the self.'

AA: In later years he had a very sour look on his face.

SFH: Of course, he was sour – a very unhappy and miserable man!

AA: Why did anybody want to be in his company?

SFH: Because of his knowledge of the self. He had recognized the dreadfulness of the self. He had recognized how awful, how dark is this identity with the self. That's all.

AA: Reason, emotion, psychology, pleasure.

SFH: All of it, and he was really in the present.

AA: That must be so – he was picked up when he was 10 years old. Whoever picked him up, must have seen the potential in him.

SFH: Annie Besant and Leadbetter.

AA: Must have seen this in him.

SFH: You know, again, hundreds of children like this grown up nicely, beautifully...the father was a gardener in the theosophy society, a cleaning boy: they all want god on earth. All want the Messiah; we all want Jesus, we want the *Khalifa*, the Mahdi, the Jerusalem. When we kill each other in the millions for that. It is the saddest city on earth. More slaughter – not a single prophet was there unless he was cut to pieces – that's Jerusalem.

AA: Dark Satanic Mills, Blake calls it –

SFH: We want the – because the other side of us beckons all the time. Allah is in you; Allah is here; so we want it physically here and we make it sacred and if you cut it, I'll cut your hand.

Societies, Nations, and Civilizations

AA: Shaykhna, I think there are two areas which *Insha' Allah* I'd like to explore with your permission. The first is to do with societies and nations and civilizations. And the second is to do with the faculty of the imaginal.

To start first with civilizations and cultures and nations and so on. When you map out the pattern of the self and consciousness, both in its limited and its universal form, and the self/soul relationship, there is obviously an element of the human agency, the human being as an agent is able to, as it were, deal with and negotiate as the means, as the *qudra*, to negotiate and to build these aspects of his or her reality in the context of the Absolute. So there is an agency.

When you move to nations and civilizations, and cultures, the agency goes away. There is no special agent that you can point to or work around, or build the focus of your attempt to understand experience. It becomes more amorphous. The agent becomes a group or collectivity. Nearly all the major texts talk also about the actions of the Absolute through nations and civilizations' rise and fall, the way that they evolve, the way that they interact – this has also been a thread of course in philosophical thought, whether related to the Absolute or not is another matter. In many ways the philosophy of history is a kind of mundane metaphysical reflection on that – I'm sorry if the question is as long – you have people like, for example, Hegel, who tried to come to terms with the action of what he calls 'spirit', through time and events, specially when it relates not to the individual activity.

So the same way that the model of the individual resonates with particular aspects of the self, the model of the spirit in action resonates through – basically through institutions that, collectively, form as it were a receptacle for the action of the Absolute. Nations and civilizations are not seen in these terms, but seen in institutional terms. The state, for example, becomes a receptacle for God or Allah's justice can be played out.

Individuality and Collectivity

AA: My first question is: do you also see it in this light? Do you see actions of the Absolute only through individuals as receptacles, or also through forms that can be 'perfected'? Non-human forms.

SFH: I see that whatever there is, seen and unseen, individual or collective, has one source, and is permeated by the powers and forces that emanate from that one source. It appears to be different in its output or its agency, as you say, and the entire business, the microcosmic/macrocosmic, individual, collective, nation, is all totally imbibed by that original, if you like, invisible pattern that is imbibed in it. Now the collective, of course, has slightly different ways of manifesting its power and the way it unfolds, and the speed at which it can re-act, or not, but it's part of that dualism. There's an individual and there is the collective. Again, these two resonate with each other, and reinforce each other, or the other way round. But they're all part and parcel of the same thing. There's only the Absolute. There is only that Supreme Cosmic Consciousness, and it filters and eventually appears in a manner that we think this is a different thing because it's a political issue, a different thing because it's an economic issue, a different thing because it's an environmental issue. That is the final appearance, only the face of it. The reality is the same as you dig deeper.

AA: But most – nearly all of your writings are to do with the individual – sometimes you extend it to families.

SFH: Sure.

AA: But the units that I'm referring to are larger. I just would like to know, for example, some of the actions of Allah SWT as we understand them in our limited form are also more appropriately reflected in the actions of the collective; for example, justice. The justice of the individual towards himself or herself is essential. But there is limited availability or possibility of extending the orbit of justice of the individual beyond very few people. You can't be just, say, to a person 500 miles away with whom you've had no contact. But the collective institutions – their span is greater. So if we're talking about in a crude way – if one thinks of these collective institutions – when I say institutions, I mean a collective form. If you can think of them as the 'Medinan reality'. The Medinan reality also is a receptacle for Allah's justice, as is the individual, as is everything else. But in human societies these institutions loom very, very large. My question relates to the recognition of the perfectibility in the individual as the key to resolving the dissolution of the illusion. Is there a parallel to that? Or is that a futile attempt?

SFH: I'm not saying that the collective is only the addition of all individuals. It has got other factors as well. In other words, it has in it some other multiply effect or whatever, but it parallels that. I don't see anything other than resonance between the individuals, it then becomes a few more individuals, and collective individuals, and then you have got a community or a nation, and then you have the whole world.

Going back to the issue of justice, we're too far away from the Source. That's why we can't see the wood for the trees. And it will end up becoming more and more polemics or academic issues – I really have no interest in that, because of my seeing the presence of the Light of the Absolute, which is the key to understanding any of these issues. Take, for example, justice. What is the root of justice, or injustice? Like the Absolute, we can only understand it through the relative. So I go to the *La ila* – what is injustice? Seeing myself separate from the One and only total, absolute, space-less, timeless realism – that's injustice. Everything else comes from that, and ends up in a valley that you cannot even describe.

Injustice is: my seeing myself as being an independent agent or want to be an independent agent, and have a will of my own. That is injustice. And that will perpetrate also to communities and others. I can't describe the chain – I haven't looked into it; nor have I been interested in it, but I see this is what it is. The same way as an individual tries to act slightly more justly and never manages it, the communities also try to act justly and never able to manage it. They try to eradicate outer poverty but the inner poverty is never addressed; outer poverty will continue, and will grow, one way or the other. It manifests in other forms. You have now got longevity, but there are also far more sicknesses and illnesses and problems coming with it.

The ultimate thing is the Absolute, the beginning, the end, and in-between. And if we do not yield to that, we will never be able to truly find, if you like, a way out of it. We try all the time to fix something, and something else goes on, we fix that and something else comes up – we become robotic insinuators of something that is beyond us. It won't work. It doesn't mean that we should not try to improve visible justice, or a bit of equality or a bit of firmness – that's necessary, but at the end of the day, it will never work, because the foundation is not right. The foundation is that individually and collectively we are here to complete an aspect of consciousness. And that is to experience the presence of Supreme Consciousness. If you don't have that as your constant reference point, then it becomes a secondary reference point. If you want to have any sustainability of well-beingness or contentment, or happiness, this is the route to take. If you try to patch up a bit of this and a bit of that so it's slightly better than it was 100 years ago, fine, and also that's not a bad thing either, but at the end of the day, the reference is that: being attuned to a Cosmic Consciousness that has within it the elements of infinity, durability etc. etc.

Then it doesn't really matter so much whether you've lived longer or shorter, or you have more power in your hands or less power, so long as you have been constantly energized and replenished by for want of a better word, God-consciousness. That's it. As long as that is experiential and certain, then none of the other usual uncertainties in the world will affect you so badly. They will be taken as an event, without a huge impact on one's life or psychology or whatever. So I see the individual and the collective inseparable and they have the same essential meaning and essential pattern.

AA: However do you mind if I push you a bit on this? The fact that you've articulated the reality of these things; you can call this the 'metaphysics of spirituality', simply by giving it verbal linguistic form. It seems to me that your teachings are supremely focused on the individual, and it could be that this is a fact, could be this is the reality – that there is no reality to a collective except inasmuch as groups of like-minded, like-hearted individuals. But like-minded, like-hearted individuals do not necessarily produce the good collective, leadership, the perfect man in government.

When I say institutions, Shaykhna, I don't mean educational institutions – I am talking about the nexus of collective relationships that keep the scaffolding of social life alive. The central point is law, what regulates it. Now a collective of realized individuals on the up side, probably is able to live a collectively conscious life, but inasmuch as there are variations of receptivity, consciousness and so on, even a near-complete yielding to the one reality, doesn't necessarily create, at a limited level, the kind of – let's call it a good society – that is able to provide a framework for these people to perpetuate and continue.

Realization at one level doesn't necessarily transfer inter-generationally. And I have noticed that – this is something that I am very much interested in, probably more so than *ya'ni* in terms of exposition; because I have taken – I think most people looking at the individual mapping that you have provided, there is not much wanting; self/soul limited consciousness, universal consciousness – these are all aspects of the same, or elaborations of the same.

There is a huge gap that is filled by all kinds of mischief-makers. In this gap of the collective, you can throw in all kinds of things, religion, theories of power, theories of Islamic government and theories of religious government, civilizations, nations, races – it's all in there. And the way it has expressed itself – I have not seen or experienced anything in the last two hundred years that tries to see how the thread of the Absolute reverberates in society, nations and cultures – Hegel is one. Probably in his own limited way, Shaykh Abdalqadir; his talk about the *dawla*; it seems the *dawla* probably is somewhat on these lines – I don't know – we will have to ask him – but does that interest you?

SFH: It interests me inasmuch as the leadership of a society accepts the basic fundamental fairness, in that everybody is endowed potentially with an inner reality they can aspire to, but not everybody is going to move, if you like, to even a middle or balanced situation towards realizing their inner state.

It interests me in that if the leadership is aware of the instant judgment against them by themselves and the punishment that they will be building up in their own balance within themselves, then the system in terms of its durability, its goodness, will be more stable and just – it will have a self-sustaining state, and it will be a good situation for anybody to thrive. My interest in the collective is that if you enable individuals to strive to whatever extent towards achieving the excellence they are capable of, for, to change the situation, I think most jobs will be fulfilled, most people will be fulfilled, and there will be flexibility – you wanted to do this and that and the other, but now you want to sit and do something else – write or teach or – as long as the goal is ultimately realizing the presence of that Absolute in every aspect of life.

If we bear in mind that ultimately there is only that, then there'll be considerable flexibility, and also considerable harmony in the self-adjustment of it. The state must regulate aspects to do with, as you said, mischief-makers, abuse, whatever, but at a very crude basic level, and it has to be provided, for the poor to be provided, otherwise, they will be mischief-makers or whatever.

But unless the whole spectrum is there – in my own mind, Karbala, as a kid, I think it was really an ideal, if you like, city-state. There wasn't a great deal of money exchange. People had considerable self-projected element of maintaining – as far as I could judge, as a youngster, as good a conduct as you could ever imagine. Most people were policing themselves or things around them for the good, and occasionally when they could not, and someone was not causing a lot of harm, they'd say; 'leave him, Allah will take care of him.'

Again, awareness of the presence of the Absolute was there.

They'd say, 'we have done what we can, we have reminded him, but he is not causing a lot of harm, whatever, he will punish himself.'

So there was, to my mind a very organic and a very wholesome way of governance, which was based on the awareness of Allah's presence amongst them. And flexibility and sense of fairness: 'why do you harm them so much? You have done the best; It's enough' It was towards the end of a long – many, many centuries, possibly, of the caravan that has moved – could not stand like a small delicate desert plant facing major changes in the climate, which is coming through central government and other things. I don't think it could last. It didn't have the sophistication to deal with what was coming. It was home-spun; it grew slowly, organically, people knew each other, if not, they knew somebody else who knew; so there was quite a lot of natural balance in it: people knew their own position, in terms of skills, economic wealth, ownership, knowledge.

So I experienced a governance that was based on first and foremost an individual being totally awakened and responsible, and family, and then extended family, and there were also many tribes in Karbala. So many of the *muhallas* were self-governed, and it was co-existence based on a very coherent path, which is the practice of Islam and adhering to it, and that was it.

So I don't see a great deal of separation in a model that I grew up in. But nowadays with the complexities we have, I think it has to be looked at from another extreme. First, maintaining basic, if you like, so-called democratic type of government, and then allowing something else to take place within it – it doesn't again impinge on others.

I think that atmosphere actually is better for the original Islam to grow again. I think it will grow better in a far more vibrant environment – and basically accepting diversity and tolerance, rather than 'let us also be tolerant.' So I think really again, Allah has done it. Allah's work is done. We did not as Muslims or religious people or whatever, bring about a universal way of conducting things. It was obviously in some cities, some places, through the history, but it didn't happen as a collective, so I think it's happening now.

The only thing that is not allowing the spiritual side also to grow, is the excessive demand on people's material productivity. It doesn't give people a chance, hours to wander, study and reflect. It's too oppressive – the style of life we are in. You can't live simply; you can't be in a little cottage and have no bank account. That is where I think we will suffer. That's where I think humanity is suffering, not allowing anyone who wants to grow spiritually – it's not just opting out, not just being marginalized; just not allowing a modification of this relentless way of life and work and holidays and in between. I think this is artificial and producing a lot of sicknesses and I think it will crack in one way or the other.

Establishment of a Medinan Society

AA: Shaykhna, you described Karbala in your writing – like a desert rose meeting a scorching wind – it's consumed; and re-creating it in the form of small communities, spiritual communities. You earlier on decided it is going to fail; but it seems that the way that your communities have evolved, the disappearance of these holistic, integrated, self-regulated communities, is in one of three or four directions. None of them seems to be conducive as a scaffold.

The one that has some resonance with us is the attempt to frame from the top, as it were, the kind of Medinan society that has been envisaged by the idealists of the Islamists and took a certain form in Iran and continues to be of some, less, decreasing appeal. In most countries these self-regulating communities, let's call them pre-modern, have been replaced by mega-cities with all kinds of chaos and huge demands and environmental crises and so on. And in parts of the West it has been met by a kind of responsible, now becoming ever more difficult, welfarism. The way that you seem to be describing it is that it's a kind of mechanism that will arise, necessarily, when enough people awaken – that they will sort of coagulate together in a kind of voluntarist way. Is that your understanding?

SFH: No – I think every individual is a universe; I don't think it will be the way you describe it. This natural coagulation of people of certain interests or hobby or orientation is natural for them to be together. Again I use the city of Fez as a model – I think it represents a very good model for cities. One district for example trades in wood, and the other one has the cloth merchants. Another district is the people who are more men of knowledge, or whatever. So it's a natural tendency. But I don't think it will be such that you will deprive individuals from also having that universality. Every one of us would like to give something, would like to have charity, to exchange. We like to have the heart open up: you can't centralize it; you can't make the government in charge of welfare. I like to be involved in the welfare; everybody else would – it's organic and it brings about much better cohesion and even better health. So I think to centralize a lot of these social services and this and that – it may be necessary as a kind of fail-safe mechanism, but for it to all encompassing can be counter-productive.

Once not long ago I calculated the cost of placing an orphan, someone whom the social services in England had taken on at the age of about 5 or 6 and placing this child for adoption the cost was about £200,000. And also the outcome is not going to be that rewarding either. Because we're not allowing an organic way of people to deal with our neighbors, and others.

This country, as it is now, there are a few million orphans, and every month there are thousands of babies thrown into the street – there's no agency – so once the social order disintegrates, we have expectations for a central agency to take over. For maintaining a minimum, it's fine, but people need to participate. The collective is *me*, also, so I can't be in isolation from it.

Then, according to my own propensity, I would be more inclined towards possibly more action, or a special type of action: in other words, what I am saying is that there would be room for everyone. It isn't going to be all of a sudden half the population sitting in meditation and looking mystical and saintly. I don't think it will be like that. Also the question of higher knowledge and awareness will be very common. I don't think it will be the preserve of the few; I think everybody will know – don't you know that there is only One – and I am here temporarily, and I am returning back to to the One, but I am also enjoying my simple menial work in the office. Perfectly all right. I don't think it will be an extension of what we had imagined of, if you like, the Prophetic models and the few who played a big role – as being role models. I don't think it will be like that. I think it will be different.

I think it will come collectively in terms of whatever there is on earth, to a zone where so-called spirituality and awakening to the Absolute will be quite normal, quite understandable, to different degrees and it will not change much people's lives. The only thing is that for it to be really normal, you need to have flexibility in terms of the economic and monetaristic and those mechanisms, not to be totally utterly a slave to the clock. Also realizing the need for a clock. The factory or whatever has an advantage – a certain time for them to open or close, but it's become excessive. I think we are reaching a point of extreme – not allowing the spiritual side of man to be nourished. We have deprived humanity of that, individually and collectively.

What is Shari`ah

AA: The process of regulation and sanctions of human relations, irrespective of their degree of awakening is the fundamental – or giving it a, as it were, a sacred or divine precept, is the claim of the *Shari`ah*, that the *Shari`ah* in its social aspect does that. These forms in which it came or is coming, irrespective of whether or not we are talking about the historical *Shari`ah* of Medina – but let us assume that the regulation and sanction of relations between individuals is governed by a precept that is rooted in knowledge of the Absolute, whether expressed or not – the degree of relativity is a question of either one side moves on to the other side. You seem to be saying that as we move to a kind of distributive knowledge, it's no longer the preserve of the elite or the few; it spreads out. The *Shari`ah* itself as understood not in the classical or conventional terms, but understood as a framework of sanctions and regulations, seems to have no purpose then.

SFH: No, without *Shari`ah* there will be no life.

AA: What is *Shari`ah*?

SFH: *Shari`ah* is the set of rules, regulations, codes, that enables individuals, communities, families, societies, whatever, to function in a manner that allows spiritual awakening, that allows the practices of excellence; it allows a certain measure of harmony, peace and well-beingness, so that the outer and inner of the individual begin to resonate and thrive, so that they attain the optimum possible point of *Insaan al-Kamil*. Without *Shari`ah* you can't live, but *Shari`ah* without *Haqiqah* also resonating with it, ends up being quite turgid and rigid, frigid and also brittle. You need both.

AA: The breath of *Rahman* suffuses the *Shari`ah*, but all the quarrels we've had, not just within the world of Islam, but everywhere, is to do with what is this *Shari`ah*. Is it social democracy, a Nazi system, Islamic government? In human beings the scale is the individual; that's how it is measured. It is the individual using his false sense of autonomy that opens the Absolute to its full realization. It has always been realized that through limited consciousness that full realization unfolds. Therefore, at the level of the *Shari`ah* we are all over the place, because we don't know either the appropriate form or the appropriate mechanism or the appropriate receptacle.

SFH: Unless it is infused with *Haqiqah*, it will be as you say and that is the situation as we observe. In the case of early Islam, or Muhammadi Islam, it was almost inseparable. *Shari`ah/Haqiqah*; Mecca/Medina were resonating. Also, it worked in the case of the role models of many people, whether they would elevate you or otherwise, or wherever it worked. So what has been missing is that we have begun more and more to separate *'Irfan* from theology, from the laws; for convenience or whatever reason, we have split it; life is not split-able. I am made of matter, energies and a subtle force, which I call spiritual, if you like, presence. So I am one, but only for the sake of focusing, I say, 'No I only have pain in my toes, my physical, my *Shari`ah* toe.' I think we have deviated from that for centuries. That's why I think the new wave will come. We'll be far more unitive without trying to patch what has been splitting for centuries together. I think people will regard it: if you do this, then you have this – a small little minority will be completely extinct. This was not considered a hundred years ago, but now they do. There is a small little group of people who focus on the *Shari`ah* without much *Haqiqah*. So you must try and allow them to continue to act the way they do, until of course the economic situation changes and clobbers it in a different way or eradicates it.

We have reduced – this is the final straw in the whole thing – we have reduced the human entities to just a functional, material, and survival entities. We are also making a mockery of timelessness and calling it 'longevity.' It's timeless, but we have now said, 'It's longer', as though there is a merit in that. We have been very clumsy and I think our science and also our philosophies in the last 50-100 years have not really lent themselves enough for this.

I think unless there are major breaks in the whole system, we will not realize that *Shari`ah* without *Haqiqah* is barren and won't work, won't last. It must allow certain freedoms to the individuals to have less of a full engagement – but not opt out completely – in the productive process, if this is what they want. We have deprived humanity of people who are reflective, who are able to have insights and so on. We have reduced it to a far more mechanistic way; we have made the human being a plumbing job.

Realization of Divinity/Homo Spiritual

AA: *Ya`ani*, in the Western world generally, as it were, God, or the notion of divinity, has been jettisoned from public space, because it creates more disaffection and discord. And collective institutions, especially the state, are fundamentally expedient. Relationships that are expedient change – designed to minimize harm and maximize welfare. While in fact it's often not like that. Other forms tend to sanctify these nations, and the nation is then elevated, and becomes kind of semi-divine. If you are part of this nation, which has in it godly attributes, or expressed in godly attributes, or builds its consciousness around God-consciousness, then it is a privileged nation. And then you have other situations now, where you cannot really escape the outer reference to divinity and sanctity, frankly, in an oppressive way. None of these things, none of these roots, seem to create a framework for what you want, or what you think human beings want, that is, a framework that would allow them to live autonomously, consciously, do what they have to do, but keep absolute awareness.

SFH: I think it's coming: it's not what I want, but it wants itself, and it has been coming very rapidly. I think a few hundred years, a few centuries – it's nothing in the life of man. I think we construed because of the size – geographical, objective positioning, we construed these villages so drastically different, and added to it the complexity of language and other things; so we thought, this is different, that is different, this and that: a hundred years ago there was not a single book that had in it a good description of world – now we take it for granted;

nowadays youngsters know a whole lot. And there are all sorts of interfaith activities, and I think we are very rapidly coming to the point of realization, without saying it, without arguing and being heated about it, that there is an Absolute, that there is timelessness, that there are these dimensions there.

So with quantum physics and all of the technologies we have now, they are all based on uncertainties, all based on a laser, which is based on uncertainty. I think it's coming to a point where the historical issues of religion and the Absolute and the relative, and the practices – *Shari`ah* – all of this will fall by the wayside. We are coming to a point where most educated, intelligent, healthy young people realize that: 'I have a structure, but I also have a feeling and I need the two,' – and the feeling also touches intuitiveness – I have a hunch.

I think we're coming to a zone of putting humpty-dumpty together again, after a few centuries of making him, and hoping that he's, *homo economical*. Of course he's *homo economic*, but he's also *homo spiritualis*. We have it all; we are a microcosm. So it isn't what *I* want – it's naturally happening. In all of these systems we will adjust, we will learn from each other what they have been. I'm not saying we'll end up having nirvana. It's going to be a better atmosphere, than has been, say, in the last 2 or 3 hundred years. I think there'll be more acceptance, genuine acceptance and tolerance, and people will see benefits of diversity. If you take a simple issue of new restaurants or foods: nobody would have believed in England 100 years ago that you would have all the diversity there is now. Thirty years ago very few people would have imagined they would go and eat in a Vietnamese restaurant, the other side of the world from Vietnam. They would've said, 'who are Vietnamese? Where is even Vietnam?'

I think we are reaching a point where we're trying to re-infect, re-write the map of man; and I think that's simple, it's both physical and non-physical; worldly and non-worldly; he needs the collective; he needs to have collective laws to safeguard, especially the weak and the meek and the poor. I think it's happening. I think *Shari`ah* is there in different forms – the country laws are none other than *Shari`ah*. Also, they are not against *Haqiqah* either. The only issue is this high-handed capitalistic monolith, that dictates that everyone has to be this and that – there's no room for someone who is not interested, who may be interested in something else, not just as a drop-out. It is that small percentage of population that is not interested in moneymaking, building this or that, and have got that inner quality: they are the pollinators of something else. These people will, I think in time, be given places at universities and other places and so on. 2-300 years ago there were still some monasteries, but no longer. We are depriving humanity of spirituality – some of whom have a far clearer understanding of the sacred, whether, if you like, it is genetically or due to other reasons.

Collectivity and the Recognition of the Absolute

AA: It's becoming clearer to me what your thinking is regarding the collective – that you see it as the rise of *homo spiritualis*, the ascent of the ape. But the apes are still limited, and the early societies, hunter-gatherer, settled agriculture and so on, somehow reached the kind of effective idealism, which is the expression of Karbala – a society big enough to sustain variety, and small enough to be self-governing. And that all in between is a kind of diversion, a kind of background noise, rise and fall of countries, rise and fall of cities and nations, empires and so on; and at the end of the cycle, you have a much larger number of people concerned – instead of a few 100,000, maybe a 100 billion, or 20 billion – a huge number, the vast majority of which seem to be enlightened, seem to be peaceable, and seem to be concerned mainly with their spiritual existence related to the Absolute, with acknowledgement of the Absolute. And it sounds like H.G. Wells, the Time Machine. This is one of the outcomes. The other outcome of course was a much more degraded, and degrading condition for humans. One outcome is spiritualized beings going on with their daily lives, lightly governed, with a great deal of personal freedom, no material wants – not chemically induced enlightenment as in Huxley. And on the other side, you have this brutish, bestial form of people, just trying to survive in this thicket, chaos and dystopia. You seem to be on the first.

SFH: No, I don't. I don't see it all like you have just said. I see most individuals, practically, not all human beings, have to go through the whole cycle; otherwise earlier on you will be concerned about the material side – that will be your main thing, but gradually you move on to the subtler – form ends up with meaning.

I see an amalgamation of all of these. I don't condemn anyone. I think each one has caught a glimpse of something that is within that as we are emerging. Also, I don't see it as a utopian idealistic thing at all. I see this life on this earth as a struggle. I think life is difficult; altogether life is difficult for everyone – the simple, the complicated, the wealthy and the poor, and it's its nature. I think the inherent difficulty of life for the individual or collective, is part and parcel of that challenge that without battling between the Absolute and the relative. The Absolute is my own source that gives me life. But I have to function in the relative, I have to reconcile these. It's not easy. I am the battlefield myself. I do not see at all this fine dandy, everybody walking around, sauntering and greeting everybody else – there's no such thing. But there will be people – many people – who will reach that state. But they start somewhere else. It's a large laboratory, so there's an evolution within it. There is a constant cycle, and no two people are the same – everybody has to go through that cycle to a certain extent. Nobody is deprived of any part of it, but some people do it easier, more elegantly, with greater, if you like, smooth passage. Others do it more difficultly. So I see this is the preparation of the cycle towards recognition of the Absolute, and the human being is the pinnacle of the possibility of that recognition. And I think we have moved a great deal in a very speedy way towards seeing, realizing that nowadays what people talk about was an anathema 2 or 300 years ago: that all religions have the same source that they are all trying to indicate one mysterious force that permeates all existence – science is doing it.

So I think, as I said, the biggest obstacle is not allowing individuals who are genuine in their propensity, to function. They are completely marginalized. They do not want to be in the economic so-called rat race. But they are not allowed. I am not advocating a safety net to accommodate them or calling for new monasteries, but there must be flexibility within the system to allow people to work part-time, to allow people to migrate, change places, or whatever, and to be a bit more flexible on these things, rather than being too rigid and limited in their choices. And that will only come again if it's more organically governed, rather than too hard and fast as it has become now – it's too mechanistic.

Haal and Maqaam of Society

AA: We'll talk about economics later. Going back to this constant referential point, Allah, the Absolute, it seems to me that you don't see any fundamental difference between the way in which human individuals awaken through a series of, let's call them, reflection points or crises, or spiritual crises or a process of accumulation of circumstances and conditions, each of which triggers the *haal* and the *maqaam*; it is a series of stages not seen mechanistically. The way I understand you is that you take that and project it on a much larger screen, and you have the same essential experiences at the social collective level, but the scale of measurement is different, and the way it unfolds is different. For example, for societies to abandon war, they have to go through a process whereby wars become nearly totally consuming, and then they move beyond that. So it is as it were, the *maqaams* of society and the *haals* of society mirror those of individuals but written on a different map. Is that correct?

SFH: To a great extent that is true, but it's not the whole story again. I again go back to the inner source, the primary source of warfare.

Warfare begins with the injustice, the illusion that I am separate from you, and I have independence. Therefore I begin to have the seeds of fear, and anger and all these other things. If I want to be independent and in control, I'll see you and the neighbor as a threat, rather than seeking co-operation and a healthy relationship; that is, I'll see otherness. So it begins with the rise of the identity and the ego, which is necessary for me to realize the Absolute.

Separation, individuation is a necessary start, the shadow that enables the reflector, thinker, the mature person, to realize it's a shadow and the light is that which is emanating from the oneness and the sameness.

So the root of warfare and injustice – and all conflicts, is the same: the illusion of separation and the illusion of the time frames. Until I begin to taste and experience the vastness, the infinitude and timelessness, I will always be in fear and anxiety, and that is the source of warfare within me and within communities. Once this map becomes more available to others – it doesn't necessarily mean everybody will live according to it or know it – but at least the diagram will be available to show them that this is the beginning. The continental philosophy has done quite a lot on that, in the last 40-50 years. But there's the question of the otherness. And this has become more and more current amongst the young educated, well-educated people. So I think it will prevail. I think more and more young educated people begin to see the fallacy of this high-handedness, or if you like, the current amalgamation between politics and economics. I'm not saying this is now a common thing, but I have seen enough people to be convinced that with intelligence more and more people will see the absurdity of this. They put up with the profile of celebrities, but they don't fall into it. 50 years ago an advertisement, a celebrity saying, 'I am doing this!', and everybody would want to do the same. No longer. They see, they laugh and ignore. So there has been a major shift in consciousness in human beings, especially amongst the young. And I think this will continue to bring about – the question of, like, vice and virtue – what is a vice today, was a virtue yesterday. Cynicism, skepticism, so there is terrible dissent, which I actually think, is the cause of liberation now. People are much more cynical. 50 years ago politicians were far more trusted. The most trusted people were teachers, doctors, and bank managers: one after the other all these holy cows have been slaughtered.

There's amazing change, and we want to believe in a sense of knowledge. We want to know something that is real, something that is the Absolute. I think that is coming. Maybe the names have to be changed – call it Absolute, instead of God, or Supreme Consciousness, or whatever. I see there will be modifications of these systems; I also come to the same conclusion from watching the number of NGO type of organizations or voluntary work that people do. The percentage of these, especially Western economies, where voluntary work is contributing more and more of the percentage of the total economy, is growing at immense speed. These are all good signs. What appears to be horrible, global world, I really read in it that it's the victory of God.

Seeing La Ghalib illa Allah

AA: Your essential optimism comes from the knowledge, the certainty, of *La Ghalib illa Allah*[125].

SFH: Absolutely.

AA: *La Ghalib illa Allah* can also lead to .... becoming ... *ya`tee Allahu biqawmin yuhibbuhum wayuhibbunahu*[126].

SFH: And that's happening. And this is not from Mars – this is what's happening here. Our own children with their revolts and rebelliousness. I think it upsets one, because one wants harmony and peace now, but actually it betrays harmony and peace that is coming.

AA: *La Ghalib illa Allah* also means to me that the way in which human beings have organized or disorganized their lives will be destroyed. So destruction is coming.

SFH: Sure. No doubt about it. I am actually convinced there will be major, major destruction in the world.

AA: So the essential optimism is to do with *La Ghalib illa Allah*.

SFH: That is the only optimism, absolutely. And the optimism is that I will come to know it. That's another optimism also.

AA: In my limited way I am trying to understand how *La Ghalib illa Allah*, which is an absolute statement, relativizes my life.

SFH: Precisely, so when I see myself acting along the will of Allah, I also see that I've succeeded. But also Allah's mercy is such that I'll be given another dose of humbleness, humility, in that I will lose after every victory. It's wonderful; wherever you look is perfection.

---

[125] "There is no Victor but Allah." (This was the motto of the Nasrid dynasty, which is found all over the walls of the Alhambra.)
[126] "Allah brings a people whom He loves and who love Him." (Qur'an 5:54)

AA: The story in between though is of interest to me. May be not to you!

SFH: No it isn't – the in-between is bracketed by this – accepted as part and parcel of the package.

AA: Of course it's bracketed, and it's always there. I don't know how one can continue this line of reasoning, because it has no reason to it; it's only a line.

SFH: No, you go beyond reason. Reason is used for minute issues – is it the right time? What day is it? Simple.

AA: But people take even spiritual within reason, and take these brackets and try to project them forwards and backwards – backwards by reading history and studying, forwards by projecting it onto the future, but not necessarily understanding that this is the singularity that goes back and forth.

SFH: Absolutely. There is only that. There is only singularity. There is only Oneness, and I think a lot of these terms that we have inherited from rigid religious and cultural background, will diffuse into some other terms, which will make it seamless. All of these terms – this is now *spiritual*, this is *secular*; this is *celestial*, this is *terrestrial*; this is *earthly*, this is *heavenly* – cause more divisions. The root of everything is heavenly; our earth is heavenly; stardust, physicality; the water is heavenly; so we are earthly/heavenly at the same time. On minute issues, childish issues, we are earthly – it's for survival. Once you move from that we want *arrival*. We want salvation, we want liberation; we want that, if you like, unfoldment. Everybody is programmed – we are driven towards that. And if our economic and political systems do not allow that, then they will break. They will have to modify; otherwise, they won't work.

Permanence/Oneness/Collective Consciousness

AA: And in the same way I assume that when you discuss the individual self wanting the everlasting, and permanent, it seems at the level of society the same thing is happening.

SFH: Sure.

AA: You start aggrandizing nations, races and religions, and giving them a permanence, which they don't really deserve.

SFH: We want the permanent; everybody wants that, through anything – through memory, through state, through color, race, and language. We love the permanent, we love the eternal, and we love the two seas, ever, ever continuing, connected, connected. We want to get out of the box of space and time. That is the key issue. If I really sum up, whatever I've learnt, it is that. Every individual, every society, every collective, every nation, every religious or non-religious person, wants out of this constriction, limitation of space and time. Most of our literature, most of our writings and discourses imagine space and time as a place to get out of space and time. Our entertainment, our holidays, our drugs, our drinks, our alcohol are all based on a tiny little glimpse of so-called temporary liberation from space and time, and to be conscious of it. So that is the third 'C'.

AA: That's what *laqad khalaqnakum shu`uban wa qaba'ila lita`arafu*.[127]

SFH: Partly, from the collective sense, yes.

AA: It's to do with consciousness.

SFH: *Karam* also means generosity – Allah is more generous with those who are more attuned to the ultimate purpose – yes.

---

[127] Full Qur'anic verse: *inna khalaqnakum min dhakarin wa untha waja`alnaakum shu`uban wa qaba'ila lita`arafu.* ("We have created you of nations and tribes so that you may get to know one another." – Qur'an 49:13)

AA: So there is therefore a collective consciousness.

SFH: No doubt.

AA: With a dimension that seeks the Absolute.

SFH: Absolutely. No doubt about it. Collective consciousness does exist.

AA: It's not limited to the individual.

SFH: Not at all! And it also has its own dynamics.

AA: But you have not, in your own teachings and work devoted much attention to this.

SFH: Except that I intuitively referred to it.

AA: No models, paradigms.

SFH: Not at all! Because the foundation is not there. It must start with allowing individuals to mutate into that more. You need an atmosphere that will enable the individual to mutate into that realization. If there were enough of them – if there were ten thousand Dalai Lamas in every religion or whatever, I think there would have been far, far more, if you like, higher quality human beings, above the angels as we pretend to be, as we are told we can be. But we don't allow it. Man doesn't behave well in a factory – we have reduced human beings to little economic rats. This is what it is. Our sciences, especially medical sciences, reflect that. Because that works in a limited way, but it doesn't work across the board. So we have concentrated too much on where it works. It's like Mullah Nasruddin's ring. He is looking where it's convenient, but he has lost it somewhere else.

Having longer living people causes more problems for everyone – the family, the state, everybody. I'm not saying living long is a bad thing, because the *ruh* is living forever. But if you realize that, it doesn't really matter if you die at 40 or 80. We have not allowed enough individuals – we have not created an atmosphere that allows enough individuals to wake up to the Divine Reality. Too much humanity; very little divinity. And it is unavoidable, because it was abused in the past. In the name of the Divine there has also been more warfare, and we know that as well. But now it's coming to another zone. That's why I say it has been horizontal for thousands of years. Now it will be seen that it's going to be vertical; without our ability to see how it is happening, individuals, without having had 50 years of theological study or being in a monastery, realizing that there is only One. Individuals will begin to be more and more accountable within themselves. I think it's coming a lot from the academic world.

AA: *La Ghalib illa Allah* – whichever way you go.

SFH: That's right. Instead of it being a monastic situation, I think more and more universities and think tanks and institutions are now into this.

AA: *La Ghalib illa Allah*. At the level of seeing these places, they are terrible places…!

SFH: No, but within that it allows individuals to grow, but at least the time and space will allow it.

AA: The conditions are there. It's always used and abused –

SFH: Sure, again the human side. Human mischief. Also research institutions, again the same thing; within it every now and then you find something telling.

AA: The end must be a "New Creation." You said people are moving away but maybe you see it one step further.

SFH: Literally, they are moving into it but their heart is not in it. And I think the heart has also got a lot of power.

AA: Minor rock singers turn up and there are 40,000 people.

SFH: They want something that touches their heart, to be out of the box. I don't necessarily consider this as a bad thing.

AA: The sign is good Shaykhna, but surely it's the way it's expressed.

SFH: Because there is no alternative – the alternative has not been allowed.

AA: Mad competition.

SFH: The alternative has not been allowed – living the *dīn* – didn't happen – again human mischief played its role in that, reducing it into rigid and turgid and frigid – it's human nature; it will take time; it's evolution.

Sacred History/Myths and Legends

AA: Would you like to talk about capitalism?

SFH: *Bismillah*.

AA: Shaykhna, there's something called sacred history which is a clumsy word for fables and stories and parables which you have in sacred texts. The Qur'an has stories about prophets, sages and so on. They seem to have also taken place in historical time; what is your understanding? I mean, apart from ethical or pedagogical purposes, didactic purposes, as examples, *mithal* and so on. What is the reality of sacred history?

SFH: It is the interface. It is the *barzakh*. We want to believe. Every one of us wants to believe there is a father in heaven, a mother on earth; there is some guardian, there is Jerusalem, the perfect person: we all want to believe – it's perfection. We want to believe in God. We want to believe in God's attributes, His justice, and His retribution. We are designed that way. Legend or myth sometimes becomes much more important than the so-called factual real. What is a fact? Two people see the same, but they interpret it differently. All of these have got their play in the evolvement of human beings. It is work in progress. Human beings' life on earth is work in progress. Back to its source with awareness of it and cognizance of it and awakening to it. That's how I see it. So all of these have their place.

AA: As I understand it, legend would be truth, as it were, captured over time.

SFH: There is nothing other than Absolute Truth: it gets diluted when it emanates from the Absolute Source, which is ever present. The event is true, but it is a diluted aspect of that. Everything carries the spark of the sacred; the sacred penetrates the known and the unknown, the seen and the unseen; the universe and the multiverse. There is only the sacred, but because it becomes so diluted, then we say, 'oh no, this is profane.' How can you know it's profane unless there is a spark of the sacred in it? How can you know it is bad unless there is a spark of goodness in it? That realization that it is bad is the spark of the goodness in the bad. So these fables do exaggerate some of these things, which are interesting – the legends or the myths. Myth is a reality, more real than the events, so they try to highlight.

AA: What of the myth of Adam? If you use the word 'myth' now, it means some kind of fantasy.

SFH: Fine, because of the language changes; the language has changed – myth didn't mean that in its original Greek. It's an exaggerated version of what we term normal day events, with a stronger, if you like, ethical, moral effect of sacredness. That's it.

AA: Do you see myth and legend as an essential way in which human beings can understand or relate to the Absolute?

SFH: Yes – it's part of our heritage, part of human wealth. But a time is coming that you spontaneously see the spark of the Origin or the Absolute in it, or the Sacred. And I think a time will come that most people won't refer to it any more as the sacred – this is more sacred, this is less sacred. The more it is tangible, the more it's to do with the senses, the more we think it is less sacred. The more it's to do with ideation or mental, the more we think it is sacred. The more it's to do with the transcendental; we think it is more and more sacred. There is only One. And that One disguises itself appearing as a physical or mental or pure energy. I think this simple map will prevail. And this is the map of the Prophet, without using this language, because we did not have the amenities, the technology, the physical things that we have nowadays.

Hardly anybody talks about transmission; hardly anybody talks about half-life, or whatever; we are in another era. The truth is the same. Reality is the same, but we need to use modern language to express it. We're still using archaic language to express the immutable – there is a tendency to reject the Sacred because so much abuse has been perpetrated in the name of religion, the name of *Shari`ah* or *Haqiqah*. I think the level of intelligence and our thinking process changes, and now it is nothing like what it was a hundred years ago. The word transmission, reception, background noise, cosmic ray, all of these change. We are living in another world, and we're not catering for our inner emotions. We are very contorted in our technologies and our outer life is not in line with our intuition and our heart. The heart is atrophied. That's why we say we are degraded. I accept that. It's the heart. That spontaneity – there is no time left to us. It has not been exercised. It's all mind, mind, mind, limbs, mind, action, action, and output.

AA: It seems that these myths and legends and all the great traditions have a powerful didactic purpose in a certain repetitive theme, like the theme of creation: it comes in different shapes and forms, but it all points to a reality that is expressed culturally in different ways. Is that something you'd accept?

SFH: True, I accept that.

AA: And also the theme of heroes and…

SFH: Yes. Well, we have in this culture, not too dissimilar a thing through literature, but a lot of it also is in a way, on the dark side. The form of short stories, novels, and also creative writing, and all of that.

We have that also. But in the past it was much more elevating. Now it is half and half. We have a lot of pulp fiction.

Universality of Religions

AA: At some point, Shaykhna, you seem to – I don't want to use these terms – agree or disagree with this or that school – but obviously finding the root of all spiritual traditions, emanating from one source and expressed in different ways – some people have made basically a religion out of it; in the sense that there is a commonly held belief that the closer you are to the origins, the source of the unfolding of these religions, the closer you are to expressing reality in its meaningful form. You were saying also that you wanted to understand how the Prophet was living and acting in his last months. So the implication is that there's something more perfect then, in terms of understanding, than it is now. So if somebody gives you very detailed exposition of what happened there and a fulsome picture and so on, it would allow you to understand the workings of the Absolute.

SFH: No, my interest in that specific issue is to understand his state and feeling and thought at the time, and also his utterances and traditions that came out in the last years, is simply to help the rank and file of the Muslims who are by far more divisive now than they were a long time ago. It's to show them that it is part of nature, when a lot of new people come, when there is dispersion, a wider number, you will get divisiveness, and that is what also happened in this time period. I wasn't trying to do anything else other than to illustrate that he also – this being with total utter resonance with *Haqq* – realized that what had happened the last two or three years, the huge influx of people with no background, no education – he was, in a way, concerned about safe-guarding the *badha* of Islam, the inner core and teachings, and that's why he also insisted on adhering to *Ahl al-Bayt* and the Qur'an. So it was really to illustrate that.

There are two different things: one is wanting to get close to the source, so people end up being a bit like theosophists – all is one and one is all – this is different from having touched that. Then you will realize that division is also part of it. Differentiation is part of it. So-called world religions or paths, they are not the same. They emanated from the same, yes. Indicating the same, One, yes. But they are not the same. They've got a cultural bias, a linguistic bias, and a geographical bias.

AA: What would you say to people like Schuon or Nasr that the exteriorization of these forms are varied, but because they all have an essentially similar core, the proper course is to be as close as possible to the esoteric or inner core of these spiritual traditions, in order for you to be most authentic.

SFH: No, I would say, 'it's good for you and maybe good for many other people, fine.' I would not say, 'this is the *Hanif* or whatever.' Good for them. There will be people who are oriented that way, fine. I think they start tolerating some others and respecting them, fine. But I don't see anything wrong with that. It's a relative truth.

AA: The flipside of that is like the Salafis who look for the exterior.

SFH: Exactly. The flipside – absolutely. Fine, but don't try to stereotype; there are as many ways as there are breaths. The direction is fine, yes. There is only one Essence – all what they are saying is *La ilaha-il-Allah*.

AA: But both the Salafis and the other extreme, the esoteric, confine it to a spiritual tradition. You can't pick and choose. If you want to follow the exterior forms of religion, you go as close as possible to its origin, and try to approximate that in your daily life. And the esoteric or perennial schools look at it the other way.

SFH: The truth of it is that every tradition is like a little drop of rain that ends up somewhere and goes into a river. You need to lead to a river to reach the ocean, from which you emerged anyway, from Allah. So I don't deny that the need for a path, the need for confinement, that's also needed. But you can't say it's the only one. That's the difference. You can't say this is the only river that goes back to the ocean. You can't say that.

AA: But I suppose the differences are, that one limits effects to the individuals, to a very small group of people, while the other one insists on certain behavioral standards.

SFH: Sure. Again, it appeals to certain people; as long as it doesn't impose, doesn't encroach. I don't think there's anything wrong with it.

AA: But Salafism does impose.

SFH: That's why it's a problem, and why it has to be stopped from that, to stop its imposition.

AA: So the idea of living your life according to the apparent behavior of the early adherents of a religious tradition, whoever is the earliest proponent of the particular tradition, doesn't have much resonance with you.

SFH: It won't work. Can't work. If it is a matter of an individual propensity, taste, etc.

AA: So why have these movements grown so remarkably?

SFH: Desperation. Again, it is religious tourism. When you hear that there are so many millions going to Mecca, or Karbala or wherever, it's an indication of thirst. It's not an indication of success of a sect or a religion. It's an indication of thirst of people. People want to be liberated, from the illusion, the depression of space and time. It's depressing. Life is hard. It's difficult: we want to know – not just believe – that there is justice, there is goodness; Allah is there and I am returning to that, and that sort of thing. So these are the proofs of it.

Fundamentalism

AA: But why choose this very, very rigid, restrictive, in many ways imprisoning form? It plays no part in this kind of self-knowledge. Why is it that you have a Salafi Tablighi mosque which has thousands of people there on Friday? Next to it there's a Sufi *zawiya* with maybe 20 people. Why do people find succor there?

SFH: We are not evolved yet. I think it's a matter of time; give it a few thousand years.

AA: Could be the other way round.

SFH: No, I think it's evolution. More people, billions and billions of people – they want to be fixed; they want to say, 'this is it – you have no alternative.' So the mind stops. When your mind stops, there is a bit of a relief. It's not a life. And that's what the majority of people are. Qur'an tells you that. Fix it. Fix rigidity, so there's safety in that. Apparent short-term safety. It's appealing. It's the only way; everybody else is at a loss and they are all in hell. Great. We are the chosen people. Everybody wants to be the chosen people.

AA: The growth is very alarming.

SFH: Indeed. Growth in the population of the world is even more alarming. It's a reflection of that.

AA: It's a sort of global phenomenon: turning towards this kind of fundamentalism.

SFH: Sure.

AA: But to you this is just an irrelevant phenomenon.

SFH: Yes – but it would seem alarming if you thought in terms of, you know, one or two centuries or whatever, I don't know the time scale. Allah knows the time.

AA: We are in this time....

SFH: Sure, absolutely; I accept that.

AA: We have to deal with what's happening.

SFH: No doubt about it. Also, we have to read it more – that it is going to increase, because people want to have that fixation.

Putting Back Together the Medina Model

AA: One of your early teachers, Shaykh Abdalqadir, has made a great virtue of following the path of *Ahl al-Medina*, supposedly the denizens of the perfect society. You think that this is just Quixotic?

SFH: No, I think it has truth in it, but I don't think it's relevant. Also, I think it has been very selective. All human beings want eternity, and eternity seems reflected in something that is older, most ancient. And, as a result of that we become very selective. We pick aspects of the old that's disappearing and stick them together, and create a model that wasn't in actuality really there. So we pick up the best parts and we stitch them together, and we try to airbrush out of existence all of the other things. So I think it is a convenient thing of creating a model that is not totally fictitious, but it is not real and also not applicable. I don't think it's a bad attempt but I don't think it's doable.

AA: I recall you said once that this is probably the appropriate thing for people coming from a broken European background who need discipline – an ennobling figure to relate to.

SFH: Sure. And it's good news to them; yes, absolutely. Be cheerful about it. But it's possible if it was possible, it will become possible again.

AA: It seemed to have helped these people.

SFH: No doubt – palliative, helpful, no doubt.

AA: But as you said, airbrushing is a very good word to use here, because there's a kind of willful neglect of the harsh fact. For example the perfectibility of *sahaba*....

SFH: Medina too. There was mayhem. But why did they leave Medina? Why did they go to Kufa? There was nothing other than discord.

AA: – and the historical evidence seems to be that Mu`awiya poisoned Ayesha.

SFH: We are scared to disturb it – we have this illusion that it was ever perfect. Perfect within it being somewhat peripherally, with quite a lot of imperfections. We're not reading the model right, reading the map right.

AA: I keep on coming back to this question – maybe it's not appropriate, but I'll ask it: You said we are not reading the model right. It seems very, very few people can read the model right.

SFH: It's not available; it hasn't not been there. The model that's understandable to the present-day man has not been there – I have not seen it. It's not available, it's not easy to see that. Look, from Oneness emerge all the dualities and diversities and so on. And they balance each other. I haven't seen it so clearly stated or lived, referred to as its Qur'anic-based or spiritually-based, revealed by the prophets.

AA: It's fizzled out into a kind of institutionalized, bowdlerized, and trivialized model.

SFH: Sure. Politicized.

AA: If you look at – the other day we were at this celebration of music – Vivekananda and Rama Krishna, probably in their own way, true men of Allah, of *haqq*; but if you look at what happened to the legacy, 50 years later, it seems to be lost.

SFH: True. We want to hang on that we think are the best people, but we have neglected our heritage – now we have to return to the machete, or with machine gun, or something. Our people were the best; they were done in. Now it's our turn. It's typical *nafsi*, typical ego.

AA: It seems to be fated to so-called spiritual communities that they inevitably decay, including great religions.

SFH: Sure.

AA: You have a person, an individual, his light, reflected light continues for one generation and then everything turns to dust afterwards.

SFH: True.

State of Islam

AA: We talked about the decay of religion, including Islam, being far, far earlier in its history than commonly believed, commonly accepted, and that these golden ages were exaggerated.

SFH: Exaggerated. I even say that Islam was stillborn: it was announced and may arrive now, and we should be able to read it. Read it according to our time and live it, rather than just recite it, as most of the *hafizes* do. Again, it's an evolutionary issue, work in progress. One side of it is very dark and depressing. But look within it and see what Allah's statements are. And put it in perspective for human kind, and the rise of homo sapiens. Suddenly you find, if you like, the children of Adam as *godlings*, as people who are self-aware, self responsible, and realize this life is only a tiny little prelude as a transition to another zone. It's not a small thing, and maybe it's beginning now.

AA: The most evocative description of Prophet Muhammad in the Qur'an is *Shahidan wa Mubashshiran wa Nadheera*[128]. I don't think he's ever referred to as a *qa'id* or leader.

SFH: None of that, and we think in terms of our own culture all the time, and he strategized – there was no such thing: he moved from one moment to the other. In the battle of Uhad, he saw the people were so full of themselves that they wanted to repeat Badr, and so on. And he

---

[128] "A Witnesser and a Bringer of good tidings and a Warner." (Qur'an 33:45)

allowed them against his own will and everybody suffered because of it. He was reading what Allah's decree was. And Allah's decree fixed up everything for everybody else as well by reflectiveness. This is what they need – goodness, and we'll do it. It's not punishing – *Thumma anzala `alaykum min ba`di alghammi amanatan nu`aasan yaghsha ta-ifatan minkum ayah* 154 Surat *Ali `Imran*.[129] Incredible! It describes the whole scene after the battle – then slumber came upon them – it's all there. This one *ayah* describes the entire business of decree, destiny, your choice, and his choice, Allah's choice and Muhammad's choice. Incredible. One long *ayah* – everything to do with your choice, my choice, and his choice, is in there. And it also has our evaluation in it. They say people who suffered, they said, 'If we had not come out from our homes, we would not have suffered.'[130] He said, *Qul* '– even if you were in *buyut muhassaha*, secure houses, if death had been decreed for you, it will take you.'[131] In other words, the decree of Allah is different from your extent of choices. You have to choose, but your choices are minute things in Allah's decree. So you have to read His decree also. Do your will, but also read His will. We don't do that. We don't refer it back to His will. This is the demise of the Muslims. They don't ever ask, 'What does Allah want out of this situation?' It's all the time what THEY want. 'Reproduce Medina, reproduce this, more mosques, bigger mosques.' It's also too late for the mosques to be tourist attractions. They are huge, but they are empty.

AA: It's to do with the loss of consciousness.

SFH: Yes, absolutely.

AA: Which has atrophied.

---

[129] "After sorrow, He caused calm to descend upon you, a sleep that overtook some of you." (Qur'an 3:154)
[130] See Qur'an 3:154
[131] See Qur'an 3:154

A State that is Islamic

SFH: More and more, we want an 'Islamic' state, and triumph. We don't want to live the state of Islam, because that's more difficult. I have to get rid of *me*. I have to get rid of *me*, to be in the state of submission. It's not easy. But demanding and sloganing an 'Islamic' state is easier.

AA: But at some point, you were partial to the idea of a state that is Islamic.

SFH: It's not a 'state' *per se*. Rather, it's an economic and political system that provides an atmosphere to those whose orientation is enlightenment to develop spiritually. That really has been, if you like, my main hope throughout my life. To have a system, a situation which enables individuals, not to be religious or spiritual, just for them to be men of Allah. Simple. It doesn't have to come through reading the Qur'an in 60 volumes. No, it's for a simple person who reflects that truth to flourish. It's for the simple beings. Allow such people to grow spiritually.

AA: You are talking in fact about a revolution in consciousness.

SFH: Definitely. Also, the Western reaction to it was the fear that this could be an alternative system. Earlier on, I think this was the biggest fear, especially when they demanded payment in another currency than the dollar. Once they realized, no, this is another government they unleashed Saddam to pull their teeth out. We are not ready; the people are not ready for an alternative system to the brutality of pure monetaristic control. Not ready. Evolutionarily we are not there yet.

AA: Also Shaykhna, at some point the path you were looking at, the possibility of turning leaders more to exploring their own spirituality, and in the process liberating their people.

SFH: True, true.

AA: Even those who had a great deal of power, and appear to be despicable in their actions. You saw in them that potential. Do you still see that?

SFH: No, I don't. I think it's too late. Now we have a monolithic system. I think for the time being I wouldn't have gone to any leader if they didn't have that basic inner goodness or a heart for the poor and the destitute. If they had been simply brutal, I wouldn't have had any resonance with them. I think at the moment we are heading towards a global monolithic system, which may begin to have some tolerance for something else, and something else may emerge. But at the moment I think it is monolithic, total utter control mechanisms.

Political Economy/Obsessions

AA: Which brings us to the issue of political economy, economics – this has been a constant theme – the degrading aspects of the capitalist – degrading to the human spirit – what you call the monolithic techno-usurious capitalist – any system – any economic system deals with the fundamental aspects of work and wealth – materials, distribution, division and accumulation, a fundamental aspect of human life, which you cannot avoid. So why is it that this system is so – why is the process of accumulation so manic?

SFH: Because we are obsessed; every human being is obsessed – so they become obsessed with the obvious, the outer. The obsession really is with the soul, obsession is with God, with light: obsession is with eternity. Obsession is to get out of the box of space and time. But there is no clear map and that's not easy. You have to turn away from the so-called 'you'; not easy to do. So you start building the so-called 'you' and get obsessed with your ego. And you justify it: 'I'm doing a lot of charity. I am saying this and that.' We are all obsessed. Human being is an obsessive being. You have to be passionate; this is your heart. The heart is the house of your soul and that is the source of your life. We are obsessed, every one of us. Either obsessed with desires or obsessed with having no desires; which is another obsession. I remember meeting this wonderful British *sanyasi* in India, whose obsession was to go to the post office once a week to receive from a very wealthy family a big box of special Swiss chocolates that were especially for him. That was his obsession. He stopped caring about food, but was obsessive about chocolates – we are obsessed beings. We cannot not be obsessed, whether it is physical, material, mental or spiritual. So it is lop-sided. There's nothing wrong with wealth…

AA: The obsession is mis-channelled.

SFH: Precisely. I like greed. Greed is God's creation. But greed for what? Greed for that knowledge, that inner state. Not greed for more accumulation. Greed is not bad. It's a necessity. Nothing is bad. Put it in its context and it becomes either very good or very bad. It's again context, context, context. Be greedy for your inner state of light. And you'll become less and less greedy for outer accumulation. Nothing wrong with wealth *per se*. Imam Ali sums it all up – he says: 'Asceticism does not mean you own nothing; it means that nothing owns you.' I remember meeting a fellow not long ago, who was probably the largest merchant – and still is – of carpets in Iran. He used to have 20, 30 direct branches all over the world. 20/30 in America alone. A man in his eighties. And now, he says he has shut them all and his obsession is that once a month, he takes a million or 2 dollars in suitcases to go for his hundreds of other orphanages, many of which were in Iraq and elsewhere. He enjoys that. A lot of wealth; he himself is a very simple person, can hardly eat. So it's your relationship with the wealth and power, and control. It's sad when you see people who've been trained all their lives in business to control, control, and they don't reach a point of seeing a higher Controller. Bigger controller than them. Really sad. I've seen many of them.

AA: These systems are no longer, mostly no longer, subject to individual whims and desires. They have a reality of their own. It's like a gigantic machine.

SFH: True. Absolutely. It's again – and this is where it comes in: 'pay Jesus his due', and 'give to Caesar what belongs to Caesar' – this is it.

It's Shaytanic; you have to pay your due; you have no option. It's monolithic and total and absolute. And therefore it will crack. It can't last. And this fashion is only acknowledging the human, accumulative material and animal side; it does not give leeway for the other side. It doesn't work. It can't.

AA: The culture celebrates it and produces 100 millionaires –

SFH: Absolutely. I remember once the credit card came, it was American Express – I realized then an immediate shift in the whole scene, as though it was the final stamp – 'if you are not within this system fully corporatized, you will not survive, and so on' – everything seemed to have shifted as an indicator. Inflation jumped 4-5%: the services in hotels changed; no more business account; it was no longer direct, no longer personal.
   No we are moving more and more towards that zone.

AA: You see in it built-in destructiveness.

SFH: No doubt – like everything else.

AA: Outer destructiveness.

SFH: I don't know, I can't tell, I can't see. I wouldn't be surprised if it came from somewhere that would be surprising to us. Like most tipping points in life, they come from where we have not measured it.

AA: I think it's an extremely resilient system because in my lifetime it has gone through 4 or 5 terminal crises, but recovered.

SFH: Because human needs and love for *duniya* and accumulation is very resilient. And that will continue. But it will allow within it certain latitude – it will be a bit more diffused and it will be more accomodating. Then slowly by slowly in time with evolution that will be more appealing, if it does allow the balance of humanity and spirituality. Then it will win. But we're nowhere near there.

Money/Quest for the Durable

AA: They say, 'man is the measure of all things'. Now it seems money is the measure of all things. Again, it seems to me an accelerating process in the last 20 years – 40 years. Probably more so than any other time in history, not, I would say, limited to individuals, the rich merchants, emperors, capitalists – it seems to be a globalized obsession, and has destroyed, places like India. There's no doubt the middle classes have turned away from any long term engagement with spirituality, and moved to money making.

SFH: Yes. But to come from where it started – I think there'll be more and more, possibly with individuals, not with such high profiles as Bill Gates, but we need a few thousand Dalai Lamas, a few thousand Bill Gates and others, who also look for the alternatives. There have been people like them, but I think there will be a few more exceptions that prove the rule, and they'll become more and more, if you like, not so abnormal.

AA: I find it a bit repulsive to see the rich people – celebrities and so on, go around fishing for spiritual highs and then abandoning it and moving on.

SFH: This is again a human obsession. They want to have something that's more durable. I think we have not yet reached the pinnacle of vulgarity in a global sense, because, again, due to the numbers. 200 years ago you would not have been able to have this sort of delineation. There would be a city and within it a few people – now we have a huge population – globally. So in the short term it's depressing and dark, but in the long term the whole of humanity now is awakened to it. So again, it's Allah's plot. From the point of view of a few generations, it's quite frightening, but if you look at it in terms of a thousand years, not at all. The whole humanity will move towards the higher. The whole system will shift and will be, if you like, the true *dīn*, not religiosity. People will be discriminating themselves, because they want that reliable inner balance which brings about dignity and respect to the individual, accepting limitations and allowing the point of excellence, rather than just materialistic pursuit and success, in terms of numbers. Very vulgar.

Wealth/Qibla of Higher Consciousness

AA: Your own exposition on wealth and moving away from obsessive materialism and accumulation attached to it is mirrored in your own life. Did you find it difficult at some point or was it easy for you?

SFH: No. I followed the system. I wasn't willing to pay the price for it. All the absurdities and superficialities and waste that come with it. What really helped me the most was the waste, whether it was in a lavish meal or in the 10 star restaurants, I could not take it.

AA: Imbalance.

SFH: Totally – that has remained. I returned once from America on QE2 and I had Shaykh Abdalqadir and his entourage with me – I paid for them all. I was travelling first class and so was he – and I seldom remember being as unhappy as I was on that trip. He was very happy. He'd wanted that. He'd not had it. For him it was a bit of an exposure. For me it was the disgusting state that I was in. It was my fault, part of it. Really, I was so unhappy because of the waste, the excesses, and everything was part of the same package – the 3 or 4 different varieties of champagne and the caviar. So I couldn't take it. It was very natural for me to walk away. The downside of it came with it was far, far more disgusting, horrible, unacceptable, than the nice aspect of it.

AA: You had the luxury, the sense of being distinctive – all this was...

SFH: Not interested – it repelled me – made me literally sick. It was a bit of a renaissance of how I felt with the IPC in Iraq – being also very special people; one of only 200 people in the whole country – pampered and so on – disgusting.

AA: I think this is a very acute observation looking in the mirror amongst may be others – the repulsiveness of power and wealth when it's misdirected. It has a peculiar repulsiveness.

SFH: Or if it has not got that *Qibla* of something higher, for higher consciousness, for God's sake. If it is not lasting, it will be repulsive.

AA: I have not seen yet a wealthy man who has got that *Qibla* – unless it's inherited.

SFH: You're right, but I mentioned to you the example of the carpet merchant. He had it. He was regarded as the wealthiest, biggest merchant – but it didn't touch him. There was another man also who had the largest shoe manufacturing – there was not a single carpet in his house. So there are a few people who have got it – more and more of these examples will come from the West as well.

AA: The abuse of power and wealth is really one of the fundamental distortions in human history. Wealth creates the illusion of perpetuity – that you are eternal – and power gives you the illusion of control over your fate. Would you say it is correct?

SFH: If one gets married or has an accident or something happens, it awakens the person, then there's nothing wrong with any of that.

AA: Nothing wrong, but very rare, unless it's inherited.

SFH: It is rare.

AA: In which case a person is disgusted by what his father has done.

SFH: True.

AA: like John Rockefeller II. He gave away all his wealth.

SFH: And many others. I think you don't need too many examples or role models and so on, but at the moment the current trend is hoarding, herd mentality of hoarding wealth.

AA: Why is hoarding so particularly noticeable in so-called Muslim countries? If you take charitable giving as an indicator. Bill Gates gave all his money away; so did Warren Buffet. You find massive works of charity and service. I think Gates' charity in medical fields is remarkable; but you find the meanness of the extremely wealthy in Muslim countries very noticeable.

SFH: Their wealth is recent and insecure – and they're still after whatever version they have of the Muslim state; it's power assertion – 'it's us, we are superior' – a bit of a legacy. I think it's very recent, not even 20 years, 30 years – it needs time.

AA: You don't see it as part of the distortion and degradation of religion?

SFH: That also – of course – they use religion to justify a lot of that. Of course it's part of that. It needs time. It's work in progress. Give it two or three more generations. We don't know what Allah's plot is. We don't know what the great grandchildren of some of these people will be doing, where and how.

AA: I can't understand the meaning of a person leaving $250 million to his children – I really don't – it goes beyond my comprehension, and I don't know how to explain it. I find it such a perversion.

SFH: It is that.

Imaginal and Natural Sciences

AA: Shaykhna, we have covered a great deal of ground and nearly all the major concerns that I, and possibly readers, would have, and covered, I think, in a fulsome way. I hope it shows the full range and full spectrum of your thought and progress over time. And of course we cannot understand your *haal*, your current condition, or your current station. We can get glimpses of it. I think it will appear in the text.

The subject I would like to talk about now, Insha'Allah, is to do with the matter of the imaginal and imagination, and science – science understood as natural science, the science post Descartes, empirical science, based on experimentation, which seems to have taken over the definition of what useful knowledge means. Now there have been a number of challenges to the conventional understanding of science; that is, it defines itself and limits its range of truth to the observable, the measurable, the empirical. It's been challenged by a few well-known and not so well-known scientists, physicists and so on, that have come really tantalizingly close to describing in language that can resonate with those who have a grounding or rooting in the natural sciences, physics and so on. David Bohm is one that comes to mind, but there are others, including, I think, John Polkinghorne, who was a Regius professor of Physics, but left his position in Cambridge to become an ordained churchman.

Khayaal/The Two Spheres/Connectedness

The key observations that have come from this quantum mechanical field theory, if you want to call it that, is the meaning and nature of the order that underlies what is measurable and what is quantifiable, and the order that underlies within it, and so on. I have found it a very, very useful way of trying to bridge the science/art type of binary division that has emerged in the last 50 years, particularly when it comes to the matter of imagination, or the *khayaal* as it's known in classical literature, clumsily translated as the 'imaginal'. So if we see the idea of connectedness – if everything is interconnected, and there's rootedness of all manifest and non-manifest beings in this common thread that connects them, imagination must be a form by which the truth is grasped, but not through empirical mechanism, or not through the effect of empirical mechanism on consciousness. Would you say that's the case?

SFH: I accept that. I also share with you a simple model that has been in my mind for a long time: and that is the two spheres. One of them is the sphere of *haqq*, which is immense and boundless, not subject to the limitation of the speed of light or time. And our consciousness is another small sphere, which is overlapping with its mother sphere. There is that overlapping point where the two spheres meet: this is where the imaginal is at home. This is the purpose of the imaginal – to connect the discernible, the measurable, the causal, the scientific, the empirical, with another zone, which is beyond the definitions of quantum mechanics or general relativity theory of Einstein. And it is that edge; it is where the speed exceeds that light. The two overlap, and this is where the imaginal helps us, to see it in a very, if you like, uncertain way, navigate in that no-man's zone. To realize that, in truth, what we were at home with, comfortable with, a certain reliability, causality, rationality, reason, stability – we are only a tiny, tiny little dot in this infinite ocean of immeasurability.

So the imaginal is the key in transition – it's a fuel we need in order to get out of the gravitational pull of the earth and its attraction. Because it's our home: huge memory, collective memory, millions of years; so I share with the wasp the breeze that comes – the wasp knows this breeze means something – the beginning of autumn – in a romantic bee subconscious way, I too find that there is a message in it. But once I move out of this lovely earth, which we love and adore and kill each other for, (everybody takes it as their own) then I need the imaginal. I need that *barzakhiya*.

The thing with the imaginal is that it comes with *wahm*, it comes with a value system, and in the teachings in Islam, and in also other esoteric teachings, it's one you need to cut. *Wahm* is a value I attribute to a situation, whether physical or imaginal: it's important – I have to cut that out. I must not give it a value – I must allow the imaginal to take me into its bliss, and then I will realize that all of what I considered to be real, rational, important, was totally, utterly insignificant. It is just like a little passing cloud, as the Qur'an describes.

AA: If you talk about the *imaginal* – it's not a common word, not used colloquially; what is used colloquially is *imagination*, creativity, and of course it is self-referential, in the sense that it is a form which takes its source from energy and its sources of imagination, creativity in itself. And when that's expressed, it's a kind of limitation – the idea that Allah is the *Khaliq*, or *Jamal*, and therefore, has no purpose beyond just titillation. The poet Coleridge divided imagination into two levels: one is this level, which he calls secondary imagination, which has no lasting value; and primary imagination, which he directly roots in the ultimate creative imagination and creative intent. So the intent to be creative underlies the way creativity unfolds. And I think it is this that most people, when you talk about the recovery of the imaginal, let's say, in spiritual traditions, particularly in Islam, is that, because it is self-referential, it is also subject to critics' views and subject to the eye of the beholder: 'beauty is in the eye of the beholder'; and it seems to have cemented itself as a form of empirical imagination. Would you say that this is the case?

SFH: It is a good bifurcation of reality, but I again repeat what I think can bring about a better and broad understanding: that this so-called reality of ours – causality, physicality, which is really governed by the non-physical, the subtle, difficult to discern, the spirit or the soul, within me, or whatever comes from above, or the cosmos. This reality is a tiny insignificant sphere, which derives its energy and its temporary reality from that boundless Infinite Reality. It is the interspace where the two meet; this is where the imaginal, which you can divide into numerous different zones – one of it is much more attached to the duality of the earthliness, and another part of it is actually emanating from a higher, if you like, closer, to that indiscernible Oneness. And maybe even you can have many other divisions, many other, if you like, possible zones. All I can say is that, if you get out of the box, of the limitations of the mind, whose essential purpose is to enforce earthly reality – survival, based on duality. I and life, I and you, and I and others, are separate. My mind is there to make sense out of this. Because in truth, it is nonsense. There is only One. The mind is that transformer, diluter of this high voltage of Oneness, in order for it to accept this illusion of otherness. The imaginal is the beginning of a release from that box. That's what I see.

AA: Well, according to this school, admittedly a minority school of physics, this faculty is absolutely essential, if you are able to engage with the various orders mathematically.

SFH: Correct.

AA: Because the way that I understand it is that the wrong turn which science took, was not so much the time of Descartes and Bacon, but rather in the way that they treated the elements of indeterminacy and uncertainty that emerged with the quantum era, quantum mechanical era, and that there were multiple paths they had taken, the chosen path, which eliminated an attempt to engage with what is not measurable, even mathematics. Do you accept, for example, an approximation of what you're saying in natural scientific terms? The model that has a process that was postulated by David Bohm, explicit order, implicit order, super implicit order, and so on, ad infinitum. He seems to be saying in mathematical, physical terms what you're saying in metaphysical, spiritual terms.

SFH: I think David Bohm was unique in trying to connect the two ends of the imaginal: the one end that is rooted on earthiness – we can discern it and allude to it in a way. The other end is, if you like, connected to the Absolute. I think it was a valuable and most courageous attempt to do that. But people did not take it on to develop it. I have a feeling also that the fallout from string theory and many other such attempts on the mathematical side also, although they seem to have reached a cul-de-sac, but I think all of this is going to contribute to us allowing ourselves, in our mind even, to allow another mind, not a boxed mind. Allowing another echo of the mind. Because there are again two minds – Imam Ali says, 'I saw mind as two. One that listens and one that is imprinted on you.' I believe in that: these people were the translators, transformers. So he said, 'I see your intellect, your reason, your mind as two. One of them is imprinted in you from the unseen, from your *ruh*, and another one is confirmed in your physical reality.' And if it is not imprinted on you, your physical reality would not have taken hold of you and you would be thinking, 'this is the only reality'.... and I think it will come. Also, because it may have commercial implications. It may have practical implications – as 50, 60, 70 years ago, nobody would have imagined that laser was going to be the foundation of what we are living now: if you just take that out of our day to day, it'll seem as though we were returning to the stone age.

Field of Consciousness

AA: There seems to be – his and others, a kind of, not a mystical science; it's in fact a scientific form of mysticism, with the sense of mystery. What is also parallel to what you're saying, is that he posits these different zones of consciousness.

SFH: Correct.

AA: Therefore it is pointless to bring in key actors, from one to the Absolute.

SFH: Where I think science missed the boat, and is still missing it, is not allowing the balloon of consciousness, our consciousness, to go into zones that are not necessarily retrievable or can even send signals that we can fully understand. Allow it. Go to the field of consciousness, you never know. We are too scared to explore. We have anchored everything into this duality. Up to a point it is fine, but allow certain research, certain creativity within the field of mathematical model building or computer model building, or whatever. And in fact the great leaps that have taken place industrially and financially have been due to that. A man like Steve Jobs – the amazing things that happened, say, with Apple – it's a phenomenon. A company that didn't exist a few years ago now is the largest in the world. People have to take notice of that. One man who was, in a way, from a certain point, unhinged. Three times he comes back. It is an unbelievable phenomenon. If we allow dozens of such things within science, within the field of consciousness, things will change – it's beginning to happen. Don't forget, the field of consciousness wasn't even referred to until the mid-80s, 1980s. It's very recent.

AA: But it seems that the way that research on consciousness is going, is within this empirical science.

SFH: Sure. It has to start somewhere.

AA: Basically trying to find consciousness within matter, which may be the case at this level.

SFH: Nothing wrong with it, I think it will lead to others. I think all of these are reaching a point of diminishing returns. In physics, after the Second World War, all the physicists were considered to be the ultimate heroes, they walked with a swagger, because of the atom bomb; but it's coming to an end. It's almost becoming now of negligible true interest in terms of it being backed up by funding and so on. I think we will be more and more tolerant in the cutting edge of, if you like, thinking, of philosophy of science, of possibilities. In allowing this more and more. It hasn't begun yet...

AA: ....evolution?

SFH: No, I think it will come on its own – it'll seep through.

AA: Because they have to move and measure.

SFH: No, we allow that. I don't think there's anything wrong with that. There is another major sphere, whose rules and regulations are different. So you have to step into it without shoes; you have to jump into it. And then hopefully some voice, or some signals will come back and say, 'Look I'm seeing things that were not seen before,' then the impact will be great.

Zonal Consciousness/Corporate World/Polymathism

AA: The leap of the imagination is a figure of speech. Actually it's more like a leap of zonal consciousness rather than imagination.

SFH: Yes, yes. And I think it will come from within the corporate world. I wouldn't be surprised if a company within the corporate world allowed its senior and other executives to have some sort of a biofeedback mechanism. Every two hours for five minutes, they are completely zonked out, thoughtless, by through some sort of electronic means, that they are so refreshed that they view everything as though it's just begun now. I think that company or that activity or that group will be in every way, leaps and bounds ahead, specially if they are involved in creative research, or whatever. And I think it's just around the corner – I don't know how it will come. We have to consciously be able to stop the consciousness of duality.

AA: The underlying – not reason – but one of the purposes I'm trying to structure the conversation along these lines – is these two worlds which appear to be completely antithetical – one world of measurement, structure, observation, experimentation, a kind of truth that is projected, and classically these worlds are united to some extent, in the sense that empirical observation were not the foundation of knowledge. Knowledge came from a different source. And if you take an equation, which I've worked out, if you speak about knowledge of God, or knowledge of different zonal consciousness, it's a kind of attempt to comprehend the outside order. The reverse is also true. One of the reasons why we've locked ourselves at this first level of consciousness is because what were seen to be eternal questions were addressed in a non-measurable, non-empirical way, and satisfying explanations were found. Now that measuring, observing and quantifying seem to have put some of the naturalistic explanations to rest, it has taken a life of its own. Would you say that we need some kind of reversal of this formula?

SFH: No, I don't think reversal – this distraction was natural, like a landing stage; then we'll move on. It is not going to give you that personal, direct, experiential realization of the Absolute. So, therefore, it's like a cul-de-sac in a way. I think we'll move on.

AA: But this level of consciousness is to do with empiricism – which cannot at all propel you to another level.

SFH: No, it will. Once I am in it, once I have been given sufficient time to reflect upon it, and be genuine in my assessment of it, also regarding my other intelligences; in other words, I must refer not only to my IQ, but also to my emotional intelligence, my spiritual intelligence and to my genuine inner questioning, like, 'am I happy? Am I content? Am I ready to live? Ready to die? Have I gone beyond just tolerating others? Have I really realized there is no 'other'?' This is what's going to be driving us. We will come out of that, if you like, landing plateau. I think it's essential for us to reach a point of rationality. Acceptance of a certain commonality of the mind, and this is as far as the mind and intellect can go, and we've taken it now almost globally. We're not quite there yet.

In the meantime you have a few breakthroughs, like David Bohm and a few others, and a few eccentrics – and Steve Jobs in a practical sense. It's happening: human beings will not stop until the being realizes there is One *being-ness*. And his being-ness is entirely there as an echo, as a holographic tiny representation of this Cosmic Being. When that has been – initially it's a *haal* – touching – it's a state until it becomes a *maqaam* – then there is nothing more.

That is the *Insaan al-Kamil* – that's it. That is the purpose, that is the yoga, and that is the completion of it. Unless there are people who have done this within themselves from different streams of professions, skills and background – science, technology, arts, literature, so-called spirituality – and then we begin to realize the entire business was emanated, has emanated from that essential mysterious Oneness, bifurcated into infinite varieties of dualities, sustained, energized by the same Oneness, which is not subject to space and time or speed of light. Once there are enough people, a few hundred of them amongst industrialists, scientists, so called religious people, politicians – once that happens, then we are no longer going to say this is now a religious matter, this is a spiritual matter; we'll be less divisive when it comes to truth. The further we are away from truth, the more we are divisive, pigeonholing. It's fine, but soon that will reach a point in many areas that it is no longer giving us any real excitement. As it is now, it's become hair-splitting. Look at the last 20, 30 years of top PhD. Dissertations – a few thousand of them around the world – we find them insignificant. Whereas it wasn't the case 50 years ago. It's reaching a point of no return, so there has to be a breakthrough and it will come from, if you like, *barzakhi* zone, almost invisible. And it will also have its own quasi-scientific, if you like, foundation. It will have its own language.

As it is, in many, many of the sciences where it is multi-faceted, where there are 5 or 6 disciplines impinging on each other. In the oil industry, working as an oil geologist, an oilman on the rig, the geologist hardly spoke to the paleontologist. They were dealing with the same thing and their objective was to discern how deep to dig, and if we were near enough to break through the cap rock, or not. Each one of them was king on their own. That was just 40 years ago. No longer. You cannot now be a paleontologist unless you have all the other multi-disciplines. Polymathism is now most common. I think we are coming to an interesting point.

AA: I'm sure you're right, but I see the opposite. I'm just looking at the product of a PhD thesis. It's more dealing with insignificant minutiae because the standard of knowledge has gone down.

SFH: Sure, you have to do that to get your PhD and get your tenure. Once you are at the edge of that, then polymathism will be your main field.

Revolution in Perspective

AA: But it seems that we are, as you said, at the cusp of a kind of revolution in perspective. And that revolution, as you say, is that while in the past it was the odd philosopher, the odd meta-physician, the odd natural scientist, but then the dam broke. Then it spread slowly, and then accelerated into society, something akin to that happened?

Imaginal and Natural Sciences

SFH: A hybrid is coming; and I don't think it will be a revolution, it will be a big bang; I think it will take us almost unawares; I feel it's coming.

AA: It's incremental progress, and this system will privilege a form of consciousness that would be attuned with higher levels of enfolding orders.

SFH: Absolutely. Did you know that professors of meditation are now teaching in many universities? There are now full time paid professors of meditation in many universities. This is a new phenomenon. 30 years ago it would have been considered quackery.

AA: With respect, it is still to do with personal well-being. It is to get away from their anger – anxiety.

SFH: Fine, great, brilliant. It is also to enhance creativity. Fine, they have to begin somewhere.

AA: Self-referential – Back to the self-referential. I don't want to be the spoiler – the fly in the ointment, but it must happen that way; otherwise I think it will end up in a kind of just going round and round –

SFH: Be the fly in the ointment, and fly; your wings will also spread the perfume you've had from the ointment. It's brilliant. What is wrong with that? I really see goodness – when it comes to the Supreme Consciousness, I see goodness in what everybody else finds in it as repressive or depressive, or negative – I don't see that – I see goodness. *Wa la Ghalib illa Allah*.[132] I honestly see the hand of the invisible in what appears to be despicable.

AA: Because you see the connectedness!

SFH: Totally. Inseparateness.

---

[132] "And there is no Victor but Allah."

AA: And therefore, everything that is manifest, they are just ripples on the surface.

SFH: Precisely. But it appears to the mind and the mental survival mechanism as being a bit too far off. I follow the Qur'an; I live it; when it says they see it far, and you see it near. I see it near to such an extent that there is no distance; it's already done, as in *jaffa al-qalam*.

We are a Photon and a Wave

AA: Going back to my undergraduate physics we had to read the volume ....and one of them was an experiment on a crystal – as you reduce it down to absolute zero, electronic action stops. From the point of view of the crystal, there is only a vacuum; from the point of view of the electron, though, there are imperfections all over the place. So you are asking us to be an electron, not both.

SFH: We are both. I am an entity; I have an identity; I am a photon and have a wave function at the same time. This is what we have deprived human beings of – that heritage.

AA: They only see the photon.

SFH: Exactly. I do not deny I am a photon: a third or half of my life was to identify with the photon. It's personality, its culture, religion, identity; its excesses, its failures, its strengths and its weaknesses – nothing wrong with that. But the reality of the photon is a wave function. And if nobody is looking at me, I am a wave function. Once you look at me, then I am a photon. Once you identify me, then I am a status: am I good, am I bad, does he like me, does he hate me, is he going to kill me or is he going to feed me? Duality. Once you look at me, it's duality. If you don't look at me, I am away from you.

AA: But you have to get away even from duality and wave function. This entire concept is in many ways, linear and there's a linearity going on.

SFH: It already is programmed to make me get away from it, because of suffering. It repels me – it is already programmed, written: *al-qalam* – the pen is dry. The system is already totally both implicit and explicit. It's done already. I just have to follow it: this is submission, but I don't follow it. This is *islam*.

AA: Interesting. Stopping time.

SFH: The key is stopping time. If I do not stop time, I will carry on and self-destruct. I will be distracted, and that is destruction.

Time Connects Movement

AA: Time connects movement; one should not look at the event, but look at the connectedness of movement that caused that event.

SFH: I look at the event, but I see that the event is utterly connected – the event is sacred. All of it is sacred. There is no profane. From the point of view of truth, there is no profane, only One. But only at the realm, the sphere of duality: this is better, this is good – I don't deny that – that's fine. It's child's play. We must allow the child to play. But for how long do you want to remain a child? You're losing your teeth; you're losing your hair – at the end you're getting close to departure. Have you realized there is no such thing as departure in truth? Have you realized that your soul is eternal? Not caught by time and space. If you haven't realized that, you have not completed your journey. Purposefulness in life is only that. Not purpose to achieve something: there's nothing wrong with achieving something, or not achieving something, and sitting quietly *per se*. 'In praise of Idleness', which I thought was the best book Bertrand Russell produced. It is not the outer things. Ask yourself: Have you been loyal to yourself? Have you been just to yourself? Have you brought justice to yourself? If you have not, then you are perpetrating injustice.

The Heart, The Soul, and The Self

AA: I'm trying to draw you into, as it were, epistemology of the soul, trying to be formulated in terms that maybe others can understand, in terms of science, natural science. Is the soul then the interconnectedness of things as well as the leap from one order to the next ad infinitum?

SFH: Yes, absolutely.

AA: So it can be grounded in an attempt, a kind of mathematical point, which will be limited by that.

SFH: Yes, the soul is the source of whatever level you want to look at – the soul-called reality. It connects the Absolute Reality to the most relative, which is the so-called 'I'. It is my personal god. It is the manifestation of God in me. Through that I know that I am the most exclusive. Through that I also know that everything in the universe is inclusive, and beyond. Inclusive of the Absolute. It is the most exclusive and the most inclusive, and boundless. It is through that agency that I can experience the photon, its limitations and the limiting factors of space and time, and the speed of light. It is through the courtesy of that, that I have been allowed to have this little perch for a while. But if that perch doesn't lead me to that infinite horizon, then I'll remain dissatisfied. Remain discontented. And I remain feeling I have been done in. I remain looking for reasons to accuse others and establish my victimhood, my sacred, if you like, cry; until I realize and taste that infinitude, which has been emitting in me, but it has to take root somewhere; it has to have germinated out of duality, out of man and woman in the womb – one out of two. And that one must realize that there is only One. And it carries on perpetuating the two, in a sense.

   It's that which is, if you like, understandable by heart, more than by head. If that which is understandable by heart does not become my main diet, then I'm not alive. The Qur'an, all of the other literatures teach the same, and allows us to be born again. What does it mean? That this life is biological; it's a good start, but I must realize there is something in me that never dies. Then I am relieved – re-lived – and then I put up with it all. It doesn't become drudgery; it becomes a temporary phase in order to return to the absolute paradise, which is a Persian word, also. We're all yearning for paradise, because paradise is yearning for us. The pattern, the reality and the model of paradise are in my heart. And that's why the Qur'an says, '[those in Paradise,] they say, *rabbana atmim lana nurana*,'[133] they say, again in the Qur'an; '*Hathaallathee ruziqna min qablu*'[134] – we have tasted all of these fruits before. We have tasted all of these, if you like, joys, or blisses; we don't want this; we want absolute light – '*atmim lana nurana.*' Brilliant metaphorical or symbolic. Qur'an gives the whole thing. But you need, if you can get, ten top physicists, mathematicians, who really trust it, believe in it, and dive into it. I tell you, you will come up with amazing, a thousand times more than David Bohm.

AA: David Bohm is just one of those – not many but – several.

The Absolute Dominates Over the Relative

SFH: I know – but you need to have access to that. First, go into that theory. Assume that, yes, the Absolute dominates over the relative; the relative is insignificant; it is just a little illusion; it is the cave of Plato, as far as the reality is concerned. They are only passing shadows – you are chained to space and time, looking at the walls. And it's a good illusion, a good myth, but it has a purpose – that the conclusion was before it. The conclusion is none other than the One, and you have been given a flicker of a shadow, to realize the One. All of these issues of self-realization emancipation and enlightenment mean nothing other than inadvertently, simply being able to step out of the box of duality, and your identity and the *photonism*. To realizing the entire thing is wave upon wave upon wave of functions, and that's it. But nothing matters.

AA: But, still, the language you use, the metaphors are extremely powerful. One of the – the term 'Light' being the grounds of creation and existence is found very positive in the Qur'an and all the spiritual

---

[133] "Our Lord, perfect our light." (Qur'an 66:8)
[134] "This is what we were provided with before." (Qur'an 2:25)

traditions, light is a fundamental principle of any kind of physical feeling. So of course you don't posit the Absolute versus the relative; you posit orders within orders and fields within fields. And this is the language; when you move from the metaphorical language to the more scientific language, by increasing the use of terms like consciousness, limited consciousness, conditioned consciousness, you've taken on, as it were, the way in which you can dialogue with people; you've expanded the base. When you say heart, it is a fuzzy thing and lovey dovey thing – it doesn't.... but to the heart, it's that connecting thread that can make these leaps.

SFH: No, I define it quite clearly in my bit of cosmology, that I find workable, I define the heart as this metaphorical vehicle or faculty that contains this metaphorical thing we call 'soul', or 'spirit'. It is how the unfathomable, mysterious, sacred entity, which is the Light of lights, infinite varieties of light, is fathomed. You can talk about the lights nearer to the shadow, that's fine. You can define them, and talk about different levels of lights, different layers of lights, but only at the lower end.

Once you reach a point, I think it will become counter-productive to continue trying to pigeonhole it. The spirit, the soul, contains all of these thousands of layers and levels of *being*. In my particular case, as a human being, my job is not to speculate about what is the spirit, what is the soul; my job is to make sure that the vehicle, the faculty, the organ, metaphorically, that contains it, is pure. That's all.

All religions are the same. Service to others, serving humanity, selfless service – all of that means purify that metaphorical vehicle. Have no rancor, anger, expectations, desires, lust, all of these things, because then the light of light, which is your soul, will not beam its multi-faceted way to the rest of you.

Every organ – physical organ – receives its portion of life and energy from the source, but if my heart is full of anger, pus, animosity, hatred, sadness, grief, I am not being enlightened. And that is why at a human level, at a spiritual level, at any other level, my first job is to have a clear mind, so I can see the play of duality, and the singsong and the swinging of it. Then with it comes my duty to purify my heart, so that the light of the soul can impinge upon the mind and everything else; so that I am a full being.

The only thing I can share, if at all, is a simple map, a simple diagram. I'm not coming up with anything fantastic or impossible to fathom. I'm saying, oh you human being, you are a photon, and you are also a wave function. You are an identity and you are a reality, which is unfathomable. It is divine, spiritual, call it what you like. If you manage to put these two together, then you are getting into a coherent wholeness, closer to wholesomeness; then you are getting closer to completing by will, by your will, due to your suffering, due to your intellectual drive. By that you are coming to realize the oneness that you are.

AA: Wonderful!! What can you say? This is a wonderful summation. You see it near – this break of the dam, maybe because you see it with the eye of *haqq*, and others see it further away from it.

SFH: I won't dismiss anything that exists at any level of reality; I won't dismiss any of the things that any human being experiences – it has a reality. But which is more durable? Which is more sustainable? Which is more authentic? Which is more self-generating? I call that absolute reality in you. I don't deny that you are suffering now from an outcome that your mind gave it importance. Your *khayaal* and your *wahm* – this is the most important thing – that you change the regime – fine. But have I changed myself, my own outlook? Which lens am I looking at?

I come from a heritage that I truly utterly know the authenticity of when Ali says: 'I didn't see a thing unless I saw Allah before it, within it and after it.' He means, 'I didn't look at anything, unless I looked at it with the eye of Supreme Consciousness, and then I saw Supreme Consciousness in it in its process; and I saw Supreme Consciousness as its perfection after it has gone.' That's it. Slight change in the language. That's all. Instead of Allah, I say, 'Supreme Consciousness'. So that's simple. It's not a big deal. I'm not coming up with anything new. I'm just coming up with something that benefitted me in my short life, without denying anything, seen or unseen.

But more than that as time goes by, being deferential to that which is original, not subject to change, and constant. That is the light, the higher element, if you like, of spirit or soul in me. Don't deny '*Fa bi ayyi alaai rabbikuma tukazibaan*'[135] How can I deny the suffering of somebody who is hungry? Their consciousness is focused to remove that which gives them the illusion of separation and death. Or pain. We have to attend to it. It's wonderful to attend – you – *wa thiyabaka fatahhir*[136] – you start by purifying the outer garment, and then your mind and then your heart, and then you'll find in truth all of it is sacred and eternally pure. Otherwise, I fall into this dreadful idea of white and be pure and the piety syndrome – horrible. It's essential for a kid, not for a grown-up, not for somebody at the door of *Ka'ba*, where they come in with their pomposity.

AA: I think we've left that one behind.

SFH: *Bismillah* – you are right.

God of Science

AA: I'm trying to see how this teaching, which seems to be self-evident manifests – Imam Ali had the highest form of possible limited consciousness as it merges into the Absolute, without any science, without having gone to MIT. But there are many people of science who are influenced by science; there are many people who are semi-literate, who worship the forms in which the scientific endeavors function; this is the new god.

SFH: Sure.

AA: The new god says certain things. The new god is in the process of being undermined – it has to be dethroned, like all systems, from within – something has to give within it that will allow it to crack. And certain aspects of it – light for example, is a metaphor of the ultimate creative principle, is also fundamental and moves in ways that are not too different from the way that was experienced in a more authentic and

---

[135] "So which of the favors of your Lord would you deny?" (Qur'an 55:13)
[136] "And purify your garments." (Qur'an 74:4)

truthful and real way by Imam Ali, or by you in a different context. So, one reason I am pushing in this direction, is to make people move from imagining to the imaginal. You imagine emptiness as a void, the imaginal sees it as the flip side of plenitude... it is just completely opposite.

SFH: and so does science – science also says there is no such thing as absolute vacuum.

AA: These metaphors – if they are re-configured, re-constituted, frames, which people now find holy, holy science, because that's what it is – and make people become deniers – deniers of the validity or reasonability of the Absolute, because it's immeasurable. But if immeasurability is explicitly stated in the implicit order of things, then you have no choice but to bow to it.

Connection with the Absolute Consciousness

SFH: This is at the duality level. I think it's brilliant. But I think what you have also touched upon earlier, and a few times, is that at this level, we suddenly connect with a much higher level, if we can find ways and means to assist individuals to experience timelessness and the absolute void or oblivion, without drugs – the more people have tasted, have experienced that, I think the more likely that this bridge will be made.

AA: Sorry, but meditation now has been seized by people – 98% of people who practice meditation in the West, which is probably the greatest number outside places like India, and maybe a few Buddhist centers, do it in terms of its material utility. They never relate it to at a spiritual level.

SFH: Good. I am not against that. Fine. It's a good start. It's a very good point, because it's clearing the mind and possibly beginning to touch on the zone of the heart. I'm all for that.

AA: But the technique does not bring you to the real – it's only mental.

SFH: There is only the Real. Any technique that gives you – puts you at the border of oblivion, I think is good. And I think biofeedback and other techniques – the same way as we have managed to shrink space, we may manage to shrink time. When that happens without revolution, without a big bang, I think you'll suddenly find entry points into the so-called preserve of the previous castle of science, and think they have been broken through. That barrier will have been broken through. Because of the effect of it, the result of it. It will show. If in a corporation you can have people, every hour or two, have 5-10 minutes of true thoughtlessness, I tell you, you'll find far less egotistic battles, far less – efficiency will increase with leaps and bounds, without us being able to know why. All what we need is to re-calibrate the mind and the heart. The mind has to be clear and stopped, and the heart must be pure and accessing the zone of the soul which is within it.

AA: Maybe it will come, Insha'Allah.

SFH: I think it's coming – the fact that you've just mentioned so many people take to meditation – it's the first step. It's an expression of desire to be mindless.

AA: But we end up again being dominated by the pleasure principle.

SFH: Not ... but pleasure would always have displeasure. It will move to another zone which I call bliss – indescribable. Nothing wrong with pleasure. Pleasure has now reached a point where people are frightened of it because it comes with a package of displeasure, whereas bliss is unific. Pleasure is duality. Bliss or whatever name you like to give it, is unific, to do with the *ruh*. These are again terms not yet become popular, not become defined. But we have to define them as we get closer to them. At the moment it's not needed to be defined, because we have lumped in joy, pleasure, all of the other things into the same clump, you know. Gay – all these words – now we're beginning to be closer to re-define them. Where do they belong? Pleasure is childish because you'll have displeasure. Joy – bliss – I think we're beginning to define and understand them.

AA: ... *Haqq* ... Within the eye of Truth ... We see it near and they see it far...

SFH: Exactly.... what's a few hundred years between friends?

AA: We're defined of course by our life span.

SFH: No, we're defined by our *ruh*, that in itself defines the apparent of our lives.

AA: Sorry – I'll re-phrase that – I meant limited consciousness.

SFH: Absolutely. That's fine. No, it's horrific if you tell me that I'm *defined* – it's a waste of time – damn such a god. Who has defined it by my birth and death? Unacceptable. I won't worship such a god. I worship that Reality that has no beginning and no end, and defies all possibilities to pigeonhole it. And it's from that reality that I'm deriving my life, and my personal life is bracketed between birth and death, in order for me to see the infinite life on the horizon. Once I have seen infinite life then my personal life becomes insignificant.

AA: If you are sure that the atom yields to these multi layers of orders, then it becomes easier for the limited consciousness to yield to the Absolute Consciousness.

SFH: Brilliant! Brilliant! I am your student. I am your follower!

AA: That's all adhocism!

SFH: No, but you are doing magnificently. This is important. This is making bridges and at least that no man's land, the zone of *barzakhiya*, a bit more accessible. It's highway code. This is brilliant.

AA: Frankly, I find it more fruitful than the attempt to re-create, as it were, the sacred science...

SFH: Absolutely. Because it's personal, and experiential. It has a reality that you can't take away from the person any more...

AA: In the sense that is a form of exhaustion of empirical science, rather than positing an alternative traditional science, like Seyyed Hossein Nasr.

SFH: All of that has helped me up to this point, but now I am entering into a zone of oblivion in my prostration. Nobody can take it away from me.

AA: So "I exhausted him as he tried to rise"[137] does not only apply to the individual – it applies to anything including science the way in which it has evolved, the technological imperative behind science.

SFH: One of the other meanings of that is that if you are thinking of climbing the ladder of return back to paradise, or the arc of ascent, you will be exhausted. You must go inwardly and give up. And that's where *Islam, Iman, Ihsan* comes into play.

Spiritual Cocktail

AA: It would seem that if you say, just a simple formulation, a new spin, or new understanding of quantum mechanics or field theory, plus what meditation, plus ethics might be teaching you.

SFH: Brilliant. That's a good mix, a nice cocktail.

AA: I think it would be accepted by anybody.

SFH: Nice cocktail. Absolutely. And it will be more and more accepted by people it serves well within their narrow field of science, because that's a refuge – narrowness is a refuge from the distraction of...

---

[137] See Qur'an 74:17.

AA: Look at technology, I mean utility. Science is a utility function of technology. Everything has to be practical, usable.

SFH: Which is fine, provided you give them more space and time, rather than deadlines and all of that. Too early dictation of outcomes is a killer. Allow it –

AA: I remember you said this is a form of theft – not allowed. It's like meditation to improve your aggressiveness and bond dealing – this is not allowed, even though it opens up a channel –

SFH: It will make your dealing higher, but your fall will be bigger. It has its own self-destructive force.

AA: My son worked for a while for Lehmann Brothers and luckily left before it collapsed. Meditation and focus were a very important part of their training.

SFH: And also the chairman always has something to say; he is allowed to say anything, if it was in his mind it was not positive. Positive thinking – what do you mean by positive thinking? Positive thinking has got negative thinking.

AA: It's to do with money – accumulation.

SFH: Unavoidable. It has its own self-destructive mechanism, which speeds up from there. It's illicit. It's again – Qur'an says, 'enter the house from its door,' *wa'tu al-buyuta min abwaabiha*[138] – this is entering by the window – it doesn't work.

Attempts to See Light

AA: A great thing to see a conversation between Krishnamurti and David Bohm – extremely strained, and in many ways I found there was

---

[138] "So enter your houses by their [main] doors." (Qur'an 2:189)

one attempt to see light, and another exasperation, so it wasn't at all pleasant.

SFH: No, again because Krishnamurti was fixed in his domain. He was a really high Buddhist priest.

AA: He was spiritually sour –

SFH: -and Buddhistic. He was not Hindu – high Buddhism. It's coming; it's opening; all of this is beginning to be more and more commonly available on YouTube and so on. These are good signs.

AA: The spectrum shifts here. Most people when they talk about science and the Qur'an, they want to find proof, empirical proof, though it's the other way around.

SFH: No, there are a lot of that is coming from Turkey. Not interesting.

AA: These are all dead ends.

SFH: Dead ends – not interesting. But they contribute to the revival …

AA: end up in a cul-de-sac and have to come back, so it's all a process of "…I shall exhaust him"…I love that...

SFH: If you are climbing you will be in every way exhausted. Climb in. Drop in. Don't climb up. No rush, no time. Stop! Be!

AA: Those who used to prescribe opiates as a way to experience the higher consciousness used to say 'turn on, tune in and drop out!' So where do opiates fit into all this?

SFH: It is beyond – it has an impression, all this. There may be some chemical changes that take place, which is not that different from the changes that these hallucinogenic drugs and so on, do. I'm sure there is a lot of resonance. The only thing is, the side effects. And I am dropping in without dropping out. I am dropping up without dropping sideways. It has to be synergetic.

AA: It's about sustainability.

SFH: Key. That's the most important thing. Exactly, not only that – it destroys other things. I don't like the side effects. I want to have access to that zone, which the best of drugs or anesthetics tries to give me – I want to have access to it all the time. It is there that I am addressing some other zone. Access to it is not being higher or more rare. No, I have to stop connecting with the familiar. No, I have to stop – utter stopping of thought, again time. If I manage to stop time and the ticking of my mind and the illusion of time, then I'll be replenished, re-energized, re-vitalized, re-calibrated.

Glossary

A–
'Abaya – Cloak – a robe-like dress worn by some Muslim women
'Abd – Servant (usually, *'Abd Allah/'Abdullah* – God's servant)
Adaab – Courtesies (sing. *Adab*)
Adhan – Call to prayer
'Adl – Justice
'Adam – The Void
Ahl al-Bayt – Family of the household of the Prophet Muhammad
Akhawat – Sisters
Akhir – The Last
Akhira – The Hereafter
Akhlaq – Manners
Akiriyah – End points
Al-'Adheem – The Magnificent
Al-Anwaar – The Lights
Al-Baqi – The Everlasting/The Ever-Present
Al-Haqq – The Truth/The Reality
Al-Mutakallim – The Speaker
Al-Qalam – The pen (Surah 68)
Al-Qawiy – The Strong
Al-Qayyum – The Eternal
Al-Salaam – The Peace
Al-Wasi' – The All-Encompassing
Al-Wadud – The Loving
Al-fana' fi al-Shaykh – Annihilate into the Shaykh
Alhamdulillah – Praise be to God
'Alim – Scholar, usually of religion
'Alim al-Ghaib – The realm beyond our basic senses (the Unseen World)
Allahu Akbar – God is greater than everything
Amana – Trust
Anwaar – A collection of lights
Aqiq – A type of religious ring for men

'Aql – Commonly refers to "reason" and "intelligence". Literally: "To bind" – the faculty which binds man to God, to his Origin
Ar-Rahim – The Merciful
Ar-Rahman – The Beneficent
'Arif – A wise person; a person of enlightenment, of higher consciousness
'Arifin – pl. of *'Arif*
Arwah – Souls (sing. *Ruh*)
Asdiqa – Friends
'Ashura – 10th of the first month (Muharram) of the Islamic calendar
Aslam – To surrender
Asma' – Names
Asma al-Husna – The most beautiful names (of Allah)
Asrar al-'Ibadat – The secrets of devotion
at-tahqiq al-khiz – The false confirmation
Awliya – Friends of God (sing. *Wali*)
Awwal – The First
Ayah – A verse of the Qur'an (pl. *Ayaat*)
Ayat al-Kubra – Magnificent *ayah*
'Ayn al-Basirah – The eye of perception, insight and foresight of the transcendental truth
'Ayn Allah – Allah's Vision
'Ayn al-Yaqin – The vision of certainty

B–
Baab/Bab – Door
Baatil – Not real
Baba Jaan – A term that is used to refer to someone out of respect, usually to an older man
Badha – purity
Bahr al-Ulum – A leading Iraqi *'alim*
Baiwa – Purity
Bala' – Something greatly unwanted/undesired
Baqa' – Everlasting-ness/Permanence (*Al-Baqi* – The Everlasting)
Baqi – The Ever-Present
Baraka – Blessing

Glossary

Barani – A reception room
Barzakh – Interface between this life and the Hereafter (also *Barzakhi*)
Barzakhiya – The quality/state of *Barzakh*
Basir – All-Seeing (*al-Basir* – The All Seeing – one of Allah's names)
Batin/Baatin – The Hidden
Batiniyya – Inner state
Ba'uda – Far
Baya/Bayah – Oath of allegiance
Bazaari (Persian) – The name given to the merchants' class and workers of bazaars
Bismillah – In the name of God
Burani – Receiving room/Outer reception area
Buyut Muhassa – Secure houses

C–
Chai Khanas – Tea houses

D–
Da`wa – To invite (usually to a religious path)
Dar al-Hikma – The Abode of Wisdom
Dawla – Riches
Dīn – Religion, in a comprehensive way
Dīn al-Hanif – Religion of pure monotheism (of Abraham)
Dhahir – The Manifest/The Outer
Dhawq – Taste (the presence of Allah)
Dhikr – Lit. Remembrance, usually of Allah, often done by the Sufis
Diwina – Mad
Doppleganger – An exact image of (something/someone), i.e., a double (in German)
Du`a – Supplication
Duniya – This life (as opposed to the Hereafter)

F–
Fajr – Dawn prayer
Fana' – Annihilation (of the *nafs*)
Faqir – Ascetic

Glossary

Faskh al-`Awa'id – Breaking of habits
Fatiha – The opening chapter of the Qur'an
Fajr – The dawn prayer
Fitr – Crack
Fitra/Fitrah – Innate disposition/Crack
Fitri – Natural, Innate
Fiqh – Islamic jurisprudence (usually a School of Thought)
Fu'ad – The inner heart
Futuwwa – Chivalry/Virtue (Sufi term)

G–
Ghaib – Unseen
Ghusl – Bath

H–
Haal – Spiritual state
Hadhrat ar-Rabbaaniyya – The Divine Presence
Hafidha – Memory
Hafiz – A person who has memorized (usually the Qur'an)
Hahut – The Realm of Majesty
Haira – Perplexity
Hajjar – Stone
Hakim – A person who practices traditional medicine (lit. A wise person. Pl. *Hukama*)
Halaal – Permissible
Haqiqah – Inner reality
Haqiqi – Pertaining to *Haqq*
Haqq – Truth; Reality. One of Allah's names is *Al-Haqq*, meaning, Absolute Truth
Haqq al-Yaqin – The level of certainty gained through experience
Harakat al-Jawariyyah – Movement of the Essence
Haram – Forbidden (Also refers to a sacred place)
Haush – House
Hawza – Seminary to train Shi`a Muslims
Hayat – Life (as opposed to Death)
Hayyu – From *Al-Hayy* (The Everlasting)

Hijab – Barrier
Hijra – Migration
Hikma/Hikmah – Wisdom/(also traditional medicine practiced in South Asia)
Hisaab – Arithmetic
Hiss al-Mushtaraq – Common sense
Hud – Surah 11 of the Qur'an – Prophet Hud
Hudhur – Presence
Hukama – Wise people/Philosopher
Hukuma Islamiyya – Islamic government
Huzn – Sadness/Sorrow

I–
`Ibadat/`Ibada – Worship
Idraak – Perception/Awareness/Knowing
Iha' – Revelation
Ihsan – Perfection/Excellence
Ijaza – Permission
Ikhlas – Sincerity
`Ilm – Knowledge
`Ilm al-Yaqin – Certainty of knowledge
Iman – Faith; Inner conviction
Insaan – Human being
Insaan al-Kamil – The Perfect Man (aka, The Universal Man)
Insaniyya – Humanity
Insha'Allah – God willing
Iqra' – Read
Irada – Will/Desire/Intention
*`Irfan* – Gnosis/Inner dimension of Shi`a Islam
Islam al-Batin – Inner Islam
Islam al-Dhahir – Outer Islam
Ista`daad – Preparedness

J–
Jabaruti – Realm of power
Jaffa al-qalam – The pen is dry

Jalal – Majestic
Jama` – Congregation
Jamal – Beauty/Beautiful
Jami` – The Gatherer
Janaza – Funeral
Jannah – Paradise
Jihad – Striving
Jum`a* – Congregational prayer on Fridays (lit. Friday; related to *Jama`)

K–
Ka`ba – The large cube-shaped building inside the al-Masjid al-Haram mosque in Mecca
Kacha - Countraband
Karaha/Karahan – By hook or by crook
Karam – Generosity
Kashkol – A bowl
Khalas – Stop it/Finish/Enough
Khalifa – Successor
Khalifah tul-Allah – Allah's successor
Khaliq – Creator
Khalwa – Spiritual retreat, done alone
Khana – Place
Khawf – Fear
Khayaal – Thought/Imagination
Khidma – Servicing others
Khilafah/Khilafat – Caliphate
Khudba – Sermon
Kitaab – Book (usually referred to revealed books)
Kuffar – Non-believers (lit. Those who cover up; sing. *Kaafir*)
Kufr al-Khafi – Hidden *kufr* (infidelity)
Kuliyat – Wisdom
Kuliyat al-Hikma – Wisdom College
Kun – Be (The word 'Be' used by Allah to cause something to come to existence)
Kurta – Long shirt, usually worn by people of South Asia

Kushte – Traditional medicines, usually made by the *hakims* in the Indian subcontinent

L–
Lablabi – Lentils
Lahut – Realm of Light
La ilaha-il-Allah – There is no god but God (Or: There is no reality but the Reality)
Laqab – A descriptive name given to a person
Laylat al-Qadr – Night of Destiny/Power/Ascent
Lutf – Pleasure

M–
Ma`na – Meaning
Madrasa – School, usually religious
Maghrib – Sunset prayer; also refers to the direction, west
Majidis – An old Ottoman gold coin
Majlis – Gathering
Majm`a – Gathered
Maknoon – Pressed
Malakut – Angels (sing. *Mulk*)
Malakuti – Angelic
Malamati – Blameworthy people
Maqaam – Spiritual station (pl. *Maqamaat*)
*Marja`* – Highest level religious legal authority in Shi`a Islam (pl. *maraji`*)
Mastaba – A type of tomb (lit. eternal house)
Majidis – Gold coins
Maragh – Stew
Mawlawi – Religious leaders
Mawqif – A halting place
Mihrab – A semicircular niche in the wall of a mosque that indicates the *qibla*.
Miswaak – Teeth cleaning tree twig
Mithal – Example/Similitude
Mizaan – Spiritual scale

Mufakkira – Faculty of thinking/reflection
Muhabba – Love
Muhallas – Neighborhoods
Muhasaba – Self critique
Muhkamat – The explicit verses
Mujtahid – A Muslim jurist who can make independent rulings (*ijtihad*)
Mulk – Angel (pl. *Malakut*)
Mulki – Angelic
Mullahdom – Domain of the Mullahs
Muraqaba – Meditation
Murid – A disciple, usually of a Sufi master
Mushaf – Pages
Mushrik – One who associate others with God (pl. *Mushrikun*)
Mutaghayer – Ever-changing
Mutakallim – Speaker (See *Al-Mutakallim*)
Mutashabihat – The relative verses
Mutawasia – Middle school
Muttaqi – A pious person/A God-conscious person
Muwadda – Love/Nearness

N–
Na Kujabaad – Land of Nowhere
Naba' – Message/News
Nadhr – Sacrifice/Oath
Nafs – Self (Usually the Lower)
Nafsi – Related to the *nafs*
Niyya – Intention
Nur – Light
Nur al-Anwaar – Light of lights

P–
Pushiye – Face covering

Q–
Qa'id – Leader
Qadir – Powerful

Qaht al-rijal – So few men
Qalandar – Wandering Sufi dervish
Qalb – (Spiritual) Heart
Qarin – Companion Self
Qibla – Direction (also refers to the *Ka`aba*)
Qira' – Reading (of anything, but in some context, it is of the Qur'an)
Qiyama – The Hereafter, usually within the context of the Day of Judgment
Qudra – Power/Control
Qur'an bil Qur'an – Qur'an by the Qur'an (usually, in relation to understanding of it)
Qurayyas – Readings on Imam Hussein's life

R–
Rabbani – From the *Rabb* (The Sustainer)
Rahma – Mercy
Rahman – Merciful
Rais – A leader
Raja' – Hope
Raka` – One unit of *Salaat*
Ribat – Fortress
Risala – Magazine
Raoufiyya – Kind and gentle
Rububiyya – Lordship
Ruh – Soul/Spirit (pl. *Arwah*)
Ruhan-ruh – *Ruh* of *Ruh*
Ruhani – Spiritual
Ruhaniya – Spirituality

S–
Sadaka – Friendship
Sadiqa – Friend
Sahaba – Companions of the Prophet
Sajdah – Prostration (Disappearance into one's nothingness)
Salaat – Formal Muslim prayer

Glossary

Sami`* – All-Hearing (*al-Sami` – The All Hearing – one of Allah's names)
Sanyasi – A Hindu ascetic
Sarrab – Exchange dealer/banker
Seerah – Biography of the Prophet Muhammad (PBUH)
Sha`ban – Eighth month of the Islamic calendar
Shadhar – Semi-precious stones
Shahadah – Islamic creed declaring belief in the oneness of God and the acceptance of Muhammad as God's messenger
Shahid – A witness
Shar` – Path
Shari`ah – Outer form of a religion (lit. The way)
Shatana – To stay afar
Shaykh – Sufi master/teacher
Shaytan – Satan
Shaytanic – Satanic/Devilish
Shubbak – Louvers
Shuyukh – pl. of *Shaykh*
Sibghat Allah – The colors of Allah
Sidrat Allah – Tree of Allah
Sidrat al-Muntaha – A Lote tree that marks the end of the seventh heaven, the boundary where no creation can pass
Simsim – Sesame
Simsimiyya – Bars of sesame, sugar and honey
Sirdabs – Basements
Siyaha – Travelling
Siyaha fil ardh – Travelling around the world
Subhanallah – Glory be to God
Suluk – Well treatment/Spiritual pathway
Sura – A chapter of the Qur'an
SWT – *Subhanahu Wa Ta`ala* (Glory to Him, the Exalted)

T–
Ta`wil – Interpretation
Tafaasir – See *Tafsir*
Tafsir – Commentary of the Qur'an (pl. *Tafaasir*)

Tahlia/Tahliya – Sweetening
Tajlia/Tajliya – To transcend
Tajrid – Divesting
Takalluf – To be accountable
Takhlia/Takhliya – Emptying out (lit. being alone; solitude)
Takhlih – Emptying out
Tariqah – Formal, structured, spiritual practical path in Islam (lit. The way)
Tarteeb – Arrangement
Tasawwuf – Sufism
Tasbih – Prayer beads
Tasfia/Tasfiya – Purifying
Tashbih – To approximate
Tatt'aruf – Extremes
Tawakkul – Trust (in Allah) and Reliance on Him
Tawassul – Use of some means to arrive at or obtain favor of Allah
Tawhīd – Oneness (Divine Unity)
Tawhīdi – State of oneness
Thanawiyya – Secondary school
Thawab – Reward
Turshi – Iraqi pickles

U–
'Ulama – Scholars (sing. *`Alim*)
Ummah – Community (of Muslims)
Ummahat al-Asma – Mothers of (Allah's) names
Ummatan Wasata – The middle people

V–
Vilayat al-Faqih – Rule of the jurist

W–
Wasita – Intermediation
Wahm – Imagination
Wajhain – To aspects
Wali – Friend of God (pl. *Awliya*)

Wilaya – The authority of the *wali*
Wird – A form of *dhikr*
Wudhu – Ritual washing done before *Salaat*
Wujudi – Existential
Wuratha – Inheritors

Y–
Ya`ni – Meaning
Yaad Allah – Remembrance of Allah
Yaqeen – Inner conviction and certainty
Yuhamic – Don't fret

Z–
Zahid – Ascetic
Zawiya – A Sufi lodge, akin to the term *Tekke/Tekyeh* in Iran, Turkey and the former Ottoman areas, as well as *Khanqah* or *Dargah* used in various parts of Asia
Zuhd – Asceticism/Renunciation

eBooks By Zahra Publications

General eBooks on Islam

Living Islam – East and West
Shaykh Fadhlalla Haeri

Ageless and universal wisdom set against the backdrop of a changing world: application of this knowledge to one's own life is most appropriate.

The Elements of Islam
Shaykh Fadhlalla Haeri

An introduction to Islam through an overview of the universality and light of the prophetic message.

The Qur'an & Its Teachings

Journey of the Universe as Expounded in the Qur'an
Shaykh Fadhlalla Haeri

The Qur'an traces the journey of all creation, seeing the physical, biological and geological voyage of life as paralleled by the inner spiritual evolution of woman/man.

Keys to the Qur'an: Volume 1: Commentary on Surah Al-Fatiha and Surah Al-Baqarah
Shaykh Fadhlalla Haeri

The first two chapters of the Qur'an give guidance regarding inner and outer struggle. Emphasis is on understanding key Qur'anic terms.

Keys to the Qur'an: Volume 2: Commentary on Surah Ale-`Imran
Shaykh Fadhlalla Haeri

A commentary on the third chapter of the Qur'an, the family of `Imran which includes the story of Mary, mother of `Isa (Jesus).

Keys to the Qur'an: Volume 3: Commentary on Surah Yasin
Shaykh Fadhlalla Haeri

Commentary on chapter *Yasin*. This is traditionally read over the dead person: if we want to know the meaning of life, we have to learn about death.

Keys to the Qur'an: Volume 4: Commentary on Surahs Al-`Ankabut, Al-Rahman, Al-Waqi`ah and Al-Mulk
Shaykh Fadhlalla Haeri

The Shaykh uncovers inner meanings, roots and subtleties of the Qur'anic Arabic terminology in these four selected Surahs.

Keys to the Qur'an: Volume 5: Commentary on Juz' `Amma
Shaykh Fadhlalla Haeri

Insight into the last *Juz'* of Qur'an, with the objective of exploring the deeper meanings of Qur'anic Revelations.

The Essential Message of the Qur'an
Shaykh Fadhlalla Haeri

Teachings from the Qur'an such as purpose of creation, Attributes of the Creator, nature of human beings, decrees governing the laws of the universe, life and death.

The Qur'an in Islam: Its Impact & Influence on the Life of Muslims
`Allamah Sayyid M. H. Tabataba`i

`Allamah Sayyid M. H. Tabataba`i shows in this gem how the Qur'an contains the fundamental roots of Islam and the proof of prophethood as the Word of God.

The Qur'anic Prescription for Life
Shaykh Fadhlalla Haeri

Understanding the Qur'an is made accessible with easy reference to key issues concerning life and the path of Islam.

The Story of Creation in the Qur'an
Shaykh Fadhlalla Haeri

An exposition of the Qur'anic verses relating to the nature of physical phenomena, including the origins of the universe, the nature of light, matter, space and time, and the evolution of biological and sentient beings.

eBooks By Zahra Publications

Sufism & Islamic Psychology and Philosophy

Beginning's End
Shaykh Fadhlalla Haeri

This is a contemporary outlook on Sufi sciences of self knowledge, exposing the challenge of our modern lifestyle that is out of balance.

Cosmology of the Self
Shaykh Fadhlalla Haeri

Islamic teachings of *Tawhīd* (Unity) with insights into the human self: understanding the inner landscape is essential foundation for progress on the path of knowledge.

Decree and Destiny (Original and a Revised Version)
Shaykh Fadhlalla Haeri

A lucid exposition of the extensive body of Islamic thought on the issue of free will and determinism.

Happiness in Life and After Death – An Islamic Sufi View
Shaykh Fadhlalla Haeri

This book offers revelations and spiritual teachings that map a basic path towards wholesome living without forgetting death: cultivating a constant awareness of one's dual nature.

Leaves from a Sufi Journal
Shaykh Fadhlalla Haeri

A unique collection of articles presenting an outstanding introduction to the areas of Sufism and original Islamic teachings.

The Elements of Sufism
Shaykh Fadhlalla Haeri

Sufism is the heart of Islam. This introduction describes its origins, practices, historical background and its spread throughout the world.

The Garden of Meaning
Shaykh Fadhlalla Haeri

This book is about two gardens, one visible and fragrant, the other less visible but eternal. The beauty and harmony of both gardens are exposited in this magisterial volume, linking outer to inner, physics to metaphysics, self to cosmos.

The Journey of the Self
Shaykh Fadhlalla Haeri

After introducing the basic model of the self, there follows a simple yet complete outline of the self's emergence, development, sustenance, and growth toward its highest potential.

The Sufi Way to Self-Unfoldment
Shaykh Fadhlalla Haeri

Unfolding inner meanings of the Islamic ritual practices towards the intended ultimate purpose to live a life honorable and fearless, with no darkness, ignorance or abuse.

Witnessing Perfection
Shaykh Fadhlalla Haeri

Delves into the universal question of Deity and the purpose of life. Durable contentment is a result of 'perfected vision'.

Practices & Teachings of Islam

Calling Allah by His Most Beautiful Names
Shaykh Fadhlalla Haeri

Attributes or Qualities resonate from their Majestic and Beautiful Higher Realm into the heart of the active seeker, and through it back into the world.

Fasting in Islam
Shaykh Fadhlalla Haeri

This is a comprehensive guide to fasting in all its aspects, with a description of fasting in different faith traditions, its spiritual benefits, rules and regulations.

Prophetic Traditions in Islam: On the Authority of the Family of the Prophet
Shaykh Fadhlalla Haeri

Offers a comprehensive selection of Islamic teachings arranged according to topics dealing with belief and worship, moral, social and spiritual values.

The Wisdom (Hikam) of Ibn `Ata'allah: Translation and Commentary
Translation & Commentary by Shaykh Fadhlalla Haeri

These aphorisms of Ibn `Ata'Allah, a Shadili Shaykh, reveal the breadth and depth of an enlightened being who reflects divine unity and inner transformation through worship.

The Inner Meanings of Worship in Islam: A Personal Selection of Guidance for the Wayfarer
Shaykh Fadhlalla Haeri

Here is guidance for those who journey along this path, from the Qur'an, the Prophet's traditions, narrations from the *Ahl al-Bayt*, and seminal works from among the *Ahl al-Tasawwuf* of all schools of thought.

The Lantern of The Path
Imam Ja`far Al-Sadiq (Translated By Shaykh Fadhlalla Haeri)

Each one of the ninety-nine chapter of this book is a threshold to the next, guiding the reader through the broad spectrum of ageless wisdom, like a lantern along the path of reality.

The Pilgrimage of Islam
Shaykh Fadhlalla Haeri

This is a specialized book on spiritual journeying, offering the sincere seeker keys to inner transformation.

The Sayings & Wisdom of Imam `Ali
Compiled By: Shaykh Fadhlalla Haeri
Translated By: Asadullah ad-Dhaakir Yate

Carefully translated into modern English, a selection of this great man's sayings gathered together from authentic and reliable sources.

Transformative Worship in Islam: Experiencing Perfection
Shaykh Fadhlalla Haeri with Muna H. Bilgrami

This book uniquely bridges the traditional practices and beliefs, culture and language of Islam with the transformative spiritual states described by the Sufis and Gnostics.

eBooks By Zahra Publications

Talks, Interviews & Courses

Ask Course ONE: The Sufi Map of the Self
Shaykh Fadhlalla Haeri

This workbook explores the entire cosmology of the self through time, and maps the evolution of the self from before birth through life, death and beyond.

Ask Course TWO: The Prophetic Way of Life
Shaykh Fadhlalla Haeri

This workbook explores how the code of ethics that govern religious practice and the Prophetic ways are in fact transformational tools to enlightened awakening.

Friday Discourses: Volume 1
Shaykh Fadhlalla Haeri

The Shaykh addresses many topics that influence Muslims at the core of what it means to be a Muslim in today's global village.

Songs of Iman on the Roads of Pakistan
Shaykh Fadhlalla Haeri

A series of talks given on the divergence between 'faith' and 'unbelief' during a tour of the country in 1982 which becomes a reflection of the condition occurring in the rest of the world today.

The Connection Between the Absolute and the Relative
Shaykh Fadhlalla Haeri

This is a 1990 conversation with Shaykh Fadhlalla Haeri, in which he talks about wide-ranging topics on Islam and presents it as the archetypal, universal, Adamic path that began when humanity rose in consciousness to recognize duality and began its journey from the relative back to Absolute Unity.

Also available on paperback.

The Spiritual Path: A Conversation with Shaykh Fadhlalla Haeri On His Life, Thought and Work
Professor Ali A. Allawi

In this wide-ranging conversation with Professor Ali Allawi, Shaykh Fadhlalla Haeri talks about his life story and the spiritual journey that he embarked on and the path he has been on ever since.

Also available on paperback.

Poetry, Aphorisms & Inspirational

101 Helpful Illusions
Shaykh Fadhlalla Haeri

Everything in creation has a purpose relevant to ultimate spiritual Truth. This book highlights natural veils to be transcended by disciplined courage, wisdom and insight.

Beyond Windows
Shaykh Fadhlalla Haeri

Offering moving and profound insights of compassion and spirituality through these anthologies of connections between slave self and Eternal Lord.

Bursts of Silence
Shaykh Fadhlalla Haeri

Inspired aphorisms provide keys to doors of inner knowledge, as well as antidotes to distraction and confusion.

Pointers to Presence
Shaykh Fadhlalla Haeri

A collection of aphorisms providing insights into consciousness and are pointers to spiritual awakening.

Ripples of Light
Shaykh Fadhlalla Haeri

Inspired aphorisms which become remedies for hearts that seek the truth.

Sound Waves
Shaykh Fadhlalla Haeri

A collection of aphorisms that help us reflect and discover the intricate connection between self and soul.

Sublime Gems: Selected Teachings of Shaykh Abd al-Qadir al-Jilani
Shaykh Abd al-Qadir al-Jilani

A collection of extracted spiritual nourishment from Shaykh Abd al-Qadir al-Jilani's existing works.

Autobiography

Son of Karbala
Shaykh Fadhlalla Haeri

The atmosphere of an Iraq in transition is brought to life and used as a backdrop for the Shaykh's own personal quest for self-discovery and spiritual truth.

Health Sciences and Islamic History

Health Sciences in Early Islam – Volumes 1 & 2
Collected Papers By: Sami K. Hamarneh
Edited By: Munawar A. Anees
Foreword By: Shaykh Fadhlalla Haeri

Health Sciences in Early Islam is a pioneering study of Islamic medicine that opens up new chapters of knowledge in the history of the healing sciences. This two volume work covers the development of Islamic medicine between the 6th and 12th centuries A.D.

www.ingramcontent.com/pod-product-compliance
Lightning Source LLC
Chambersburg PA
CBHW021133230426
43667CB00005B/93